INTERNATIONAL SHIPPING CARTELS

International Shipping Cartels:

A Study of Industrial Self-Regulation by Shipping Conferences

~~~~~~~~~~~~~~~~~~~~~~~~~~

BY DANIEL MARX, JR.

PRINCETON, NEW JERSEY
PRINCETON UNIVERSITY PRESS
1953

387.51
M392i

387.51
M392i

Printed in the United States of America by Princeton
University Press at Princeton, New Jersey

To
WINFIELD W. RIEFLER
whose understanding and encouragement
helped make this book a reality

PREFACE

SHIPPING conferences are among the earliest cartels in international trade. The purpose of this volume has been to describe and analyze as objectively as possible the functioning of these organizations for self-regulation. Are shipping conferences necessary? Do they possess the inherent vice of unregulated monopolies? Should they be abolished, or tolerated, or regulated? These are some of the questions this book attempts to answer. Readers who desire a survey of the author's conclusions before reading the more detailed descriptive and analytical portions may wish to turn first to Chapter XIV.

Chapter I briefly presents the problem, and Chapters II and III present background material. The next three chapters describe the results of official investigations of shipping conferences by Great Britain, the United States, and other countries. Chapters VII, VIII, and IX portray the nature of shipping agreements in the foreign trade of the United States, and the regulation by this nation of its overseas shipping. Chapter IX also includes an analysis of non-conference liner competition. Chapter X discusses tying arrangements, and Chapter XI considers the competition of tramp vessels. Chapter XII analyzes the economics of shipping conferences. Chapter XIII describes the proposed Intergovernmental Maritime Consultative Organization, and contrasts the regulation of ocean transport with the international control of aviation and with international commodity agreements. In addition to a summary, the concluding chapter considers various alternatives and presents the author's conclusions.

It is hoped that this study may be of interest to industries besides shipping. Many of the problems with which this volume is concerned are common to air transportation, industrial cartels, and commodity agreements.

It is also hoped that this volume will be of interest to businessmen and to government officials as well as to economists and political scientists. As a result some readers may find the background material of Chapters II and III old stuff and a bit academic for their taste. An effort has been made to avoid the excessive use of jargon peculiar to shipmen or to economists; but where a word or phrase seemed to provide a convenient and not too esoteric shorthand exceptions have been made. Most of the economic terms that have been employed are defined in Chapter II where they first appear.

The author is deeply indebted to the Institute for Advanced Study for having favored him with a membership which carried with it the privilege of living and working in its stimulating environment for a year and a half.

The author is also profoundly grateful to the John Simon Guggenheim Memorial Foundation for having honored him with a fellowship for the year 1950.

A grant-in-aid from the American Philosophical Society, which financed the collection of data and defrayed the costs of typing the final manuscript, assisted materially in the preparation of this volume, and is keenly appreciated.

In addition, the author also wishes to acknowledge the debt he owes to Professor Walter W. Stewart of the Institute for Advanced Study for having read portions of the manuscript and for his extremely helpful comments and suggestions on these and other matters. Thanks are also due to Professor Edward M. Earle of the Institute for his cooperation and numerous kindnesses.

The preparation of several chapters would have been far more difficult had it not been for the helpfulness of Mr. Ralph H. Hallett, chief of the Office of Regulation of the Federal Maritime Board, and the painstaking assistance of Mr. L. E. Ranck and Mr. Norman Levey of that organization. May these few words convey my deep sense of obligation to them for their valuable assistance.

Thanks are also due to Princeton University and Harvard University for providing the author with the opportunity to try out some of the ideas developed in this volume at their Social Science Seminar and Transportation Seminar respectively.

The cooperation of numerous other persons, who contributed information or ideas either by conversation or correspondence, should also be acknowledged. This is an invidious task for one with an all too fallible memory; the author begs the indulgence of those few who may have been overlooked. Stimulating and informative conversations relevant to this study are pleasurably recalled to have taken place with the following: Mr. John Palfrey, Mr. Harvey Klemmer, and Dr. Walter A. Radius of Washington, D.C.; Professor Ansley J. Coale of Princeton; Professor John C. Cooper of McGill; Professors Walter Isard and Edward S. Mason of Harvard; Professor

Lionel Robbins of the London School of Economics; Sir Henry Clay and Mr. John Fforde of Oxford University; Mr. Morris Rosenthal, president, National Council of American Importers; Mr. Matthew S. Crinkley, vice president, Isbrandtsen Co., Inc.; Mr. C. Duran-Ballen, Consul General of Ecuador; Mr. Charles L. Wheeler, executive vice president, Pope and Talbot Lines; Messrs. J. F. McArt and R. F. Burley, chairmen of several conferences.

In London much assistance was provided by Mr. Fred V. Cross of the British Ministry of Transport, Mr. Martin Hill of the Liverpool Steamship Owners Association, Professor M. G. Kendall, and Mr. Hector Gripaios. An unforgettable visit to the Baltic Exchange was personally and most graciously conducted by Mr. Hubert Roberts.

Information regarding pertinent policies of their governments was sent to me by: Mr. J. U. Garside, commercial counselor, Australian Embassy, Washington; Mr. W. A. Horrocks, commercial secretary, Embassy of the Union of South Africa, Washington; Mr. José Gil-Borges, commercial counselor, Venezuelan Embassy, Washington; Mr. Ruy Leitao, assistant commercial attaché, Portuguese Embassy, Washington; Mr. R. W. Marshall, commercial attaché, New Zealand Embassy, Washington; Mr. G. W. Clinkard, Secretary of Industries and Commerce, Wellington, N.Z.; and Mr. A. S. Whiteley, deputy commissioner, Combines Investigation Act, Ottawa, Canada.

Thanks are also due the Library of Congress for the use of its fine facilities, to Dartmouth College for its liberal leave policy, and to my colleagues who arranged for the necessary adjustments in staffing.

Finally, my gratitude to Miss Elizabeth I. Horton, Miss Jocelyn Farr, and Miss Beatrice H. Miers for their assistance in typing and to Mrs. Daniel Marx, Jr. for help with the indexing can at best be inadequately described.

With all this assistance in mind the reader might be led to expect a volume of peculiar and extraordinary merit. Lest his disappointment be too keen, let him remember that the book itself is entirely the author's own, and that no one else can be considered responsible for omissions or for any errors of fact or interpretation.

D.M., JR.

February 1952

CONTENTS

xi

CONTENTS

CONTENTS

organizations contrasted; Ocean rate regulation and international commodity agreements; Conclusion

INTERNATIONAL SHIPPING CARTELS

CHAPTER I

INTRODUCTION

SHIPPING CONFERENCES are among the earliest cartels in international trade. Shipping conferences, or rings as they are sometimes called, are agreements organized by shipping lines to restrict or eliminate competition, to regulate and rationalize sailing schedules and ports of call, and occasionally to arrange for the pooling of cargo, freight monies, or net earnings. They generally control prices, i.e. freight rates and passenger fares. The nature of their organization varies considerably, depending on the market structure of the trade route. Some have been conferences quite literally—informal oral conferences—but many have employed written agreements establishing a permanent body with a chairman or secretary, and containing carefully described rights and obligations of the conference membership. Penalties for violations of the agreement are sometimes stipulated and in such cases the posting of cash or a fulfillment bond is usually required. Arrangements to refer disputes to arbitration have been fairly typical of conference agreements for many years. Procedures for combatting competition from ship operators who are not conference members are at times a part of the agreement, and various tying arrangements with shippers are extremely common. Shipping conferences should not be confused with combinations of shipping companies in which ownership is merged. The latter have also been common in ocean transport, but have rarely been able by themselves to prevent cutthroat competition. The shipping conference or ring in which the participants remain separate and independently owned enterprises has been the more effective means of restricting competition; and it is with this form of organization that this volume is concerned.

The basic purpose of shipping conferences is to minimize losses or to maximize profits. Historically it seems that most conference agreements were prompted by the necessity of stopping, or at least of avoiding, the insanity of cutthroat competition which is so apt to occur in industries characterized by increasing returns and decreasing costs. In short, the conference system provides a method for the self-regulation of an industry most of which is subject to the multiple jurisdiction of several sovereign nations with disparate legal codes and diverse commercial practices. A Norwegian shipping line may, for example, in competition with lines of various other nations, charter a British ship to carry cargo from New York to Buenos Aires via Rio de Janeiro, Brazil, and Montevideo, Uruguay. The conference system, it is generally agreed, has brought a substantial amount of order out of what might otherwise have been chaos, although rate wars and destructive cutthroat competition still occur from time to time. In achieving this goal, however, the power to regulate is concentrated in the hands of private interests, and although the great majority of conferences originated for protection against destructive competition and not for aggressive predatory purposes, there is no reason outside the actual and potential competition on each trade route to prevent the members from shifting the emphasis of their activities, once an element of monopoly power has been achieved, from minimizing losses to maximizing gains.

It is not astonishing, therefore, to find considerable discontent on the part of some shippers who have charged that the monopoly power of the conferences has led to abuses. As early as 1906 the British government started a thorough investigation of the subject, and the United States government in 1912 began a comprehensive study of the situation in American commerce. The Royal Commission on Shipping Rings reported to his Britannic Majesty in 1909, and the Alexander Committee,[1] which was charged by the Committee on Merchant Marine and Fisheries of the House of Representatives of the Congress of the United States to investigate all types of shipping combinations, issued their report in 1914. The consensus of these reports was that shipping conferences were necessary to assure stability of rates, regularity of service, and improved facilities; but that these organizations contained the inherent vice of monopoly power. There was considerable divergence of opinion between the majority and the minority reports of the Royal Commission regarding the relative weights to be attached to the alleged advantages and abuses; and there were substantial differences in the remedial procedures favored by the British and those proposed by the Congressional Committee.

The passage of time alone warrants a reexamination of the advantages and disadvantages that were claimed, especially since there

[1] Named after its chairman, Representative Joshua W. Alexander of Missouri.

4

have been substantial changes both in the shipping industry and in the structure of the world economy. Examples of these changes include: the increased subsidization and nationalization of shipping; the development of international tramp shipping pools; and the growth of new forms of trade and exchange barriers and the discriminatory practices associated with them. An examination of the efforts at unilateral control of the industry by such countries as the United States, Australia, and the Union of South Africa is also in order. The United States Federal Maritime Board and its predecessors have accumulated, as a result of the authority granted them by the Shipping Act of 1916, much evidence and experience regarding the operations of shipping conferences concerned with trade to and from United States ports.

Shipping conferences appear to achieve their greatest activity in commercially stormy weather when the supply of shipping is superfluous and rate-cutting is threatened or rampant. When space is tight the conferences have occasionally discontinued granting rebates and other preferences to contract shippers and in extreme cases have disbanded. During World War II many conferences continued to operate, although they ceased to be rate-making institutions as government control took over this function. In other cases conferences suspended operations completely, but generally the basic agreements were kept intact to be resumed by such members as were able to run ships after the termination of hostilities and the restoration of some semblance of normality.

In the period between the two great wars an undercurrent of dissatisfaction broke the surface calm of the shipping industry in various parts of the world, with the result that several countries took specific action to control the activities of shipping conferences. It is perhaps not without significance that, in comparison with the relative satisfaction with the operation of conferences on the part of shipowning Great Britain, some British Dominions have found it advisable to subject these organizations to scrutiny and control. During the war complete government control was the practice, and for the Allies coordination was provided by the Combined Shipping Adjustment Board. Authority over rates, however, was left under national control, and was exercised primarily by the United States War Shipping Administration and the British Ministry of War Transport. After the war these controls were gradually relaxed as the supply of shipping became more abundant in relation to the demand for it; although, with national trading monopolies exercising a larger influence than prewar, with exchange control becoming a widespread phenomenon, and with American-vessel participation being stipulated for cargoes such as Marshall Plan goods financed by the United States Government, elements of government influence continued to linger in the postwar freight market. The purpose of this volume, however, is not to study wartime controls, but to consider the operation of conference agreements between shipping companies under more "normal" (which may roughly be defined as peacetime) conditions.

Are shipping conferences still a necessity and do they continue to possess the inherent vice of unregulated monopoly power? Should shipping conferences be abolished, or should they be let alone, or should they be regulated? These are some of the questions this book attempts to answer. The timeliness of such a survey is attested to by the drafting of a charter in 1948 for an Intergovernmental Maritime Consultative Organization as an independent agency cooperating with the United Nations; by Article 53 of the Charter drafted at Havana for the proposed International Trade Organization, which is concerned, among other things, with restrictive business practices in international transportation; and by litigation recently brought by the United States Department of Justice against conferences employing the "exclusive patronage contract" system.

The questions asked in the foregoing paragraph are often glibly and dogmatically answered. Statements supporting the *status quo* as well as hostile comments are never hard to find. The abundance of evidence favorable to shipping conferences and the copious supply of that which is condemnatory would have made this investigation simpler and shorter if the task had been approached with a preconceived notion of the merits of the case. Furthermore, the results of such an "inspired" search could probably have been presented with the directness and clarity that so often attend predilection and oversimplification. While it would be arrogant for the author to claim he is devoid of all prejudice, it is his sincere opinion that none of his biases has materially affected this study. His goal has been to understand, not to mock, lament, or praise.

CHAPTER II

BASIC ECONOMIC FACTORS

OCEAN SHIPPING consists of a family of industries, some closely, others remotely, related. As in human kinships, the intimacy of relationship of the shipping family varies, depending on whether their paths cross often or seldom. The family includes such proud though sometimes impoverished members as the large luxury passenger liners as well as the tramp vessel which, though often called lowly, is a respectable and respected member of the clan. The family also includes combination passenger-cargo vessels, dry cargo liners, reefer and refrigerator ships, tankers, ore carriers, and various combinations of the foregoing. For reasons probably best understood by marine insurance underwriters, a vessel with accommodations for more than twelve passengers is known as a combination passenger-cargo ship unless the relative importance of the passenger business transcends some mystical, undefined margin, in which case the full dignity of the title—passenger liner—is conferred. Reefer vessels carry chilled cargo, while refrigerator vessels are able to carry frozen or chilled cargo. The distinction between the ordinary cargo liner and a tramp vessel is so nebulous that it is impossible to formulate precise definitions.[1] While tramp vessels on the average are apt to be both smaller and slower than their bigger and faster brothers operating in regular scheduled service by a shipping "line," and therefore known as liners,

[1] The difficulty of distinguishing between tramps and liners is illustrated by the experience of the British when they inaugurated a tramp subsidy in 1935 (see Chap. XI). Since no definitions would work satisfactorily, they were forced to write up a complex set of rules to limit eligibility. Mr. C. Ernest Fayle, an English writer on maritime subjects, describes the situation quite well when he states, "Strictly speaking, a liner service implies today a fleet of ships, under common ownership or management, which provides a fixed service, at regular intervals, between named ports, and offer themselves as common carriers of any goods or passengers requiring shipment between those ports and ready for transit by their sailing dates. A fixed itinerary, inclusion in a regular service, and the obligation to accept cargo from all comers and to sail, whether filled or not, on the date fixed by a published schedule; these, and not the size and speed of the ships nor the number of vessels in the fleet are what distinguished the 'liner' from the 'tramp,' 'seeker,' or 'general trader'—the ship which can be hired as a whole, by the voyage or the month, to load such cargo and to carry it between such ports as the charterer may require." *A Short History of the World's Shipping Industry* (London: George Allen & Unwin, Ltd., 1933), pp. 253-254.

numerous ships are transferred from one category to the other as business conditions change. Tankers, as the name implies, are vessels equipped to handle bulk liquid cargoes. While their principal business consists of the transportation of petroleum and its products, tank ships also convey a variety of liquid cargoes which move in large volume, e.g. molasses and creosote. Ore carriers, as the name indicates, are vessels primarily employed in carrying bulk ore cargoes. They are often especially designed to carry cargo of considerable density, i.e. cargo whose weight is large relative to its bulk.

The closeness or remoteness of the relationship of these carriers to each other depends on the degree of competition among them. Passenger and cargo liners rarely carry shipments of coal or ores. Coal is generally carried by tramps, and ore by tramps or by especially designed ore vessels operated by concerns directly interested in the cargo. Grains, on the other hand, while they constitute one of the most important tramp cargoes, are also carried by passenger liners, combination liners, and cargo liners—in short, by all members of the liner family. Reefer and refrigerator carriers generally operate, as liners, on regular schedules, and in addition frequently carry ordinary cargo in space not devoted to chilled or frozen commodities. They generally carry ordinary cargo on the return voyage. Ore carriers may operate on a similar basis though they frequently return in ballast. Tankships are the most exclusive members of the shipping family and generally confine their business to the conveyance of bulk liquid cargoes, although some tankers have limited internal accommodations for dry cargo, as well as some space available on deck, though this latter is rarely used. Many dry cargo vessels are equipped with deep tanks which permit them to handle relatively small quantities of bulk liquid cargoes. The degree of competition varies not only with respect to the commodities transported but with the ocean route, or trade as it is called, as well.

Since this study is concerned with shipping conferences it is primarily interested in ships which operate as liners and such other vessels as customarily compete with them. As previously indicated, liners include passenger vessels, combination cargo-passenger vessels (generally referred to as combination vessels), reefer and refrigerator vessels (which incidentally also frequently have sufficient accommodations for passengers to be classified as combination vessels), and ordinary cargo liners carrying twelve or less passengers. Whenever competition is provided by tramp vessels (ordinary cargo car-

8

riers not operating on a scheduled service) their activities must also be considered.

Ocean shipping produces different products, all of which may be described as transportation service, which, in technical economic language, is described as the creation of place utility. While the creation of place utility is the universal function of all shipping, the speed of a vessel is important and high speeds frequently command higher rates. Therefore, shipping may at times also be said to create time utility. In some relatively rare cases ocean transportation also creates form utility; an example of this is when wines or distilled spirits are placed in a vessel for a long voyage because the vessel's motion expedites the aging process. While it is true, nevertheless, that ocean shipping is primarily involved in the creation of place utility, the product or service rendered frequently varies with the cargo carried. The carriage of passengers is obviously a service quite different from the carriage of cargo, and the difference between carrying bulk petroleum in a ship specially designed to transport liquids in bulk and bananas in a reefer ship designed for that purpose is equally apparent. Even if the passengers and cargo are carried on the same voyage, or if the petroleum is conveyed in the deep tanks of the reefer vessel loaded with bananas, the service or product created is different. Furthermore, the service produced on an outbound voyage differs from that produced on the homebound voyage. The carriage of cargoes on different routes, and at times transportation at different speeds, must also be considered as the production of different products. A less apparent difference occurs when two or more types of commodities are transported simultaneously by the same vessel under similar conditions between a given port of origin and a common destination. Nevertheless the service rendered in carrying a shipment of sand is neither exactly identical to nor completely homogeneous with that rendered in the movement of machinery, although both may be carried in similar space on the same vessel from the same port of origin to the same destination. The distinction in this latter case depends primarily on differences in the cost of handling each commodity and therefore it can, although real, be easily exaggerated.

PRICING OF OCEAN TRANSPORTATION

The pricing of ocean transportation, like all pricing, is subject to the forces of supply and demand; but the variables affecting its supply and demand are unusually numerous. Ocean shipping may produce one or several commodities (or types of service). It is frequently subject to joint costs.[2] Furthermore, it is often characterized by increasing returns resulting from fuller utilization of carrying capacity, and at times it can reduce average unit costs by expanding the scale of operations.[3] In addition, the mobility of its "plant" renders opportunity costs of greater significance than in the case of most manufacturing or other service industries.[4] Its products, which cannot be stored in an inventory or accumulated for future use, are capable in some instances of being differentiated, though differentiation is rarely important except in the carriage of passengers;[5] and the demand for its products, except for passengers taking a pleasure cruise, is derived from the demand for other things.

The prices of its services (known as freight rates or passenger fares) are determined in a variety of market structures, which range all the way from competition as pure and perfect as floor trading on an organized exchange will provide, to monopolies as exploitative as the elasticity of demand and business prudence will permit. The former situation applies to the fixing of tramp charters on the Baltic Shipping Exchange, though not to all such fixtures. While many tramps are fixed under conditions approximating perfect competition, most liner rates are tinged with more than a little of the monopolistic element. A "pure" monopoly condition is rarely found, and then only in relatively unimportant trades, or where government restrictions assist the monopoly in avoiding the hot, invigorating breath of some competition. In short, the liner trades, except for a few cases of pure monopoly, are basically oligopolistic[6] market structures; but since in the great majority of instances coordination is

[2] "Joint costs" are those which cannot be specifically allocated to any one of two or more goods or services resulting from the same productive process.

[3] In this volume "increasing returns" will be employed to designate the advantages accruing from fuller utilization of available, usually scheduled, carrying capacity. "Decreasing costs" will refer to the reduction in average unit costs resulting from expanding the scale of operations, i.e. the running of more or larger ships. Since the latter advantage often arises from more complete utilization of shore staff and facilities, it may differ but slightly from the former.

[4] "Opportunity cost" in the present connotation refers to the "cost" of foregoing one opportunity in order to accept another.

[5] Although there is relatively little product differentiation in the cargo markets, some exists as a result of preferable schedules, extra facilities offered shippers by the carriers, friendship, habit, convenience, and local and national patriotism. Standardization of rates, facilities, and practices tend to make all but the latter of small importance. Preference because of business connections is at times of considerable significance, and reciprocity arrangements in some trades are of great importance in the routing of shipments.

[6] "Oligopoly" is an economic term denoting a relatively small number of sellers.

provided by an association of lines, known as a shipping conference or ring, the market structure is transformed into a limited monopoly.

In the light of these conditions, it is not astonishing that the pricing of ocean transportation is a complex matter. It was previously explained that ocean shipping consists of a family of industries. We shall now examine the principal factors affecting ocean freight rates charged by ships operating as liners, although occasional comments will indicate some of the principal differences affecting rates charged by tramps.

THE PRINCIPAL COST FACTORS AFFECTING OCEAN FREIGHT RATES

The principal cost factors affecting ocean freight rates may be classified as follows:

    I.   Prime or out-of-pocket expenses.
    II. Operating expenses.
   III. Overhead expenses.
   IV. Joint costs.
    V. Opportunity costs.

I. *Prime or out-of-pocket expenses*: The first and last out-of-pocket expenses which in most cases have to be met by an ocean liner are those of loading and discharging. Unlike railroad transportation in the United States where the loading and discharging of carload lots is generally handled by the shipper or consignee, in ocean transportation such operations are customarily performed for the account of the vessel. Port facilities, efficiency of longshore labor, and the ability to handle certain types of cargo by mechanical devices rather than by hand dominate the cost of providing these services. Bulk grain, for instance, can be loaded from an elevator by gravity and unloaded ("discharged") by suction or by clamshell buckets with only a small amount of hand labor necessary for trimming the cargo. On the other hand, boxed shipments, such as canned goods, must generally be stowed in, or "broken out," of the hold by hand regardless of whether the cases are placed in or removed from the vessel by sling loads, conveyor belts, or hand trucks.

Heavy lifts and commodities of extra length often require special handling. If cargo is too heavy to be handled by the ship's tackle, it may be necessary to hire floating cranes or other special equipment. In some instances, although the vessel itself may be able to handle these heavy lifts, extra expense may be involved because of the addi-

11

tional care and time required. Other commodities because of extra length or unusually large dimensions require special handling, and special stowage, and it may be possible to carry only relatively few such items on the ship because the space which can accommodate them is limited. Some cargo requires special sorting, storing, or other extra services, such as coopering or guarding, and these services necessarily involve additional costs to the vessel. At times it is necessary for a ship to receive or deliver cargo at special docks in addition to those customarily employed and such diversions involve extra time and expense for shifting and tying up the vessel, and possibly additional port charges.

Claims for loss or damage also exert an important influence on freights. Some commodities are unusually susceptible to damage or spoilage and others are highly susceptible to pilferage. Well-packed goods tend to minimize these dangers but the inherent nature of some items still renders them more liable than others to claims. Other commodities such as acids and creosoted wood possess an inherent vice which may contaminate adjacent cargo; while other goods, such as flour and chocolate, are themselves easily contaminated. The value of the commodity also influences the size of the claim which might arise, and accordingly some items are shipped at a valuation which releases the carrier from liability in excess of a specified amount.

Special stowage is another consideration which affects costs. In addition to goods of unusually large dimensions and those easily contaminated, some cargoes require ventilation, refrigeration, or other special treatment. In contrast to the extra cost of transporting goods requiring special handling or treatment, some commodities are desirable in certain instances because they provide weight or stiffening, or are useful as dunnage in protecting fragile goods. The stowage factor of a commodity, or the relation of the weight of a unit to its cubic measurement, is always important and will be separately considered under *joint costs*.

II. *Operating expenses*: These expenses, depending on circumstances, are sometimes fixed and sometimes variable. For a liner already scheduled they represent a fixed charge to which the operator has committed himself, but for a tramp or for the sailing of a liner in addition to the regular schedule these costs are variable in nature and can be avoided, at least in part, by laying up the ship, or altered by placing it in another trade. These alternatives introduce an element of opportunity cost which will be considered separately. The direct costs of operation include fuel, water, food, supplies, crew's wages, maintenance and repair, marine insurance on the vessel, protection and indemnity insurance, etc. These expenses depend on the route to be taken, the size, speed and type of vessel, the management, and the ports of call. In addition, there are port expenses which vary considerably in different parts of the world and include such items as pilotage, lighterage, and the prompt availability of berthing space. Port regulations, as well as port charges and dues, and canal tolls,[7] all affect the operating cost of a vessel, as does the location of some ports which might lie inside of a dangerous bar or hazardous channel.

III. *Overhead expenses*: Overhead expenses include such items as management, interest on capital investment, depreciation, and some taxes. Provision must be made for the cost of maintaining shore staffs, and liner companies frequently employ salesmen, known as freight solicitors, and operate terminals. For tramps and for some liner operations these expenses are variable rather than fixed because commissions may be paid to agents at ports where the shipowner does not maintain his own organization and the payment is then generally based on the volume of cargo or the value of the freight handled at that port. Terminals at most major ports may be utilized on an *ad hoc* basis by payment of wharfage or other terminal charges.

Most overhead expenses as well as some operating expenses, such as crew's wages, it should be noted, do not vary whether the steamer is in port (unless in lay-up, in which case crew's wages are nominal) or under way on the high seas; but these expenses do vary directly though not proportionately with the size of the vessel. Within limits large vessels are cheaper to run per ton of carrying capacity than small ships. Draft limitations of some harbors and waterways, and the fact that they may be closer to the size of the typical load, thereby avoiding the necessity of sailing with considerable unused capacity or of waiting in port for more cargo, give the smaller carrier its advantages.

IV. *Joint costs*: As with other modes of transportation, shipping involves joint costs. The prospect of securing return cargo is naturally influential in determining the rates that must be charged for outgoing cargo. Obviously it is preferable for a vessel to be able to

---

[7] Some port charges and canal tolls are based on the cargo carried instead of on the vessel and can, therefore, be more properly classified as out-of-pocket expenses.

secure full cargoes both outbound and inbound, or to be able to accomplish this desideratum by engaging in a triangular, or, if necessary, more circuitous voyage. An interesting development illustrating this is the round-the-world operation of several lines.

Another element of jointness, generally of less significance to most other types of transportation, is the stowage factor or the relation of a cargo's weight to measurement. For a ship to operate at the greatest advantage it should be loaded so as to be "full and down"; that is, it should be loaded to its full capacity to carry weight and at the same time to its full cubic or space capacity. A vessel with a cargo of iron and steel products may be submerged to its Plimsoll mark (legal depth), while much of its space remains empty. On the other hand, a vessel may fill its holds with a lightweight commodity, such as loosely baled cotton, and still retain unused considerable lifting capacity. The variety of stowage factors is illustrated by the following: one ton of lumber customarily occupies 80 cubic feet of space, while wood pulp utilizes only 45 cubic feet per ton; canned goods and dried beans stow at 55 cubic feet; iron and steel bars stow at 15 cubic feet per ton; iron and steel pipe require 36; lawn mowers in boxes have a stowage factor of 71; and oil paints in barrels customarily ship with a stowage factor of 24.

For the liner with a prearranged and advertised schedule to maintain, the volume and availability of cargo is also important. Some shippers may require frequent and regular service, but their patronage may not be sufficient to load vessels remuneratively. Other shippers may provide a large volume of business at certain times but not at others. If a steady volume of basic cargo is regularly available in adequate quantity, frequent sailings can more easily be maintained on a profitable basis and the rates on all commodities consequently may be lower than if vessels are required to sail at certain seasons with unused space and weight capacity. Such cargo complementarity is another instance of jointness, and is well illustrated by the operations of some industrial carriers[8] whose efficiency of operation is improved by the existence of a predictable and steady volume of proprietary cargo.

[8] An "industrial carrier" is a transportation concern which is affiliated with a commercial or industrial enterprise whose transportation requirements constitute an important element in the business of the carrier. Industrial carriers frequently operate as common carriers and handle traffic for anyone, including competitors of its affiliate, who wishes to ship on the route or routes served. Railroad ownership of steamship lines presents a similar situation.

V. *Opportunity costs*: The mobility of vessels permits them to be shifted more easily from one area to another than is possible for most other forms of capital equipment of comparable value. Accordingly, alternate employment presents to liner operators an opportunity to shift a vessel from a depressed trade to a more active part of the world. In some instances these vessels may be operated in another service provided by the same company, or they may be chartered to other liner operators or as tramps for a period of time. The more highly specialized types of vessels are less adaptable to other uses than the general types of cargo carrier, but there are relatively few vessels that do not have some flexibility of this sort. In the case of tramps, they traditionally make it their business to try to be in that portion of the world where the most remunerative rates are to be earned. As a result, opportunity costs assume a greater importance in shipping than in most other industries, and the continued scheduling of vessels in a regular service can be maintained only by foregoing the opportunities presented by alternate employment. This does not mean that a liner operator will remove a vessel from a given trade whenever higher profits are available elsewhere; because the operator will naturally consider the long-term repercussions that such an action might have upon his relations with shippers on his customary route and his competitive position vis-à-vis other participants in the trade. Nonetheless, some shifting of vessels can easily take place and frequently does. It is not inaccurate to visualize the world's shipping tonnage as a pool from whose margins carrying capacity will flow to those areas currently offering the most attractive possibilities.

In addition to the foregoing opportunity of alternate employment, a shipowner, as other owners of capital equipment, always has the option of laying up his craft if business conditions are sufficiently bad to warrant such action. In reaching such a decision there are special "lay-up" costs to be considered, and vessels depreciate more rapidly when idle. The shipowner must also take into account in the case of a lay-up, as in the case of a transfer to another trade, the effect of his action on his patrons and competitors. It must be remembered that although alternate employment opportunities provide the supply of shipping on most routes with considerable flexibility, and that laying-up and withdrawals from lay-up impart some flexibility to the total supply of active tonnage it is only new construction and scrapping which radically affect the total. The durability of vessels and the length of time required to build new ships renders the total supply of tonnage rather stable for fairly long periods of time; and therefore total tonnage responds slowly to price (rate) changes.

A final example of opportunity costs, which has already been alluded to, is presented by cargoes which readily contaminate others and by those which are themselves easily contaminated. In such cases the ship operator may be forced to decide to carry one or the other.

THE DEMAND FACTORS AFFECTING OCEAN FREIGHT RATES

The demand for ocean transportation is, with one exception noted above, derived from the demand for the commodities carried, and is therefore affected by the elasticity of demand for the commodity itself as well as by transportation competition.[9] The unit value of a commodity offers a crude indication of the value of the service. A more accurate measure of the value of service, however, and one which sets a ceiling beyond which the freight rate cannot go without stopping the movement, may be obtained by subtracting the market value at the port of origin from the market value at the destination (after making due allowance for other costs, such as interest, insurance, marketing, etc.).[10] The elasticity of demand for ocean shipping, being a derived demand, is affected by the availability of substitutes for the commodity seeking transportation as well as by direct com-

[9] "Elasticity of demand" refers to the relationship between proportionate changes in the amount of a good or service that is purchased and proportionate changes in its price, or proportionate changes in the buyer's rate of income. When a change in price produces a more than proportionate change in the quantities bought, the demand is said to be price elastic. Conversely, when a change in price produces a less than proportionate change in the quantities bought, then demand is called price inelastic. Similarly, "income elasticity" refers to the relation of proportionate changes in quantity bought to proportionate changes in the buyer's rate of income.

[10] If a rate is based on the difference in price of a commodity in the exporting market A and the importing market B and if A is the sole source of supply, then there is circularity of reasoning involved if this price difference is used to compute the value of the service. However, if B can obtain the commodity from other sources, the value of the transport service may be an independent variable. If A is a highly important although not necessarily the only source of supply for the commodity, then the demand for the service is, like the demand in any other monopolistic or semi-monopolistic market, inclined downwards to the right, and a complete escape from circularity is not possible when employing as a criterion "value of service" in this connotation. Therefore, the unit value of the commodity itself is often used for rate-making purposes. However, competitive sources of supply may exercise far greater influence on rates than the unit value of the commodity; for when B can obtain the item in adequate volume from sources other than A, or from A via other modes of transport, the value of the service becomes a highly important rate determinant.

16

petition.[11] Direct competition may come from other carriers operating on the same route, from carriers operating via competitive gateways (e.g. there has been keen competition between United States Atlantic and Pacific ports for trade moving from the Middle West to the Orient), and from other sources of supply for the same commodity.

The elasticity of demand for ocean transportation, therefore, varies considerably from one commodity to another, and even for the same commodity it will differ at different times and on different trade routes. The cost of transportation, furthermore, represents a varying proportion of the total delivered cost of the commodities carried and will, accordingly, have a larger or smaller effect on price of the product. Illustrations of the relation of freight costs to delivered price are abundant; a few examples will suffice. The 1939 prewar freight rate on flour from United States Gulf ports to London was approximately 25 cents per hundred pounds, and although this was approximately one-sixth of its export value it is estimated that this amounted to only about 1.7 mills per pound of bread.[12] In 1939 the ocean freight on paint shipped from New York to Rio de Janeiro amounted to 7 per cent of the retail price of the commodity in the South American city and less than 8 per cent of the landed price.[13] Paint shipped from New York to Buenos Aires in 1939 paid a freight less than 4 per cent of the retail price and slightly more than 7 per cent of its landed value.[14] The ratio of freight charges to value of high-priced manufactured goods is apt to be quite small, despite rate structures which charged considerably higher freights for transporting items of high unit value. This is illustrated by the rate on typewriters shipped from New York to Rio de Janeiro and Buenos Aires where the freight amounted to less than 2 1/2 per cent of the retail price and less than 4 1/2 per cent of the landed cost at Rio de Janeiro, while at Buenos Aires these figures were approximately 2 per cent and 2 3/4 per cent respectively.[15] In the case of imports we find the rates on coffee from East Coast Colombian ports to New

[11] "Derived demand" or "indirect demand" refers to the demand for goods or services employed in the production of other goods or services.

[12] Hobart S. Perry, *Impact of the Present War on Ocean Shipping with Special Reference to the Effects of War Shipping Conditions on United States Agriculture* (Washington: U.S. Dept. of Agriculture, mimeographed 1940), pp. 71 and 86.

[13] *Inter-American Maritime Conference* (Washington: U.S. Government Printing Office, 1941), p. 185.

[14] *loc.cit.*

[15] *ibid.*, p. 186.

York to have been only slightly greater than 1/2 cent per pound from 1926 through 1939, or approximately 6 per cent of its landed value.[16] For other imports we find that crude rubber paid a prewar freight equal to approximately 3 to 4 per cent of its landed value,[17] while raw silk paid a freight equal to 1 to 3 per cent of its import value.[18] For commodities of lower unit value, ocean freights constitute a more important component, and we find that cane sugar from Cuba paid a prewar freight equal to approximately 6 per cent of its landed value.[19] Iron and steel structural shapes paid prewar freights equal to approximately 18 to 20 per cent of their value.[20] Some of the highest rate to value ratios are for commodities shipped on tramps at charter rates, so we find that while the actual rates on fuel oil and manganese ore, for example, were low,[21] they constituted approximately 22 per cent and 18 per cent of the value of these commodities.[22] The cost of transportation, therefore, is of much greater importance for some industries, some commodities, and some sources of supply, than for others. When the cost of transportation represents a small proportion of the total price at which the article is sold the demand for transport will tend to be price inelastic, whereas if the transportation cost constitutes a large proportion of the total cost then transport demand will tend to be more elastic. Although the availability of substitutes or alternate sources of supply will tend to increase the elasticity of demand for transportation, the fact remains that the freight rate is only one element, and sometimes a small element, in the final sales price; and therefore the effect of the cost of transport on the volume of business is frequently negligible.

The demand factors of ocean freight rates, like the cost factors, are highly complex and subject to numerous variables. In situations of this type, quantification which might illuminate the elasticity of demand with sufficient precision to be useful is in all likelihood not

[16] ibid., Exhibit No. 2, opp. p. 184.

[17] U.S. Tariff Commission, Transportation Costs and Value of Principal Imports (Washington, processed 1940), p. 50.

[18] op.cit., p. 45.   [19] op.cit., p. 2.   [20] op.cit., p. 35.

[21] A typical prewar rate on fuel oil from Venezuela to United States North Atlantic ports was 5 cents per 100 pounds, while manganese ore from Black Sea ports to the United States moved at around 13 cents per 100 pounds. Compare this with typical prewar rates per 100 pounds of 49 cents and 57 cents for crude rubber from the Netherlands Indies and British Malaya respectively; of $2.00 for silk from Japan to Pacific Coast ports and $4.00 to Atlantic ports; of 12 cents for sugar from Cuba; and 30 cents for structural iron and steel from Belgium.

[22] op.cit., pp. 27 and 34.

obtainable for the majority of commodities moving in world commerce. Even if such information were available, the underlying demand forces from which the demand for transportation is derived are usually subject to fluctuation to an extent which is apt to render meaningless elasticity schedules calculated for a previous period. This indeterminateness should be kept in mind when the actual rate-making practices of ocean carriers are subsequently considered. The indeterminate nature of the elasticity of demand, however, is not the only calculation in which the ship operator is faced with a lack of precision, for the same vagueness plagues many of his cost computations as well. The consequences of such indeterminateness are considered below.

SOME CONSEQUENCES OF ECONOMIC FACTORS

In addition to the arbitrariness involved in cost estimates of depreciation and obsolescence which are common to many business enterprises, shipping is characterized, as we have seen, by joint costs and opportunity costs, and in addition frequently operates under conditions of increasing returns and decreasing costs. These cost characteristics often involve ocean shipping in a choice between cutthroat competition and monopolistic arrangements.

I. *Increasing returns and decreasing costs*: An examination of a composite income statement covering 1,577 voyages of United States flag liners serving the American republics during the years 1936 through 1939 reveals that expenses directly chargeable to cargo generally ran between 25 and 30 per cent of total expenses.[23] The same source reveals that expenses chargeable to vessel operation ranged from 50 to 55 per cent and that overhead costs ran from 20 to 25 per cent.[24] These results also held for the prewar composite operation of

[23] Cargo expenses are a first approximation of out-of-pocket expenses but somewhat understate the latter, because port charges, wharfage, dockage, etc., incurred exclusively to pick up or discharge a given consignment, are not always included in the former.

[24] *Inter-American Maritime Conference, op.cit.*, pp. 319-320. These cost percentages are crude approximations and should be interpreted as indicating only roughly the relative order of magnitude of out-of-pocket, operating, and overhead expenses. The crudeness of these data arises from several causes which are enumerated here in order to enable the reader both to appreciate the limitations of these figures and to glimpse some of the difficulties which surround composite financial statistics of the shipping industry:

(1) The capacity of the vessels is not given.
(2) Some were freighters while others were combination vessels.
(3) Some were chartered while others were owned by the operators.

10 common carriers engaged in the intercoastal trade between the Atlantic and Pacific coasts of the United States via the Panama Canal.[25] Vessels operating under foreign flags with different manning and subsistence standards, different wage scales, and different capital costs, might very well not have identical cost patterns. Vessels operating as tramps will also probably show a different distribution of costs.[26] To the extent that tramps usually carry bulk shipments, their cargo or out-of-pocket expenses will tend to be lower, and as they are not required to maintain shore establishments comparable to those needed for liner operation their overhead costs are apt to be lower. Tramps, therefore, can be expected to show a higher percentage of their total costs going for operating expenses and lower ratios for out-of-pocket and overhead expenses than liners. But since tramps are not compelled to observe a schedule their operating costs tend to become variable rather than fixed; and as they are more apt to sail well loaded, they are also apt to show lower unit cost for both operation and overhead. There is no reason, moreover, to believe that American vessels operating on trade routes different from those mentioned, and carrying different types of cargo, would necessarily show the same relationship between cargo, operating, and overhead expense.[27] But since the general magnitudes probably remain roughly

---

(4) Depreciation was generally based on vessel value far below replacement cost at the end of the period; but, despite this, average profits for the four-year period were negative. Subsidies probably rectified this.

(5) The amount of unused capacity is not shown. In 1938, the average load per voyage was 159 passengers and 5,010 tons of cargo; while in 1939 the average load was 168 passengers and 5,880 tons of cargo. As a result overhead expenses and other fixed charges, excluding charter hire, dropped from 19.1 per cent of total expenses before profits in 1938 to 18.4 per cent in 1939. Profits were reported as 1.2 per cent of total expenses in 1938 and as 4.4 per cent in 1939. Since vessels were added to the route in 1939 and more voyages made than in the previous year no significant deductions can be made from the change in average load.

Nonetheless the crucial fact remains, viz., a liner operator is committed to substantial costs once his schedule is advertised, and as a result liner operation is characterized by increasing returns over a substantial range.

[25] Intercoastal Rate Structure, 2 U.S.M.C. 285 (299).

[26] As J. Russell Smith so aptly states, "The schedule is the soul of the line and it joins with many other costs to make the traffic of lines more costly than that of the individual vessel that is run with only the necessary costs of physical operation." "Ocean Freight Rates," *Political Science Quarterly*, xxi, No. 2 (1906).

[27] Postwar cost information for operators in the United States intercoastal service shows a considerable increase in the percentage of total expenses attributable to the handling of cargo, with the result that while operating expenses remain in the neighborhood of 50 per cent the percentage allocated to overhead expenses has decreased. (See Interstate Commerce Commission, *Ex Parte No. 165*, pp. 283-287; and the Bureau of Foreign and Domestic Commerce, *Industry Report, Domestic Trans-*

the same we can tentatively conclude that, once it has been determined to place a vessel on berth, roughly 70 to 75 per cent of the cost of the voyage is fixed, and only approximately 25 to 30 per cent remains of a variable nature. Liner operators with fixed schedules, therefore, have fixed expenses of this magnitude; and anything, such as subsidies or pooling agreements, which increases the rigidity of schedules tends to emphasize the costs to which the operator has committed himself. However, if a vessel has not been previously scheduled in a particular service, the percentage of total expenses which are directly chargeable to the output of the service amounts to approximately 75 to 80 per cent.[28]

The crucial fact which appears from these estimates of costs is that, once a vessel has been scheduled by a liner operator or actually placed on berth by a tramp operator, a large proportion of the total expenses of the voyage has become fixed, and until the vessel is loaded "full and down" it will be remunerative for that vessel to carry any additional cargo that can be procured so long as it pays anything in excess of the actual out-of-pocket expense involved. In trades where the flow of commerce is not balanced—and this is the case more often than not—both liners and tramps will be tempted to engage in cutthroat competition at least on the leg of the voyage on which cargo is light.

Increasing returns, especially important when fixed costs are high, depend on the existence of unused carrying capacity. Unused capacity is not only apt to occur periodically as a result of seasonal and cyclical fluctuations coupled with the imperfect mobility of vessels, but it has been a chronic condition which has plagued the industry in a large number of peacetime years. Construction stimulated by the anticipated requirements of defense and the practices of conference have, as will be shown in subsequent chapters, tended to provide a plethora of shipping tonnage. In situations of shipping scar-

---

portation, April-May, 1947, p. 10.) This situation, however, is probably not representative of world shipping conditions and is probably due to the very rapid increase in cargo handling costs at American ports and the relatively low capital charges for vessels in this service. It is estimated that cargo handling charges probably ranged between $1.00 and $7.00 a ton at this time, the lower rate being applicable to bulk commodities, and the cost for handling general cargo varying according to its nature from $3.00 to $7.00 a ton. This represents an increase of almost 100 per cent, in many cases, over prewar. (See Bureau of Foreign and Domestic Commerce, *Industry Report, Domestic Transportation*, April-May, 1946, p. 48; and Association of American Railroads, *Transportation in America*, Washington, 1947, p. 52.)

[28] Out-of-pocket expenses plus operating expenses.

city, such as existed immediately after the termination of World War II and again after the outbreak of hostilities in Korea, the tendency of the industry to operate with unused capacity is severely reduced.

Decreasing costs arise from internal and external economies not hitherto examined in this analysis. For example, overhead costs, especially for management, may not increase as rapidly as the traffic carried. If management has not been fully employed, more ships can be operated and more tonnage can be carried without commensurate additions to staff. Likewise a larger volume of traffic may enable fuller use to be made of shoreside facilities, or it may justify the employment of more efficient terminals and handling equipment.

II. *Cutthroat competition or monopolistic arrangements*: Wherever there are substantial joint costs, opportunity costs, fixed costs, or a combination of these elements in the production process of a multi-product concern, these expenses may be allocated deliberately and arbitrarily to such commodities or markets as appear expedient in order to reflect low costs and positive profits where desired as an apparent justification for cutthroat pricing and discriminatory practices. As a result, one should not be astonished to find cutthroat competition and price discrimination "justified" in this manner by ocean carriers. Such is often the case, and, as in other areas of the economy where cutthroat competition is inherent, monopolistic arrangements generally follow. In addition to combination through mergers and amalgamations these monopolistic arrangements in the shipping industry have commonly taken the form of shipping conferences or rings, a variety of "tying" devices, and pooling agreements of various sorts; and it is these latter devices to regulate or restrict competition with which this study is primarily concerned. Where competition is not perfect the entrepreneur can influence price either by his control of supply or his ability to manipulate demand through product differentiation, advertising, tying arrangements, etc. In view of the numerous variables affecting the supply of and demand for ocean transportation and the indeterminate nature of many of them, it is not astounding to find a great variety of schemes and market structures, ranging from the highly competitive to the monopolistic, and in some trades elements of both are present as different commodities are frequently accorded different treatment.

For example, on some trade routes some or all of the liner operators belong to a conference which controls rates, sailing schedules, or both; and in some instances freight revenues are pooled; while in a few trades there are no conferences. On trade routes in which we find conferences, direct competition may be provided by: (1) intra-conference rivalry; (2) operators of liners who are not conference members and who may or may not charge conference rates; (3) tramps which compete primarily in the carriage of commodities moving in bulk and whose presence frequently requires the conferences to exempt certain goods from its rate agreement; and (4) other conferences serving alternate sources or markets. All these situations will be examined in subsequent chapters.

III. *Price discrimination.* We have seen how the indeterminateness of ship operating costs and the various and indeterminate elasticities of demand for ocean transportation tend to obscure the relationship between cost and freight rates. While an ocean-going vessel might sell several products, such as refrigerator space, ventilated space, deck space, deep-tank space, as well as ordinary dry cargo space, each of these in itself represents a more or less homogeneous product. Although the expenses of loading and discharging and the claims liability involved in the carriage of bulk grain, sacks of coffee, and machinery, are quite different, there still is a distinctly homogeneous element involved in providing for the transportation of all these types of cargo. The rates charged for their conveyance, however, vary considerably, being in general influenced by the value of the commodity, and by the value of the transportation service which in turn is influenced by the availability of competitive sources of supply and transportation. To the extent that liners sell a relatively homogeneous product at rates whose difference cannot be explained by cost differences, they may be said to be engaging in price discrimination. The prevalence of monopolistic elements in the market structures where general cargo rates are determined facilitates such price discrimination. The term "price discrimination" unfortunately possesses a prejudicial normative connotation; but it need not always involve undue discrimination, and it may often aid in achieving desirable results by reducing under-utilization of existing shipping.[29]

A NOTE ON PASSENGER FARES

Basically, very much the same influences affect passenger fares as cargo rates. All passenger liners carry cargo, although the relative importance of human and inanimate freight varies considerably so

---

[29] Economists are not in universal agreement with this proposition. A brief note on this controversy appears in Appendix A.

that the weight given various supply and demand factors is quite different for luxury-liners and for ordinary combination carriers. On the cost side, passengers involve smaller loading and discharging expenses in relation to the revenue forthcoming for their passage than is the case with cargo, unless it is handled "free in and out"—that is, at the shipper's or consignee's expense. On the other hand, operating expenses are higher because subsistence and service must be provided, and because speed and regularity of sailings are of greater importance. Furthermore, sales costs are higher because of the necessity for advertising, ticket offices, and sizable commissions. In addition to the greater expense involved in the actual making of reservations and selling of tickets, there is also the element of product differentiation which tends to expand sales costs. The cuisine, service, entertainment, décor, and the thousand and one other factors that cause travelers to prefer one line to another are carefully developed and exploited. Finally, many passenger ships designed for a particular trade are so highly specialized that they frequently have less mobility than ordinary cargo ships, and this reduces the influence of opportunity costs. The greater importance of product differentiation (generally of small consequence in the goods carriage business) would by itself indicate a different demand situation since it gives more emphasis to subjective elements in shaping the demand curve than is the case for cargo where the market for the product at its destination plays a dominant role. The demand for passenger accommodations is not only derived from the needs of business and government, but consists also of the direct demand of persons desiring to travel for pleasure. Insofar as the demand of passengers is a composite demand, it resembles the multitudinous sources of demand for cargo transport; and insofar as both the price and income elasticities of the demands of both passengers and shippers are for the most part unknown, if not unknowable, the resemblance continues. However, this does not mean that the elasticities for goods and passenger transport necessarily have any similarity. Nor does it mean that the "value of service" principle of cargo rate-making permits scaling comparable to that employed for passenger fares, which are generally divided into classes with different fares for different accommodations within each class. Although differential rates are not unknown in the cargo business, and lower rates are sometimes permitted by a conference to members operating old, slow vessels, the practice is relatively rare in comparison with the almost universal application of this principle to the pricing of passenger accommodations. Finally, the passenger business is subject to much greater competition from aircraft than is true for cargo, with the exception of mail and a small quantity of express shipments.

CHAPTER III
THE GENERAL ECONOMIC AND
POLITICAL ENVIRONMENT

A NEW MULTILATERAL NETWORK of world trade came into being about 1870, largely as a result of technical improvements in production and transportation,[1] which has enabled the world to benefit materially from an almost world-wide system of geographical specialization. The advent of the steamship completely altered merchandising methods for overseas markets since steamships, independent of wind conditions, were able to adhere to fairly regular schedules. In combination with the expansion of cable and postal services, regular schedules gradually reduced one of the great speculative elements in overseas trade by permitting shipments more nearly in accord with market requirements. Furthermore, as the speed of steamers increased, the shipment of perishable commodities and goods of high value was facilitated. The most significant change of all, however, was the substantial reduction in the costs of transportation, and the resultant growth in the movement of relatively low-value commodities.[2] Dr. Wickizer describes this development graphically, "Shipping—together with railway transportation—created the world grain market and has been largely responsible for its vast expansion during the past century. Enormous improvements in ships, with corresponding changes in port facilities, cargo handling, and shipping organization, brought freight rates down to a small fraction of their former size. Great reductions in transportation costs stimulated the agricultural development of newer countries, promoted international division of labor, enlarged the productive capacity of the world, greatly reduced the hazards to world food supplies from crop failures in particular countries, and helped to create new land values in some places and at least temporarily to depreciate land values in others."[3] The

---

[1] League of Nations, *The Network of World Trade* (Geneva: 1942), p. 9.
[2] Such secular price elasticity of demand should not be confused with the inelasticity applicable in shorter periods referred to in Chapter II.
[3] V. D. Wickizer, "Shipping and Freight Rates in the Overseas Grain Trade," *Wheat Studies of the Food Research Institute*, Vol. xv, No. 2 (1938), p. 49. This excellent work has been very helpful in the preparation of this chapter.

steamer has become beyond doubt the prime conveyor of international trade; and it has been estimated that in 1937 ships carried approximately 75 per cent of the volume of the commerce moving between nations.[4] The network of world commerce gradually expanded until it embraced almost all countries, and after a temporary disruption during World War I this multilateral movement of commerce was resumed with the support of United States capital exports.[5] However, by the middle of 1928 the repatriation of liquid funds by creditor countries imposed strains on the system which culminated in the financial crisis of 1931. This breakdown led to the imposition of restrictions which increasingly disturbed the multilateral nature of world trade and thereby introduced cumulatively more clearing difficulties and still more restrictions on the transaction of foreign trade.

In addition to the foregoing developments, other fundamental changes since 1870 have affected the composition and direction of world commerce. The Suez and Panama Canals were probably the most spectacular of these other developments; but the continual introduction of new industrial and agricultural products and techniques has had a tremendous impact on the course of world commerce. The vagaries of the ordinary business cycle have also had their effect on shipping, and the Great Depression of the 1930's, aggravated by the payment difficulties previously mentioned, had serious repercussions on the shipping industry.[6]

SHIPPING AND THE LOCATION OF ECONOMIC ACTIVITY

The fact that most of the world's great cities are ocean, river, or lake ports indicates the importance of water transportation as a locational factor. The connection of one means of transportation with other means of transport, requiring a break in the service which necessitates the unloading and reloading of a shipment, such as occurs in all the great ports where water-borne traffic connects with a network of converging rail lines and highways, exercises an important influence on the location of economic activity. The cost of shift-

[4] J. Humlum, *Die Grosschiffahrtswege des Welthandels,* according to League of Nations, *World Economic Survey 1939-41* (1941), p. 243.

[5] *The Network of World Trade, loc.cit.*

[6] For a description of the effect of business cycles on shipping, see: Sven Helander, *Die Internationale Schiffahrtskrise* (Jena: Gustav Fischer, 1928). F. C. James, *Cyclical Fluctuations in the Shipping and Shipbuilding Industries* (Philadelphia: Doctoral dissertation, 1927). Tjalling Koopmans, *Tanker Freight Rates and Tankship Building* (London: P. S. King & Son, Ltd., 1939).

ing cargo from one agent of transportation to another often leads to the occurrence of processing at the transfer point. The cost of loading and reloading, relatively high in comparison with the costs of hauling, also generally makes longer journeys relatively cheaper than short ones and thereby tends to reduce the importance of distance as such. This is particularly true in sea transport, which for this reason makes a long sea-borne shipment considerably cheaper than two shorter ones of the same total distance.

The direct effect of transportation costs on industrial location is obvious for, as Ohlin points out, "the relation between costs of production at home and the supply price of 'foreign' goods, i.e. costs abroad plus transportation costs, determines whether a given commodity is to be imported, exported, or produced for the home market."[7] When the source of a raw material and the market for its product do not coincide, the source and the market exert opposing forces on the location of its processing. And in this tug-of-war, in addition to the locational pull of transfer points, transport charges themselves exert an important influence on economic location.

The policy often followed by liners, of charging what the traffic will bear, usually has the effect of requiring finished goods to pay higher rates than semi-finished articles, while the latter in turn generally are required to pay higher rates than raw materials. The result of this is to favor the location of an industry near the market for its final product, unless one of the raw materials, like coal, loses much of its weight in processing, in which case the industry tends to be oriented towards this raw material component. Reductions in the cost of transportation, however, weaken still further the attracting power of raw material sources. We find, for example, that low ocean freights have benefited European industry by permitting raw materials to be imported at delivered prices only slightly higher than those which have prevailed at their sources. Whenever raw materials can be conveyed cheaply enough, the market-orienting forces will tend to predominate. However, if European manufacturing has been favorably influenced by cheap freights, its agriculture has been adversely affected by the greater accessibility of its markets to overseas producers of such products.

Changes in freight rates tend to influence the internal prices of

[7] Bertil Ohlin, *Interregional and International Trade* (Cambridge, Mass.: Harvard University Press, 1933), p. 144. "Foreign" in this quotation refers to any other area, whether under the same or a foreign flag.

countries and, through the price mechanism, the distribution of their national income and the allocation of their resources. Increased freight rates on imports have an effect similar to the imposition of a tariff, while conversely a lowering of freights on imports exerts an influence similar to a reduction of a customs duty. A reduction in outbound freights is apt to encourage the export industries, and their expansion in turn may pull resources from other industries, particularly those in competition with imports if the latter also are charged lower freights. Shipping rates, of course, do not operate in isolation, and other factors such as fiscal and credit policy, tariff policy, and basic changes in the demand for and the cost of producing the commodities traded will generally exert a greater influence on a country's price structure. However, the locational effect of changes in ocean freights should not be overlooked, since it might be of considerable importance in countries to whom ocean-borne imports or exports are of great significance, such as Great Britain, Australia, New Zealand, Argentina, and Japan.[8] And it should be remembered that new cheap methods of transportation to the seaboard and thence to Europe made the rapid development of the American West an economic possibility. "Cheaper transfer has enlarged market areas and supply areas, allowing further concentration of market-oriented and material-oriented industries. . . . Each new transfer medium developed has had a different effect on location, reflecting its own characteristic of cost structure."[9] In short, transportation costs have had a large influence in determining the extent to which advantage could be taken of geographical specialization. The rates charged for shipping service have in turn often been importantly affected by the tendency of the supply of tonnage to be redundant—a tendency which was especially pronounced during the interwar period.

THE VOLUME OF WORLD TRADE AND THE VOLUME OF SHIPPING

The ever-changing character of world trade and the continual improvement in the efficiency of ships make long-term quantitative comparisons difficult. Suffice it to say that since 1870 the increase in the volume of international sea-borne commerce has been huge, and the expansion of the world's merchant marine enormous. Although the statistics of the quantum of world trade are at best crude esti-

[8] Ohlin, op.cit., pp. 523-528.
[9] By permission from The Location of Economic Activity, by Edgar M. Hoover. Copyright 1948. McGraw-Hill Book Company, Inc., p. 184.

mates, they do, nonetheless, have some usefulness in indicating changes of magnitude over a relatively short span of years. Besides the usual statistical difficulties involved in the use of price indices,[10] quantum-of-trade data neglect the composition and direction of the commerce conveyed. While it would be preferable to use statistics which took into account changes in the stowage factor of the cargoes carried and the miles over which they had been transported, such detailed information is not available, but some indication of their importance can be gained from considering changes that have taken place since World War I. The decline in the quantity of grains, timber, and paper imported by Western Europe has been partially offset by the longer distances separating European customers from their new suppliers. The quantity of grain moving from the Black Sea and the volume of timber and paper products from the Baltic have declined, but the shipments of grain from Argentina and Australia have increased, as have timber and paper shipments from North America.[11] The tonnage demanded for the growing trade in vegetable oils and fruit has not only increased, but Asiatic sources of vegetable oils have gained importance at the expense of African suppliers; and fruit from Palestine and the Pacific Coast of North America has entered competition with Spanish fruit.[12] On the other hand, new sources of coal and the growth of the petroleum industry have spelled serious losses to coal carriers, but the business of tankers was augmented.

The quantum of trade imported by and exported from North America fell more drastically during the Great Depression than that of other parts of the world, but in all areas the volume of industrial raw materials fell less than shipments of manufactured goods and foodstuffs.[13] The unbalance of inbound and outbound shipments was in turn aggravated on most routes by greater losses in the volume of manufactured products than of raw materials, and, since balanced loads in both directions are necessary for maximum efficiency in vessel utilization, this change had an adverse effect on the profitableness of the shipping industry. Europe has traditionally been an importer of both bulky raw materials and foodstuffs and an exporter

[10] Neither comparable nor additive quantitative data is available, so the quantum of trade is estimated by dividing value figures by a price index.

[11] T. Ouren and A. Sømme, *Trends in Inter-War Trade and Shipping* (Bergen: J. W. Eides, 1948), pp. 40-44.

[12] *loc.cit.*

[13] League of Nations, *World Production and Prices 1938-39* (Geneva: 1939), pp. 65-69.

of manufactured products which do not require as much space, while the United States has had a somewhat more balanced trade. The vast seaboard of the United States, however, is so varied that balances of inbound and outbound loads are not usually available on the same coast—the United States Atlantic range in the interwar period had a tonnage import balance, while Gulf and Pacific ports had surpluses of export tonnage. Since World War II, all United States seaboards have been showing heavy surpluses of exports over imports.

Statistics of shipping tonnage, like those concerned with the quantum of trade, are subject to numerous difficulties. In addition to different standards of vessel measurement and the relatively unsatisfactory nature of any single measurement, there have been very substantial improvements in ship architecture and engineering which render comparisons difficult when they are made to cover a considerable period of time.[14] The introduction of the steamship has already been mentioned, and as early as 1870 its influence was apparent in the rapid increase of available tonnage. The merchant fleet of the United Kingdom alone increased fivefold within the two decades following the introduction of steamers. Competition became severe, and cutthroat practices were prevalent. Consequently, the first steamship conference was organized in 1875 in the trade between India and the United Kingdom, and in 1877 this conference introduced the deferred rebate system. An oversupply of tonnage has characterized the world's ocean freight markets frequently since that time, and an appreciation of this fact is fundamental to an understanding of the recent economic history of the maritime industry. Shipping tonnage has increased spasmodically in response to cyclical factors, but particularly as a result of wars. The expansion of tonnage resulting from World War I was enormous. After the war, world trade increased while ship construction gradually tapered off, but it was not until 1937 that a shortage of carrying capacity was felt. The statistics

---

[14] Several notable improvements in ship design and propulsion adopted since World War I rendered many ships obsolete during the interwar period and make tonnage statistics increasingly unreliable for comparative purposes. Improved hull design and construction permitted more cargo to be accommodated, while increased engine speed and improved cargo-handling facilities enabled a vessel of given size to make more voyages during a given period of time. Furthermore the increased use of fuel oil and diesel propulsion permitted more dry cargo to be carried. Another highly important development has been the increased volume of bulk shipments of petroleum and its products, and the huge growth of a special type of carrier—the tanker or tank ship—to handle this business.

clearly reveal that the surplus capacity of the interwar period was primarily a legacy from the construction prompted by the war, rather than of the relative prosperity which the world experienced from 1925 to 1929. In 1914 the world total of steam and motor tonnage (over 100 gross tons) was approximately 45.4 million gross tons. By 1923 this total was about 62 million tons and reached a peak of over 69 million tons in 1931; and at the same time the average carrying capacity per gross ton and the average speed of ships was increasing rapidly. It has been estimated that in the interwar period the average speed of ships increased by 20 per cent; and while less than 4 per cent of the gross tonnage afloat burnt oil or was diesel-powered in 1914, by 1938 well over half of the tonnage was so equipped.[15] The use of liquid fuel released considerable space, previously needed for coal bunkers, for the carriage of dry cargo, since fuel and diesel oils can be carried in deep tanks—space not utilizable for the stowage of dry cargoes. From 1932 through 1934 the world tonnage of ocean vessels lost in accidents and scrapped exceeded the volume newly launched; but by 1935 the additions were virtually equal to the deletions, and the following years witnessed large increases in the world's merchant marine stimulated by the prosperity of 1937 and preparation for war. Almost the entire interwar period was characterized by a volume of carrying capacity well in excess of the requirements of world commerce.[16]

With the advent of World War II the race between submarines and the shipyards was resumed, and although the submarines took an early lead in the struggle, the shipyards, as is well known, with the assistance of devices to destroy underseas craft, won the contest by a wide margin. With the termination of hostilities, many of the victorious nations which had suffered severe losses undertook the construction of new vessels in an enthusiastic effort to restore their fleets to their previous competitive positions and to share in business

[15] League of Nations, *World Economic Survey, 1939-41* (1941), pp. 243-244. This study estimates that the freight carrying capacity of the world's shipping probably doubled between 1914 and 1939.

[16] Because of the serious shortcomings of quantum-of-trade statistics previously mentioned, and the changes in the types and efficiency of ships as well as changes in the organization of the industry, accurate comparisons of the volume of trade and the carrying capacity of shipping are extremely difficult to make. One chart showing the quantum of trade and the volume of steam and motor ocean-going tonnage (of 2,000 gross tons and over) is shown below. It should be noted that no adjustment has been made for the improvement in the efficiency (carrying capacity) of ships. The following table appears in the *Annual Report for 1939* of the Liverpool Steamship Owners' Association. Although the reliability of the results are extremely doubtful in view of

previously carried by German and Japanese vessels. By the end of 1949, the gross tonnage of steam and motor ocean-going vessels of 1,000 gross tons and over was 80.6 million tons, or approximately 26.4 per cent larger than in September 1939; and again there had been an increase in average speed. About 15.2 million gross tons, however, were laid up in 1949 in the United States reserve fleet— and remained there until the exigencies of the Korean War and the rearmament of Europe led to withdrawals.

Table III-A presents comparisons of the world's merchant shipping which show that: (1) the average size of postwar vessels was considerably larger than that of prewar vessels; and (2) the deadweight tonnage not impounded in the United States Reserve Fleet was slightly larger at the end of 1949 than it was just prior to the outbreak of war in 1939.

Returning to the depression of the 1930's, we find the shipping industry was characterized by: (1) a large volume of laid-up tonnage (in June, 1932, almost 21 per cent); (2) substantial unused carrying capacity on ships which were operating; and (3) declining revenues and financial losses.[17] The under-utilization of carrying capacity has been a serious problem to the industry, whose periods of famine have customarily exceeded its opportunities for feasting. In the depression of the 1930's, surplus capacity became quite ominous and the League of Nations reported in 1933, "There appears to be a surplus of considerably over 50 per cent of ocean-going world tonnage.

---

the long period between the base year of 1913 and the final year of 1938, they are presented here for what they might be worth.

Year	Quantum of World Trade (Sea-borne and Land)	Estimated Quantum of Sea-borne Trade	World Shipping of 2,000 Gross Tons and Over (exing U.S. Lakers)
	(1913 = 100)		
1913	100	100	100
1929	130	135	157
1932	97	101	163
1933	98	104	158
1934	102	110	152
1935	107	115	150
1936	112	120	151
1937	126	135p	154
1938*	113	121p	158

* to June 30th   p preliminary

[17] League of Nations, World Economic Survey, 1933-34 (1934), pp. 213-217.

TABLE III-A

Merchant Vessels of the World[a]

(total gross tons and total deadweight tons in thousands)

		Sept. 1, 1939	Dec. 31, 1949
(1)	Total number of vessels	12,798	12,868
(2)	" " in U.S. Reserve Fleet	113[b]	2,127
(3)	" " outside U.S. Reserve Fleet	12,685	10,741
(4)	Total gross tons	58,270	73,640
(5)	" " " in U.S. Reserve Fleet	?	15,209
(6)	" " " outside U.S. Reserve Fleet	?	58,431
(7)	Total deadweight tons	80,601	103,461
(8)	" " " in U.S. Reserve Fleet	925[c]	21,372
(9)	" " " outside U.S. Reserve Fleet	79,776	82,089
(10)	Average gross tons per vessel (4) ÷ (1)	4,553	5,800
(11)	" deadweight tons per vessel (7) ÷ (1)	6,298	8,040

a These data include seagoing iron and steel steam and motor merchant type vessels of 1,000 gross tons and over; but exclude vessels on the Great Lakes and inland waterways, and special types, such as ice breakers, cable ships, etc., as well as merchant-type vessels owned by the Armed Forces. Except where otherwise indicated they have been compiled by the United States Maritime Commission and published in Senate Rept. 2494, 81st Cong. 2nd Sess., Committee on Interstate and Foreign Commerce, *Merchant Marine Study and Investigation* (1950), pp. 126-131, 134.

b The laid-up fleet as of October 25, 1939 according to U.S. Maritime Commission, *Annual Report for 1939*, pp. 31-32.

c Based on the assumption that the average deadweight per vessel in the reserve fleet was 8184 tons. This was the average deadweight of 75 vessels sold from the reserve fleet in the fiscal year 1937. (U.S. Maritime Commission, *Annual Report for 1937*, p. 26.)

. . . Partially-employed tonnage is a very much heavier charge upon the shipping companies than tonnage actually laid up."[18] War-stimulated construction might make surplus tonnage inevitable, but excessive unused capacity on vessels which are operated is partially explained by the reactions of the industry to highly remunerative conference rates, especially when the entry of new lines is not re-

18 League of Nations, *Notes by Economic Relations Section and the Communications and Transit Section on the Merchant Shipping Crisis* (March 16, 1933, mimeographed), p. 8. In its *Annual Report for 1931-1932* (p. 56), the Chamber of Shipping of the United Kingdom reported, "In normal times there must be a reserve of space, but it may be estimated that over and above this, 20 per cent of cargo space on vessels in commission is being wasted, and 50 per cent or more of the cargo and passenger space is empty voyage after voyage. This problem of empty space is at least as grave as that of laid-up tonnage."

stricted.[19] Restricted entry, on the other hand, may lead both to greater efficiency in vessel utilization and to monopoly profits. As a result of these conditions there was an intensification of competition in some trades, and more rigorous conference activity to prevent cutthroat practices. Furthermore, something relatively new under the sun occurred during the Great Depression when tanker operators and tramp owners formed agreements to establish minimum rates and to rationalize the utilization of their tonnage. These developments are described in Chapter XI.

Table III-B presents some interesting world merchant shipping statistics for the period from 1920 to 1938. Total tonnage registered on June 30, 1949, is shown for comparative purposes. In addition to revealing some of the gaps and vagaries which plague shipping statistics,[20] this table also clearly shows that: (1) tonnage scrapped and lost annually was generally exceeded by the volume launched; (2) total tonnage on register did not vary appreciably from the early 1920's to the late 1930's, despite large fluctuations in the volume of ocean-borne cargoes that are known to have occurred; and (3) there were large fluctuations in the amount of idle tonnage. All of this is pretty much what one would expect in an industry with expensive and durable capital units of large size whose construction cycle is largely influenced by war. Ship construction during the 1920's, however, revealed considerable stability for an industry of this type. The shipbuilding industry is characterized by cycles which appear to be uniquely its own, and quite distinct from business in general and from the business of operating ships. In 1927-1930, for example, the construction of merchant vessels was well maintained, although freight rates were not; and in 1934, with costs very low, shipbuilding made a partial recovery before freight rates began their advance.[21]

---

[19] This subject is analyzed in Chapter XII.

[20] For example, the total tonnage registered in successive years does not agree with the changes one might expect to find by adding the tonnage launched and subtracting the volume lost and scrapped.

[21] See Wickizer, *op.cit.*, p. 61. The price of new vessels is flexible, and, together with the practice of some shipyards to assist liberally in the financing of new ships or to build vessels and then charter them on liberal terms in order to keep their organizations in operation, helps to explain why new tonnage keeps coming off the ways when losses are being experienced by the ship-operating industry. This should not be construed, however, to mean that the shipbuilding industry customarily operates at or near capacity, for this is far from the case; it merely means that the industry displays both considerable stability and much unused capacity in most peacetime years.

Fluctuations in the price charged for new construction is not without interest, and we are indebted to *Fairplay* for an annual price series of a new, ready, 7,500 dead-

In regard to the data on idle shipping it should be noted that the source does not specify the definition of idleness. The figures probably include some shipping which must always be out of service, such as obsolete vessels waiting to be scrapped, and vessels being repaired. The idle United States tonnage includes much old shipping which was left over from the World War I construction program and which was kept more or less permanently in a government-owned reserve fleet. A more accurate indication of the fluctuations in idle tonnage is obtained, therefore, from the column showing the amount laid up in the United Kingdom. Tonnage listed as idle, however, presents only a partial picture of surplus carrying capacity, because in all but the best years there has been serious under-utilization of the ships that are in operation. No one knows what the future will bring, but if there is peace it would not be unlikely for carrying capacity again to outrun the usual volume of world commerce. There was some evidence that this might be happening in 1949 when the tramp freight rate index compiled by the Chamber of Shipping of the United Kingdom fell from over 100.5 in February to 66.5 in November.[22] Liner rates on many routes began to soften during this period; and new construction was steadily increasing the capacity of the world's shipping.[23] The future volume of world com-

---

weight ton merchant vessel, from which the following has been chosen. (The date is the end of the year, and no adjustment seems to have been made for vessel improvements during the period.)

Year	Price in £ (000)	Year	Price in £ (000)	Year	Price in £ (000)
1900	61	1920	105	1940	150
1905	45	1925	53	1945	163
1910	40	1930	49	1946	170
1915	150	1932	32		
1919	232	1935	60		

The same source has recently published similar information for a more modern type vessel—a 9,500 ton motor-ship—which indicates postwar fluctuations.

Year	Price in £ (000)
1945	240
1946	310
1947	420
1948	425
1949	320
1950	450
1951	675

[22] It was not until the outbreak of war in Korea and the launching of the American rearmament program that tramp rates rose appreciably. See Chapter XIII.

[23] In the year which ended June 30, 1949, 3,186,000 deadweight tons of new, sea-

TABLE III-B

World Merchant Shipping Statistics, 1920-1938 and 1949
(millions of gross tons)

| | Ships of 100 Gross Tons and Upwards[a] | | | | Idle Tonnage as of January 1[b] | | |
| | On Register June 30 | | Year Ending June 30 | | | | |
Year	Total[c]	Sail	Launched[d]	Scrapped or Lost[e]	World Total	United States	United Kingdom
1920	57.3	3.4	5.9	0.5	—	—	—
1921	62.0	3.1	4.4	0.5	—	—	—
1922	64.4	3.0	2.5	0.7	10.9	5.3	1.8
1923	65.2	2.8	1.6	1.5	9.0	5.3	1.0
1924	64.0	2.5	2.2	1.6	6.8	4.3	0.9
1925	64.6	2.3	2.2	1.0	5.6	4.2	0.7
1926	64.8	2.1	1.7	1.2	5.7	4.1	0.6
1927	65.2	1.9	2.3	0.9	4.1	2.9	0.5
1928	67.0	1.8	2.7	1.2	4.3	3.0	0.5
1929	68.1	1.7	2.8	1.5	3.9	2.8	0.5
1930	69.6	1.6	2.9	1.2	3.2	2.0	0.5
1931	70.1	1.4	1.6	1.3	8.6	2.6	2.4
1932	69.7	1.4	0.7	1.7	12.2[f]	3.0[f]	3.1[f]
1933	67.9	1.3	0.5	2.7	12.6	3.6	3.1
1934	65.6	1.2	1.0	2.1	7.5	2.9	1.7
1935	64.9	1.2	1.3	1.4	6.5	2.6	1.5
1936	65.1	1.1	2.1	1.4	4.2	2.2	0.7
1937	66.3	1.0	2.7	1.0	2.8	?	0.3
1938	67.8	1.0	3.0	0.9	1.3	?	0.2
1949	83.3	0.8			15.2[g]		

[a] The data in these four columns are from *Lloyds Register of Shipping.*

[b] Data in these columns are from U.S. Dept. of Commerce, *Commerce Yearbook, 1930; World Economic Review*, 1935; and various *Annual Reports* of the Chamber of Shipping of the United Kingdom.

[c] Steam and motor tonnage is the total minus the tonnage of sailing vessels. These figures also include lake vessels, chiefly on the Great Lakes, which amounted to approximately 2.5 million tons during this period.

[d] Returns incomplete for Spain in 1937 and 1938, and for Soviet Russia except for years, 1926-29.

[e] Tonnage lost annually runs between 300,000 and 500,000 tons; the remainder was scrapped.

[f] The estimates for July 1, 1932, were respectively 14.2; 3.4; and 3.5.

[g] As of Dec. 31, 1949. See Table III-A.

going steam and motor vessels of 1,000 gross tons and over were added to the world's supply. (359,000 tons of combination passenger and cargo vessels, 1,647,000 tons of freighters; and 1,180,000 tons of tankers.) 81st Cong., 2nd Sess., S. Rept. 2494, Committee on Interstate and Foreign Commerce, Merchant Marine Study and Investigation (1950), pp. 311-312.

merce and the demands it will make on ocean shipping, however, remain an enigma.

POLITICAL FACTORS AFFECTING SHIPPING

There is perhaps no single factor that has exercised a greater effect on ocean shipping in the last thirty-five years than war. The volume of world tonnage is influenced far more by peak wartime demand than by peacetime demands. Peak wartime demand influenced by huge military requirements, by the unavailability of enemy tonnage, by operating conditions that are far from efficient, and by the urgency and uncertainties of the occasion have dictated the advisability of erring on the side of too much rather than too little. Previous wars had also strongly influenced the construction cycle for shipping, but the two global wars, as we have seen, increased the volume of tonnage tremendously despite serious war losses. The construction of enormous amounts of shipping for war subsequently affects the replacement demand since large numbers of war-built vessels are obsolete to begin with and ships built within a few years tend to depreciate in a block. As J. Einarsen has demonstrated, ship construction in Norway was marked by two cycles: replacement and new investment. The latter depends on freight rates, while the former depends on age and life expectancy. A skewed age distribution, caused by war-stimulated construction, will accentuate the replacement cycles.[24] In the United States, ship construction contracted for in wartime and ship construction sponsored by shipping subsidies whose only justification is the strategic importance of a national-flag merchant marine, have accounted for most of the American merchant fleet. The United States, however, is not the only nation to subsidize shipping, and in fact quite the opposite is true, for the majority of the world's maritime nations give assistance to their shipping. Besides restricting the domestic or cabotage trades to national flag-vessels, a practice which for better or worse is almost universal, the payment of subsidies in one form or another is very widespread and appears to have been expanding.[25] As new modern ships are

[24] J. Einarsen, "Replacement in the Shipping Industry," *Review of Economic Statistics* (1946), pp. 225-230.

[25] See Jesse E. Saugstad, *Shipping and Shipbuilding Subsidies* (Trade Promotion Series, No. 129, United States Bureau of Foreign and Domestic Commerce, 1932). During the 1930's government assistance to the ship-operating and ship-construction industries increased as the depression worsened their financial condition. Since World War II, construction aid has been granted by Australia, Italy, and the United States; operating assistance has been given by Brazil, Canada, France, and the United States;

constructed, with or without governmental assistance, competitors are required to build new vessels lest the superior efficiency of their rivals' fleets drive them out of the trade. However, old vessels are not usually scrapped automatically as new tonnage appears (although some governments have tied scrapping requirements to their construction assistance programs), so that the redundancy of shipping tends to be aggravated still further. Although vessels lost as a result of marine casualties have, because of increased ship safety, shown a downward secular trend, scrapping has generally displayed a cyclical pattern. Together with war losses, however, they have not exceeded new construction except during the worst phases of submarine warfare and during the Great Depression of the early 1930's.

Subsidies and coasting restrictions, however, are not the only techniques employed to assist national-flag shipping. Government control of foreign trade and exchange, nationalization of shipping and other industries, and discriminatory measures all play their part. Before World War II the German government controlled the combined Hamburg-American—North German Lloyd fleet, and the French Government was heavily interested in the Compagnie Générale Transatlantique. Shipping shortages during and immediately after the war, and general nationalistic considerations, stimulated numerous countries to engage in the shipping business. India, Argentina, Colombia, Brazil, Venezuela, Israel, and Eire are some of the countries that have recently entered the business, or through government action have expanded previous undertakings. To assist their national shipping, some governments have directed the routing of all government-controlled cargo to national lines. (The United States has by Acts of Congress required that half of all goods shipped under the Foreign Assistance Program [E.C.A.], the Military Aid Program, and the stockpiling program be carried in American bottoms if possible.) Some other devices have been preferential consular fees, preferential terminal facilities or assignments in crowded ports, waiving of government charges, preferential taxation, and insistence that freight on imports be paid only in the currency of the importing country. Government control of foreign trade and exchange has also been employed upon occasion to direct the routing

loans, grants, and government-guaranteed loans have been accorded by Belgium, Sweden, the Netherlands, and Norway; and tax privileges more liberal than those available to other industries have been granted by a large number of important maritime powers.

of business. Nationalization of industries and state trading monopolies often permit a country to channel traffic to lines flying its own flag. The Chamber of Shipping of the United Kingdom attributes the recrudescence of flag discrimination largely to the intervention of governments in the buying and selling of commodities and to the growth of currency restrictions.[26] The temptation for governments to patronize their own flag shipping has certainly been increased as a result of the inconvertibility of currencies in general and the dollar shortage in particular. The same is true of private shippers, for an exporter in a country practicing exchange control may have no alternative but to ship by the national flag when it becomes difficult for him to obtain the foreign currency with which to discharge his obligation to foreign shipowners. And when foreign exchange is rationed between importers, the importer who ships by the national flag is in a position, other things being equal, to buy more goods within the limits of the foreign exchange allowed him. In 1939 the Imperial Shipping Committee observed that "there is a strong *prima facie* case for the conclusion that in general the effect of foreign exchange control is to increase the proportion of trade carried under the flag of the country exercising the control";[27] and *The Economist* recently said, "So long as the necessity for exchange control exists, it will perpetuate conditions hostile to the re-establishment of a free freight market and tend to breed flag discrimination."[28] Obviously, whenever conditions exist that render the control of foreign trade and foreign exchange attractive to a country the same forces will cause it to prefer to patronize its own shipping to the fullest extent possible, and it is not astonishing if these controls of trade and exchange are employed so as to accomplish both of these closely related objectives at the same time. Furthermore, the shortage of hard currencies provides some countries with an additional incentive to enlarge their merchant marines.

SHIPPING AND THE BALANCE OF PAYMENTS

"There is an obvious gap between the sum which the exporter receives for his goods, and that which the importer pays for these same goods; the gap standing for the transportation or freight

[26] *The Economist*, March 4, 1950, p. 504.
[27] *British Shipping in the Orient* (Thirty-eighth Report of the Imperial Shipping Committee, 1939), pp. 63-64.
[28] *The Economist*, March 25, 1950, p. 665.

charge."[29] "It is this circumstance—that the expense may be incurred by residents of either country and that payments therefrom may become due either way—which is peculiar to the item of freight charges."[30] Furthermore, in the sense that the prices of imported articles are higher to the purchaser in the importing country, the cost of transportation is borne by the importing country; but these payments may affect the barter terms of trade and in so doing the exporting country may pay part or all of these charges, depending upon the relative elasticities of demand and supply.[31]

In view of the uncertainty attending the ultimate incidence of transportation expenses and other transfer costs, statistics regarding the net result of shipping charges on a country's balance of payments are customarily compiled on the arbitrary, but generally reasonable, assumption that the importer pays the freight. With this qualification in mind, it is interesting to consider: (1) the contribution to the dollar earnings of foreign countries made by United States payments for shipping services during the interwar period; and (2) the great importance of shipping in the balance of payments of countries, such as Norway and Great Britain, in which the merchant marine is a highly important component of the national economy.

From 1922 through 1939 foreign countries earned an average of about $71 million net per annum by providing the United States with ocean transportation.[32] The amount of dollars earned by foreign countries in the American overseas carrying trade depends on the volume of business, the share carried in foreign-flag bottoms, and on the level of freight rates and passenger fares. In 1937, a prosperous year, it is estimated that net payments of the United States for shipping services amounted to more than $108 million,[33] which was ap-

[29] F. W. Taussig, *International Trade* (New York: Macmillan, 1941), p. 135. Taussig quite rightly emphasized freight charges. Ocean and inland freights are often the largest elements in transfer costs which include such other expenses as insurance and interest. However, if customs duties are included in transfer costs they may outweigh freight charges by a considerable margin.

[30] *ibid.*, p. 132.

[31] *ibid.*, p. 135. Also see G. von Haberler, *The Theory of International Trade* (London: Wm. Hedge & Co., Ltd., 1937), pp. 155-159 and 171-174.

[32] John S. Smith, "Shipping Policy and Balance of Payments," *Foreign Commerce Weekly*, September 22, 1945, p. 4. *Net payments or receipts* are determined by calculating the difference between the estimated receipts from foreigners for United States shipping services rendered them plus expenditures of foreign vessels in United States ports on the one hand, and the estimated payments to foreign ship operators for services paid by residents of the United States plus the expenditures of American vessels in foreign ports on the other hand.

[33] United Nations, *Balances of Payments 1939-1945* (Geneva: 1948), p. 167.

proximately the same amount of exchange made available by American imports in that year of raw silk or tin.[34] During the 1920's and 1930's American-flag ships carried about one-third of their countries' water-borne imports and exports; but since World War II the American share has been as large as two-thirds.[35] With the restoration of the merchant fleets of other nations this fraction is dropping, but the substantial increase in the tonnage of American vessels operating in the foreign trade, coupled with statutory provisions that 50 per cent of all shipments financed by the United States Government must be carried in American bottoms, will certainly delay and possibly prevent the share of American-carried business from returning to prewar levels.

Foreign exchange earned by Norwegian shipping is of greater importance to the economy of that country than the shipping receipts of any other nation. In the period of 1936 through 1939 the Norwegian merchant marine's net earnings of foreign exchange averaged over $100 million. In both 1937 and 1939 the foreign exchange so gained amounted to approximately $120 million.[36] Much of this sum was received from services rendered to the dollar area. In 1937, for example, 12 per cent of the tonnage arriving and departing from the United States seaports flew the Norwegian flag; and in the same year approximately one-third of the Norwegian merchant marine operated on the trans-Pacific route and other Pacific trades.[37] The foreign operations of the Norwegian fleet remain highly important to that nation's economy, and in 1947 it derived some 80 per cent of its earnings from trading between foreign (non-Norwegian) ports.[38]

The estimated contribution of British shipping to the United Kingdom's balance of payments for some years between 1913 and 1938 is shown in Table III-C.

The following table indicates the traditional importance of shipping as a source of foreign exchange for the United Kingdom, although its contribution was smaller both in absolute terms and relatively to the adverse visible balance in the 1930's than in earlier

[34] John S. Smith, *op.cit.*, p. 5.
[35] *Statistical Abstract of the United States 1939* (Washington: Government Printing Office, 1940), p. 457; and the same for 1949, pp. 582-583.
[36] United Nations, *Balances of Payments 1939-1945*, p. 111. *The Economist*, Dec. 15, 1951, reported that in the first six months of 1951 foreign freight earnings of Norwegian shipping amounted to £43 million, which was almost equal to that country's entire import surplus of £43.3 million.
[37] Ouren and Sømme, *op.cit.*, p. 39.
[38] *The Economist*, March 25, 1950, pp. 665-666.

TABLE III-C

Estimated Contribution of Shipping to the United Kingdom's Balance of Payments

Year	Including disbursements of foreign ships in U.K.[a]	Ratio of Col. 1 to Adverse Visible Balance	Excluding disbursements of foreign ships in U.K.[b]
	(MILLION £)	(PER CENT)	(MILLION £)
1913	94	70	—
1920	340	91	—
1922	110	61	—
1929	130	34	—
1931	80	20	73
1932	70	25	62
1933	65	25	59
1934	70	25	64
1935	70	25	65
1936	85	24 1/2	75
1937	130	30	115
1938	100	26	90

[a] According to the Board of Trade.
[b] According to the Chamber of Shipping of the U.K.
Source: General Council of British Shipping, *British Shipping Policy* (London: 1944), p. 8.

years. These figures also indicate the importance to the United Kingdom of active trade, and of freight rates that are not unduly depressed. This is clearly revealed by comparing the results for 1929 and 1937, which were prosperous years for shipping, with the other years in the 1930's during which shipping in general was depressed. In 1949 dry-cargo and passenger shipping (tanker earnings were buried in the omnibus item, "other invisibles") earned a net credit of approximately £88 million for the United Kingdom, or about 49 per cent of the adverse visible balance for that year.[39] An unofficial estimate places the comparable credit for 1951 at about £150 million.[40] As in Norway, British shipping earns substantial revenues from the carriage of goods and passengers between other countries, and in 1947, 39 per cent of the gross freight earnings of British shipping was derived from trades not touching the United Kingdom.[41]

[39] *ibid.*, April 15, 1950, p. 843.
[40] *ibid.*, Nov. 10, 1951, p. 1136.
[41] *ibid.*, March 25, 1950, pp. 665-666.

In concluding this chapter, it seems appropriate to repeat that no single factor seems to have had an effect on the supply of shipping comparable to war and preparation for it. On the demand side of the picture, political controls have also exerted an important influence, albeit that in numerous instances they were prompted by economic considerations such as the inconvertibility of currencies. However, regardless of prime causes and basic motivation the fact remains, and it is an exceedingly important one, that the supply of shipping in peacetime has generally been considerably in excess of the demand for it.

The frequent plethora of tonnage, the importance of shipping to the balance of payments, and above all the great strategic significance of the industry have produced an integration of shipping policy with the general policy of nations. As Brig. Gen. Sir H. Osborne Mance has pointed out, international shipping competition, which was almost entirely commercial at the end of the nineteenth century, had become to no small extent political at the outbreak of the second world war.[42]

[42] *International Sea Transport* (Oxford University Press: 1945).

THE ADVENT of the steamship completely changed the methods of shipping goods. A sailing vessel customarily received its cargo at one port and did not sail until virtually fully loaded, whether chartered to carry bulk cargo or general merchandise. Dates of departure were uncertain, and arrival dates even more so; with the result that the merchant had to ship his goods in speculative anticipation of market requirements. Furthermore, sailing vessels were frequently controlled either through ownership or through charter by important merchants or mercantile companies so that sailings with space available to smaller shippers were limited and their dates unpredictable. The substitution of steam for sail and of iron (and later steel) for wood changed much of this, especially after the introduction of the compound engine. The vagaries of winds did not affect the operation of steamers appreciably, so steamers were able to maintain definite schedules. Regular schedules, the improvement in postal facilities, and the laying of transoceanic cables made it possible for the shipper to send goods to market in more accurate anticipation of requirements. This permitted an increase in the total volume of trade since the reduction of speculative elements made a reduction in costs possible. The resultant expansion in world trade and the fact that the steamship permitted greater specialization of design than the sailing vessel encouraged the development of low-cost common carrier services. More sailings permitted merchants to ship smaller lots more frequently, and this in turn gave additional impetus to the growth of common carrier service, as did the growth in individual vessel capacity which made it increasingly difficult for individual merchants dealing in general merchandise to fill or come close to filling an entire ship. At the same time the tramp steamer was demonstrating its superiority over the sailing ship, although it was in this field that windjammers held out longest. The variety of goods classified as general merchandise is large and includes most manufactured products, numerous raw materials, and semi-manufactured commodities —in fact most everything that does not customarily move in ship-load lots. The total volume of these goods is great, though individual shipments may be small and subject to fluctuation. They are apt to be shipped by numerous exporters and consigned to numerous consignees. Furthermore, they are, in many cases, goods of high value on which the loss of interest and the cost of insurance is significant. The advantages to goods of this character of the regular service of high-class steamers is obvious; and shipping companies competed vigorously for this business by building ships of increasingly higher speed which they guaranteed would sail on advertised dates whether they were full or not.

In the decade prior to the opening of the Suez Canal in 1869 and in the decade following its completion the growth in the tonnage of steamers was enormous. The steamer registered tonnage of the United Kingdom alone increased more than five-fold between 1860 (450,000 tons) and 1880 (2,720,000). The supply of shipping exceeded the demand, and bitter cutthroat competition ensued, reducing freight rates to unremunerative levels. Some lines failed, but their ships remained and the excess of supply over demand continued. The surviving shipping companies responded by combining their resources, by making special contracts with large shippers, and by forming organizations to regulate the trade and eliminate competition.

In some trades sailing vessels had early attempted tentatively to regulate sailings but without pronounced success, and although there were agreements between the representatives in New York of the steamship lines engaged in the European trade as early as 1868,[1] the first successful shipping conference is generally considered to have been the Calcutta Conference which was formed in 1875 by liner companies engaged in trade to that port from the United Kingdom. This conference agreement provided for equal rates from each of the British ports served and further stipulated that no preferential rates or concessions were to be given to any shippers. The exporters who had previously enjoyed low rates, and in some cases preferential treatment as well, immediately became discontented and made arrangements to patronize steamers run in opposition to the conference. The shipowners then attempted to negotiate special contracts

---

[1] The Transatlantic Shipping Conference formed in 1868 grew out of the disturbances caused by the Civil War. This conference attempted little in the way of rate control until 1902 when a minimum freight agreement was reached. J. Russell Smith, "Ocean Freight Rates," *Political Science Quarterly*, Vol. xxi, No. 2 (1906), pp. 253-256.

at mutually satisfactory rates with shippers who agreed to give conference carriers exclusive support. The large shippers, however, refused at first to bind themselves unless they were accorded preferential consideration, but, since the conference realized the disadvantages to itself of having the smaller shippers frozen out of the trade, the lines rejected this solution. In an effort to meet these difficulties, the deferred rebate system was introduced, in 1877. The granting of rebates to shippers after a period of "loyalty" was not in itself a novelty;[2] but deferring the payment, until the shipper had demonstrated his "loyalty" by giving the conference all his business not only for the contract period but for a subsequent period of time as well, constituted the innovation which provided the conference with an effective method of tying shippers to its members. The conference system spread rapidly and soon included most of the world's liner routes. It was frequently, but not invariably, accompanied by the deferred rebate system. Membership of the first conferences was entirely British but soon became international. The European outbound trades were the first to be organized since general merchandise constituted so much of their business. Conferences on return routes to Europe developed more slowly because of the great importance of bulk commodities in these trades which made tramp competition difficult to control.

The heavy overhead costs involved in operating liners and the numerous rate wars led to mergers as well as to the formation of conferences. Combinations involving ownership, as distinct from conferences which did not alter ownership, were achieved by direct purchase of one line by another, by the formation of pools which shared the financial results of a year's operations in different trades, or by the exchange between lines of shares of stock. Whether the merger was partial or complete they all had the same objectives: the reduction of competition, economy in operation and administration, and the spreading of risks by giving a single ownership an interest in more than one trade. In short, shipping companies operating liner services combined for the same reasons that stimulated the growth of large businesses generally. It might be noted parenthetically at this point that, despite the fact that the combination movement has continued to reduce the number of competitors, national-

[2] Rebates may have grown out of the custom of paying primage to the supercargo or captain, according to Adam W. Kirkaldy, *British Shipping: Its History, Organization and Importance* (London: 1914), pp. 182-183.

flag considerations have generally prevented combinations involving common or joint ownership from achieving a monopoly. The most ambitious international combination was probably the International Mercantile Marine created in 1902 by J. P. Morgan. The I.M.M. combined American, Belgian, and British companies and, with the Hamburg-American Line, jointly controlled the Holland America Line.

The series of mergers and amalgamations in the late 1900's and early twentieth century, by reducing the number of interests to be reconciled, facilitated the formation of tighter conferences. This concatenation of events naturally aroused suspicions concerning the shipping industry, suspicions which gained support from allegations of discrimination and other monopolistic practices made from time to time by shippers. Regardless of the defensive motivation surrounding the origin of shipping conferences, the question gradually arose as to whether they had not become aggressive. Had this institution, ostensibly started as a benevolent scheme to provide regular sailing schedules and maintain stable, reasonable rates, become a malevolent monopoly extorting shippers?

The date on which the first complaints were made is not now known, but since even the goose which laid the golden egg probably did not do so noiselessly, it is reasonable to assume that complaints about conferences and deferred rebates are as old as these institutions themselves. However, in 1897 a Blue Book entitled *The Trade of the British Empire and Foreign Competition* complained that differential freights in favor of goods from the Continent of Europe were injuring British trade; and in 1899 the Chambers of Commerce of the United Kingdom alleged that "the profits made in carrying from English ports are used, in part, to pay for the losses in giving to our foreign competitors advantageous terms."[3] At the same time the British Iron Trade Association informed the Board of Trade that these adverse differential rates were the consequence of shipping rings, as a result of which the Colonial Office made further inquiries. In 1902 questions on the subject were put in Parliament and the Board of Trade received more complaints. In the same year a commission was appointed in the Straits Settlements to study the effect of conferences on the colony's trade, and they reported secret rebates and substantial rate increases. In 1904 a conference of delegates from the South African colonies also complained about the

[3] As reported in Cd. 4669, p. 12. See next footnote for title of command paper.

rebate system, preferential rates of freight from the United States and the Continent, and secret concessions to shippers. At this same time investigations were held in New Zealand and Australia concerning deferred rebates, and in 1906 the Australian Royal Commission recommended that they should be made illegal. It was also in 1906 that a Congress of the Chambers of Commerce of the Empire protested against the payment of rebates by steamship companies; in conjunction with the higher rates charged for carrying goods from the United Kingdom, as compared with the United States, rebates were said to be injurious to the imperial trade. The deferred rebate system, however, was not unknown on United States trade routes, and American shippers were far from being universally satisfied with the growing power of the steamship lines. It is not astonishing, therefore, that the United Kingdom and the United States began investigations of the industry within a few years of each other. The Royal Commission on Shipping Rings was appointed in 1906 and issued a comprehensive report three years later.[4] In 1911 the Department of Justice of the United States government brought actions against three conferences for violations of the anti-trust law. These cases, involving the practice of granting deferred rebates, finally reached the Supreme Court, but by that time World War I was in progress and the practices complained of had been terminated; so the Supreme Court held the matter to be moot and did not render a decision on the original issue.[5] In 1912 the United States House of Representatives approved a resolution introduced by Mr. Joshua W. Alexander, chairman of the Committee on Merchant Marine and Fisheries, to have the committee investigate shipping combinations. The committee, with the assistance of Professor S. S. Huebner, conducted a thorough investigation and issued a complete report of their findings in 1914, which subsequently formed the basis for the regulatory portions of the Shipping Act of 1916.[6] It is to the reports of the

---

[4] *Report of the Royal Commission on Shipping Rings* (London, 1909). Five volumes, Cd. 4668-70, 4685-86. The Commission's recommendations are in Vol. i, Cd. 4668.

[5] U.S. v. Hamburg-American Line, et al. 239 U.S. 466; and U.S. v. Prince Line Ltd., et al. and U.S. v. American Asiatic Steamship Co., et al. 242 U.S. 537.

[6] U.S. Congress, House of Representatives' Committee on Merchant Marine & Fisheries, *Investigation of Shipping Combinations* (Washington, 1913 and 1914). Four volumes, 62nd and 63rd Cong. The first three volumes contain the hearings and other evidence collected by the Committee. Vol. No. 4 entitled *Report on Steamship Agreements and Affiliations in American Foreign and Domestic Trade*, contains the Committee's recommendations.

Royal Commission and the Alexander Committee that we shall now turn our attention.

THE ROYAL COMMISSION ON SHIPPING RINGS

The Royal Commission on Shipping Rings was appointed in 1906, in response to complaints received from commercial interests in Great Britain as well as from elsewhere in the Empire. These complaints had centered mainly about the use of deferred rebates and the disadvantageous rates with which the conferences were alleged to have been hampering Empire trade. It should be recalled that this was at a time when British manufacturers were first being effectively challenged by competition from both Germany and the United States. Extensive hearings were held at which all interested parties had an opportunity to present their views. A subcommittee held separate hearings in South Africa because of the great dissatisfaction of those colonies with the shipping situation. In addition, government departments in Great Britain and throughout the Empire were called upon to provide supplementary information. The Commission was chosen to represent the varied interests of shippers in Great Britain, of those in the colonies and dominions, and of the important British shipping industry. The frequently diverse interests of shippers in the mother country and shippers in the colonies and dominions combined with the still different interests of British shipping made the Commission's task an extremely difficult one. It is not astonishing, therefore, that the Commission failed to come to a unanimous decision and felt compelled to render two reports. The majority report was signed by eleven members, two of whom had reservations. The minority report was signed by five members, one of whom had reservations.[7]

The Commission carefully considered and described the different competitive structures of the different trade routes, and the modifications in the conference and rebate procedures that were made to meet these various market conditions. The rebate tie, for example, was found to be almost universally employed except in a few trades in which it was inapplicable. The reasons for such inapplicability were generally: (1) the absence of need for regular and fixed sail-

---

[7] In 1923 a Canadian Committee observed that "those who signed the majority report were, in considerable numbers, connected with the shipping interests, while those who signed the minority report do not appear to have had such direct or indirect interest in the matter." *Journals of the House of Commons, Dominion of Canada,* Appendix to 60th Vol. (1923), p. xi.

ings, or (2) a pronounced imbalance between the inbound and outbound volumes of business, or (3) because of the presence of large quantities of commodities peculiarly suitable for carriage by tramps. The absence of the deferred rebate in the coasting trade of the United Kingdom and in the important trans-Atlantic trade with North America was noted. It was accounted for in the former by the fact that coastal shipping either had competition from railroads or was owned by them. In the North Atlantic route the heavy requirements of the passenger business dominated the trade to such an extent that the carrying capacity available for cargo was in excess of the demand, with the result that cargo rates were so low as to make this route of little attraction to tramps. (It should be pointed out, however, that the passenger business on this route was very strictly controlled, and, since deferred rebates are not effective when the customer is not a fairly steady patron, an elaborate pooling scheme was in operation covering the revenues from the steerage business, which was the remunerative core of the trade.) The Commission also described the principal factors which determined the strength or weakness of a conference's monopoly power. Where the trade of a conference is distributed over a large number of ports, the fitful competition of tramps is not so keen, since the latter generally load and discharge at one port only. The nature of the cargo was also noted to be an important criterion, with the result that in trades where bulky commodities suitable for tramp conveyance were prevalent the hold of the conference was naturally less. The geographical position of the conference's route was also of considerable importance. Conferences whose routes are on or adjacent to one or another of the world's major highways of commerce are exposed to the competition both of tramps and of conferences operating on the adjacent routes, for vessels can be diverted at small cost to enter the domain of the "exposed" conference.

THE ALEXANDER COMMITTEE

In the United States, the Committee on Merchant Marine and Fisheries acknowledged the benefit it had derived from the work done by the Royal Commission, and proceeded to explore specifically the situation on United States trade routes. The Committee enjoyed the cooperation of United States diplomatic and consular representatives who prepared comprehensive reports on the subject, and the Department of Justice gave the Committee access to the testimony and exhibits in cases that were pending against carriers for alleged violation of the Sherman Anti-trust Law. The Committee furthermore issued detailed inquiries to the carriers and other inquiries to individual firms, forwarders, brokers, and others interested in foreign trade. They received what was considered a satisfactory number of replies. In addition, the Committee held public hearings which ran for almost two months. It was felt that by and large both ship operators and shippers had cooperated in helping the Committee obtain an accurate and comprehensive picture of conference organizations and activities in the United States trades, although it pointed out in its final report that "While numerous individual shippers voluntarily presented their grievances to the Committee, under promise of confidential treatment, very few were willing (fearing retaliation) to testify openly against the steamship line or lines upon which they were dependent for the movement of their freight."[8]

The general conference situation was found strikingly similar to that described by the Royal Commission, and the arguments presented by both shipping companies and shippers in the United States were essentially identical to the points of view of their counterparts in Great Britain.

The investigation revealed that on nearly every trade route in both the foreign and domestic commerce of the United States, practically all the established steamship lines had either been consolidated through stock ownership, or were working in harmonious cooperation through written or oral agreements, or through conference arrangements. The conference procedure was the method most often employed. Furthermore, in nearly all of the few trades where the existence of agreements or understandings was denied, the report stated, "a remarkable uniformity in rates seems to exist and not a trace of a rate war can be found. The situation has been explained to the Committee as one of 'following the leader,' the dominant carrier fixing the rates and the less important lines adopting those rates, they being allowed to exist in the trade without having an effective fight waged against them, as long as they conform to the rates and conditions established by the dominant carrier."[9] The various agreements and conference arrangements were again found to differ greatly in their details, since they were adapted to meet the needs of the different competitive conditions which prevailed on each

[8] *op.cit.*, Vol. 4, p. 5.
[9] *ibid.*, p. 294.

route. But, aside from these differences in detail, all agreements and arrangements displayed the one unmistakable purpose of controlling competition, whether it be competition between parties to the agreement or conference, or competition from carriers outside the conference. The various methods employed to meet both internal and external competition were found to be essentially the same by both the Royal Commission and the Alexander Committee.

CONFERENCE METHODS OF CONTROLLING COMPETITION

Competition among conference members was found to be regulated by: (1) rate agreements, (2) control of sailing schedules, (3) pooling, and (4) "good faith" or performance bonds. The competition of outsiders was minimized by: (1) agreements, (2) the use of "fighting ships," (3) and tying arrangements with shippers. Since all these procedures are still practiced, though no one conference usually employs all of them, they will be examined in more detail.

Rate agreements were found to consist of three principal types providing for either fixed, minimum, or differential rates. In fixed rate agreements the rates charged are generally definitely prescribed in the tariff agreed upon, and all changes must be made by the mutual consent of the conference membership. Minimum rate agreements stipulate that the members will not carry a commodity for less than the agreed rate, which can be changed only by agreement. These minimum rates are usually the actual rates charged, although when ocean freight rates are advancing rapidly the member lines may find themselves in a position to charge more. Differential rate agreements provide for lines which operate a slower, more indirect, or otherwise inferior service than other conference members to charge rates which are somewhat lower (usually 5 or 10 per cent) than the rates charged by the carriers offering superior service. Such agreements may apply to all cargo, to passenger fares, or only to certain stipulated commodities. Differential rates are customary in agreements covering passenger rates, because the type of accommodations and service offered by different vessels (even those operated by the same line) vary greatly. In all types of rate agreements exceptions are sometimes found, the most common being the exception of certain commodities from the agreement. This frequently occurs in the case of bulk commodities which move in sufficient volume to attract tramp competition, and for cargo useful as ballast.

In such instances the rate on each shipment is individually negotiated; and this is known as an "open" rate.

Another method of regulating competition between the members of a conference is to control the sailing schedules. Sometimes the total number of sailings each member line is permitted during a year is stipulated. In some cases the dates of sailing are subject to agreement. Other agreements restrict the ports of call which can be served by each member.

Pooling arrangements display a great variety but can be roughly classified as agreements to pool the available traffic, the gross passenger or freight monies, or net freight earnings after deducting expenses previously agreed upon. The organization and operation of these arrangements are similar in all important respects to the pooling practices of industrial cartels.

Some conference agreements require members to deposit a stipulated sum of money as a guaranty of their good faith. Fines can be imposed for minor infractions of the agreements, and the entire amount is subject to forfeit for major violations of the agreement.

Controlling competition from shipping companies which were not members of a particular conference often presented great difficulties because of the varied nature of the competition which might come from tramps, non-conference liners, or from competing trade routes. Competition from alternate trade routes is occasionally reduced by agreements between the conferences operating on each of the routes. These agreements sometimes equalize rates or stabilize an agreed differential between the rates charged by the two conferences.

"Fighting ships" and a variety of tying arrangements designed to secure the exclusive patronage of shippers were employed to reduce the competitive threat of non-conference carriers. A "fighting ship" is a vessel placed on berth by the conference to sail in competition with a non-conference carrier. The "fighting ship" would be scheduled to sail on the same day as the "interloper's" vessel, or several "fighting ships" would bracket the outsider's sailings. The "fighting ship" would call at the same ports as the non-conference competitor, and it would charge the same or lower rates as the outsider even if such rates were well below the conference tariff. Financial losses of the "fighting vessel" would be distributed over the several members of the conference, who would each suffer proportionately much less than the one outside line; furthermore, the conference members would often have the advantage of obtaining higher rates on their other sailings. Perhaps the most spectacular instance of this practice was the Syndikats-Rhederi, a "fighting corporation" established in 1905 by six important German lines trading out of Hamburg. The corporation purchased four small and comparatively inexpensive vessels, which, with others chartered from time to time, were hired out to the six owners of the syndicate to throttle competition. In time of "peace" the syndicate's ships engaged in regular trade on time charters.

Tying arrangements included the deferred rebate and a variety of contracts. The cardinal principle of the deferred rebate system is that a shipper who, during a particular period of time, ceases to confine his shipments exclusively to the members of the conference, loses his right to the rebate (usually 5 or 10 per cent) not only for goods shipped during that period but also on goods shipped during the previous period as well. The original rebate period usually runs for three, six or twelve months; and the deferment period generally runs for an additional three or six months. The overlapping makes it difficult for most shippers to shift their patronage to a non-conference carrier without jeopardizing the loss of a rebate which in many instances is substantial. The Shipping Act of 1916 made both the "fighting ship" and the deferred rebate illegal in United States trades, but the deferred rebate is still extensively employed throughout much of the rest of the world. This method is thought by many shipping companies to be the most effective device for the control of trade. Shippers whose business demands regular service not only are reluctant to forfeit their rebates but often have feared that conference carriers might retaliate against "disloyalty" by denying their subsequent shipments accommodation on conference vessels even at full rates. Such retaliation can be disastrous to shippers since an independent line can rarely offer sufficiently adequate service. Discriminatory treatment of this type is also made illegal in United States commerce by the Shipping Act of 1916. As previously stated, contracts present another method by which carriers can secure a shipper's exclusive patronage. The oldest form is the preferential contract, which provides large shippers with special rates lower than those generally quoted. These preferential contracts usually require either the shipper's exclusive patronage or a specified minimum volume of business. Another type of contract between a carrier and shippers was open to large and small shippers alike, and provided lower rates to contract shippers in return for their exclusive patronage for a specified period (often one year). With the development of the conference system contracts of the foregoing varieties continued to be employed but were generally modified so that the shipper could use the ships of any conference member or any steamers designated by the contracting line. A joint contract made by the conference as a whole was a logical development. Such contracts are made for the account of all member lines, each carrying the freight as it is tendered. (This practice has occasionally led to the formation of agreements to pool traffic or revenue.) These contracts are generally available to large and small shippers on the same terms, but non-signers are charged higher rates. The contracting carriers agree to provide adequate tonnage at regular intervals and the shipper promises the conference members his exclusive patronage. These exclusive patronage contracts, as this type of agreement has come to be known, have been widely adopted in United States commerce since deferred rebates are illegal, and in the course of time have undergone some interesting developments. After the Second World War they became the subject of considerable controversy.[10]

All the foregoing methods of controlling competition were found to have been useful in regularizing and rationalizing sailing dates and ports of call, and in stabilizing rates; but it was feared that they also may have succeeded in concentrating sufficient power in a few hands so that the typical abuses of monopolies would inevitably appear if they had not already done so. Therefore, the advantages and disadvantages with which the conference system was credited and charged by the Royal Commission and the Alexander Committee will now be examined, after which the recommendations made by these two investigatory groups to improve the situation will be reviewed.

ADVANTAGES AND DISADVANTAGES OF THE CONFERENCE SYSTEM

The Alexander Committee summarized the views of ship operators and shippers concerning the advantages and disadvantages of the conference system without attempting to make an explicit evaluation of its own. The Royal Commission, however, not only essayed to appraise the merits and demerits of shipping conferences but in doing so rendered a minority report which was far more critical than the conclusions of the majority. The policy recommendations, however, of the American committee and of the majority and minority

[10] This problem is more fully treated in Chapter X.

reports of the British Commission seem to present the best method of evaluating and comparing the relative importance which each group assigned to the advantages and disadvantages of the conference system as they found it in the first decade of the twentieth century. Therefore, after examining the description of the system's alleged merits and demerits, the programs advocated by each of the three reports will be considered.

With two exceptions the advantages associated with shipping conferences were the same in both the Alexander Committee and the *majority report* of the Royal Commission. Both stressed the improvement in service that resulted from (1) the greater regularity of sailings, and (2) the improved ships that were made possible by the greater security which conferences gave to capital invested in the steamship business. There also was agreement that the conference system provided greater stability of rates, a condition which all agreed was essential to the sound development of trade, provided the rates themselves were not excessive. Both reports also mentioned that conferences provided uniform rates to all shippers, but the *majority report* of the Royal Commission noted that in some cases the member companies still seemed subject to pressure from large shippers that might lead to preferential contracts or discriminatory rates. The Alexander Committee stated that conferences generally maintain rates from the United States to foreign markets on a parity with those from other countries, especially from competitive European sources. The Royal Commission found that the conference system did the same for British exporters vis-à-vis the Continent, but that United States trades enjoyed lower rates which had led to a diversion of business, in some instances, from the United Kingdom to the United States. It was thought that these lower rates from the United States might have been due to the fact that deferred rebates were not granted on these American routes, to the lower quality of the American services, and to the great bargaining strength of American "trusts." Both reports described the opportunity conferences have to reduce costs by eliminating wasteful competition between the member lines through the rationalization of sailing dates and ports of call. The reports also mentioned the advantage of conference carriers being able to "charge what the traffic will bear," since thereby they might reduce rates on articles where the higher charge would bear too heavily, and secure compensation on other items where value justified it. Furthermore, the conference lines, it was claimed, could view the trade not only as it is but as it may become, and therefore it was to their advantage to help promote future trade. The British report also mentioned that conference lines did not generally compete with their customers, for member carriers did not usually carry cargo for their own account. (There was some evidence, however, that conference ships did in a few instances carry cargo for their own account, especially bulky, low-value cargo, and thereby did compete with merchant shippers.) The American report failed to mention this point, so presumably the practice of ships carrying cargo of their owners was more prevalent in United States commerce. The Alexander Committee listed one alleged advantage which the British had the good judgment to omit; namely, that the conference system prevented the weaker lines in the various trades from being eliminated. If the weakness was in all instances due exclusively to relative financial strength this argument might possess some merit; but since competitive weakness is more frequently due to higher costs, poorer facilities and service, or both, it is difficult to argue in favor of preventing the elimination of such inefficient operators. This argument may have been included in the American report because the American operator was very apt to be the high-cost producer. The British *majority report* observed that the foregoing advantages depended upon an effective conference system, and to be effective some sort of tie on the shipper's patronage was required. However, the *majority* also observed that there was no guarantee that any of the claimed advantages would be provided by the conference. Only the rebate was guaranteed. "It is the fear of competition from without, and the existence of competition within the Conference which tend to ensure the advantages claimed for the system."[11]

The disadvantages described by the Alexander Committee emphasized the monopolistic nature of conference agreements. The possibility of excess profits being earned, of carrier indifference to delivering cargo in proper condition, arbitrariness in the settlement of claims, failure to give adequate notice of rate changes, and of retaliation and discrimination being practiced had been charged by some complainants. Rate increases were said to have been arbitrary in some cases or to have been made without adequate notice to the shippers. The secrecy with which most conferences operated and the unavailability of tariffs were objected to and fortified suspicions that

[11] *op.cit.*, Cd. 4668, p. 46.

special rates and treatment were being accorded large shippers. The deferred rebate was felt to be too strong a tie. The Royal Commission's *majority report* in spite of its belief that the deferred rebate system was necessary for effective control, agreed that the conferences had arbitrary control over the length of the deferment period and of the ports to which it applied. The *majority* also conceded that rates based on "what the traffic will bear" might at times be too high. The *majority report* made one extremely penetrating observation, which the American Committee apparently overlooked completely, to the effect that conference monopolies might earn excess profits or cause the route to be overtonnaged. They elaborated this latter point by stating that "owing to the form of competition which prevails between the members of the Conference it is possible that ships of greater value or tonnage or number than are required may be imposed upon a particular trade, with the result that the rates are higher than they ought to be, though the shipping companies may not be earning an inordinate or even reasonable profit."[12]

Although the *majority report* of the Royal Commission recognized that conditions could be quite bad when one line controlled a conference, and cited the South African Conference for being arbitrary, out of touch with opinion in South Africa, and for practicing port discrimination, their consensus was far less critical than the *minority report*. The *majority's* adverse opinion is probably best summarized in the statement: "it is obvious that in view of the power which the system gives to shipowners . . . there may always be from time to time arbitrary actions of which shippers have reasonable grounds for complaint."[13]

By way of contrast, the *minority* expressed themselves to the effect that the power to charge "what the traffic will bear" is equivalent to the power to tax a prosperous industry, and such power may be extended to tax all customers for the benefit of the monopoly since the shipping industry is not a purely philanthropic enterprise.[14] The *minority* observed that while most of the conferences have not frequently abused their powers as monopolists, there was no guarantee that they would not do so in the future. Furthermore, it was noted that some shippers, apparently in fear of reprisals, were afraid to testify. After pointing out that rate stability sometimes led to rate rigidity, and that conferences had not succeeded in abolishing all rate wars since they were apt to occur whenever a new line endeav-

[12] *ibid.*, p. 79.   [13] *ibid.*, p. 74.   [14] *ibid.*, pp. 109-110.

ored to enter the trade, the *minority report* recapitulated its position, which we repeat here in some detail because it is itself of substantial interest and because of the references in subsequent investigations to the findings of the *minority*.

"Summing up the chief conclusions at which we have arrived:

"(1) The Conference system with the deferred rebate—the natural evolution of a highly organized trade dealing with customers for the most part scattered or disorganized—has created on almost all the chief ocean routes a monopoly, the limitations upon which are in many cases illusory, and which generally tend to decline;

"(2) The system was introduced in the first instance with the object of raising rates or preventing their fall and diminishing competition;

"(3) It has been successful in raising or keeping up rates;

"(4) The public have, as a rule, to pay higher rates of freight than they would pay in an open market;

"(5) The system has been injurious to 'tramps,' the strongest element in the British mercantile marine, and it leads to waste and to higher rates of freight;

"(6) The system tends to waste in various other directions, owing to the manner in which the Rings are constituted;[15] (Since conferences are a partnership monopoly and not a sole monopoly there is less rationalization and perhaps none.)

"(7) There is no satisfactory evidence that the saving in cost, if there be any . . . exceeds the waste which is due to the system;[16]

"(9) The system tends to inflate the amount of tonnage and consequently the amount of capital invested upon which interest has to be paid;

"(10) It has diminished or tends to diminish the ports of sailing;

"(11) It gives a country such as the United States, in which the system is illegal, an advantage as compared with the United Kingdom;[17]

---

[15] The report pointed out that "The monopoly possessed by a Shipping Ring is not, as a rule, a monopoly under the control of a single head. It is really a sort of partnership in monopoly. The partners have conflicting interests as between themselves, though they are united against the outside public; and owing to this fact there frequently arises a positive temptation to waste." *ibid.*, p. 107.

[16] There was no number 8 in the report.

[17] The Royal Commission seems to have had the notion that the Sherman Act had eliminated the conference system from most all United States trades. The findings of the Alexander Committee revealed that the Royal Commission's minority had overestimated the effectiveness of the Anti-Trust Act.

"(12) It has caused in the case of South Africa a diversion of British trade;

"(13) There is no evidence that it has appreciably increased regularity of sailings or greatly improved the quality of steamers; but it has tended to bring equality and stability of rates."[18]

The *minority report,* in short, recognized the natural development of the conference system in the shipping industry. While granting that the system had tended to bring about equality and stability of rates, the minority did not believe this institution entirely free of serious defects. Before concluding this subject, a few comments on some of the points of this report are in order. Point 4, which held that as a rule the public would have to pay higher rates of freight to conference carriers than they would have to pay in the open market, not only ignores the better service usually provided by liners but also ignores the fluctuating nature of open market rates. Furthermore, freight rates displayed a definite downward trend during the first decade of the twentieth century, and at such a time conference liner rates are apt to lag behind those quoted in the open market, just as they are apt to do so when the trend of rates is upward.

Point 5 regarding the effect of the conference system on British tramp shipping must also be taken with a grain of salt, for the difficulties of tramps has been at least as much a result of technological change as of "unfair" competitive practices. Point 10 calls attention to the fact that some minor ports or outports tend to lose out to the major ports. Without engaging in debate on the benefits or evils of industrial concentration for socio-economic or military purposes, it should be noted that the omission of calls at minor ports was and is one of the ways in which conferences may reduce the wasteful competition of having ships call at innumerable places for small parcels of cargo.

The basic, though somewhat overlapping, problems with which all three reports were concerned, and which still await a completely satisfactory solution, were: (1) how to achieve a desirable degree of rate stability in an industry with liner shipping's cost characteristics without sacrificing all the advantages of the flexibility necessary for adjusting to altered demand or supply conditions; (2) how to rationalize such an industry without losing the spur to efficiency

[18] *ibid.,* p. 114.

61

provided by competition; and (3) how the concentration of power necessary to achieve the desired stability and rationalization can be prevented from perpetrating monopolistic abuses.

What in general was the final evaluation of each of the groups? If it is true, that "by their fruits ye shall know them," then the matured product of each report—its policy recommendations—should provide us with a better understanding of its attitude, tempered by what was considered politically expedient, towards the conference system.

RECOMMENDATIONS OF THE ROYAL COMMISSION'S MAJORITY REPORT

The *majority* felt that the advantages of the conference *cum* deferred rebate system were great, although excessive power, should it arise, ought to be subject to checks to prevent it from causing abuse. A board of control and the compulsory arbitration of rates were not considered feasible unless the government was prepared to guarantee adequate profits. The *majority* pointed out that the limitations on a conference's monopoly were: (1) the outside competition of tramps and new lines; (2) the inside competition between conference members in the provision of facilities and service, and sometimes even the quoting of rates; and (3) the common action taken by shippers. They stressed this latter point and recommended collective bargaining between associations of shippers recognized by the Board of Trade as representative of the whole trade on the one hand, and the conferences on the other hand, as a means of neutralizing the power of the latter. Shippers in the colonies were also advised to form such associations and to have them work in concert with their counterparts in the United Kingdom. The *majority* had some fleeting suspicion that organizations of exporters and importers would not necessarily be concerned with the interests and welfare of producers and consumers; and, therefore, suggested that the government be represented in such associations to safeguard the public interest. The self-interest of shipping companies was presumably considered sufficiently related to the commonweal so as not to require government representatives in their conferences—perhaps because the *majority* thought the shipping lines to be producers rather than middlemen. The Board of Trade, they went on to state, should be authorized to appoint conciliators; or, if both parties agreed, to appoint an arbitrator, when the conference and shippers' group are unable to reach an agreement without outside assistance.

Furthermore, the *majority report* suggested that all conferences using deferred rebates should be required to deposit with the Board of Trade all conference agreements and all understandings with lines outside the conference, all rebate circulars and claim forms, and all agreements with associations of shippers recognized by the Board. Such conferences were also to be required to publish their tariffs and file them with the Board.

Finally, it was recommended that the Board should be empowered to conduct an inquiry whenever there were grounds for believing that important national interests were affected.[19] The *majority* concluded its recommendations by stating, "It is possible that at some future time the system may assume a different character, and that in the shipping trades as in other industries there may be trusts or combinations calling for statutory regulation of a more drastic kind than that here proposed."[20]

RECOMMENDATIONS OF THE ROYAL COMMISSION'S MINORITY REPORT

The *minority* of the Royal Commission felt that the interests of producers and consumers had been neither considered nor protected by the *majority report*. They felt that the alleged advantages of the conference system were not only exaggerated by the *majority* but that they were not guaranteed by the deferred rebate contract, and were purely incidental to the governing conference objective of obtaining higher rates. They felt that good service was a condition of the trade route and not of the conference arrangement, and pointed to the excellence of service on the North Atlantic and on the coastal routes.

The *minority*, however, did not favor novel and drastic legislation, but felt that the conference lines and their customers should first be

[19] Baron Inverclyde and Mr. F. Maddison signed the majority report with reservations. Inverclyde, a prominent shipowner, objected to the publication of tariffs and classifications and to supervision by the Board of Trade. Mr. Maddison said, "I desire it to be clearly understood that I do not, in the least degree, subscribe to the view that Shipping Rings or Conferences are either necessary to, or in the interest of, the trade of the United Kingdom and the Colonies. The contrary I believe to be the fact. But, in my opinion, the evils arising out of the monopolies created by the Conferences are not so far of a character to warrant their prohibition by statute; and, for the same reason, I do not favor placing them under direct Government control." *ibid.*, p. 91. This gentleman was a labor leader, which might explain his disapproval on principle of a monopoly, while at the same time he remained reluctant to commend a policy of government control over an activity which could be claimed to be in restraint of trade.

[20] *ibid.*, p. 90.

given an opportunity to prove the value and efficacy of a real system of consultation and conciliation.[21] Their recommendations followed the pattern of those in the report submitted by the *majority*, but endeavored to remove the restrictions and reservations made by the *majority* which the minority felt would render the suggested control procedure completely nugatory. The *minority* recommended that the Board of Trade should be free to recognize any association of shippers which in its judgment was adequately representative, because it was inconceivable that the whole trade, as required by the majority, could get together. They further recommended that the Board of Trade should be free to direct an inquiry whenever it had received representations from the colonial governments, and the result of such inquiries should in all cases be promptly presented to Parliament. It was felt that the interests of producers and consumers should be considered adequate grounds for investigations and that restricting inquiries to matters affecting important national or imperial interests might exclude many important cases; and, since it was hoped that the effect of full publicity would go far to rectify inequities, the *minority* were not content to leave reporting to Parliament to the discretion of the Board. For the same reason, the *minority* recommended that annually there should be presented to Parliament—not merely deposited with the Board—a report on all conference agreements, all understandings with lines not members of the conference, all circulars and rebate claim forms, and any agreements entered into with associations of shippers recognized by the Board. The *minority* agreed with the *majority* as to the desirability of the publication of tariffs and classifications.

RECOMMENDATIONS OF THE ALEXANDER COMMITTEE

The Alexander Committee observed that the prohibition of agreements between shipping companies to regulate competition would lead to cutthroat practices, which would in turn render the maintenance of competition dubious. Furthermore, any wholesale disturbance in the shipping business would, it was felt, "deprive American exporters and importers of the advantages claimed as resulting from agreements and conferences if honestly and fairly conducted,

---

[21] Sir David Barbour signed with reservation, since he believed that "no check could be applied to the system of Shipping Rings which would be sufficient to protect the public interests without at the same time involving such an amount of interference with the business of shipowners as to make the continuance of the Rings impossible." *ibid.*, p. 114.

such as greater regularity and frequency of service, stability and uniformity of rates, economy in the cost of service, better distribution of sailings, maintenance of American and European rates to foreign markets on a parity, and equal treatment of shippers through the elimination of secret arrangements and underhanded methods of discrimination."[22] The Committee pointed out that very few shippers who communicated with it had been opposed to agreements and conferences in themselves, provided they were fairly, honestly, and openly conducted. The Committee concluded that the claimed advantages could be secured only by permitting the several lines in any given trade to cooperate through some form of rate and pooling arrangement; but the Committee continued, "the disadvantages and abuses connected with steamship agreements and conferences as now conducted are inherent, and can only be eliminated by effective government control."[23]

Consequently, the Committee offered the following recommendations for shipping in the United States foreign trade:[24]

(1) That shipping companies be brought under the supervision of the Interstate Commerce Commission as regards the regulation of rates and the approval of contracts entered into with other shipping or transportation companies.

(2) That all agreements, understandings, or conference arrangements, and all modifications and cancellations of such agreements should be filed with the Commission which should be empowered to order cancellation of any such understandings, or any parts thereof, that it found to be discriminatory or unfair, or detrimental to the commerce of the United States.

(3) That rebates on freight rates and other discrimination between shippers should be made illegal.

(4) That the Commission be empowered to investigate complaints regarding the unreasonableness of rates, and to institute proceedings on its own initiative. (The Alexander Committee added that, while this recommendation was intended to include the supervision of freight classifications, the essential differences between shipping and railroading should not be overlooked, and that it was not the purpose of this recommendation to prevent steamship lines from promptly

[22] *Report on Steamship Agreements and Affiliations in the American Foreign and Domestic Trade, op.cit.*, p. 416.
[23] *ibid.*, p. 418.
[24] Similar, but somewhat more extensive, regulation was recommended for carriers by water operating in the domestic trades of the United States.

lowering their rates to meet competitive conditions.) The Interstate Commerce Commission was also to be empowered to investigate fully all complaints (or to undertake such investigations on its own initiative) charging: (a) failure to give reasonable notice of rate increases; (b) unfair treatment of shippers in regard to space or other facilities; (c) the existence of discriminatory or unfair practices; and (d) unfairness in the settlement of claims and indifference in the landing of cargo in proper condition. The Commission was to be empowered to order the discontinuance of any such practices which it found to exist.

(5) That the use of "fighting ships" and deferred rebates be prohibited in both the export and import trade of the United States; and, moreover, that carriers be prohibited from retaliating against shippers for any reason.

(6) That adequate penalties be provided to correct and prevent the abuses previously mentioned in these recommendations.[25]

SUMMARY

Both the *majority report* made by the Royal Commission and the report of the Alexander Committee concluded that unrestricted competition in the liner shipping business was impossible. Regulation was considered necessary and self-regulation by the industry was found to have developed in the form of conferences. The Royal Commission's *majority* did not believe the monopoly power in the hands of most conferences to have been excessive or to have been abused, and felt that collective bargaining with shipper organizations would neutralize any undue power that the conferences might possess. The *majority*, furthermore, felt that a tie, such as the deferred rebate, was necessary in most instances to keep shippers from patronizing non-conference carriers, but conceded that the Board of Trade should be authorized to try to conciliate disputes and to investigate certain alleged abuses. The *minority* report proposed a similar solution, but recommended that more discretion be given to the Board of Trade except in the matter of reporting to Parliament which was to be obligatory. The American Committee deplored the deferred rebate and suggested that it be prohibited. In their positive recommendations the Americans went further than either of the Royal Commission's groups and suggested that agreements among ocean carriers, and the rates charged by carriers who were par-

[25] *ibid.*, pp. 419-421.

ties to them, should be under the supervision of the Interstate Commerce Commission. While neither of the reports of the Royal Commission was implemented by action, the report of the Alexander Committee formed the basis for the Shipping Act of 1916 which is still the basic statute governing the commercial practices of shipping in the United States trades.[26]

[26] The Shipping Act of 1916, amendments to it, and regulatory experience under it are described in Chapter VII.

CHAPTER V
BRITISH INVESTIGATIONS SINCE 1918

WORLD WAR I broke out only five years after the Royal Commission on Shipping Rings submitted its divided majority and minority reports, and thereby delayed further consideration of shipping conferences in Great Britain. However, remembrance of German liner competition and the decline of the United Kingdom's tramp shipping brought the conference problem to the surface of British postwar planning. In 1918 the reports of both the Dominions Royal Commission and the Departmental Committee on Shipping and Shipbuilding were concerned with this problem among others. The Imperial Shipping Committee was created in the same year and given authority to investigate complaints regarding ocean freights, facilities, and conditions on Empire trade routes.

The Dominions Royal Commission, which had been created shortly before the war to study various aspects of the economic life of the Dominions, stated in its final report that the question of ocean freight rates had been exciting public attention in Canada prior to hostilities and, therefore, in accordance with the wish of the Canadian government they had been specially charged to investigate this matter. The Commission added that this problem "is also one which has been brought to our notice in various aspects in the other parts of the Empire which we have visited, and we have found throughout considerable public feeling on this as well as on other shipping questions."[1] After taking evidence and considering the problem in several parts of the Empire the Commission concluded that "the operations of the steamship companies should not remain longer without some measure of Government control."[2] The Commission recommended that all written or oral agreements among shipping companies, or with shippers, or with other transportation companies, should be filed with boards to be established by the United Kingdom and the Dominion governments. These boards were to be given "full powers for taking evidence and for ordering the production of

[1] Great Britain, Dominions Royal Commission, *Final Report* (1918), p. 307.
[2] *ibid.*, pp. 408-409.

documents."[3] The boards were also to be empowered to investigate complaints and to initiate inquiries. "In particular the investigation of the Boards should extend to freight classifications and to complaints relating to the adjustment of rates between classes of commodities."[4] These investigations were expected to cover the failure to give reasonable notice of changes in classification or rates, unfair treatment of shippers in the matter of cargo space, unfair contracts with certain shippers, unfairness in the settlement of claims, and indifference to the landing of shipments in proper condition.[5] The recommended procedure was analogous to the United Kingdom's Railway and Canal Traffic Acts of 1888 and 1894, and was obviously influenced by the United States Shipping Act of 1916. The Commission suggested that "the functions of these Boards should be in the main directed to investigation and conciliation, but that they should be empowered, at their discretion, to order abolition of differential freight rates found to be inimical to Imperial trade."[6] It was recognized, however, "that some of the Governments may think it advisable to give judicial powers to their Boards, in addition to those suggested above, in order to enable them to enforce their decisions if and when conciliation fails."[7] The Commission also recommended, "That contractors for the new mail services . . . and all other subsidized services should be required to submit for approval to the Governments concerned a schedule of freight rates on the chief articles of import and export, supervision of which is important in the national interest."[8]

The Departmental Committee on Shipping and Shipbuilding, which was created to survey the postwar prospects for these two important British industries, was greatly impressed by the decline of tramp shipping and by the prewar nature of German liner competition, and considered the relation of both to shipping conferences. In its final report the Committee states, "There were . . . tendencies in the years immediately preceding the war (which have continued since its commencement) towards:

"(1) the gradual conversion, in some cases, of the tramp into a regular line;
"(2) the successful competition of an established line, where tramp vessels had succeeded in opening up a more or less regular trade; and

---

[3] *loc.cit.*   [4] *ibid.*, pp. 317-319.   [5] *loc.cit.*
[6] *ibid.*, p. 409.   [7] *ibid.*, p. 319.   [8] *ibid.*, pp. 408-409.

"(3) the absorption of tramp vessels by regular lines.

"No doubt the presence of the tramp owner acted as a wholesome check on the conference system, but there are indications that, when the lines were in a position to enter into direct competition with tramps, the former tended to win. In shipping as in other industries the modern tendency is in the direction of large organizations, and, while there is much trade which cannot be done by the lines, it is only to be expected that the lines will gradually absorb most of the trades where there is business for which it is worth their while to cater."[9]

In regard to German competition, the Committee indicated that the German lines appeared to have had the full support of their government which granted them subsidies, arranged favorable railroad rates, and operated Emigrant Control Stations so as to channel goods and steerage passengers to them. The Committee concluded, "that the German lines observed their [conference] agreements only so far as it paid them to do so."[10] The Committee viewed shipping conferences as the corollary of economic conditions and believed that it would be inexpedient to prohibit them, but in view of later developments in the conference system, principally German competition, the Committee expressed the opinion that "it is possible that the views of the Royal Commission [on Shipping Rings] might have been modified by the fuller revelation of German methods since made."[11] Therefore the Committee concluded, "In the case . . . of agreements with foreign companies, it might, in our opinion, be desirable that copies should be furnished confidentially to His Majesty's Government in order that the Departments concerned may be in possession of all the facts necessary for the safeguarding of British interests in peace and in war."[12] However, the Committee felt that the most satisfactory method of meeting the type of competition the German lines had provided was for the British lines which had already tended to form large combinations to continue this process of amalgamation and for these combinations to cooperate with each other instead of working independently. Such a suggestion naturally led the Committee to consider the regulation of rates. The Committee concluded, "We are convinced that the permanent regulation of freight rates by the Government would be highly detrimental to the wider interests of British merchants and manufacturers,

[9] Cmd. 9092 (1918), pp. 85-86.   [10] *ibid.*, p. 127.
[11] *ibid.*, p. 103.   [12] *ibid.*, p. 116.

70

whose needs can only be satisfied by a great and efficient mercantile marine. Complaints made by traders in the past have arisen largely from factors due to international competition; and we have suggested that the remedy is to be sought mainly in a better organization of British shipping. We would, however, make the following further suggestions:

"(1) A Board of Investigation appears to us desirable in the Interests alike of traders and shipowners. It should be so constituted as to be in a position to appreciate the needs both of trade and of shipping; and to give full weight to the position of this country as a maritime nation. The Board's powers should not go beyond investigation, conciliation, and where deemed expedient, the publication of its findings.

"(2) Even more important is the growth of strong trade associations among traders themselves, which, by their influence, would be able to meet the Shipping Conferences on equal terms. Co-operation on such lines is bound to conduce to the welfare of both sides."[13]

The foregoing reports clearly indicate that the problem of coping with complaints about the monopolistic character of shipping conferences, which had divided the Royal Commission on Shipping Rings in 1909, remained unsolved. The different and often conflicting interests of shipowners, manufacturers, traders, importers, and exporters, which in the United Kingdom itself might conceivably be resolved along the lines recommended by the Royal Commission's majority report, certainly could not be satisfactorily handled in this manner so far as all other members of the Empire were concerned, especially where shipowning was of relatively negligible importance or where the difficulties of establishing shippers' associations were very great. This conflict of interest between shipowner and shipper was often reflected by the different solutions to the conference problem advocated and adopted by the Dominions, and by the investigations made by the Imperial Shipping Committee; and it is therefore to these that we now turn our attention. Before doing so, however, the overriding difficulty of unilateral regulation by one nation of an industry which is multinational must be mentioned, because this obstacle as well as the danger of establishing precedents which might impair the freedom of ship operation in other parts of the world were clearly understood by the British committees which studied the matter. The British reports repeatedly stressed trade competition

[13] *ibid.*, pp. 131-132.

as an important difference between shipping and railways, and as a sufficient reason for not regulating the former. Unilateral or bilateral regulation of the rates between A and B cannot reach trade competition which brings goods from markets in other countries into A or B. The British were particularly disturbed by the fact that inter-Empire rates were sometimes higher than those applicable between Continental European ports and the Dominions, as bitter competition, especially from the German lines, provided low rates to and from the Continent. Accordingly the more stringent British recommendations were applicable only to the inter-Imperial trade. Nevertheless, both of the reports submitted in 1918, especially that of the Dominions Royal Commission, went somewhat further than the majority report of the Royal Commission on Shipping Rings in 1909. The decline in competition to be expected from tramps, the "unsportsmanlike" competition of German lines, and the complaints and evidence supporting them that had been presented by the Dominions, all played a part in explaining the swing in the direction of the recommendations favored by the minority report of the Royal Commission on Shipping Rings.

THE ORGANIZATION OF THE IMPERIAL SHIPPING COMMITTEE

The Imperial Shipping Committee was created by a resolution passed by the Imperial War Conference in 1918. While it was originally contemplated that there should be two bodies concerned with the Empire's oceanic communications, one whose duties would succeed those of the Dominions Royal Commission and be charged with considering improvements of harbor and shipping facilities, and the second with the investigation of complaints, it was decided in 1920 after protracted negotiations to invest one committee with both functions. We are primarily interested in the Imperial Shipping Committee's authority to consider complaints, which was described in its original terms of reference as follows: "To inquire into complaints from persons or bodies interested with regard to ocean freights, facilities and conditions in the inter-Imperial trade, or questions of a similar nature referred to them by any of the nominating authorities; and to report their conclusions to the governments concerned."[14] To prevent irresponsible persons from recourse to its procedure for "vexatious or idealistic purposes" the Committee subsequently ruled

[14] *Report on the Work of the Imperial Shipping Committee*, December 1932 (London: H. M. Stationery Office, 1933), p. 8.

that the "interest" of complainants in the matter under dispute must be "serious and considerable."[15]

In 1923 the imperial character of the Committee was emphasized by making it responsible to all the governments represented at the Imperial Conference instead of to the United Kingdom alone. In 1928 the Committee was also given authority to inquire into a complaint which claimed that British shipowners trading between two foreign ports were, owing to differential rates, placing at a disadvantage shippers sending goods from an Empire port to the same foreign destination. The question involved was a thorny one in that the important interests of British shipping might clash with the equally important interest of British exporters. A means of adjustment, however, was found on this occasion and an appeal to the Committee became unnecessary. In 1930 the Committee's terms of reference were extended to permit it to take into account facilities for overseas air transport.

The Committee is composed of a chairman[16] who does not represent any one part of the Empire and is not directly interested in shipping or commerce; a representative from the United Kingdom and one from each of the Dominions (even before receiving dominion status India was represented on the Committee); a representative for the colonies and protectorates; and five persons having experience in shipping and commerce, of whom two have traditionally been representative shipowners. Since 1930 provision has been made for an additional member to represent civil aviation. The Dominions have usually nominated their High Commissioners in London as representatives, although the working sessions have frequently been attended by their deputies.

It may not be without interest to readers familiar with the cost of operating American agencies to learn that in the first twelve years of the Committee's existence its average annual expenses did not exceed £2,000. This expense was met by the government of the United Kingdom except when a subcommittee visited Canada to investigate certain problems at the request of the Canadian government, in which instance the expenses involved were met by the latter.[17]

---

[15] Halford J. Mackinder, "The Imperial Shipping Committee," *Brassey's Naval and Shipping Annual*, 1929, p. 177.

[16] From its inception until 1939 Sir Halford J. Mackinder served as chairman.

[17] *Report on the Work of the Imperial Shipping Committee*, December 1932, p. 12.

PROCEDURES OF THE IMPERIAL SHIPPING COMMITTEE

As an advisory body the Committee realized from its inception that if its recommendations were to carry weight it would be desirable to reach unanimous conclusions. The Committee's ultimate weapon was publicity, so it was felt that unanimous recommendations of representatives of the Empire governments and of important shipping and commercial interests, with carefully reasoned grounds for the recommendations, were not likely to be ignored. To facilitate the obtaining of unanimous decisions the Committee made it customary to have complaints from its member governments and other bodies presented in writing and, if necessary, supported by witnesses specially sent for the purpose. This procedure relieved members of the Committee from themselves formulating a complaint and acting as an advocate—from which position it might be difficult to retire. Members representing the shipping industry were for similar reasons chosen from a panel so that an industry member would not have to sit as judge in a case when a concern in which he had an interest was a participant.

The Committee has operated on the basis of the good will of all concerned and has preferred to rely on the cooperation of shippers, shipowners, and government departments rather than have the power to compel the attendance of witnesses and to require the production of evidence. The Committee's efforts to remain on friendly terms with all is illustrated by its report on a complaint which charged that conference lines in the Australian trade had discriminated against shippers because of the latter's failure to patronize the conference carriers exclusively. After considering evidence presented by the Australian government, the Committee stated, "*It is clear some such cases have occurred.*" On the same page of its report, after referring to a shipowner's repudiation of such discrimination as unauthorized, the Committee continued to say, "We think, therefore, that *such cases as may have occurred* are due to unauthorized action on the part of subordinate officials in certain of the Conference Lines."[18]

The chairman of the Committee acts in certain ways which have been established by practice. When a complaint is received he may make a preliminary attempt at conciliation; or, where it appears that a conference between the parties is more likely to lead to a speedy

[18] *Interim Report of the Imperial Shipping Committee on the Deferred Rebate System as Obtaining in the Trade between the United Kingdom and Australia* (1921, Cmd. 1486, p. 5. Italics added).

and satisfactory solution than a formal hearing before the Committee, the chairman has been authorized to summon and preside at such a conference. The growth of precedents has enabled the chairman to settle more cases in such an informal manner. In certain instances, where it appeared desirable to do so, the chairman has been authorized to make confidential inquiries concerning the acceptability of recommendations which the Committee contemplated proposing.

Some of the Committee's findings have been released in official reports, but in a large number of cases the Committee has merely embodied its findings in a letter to the Prime Minister or the Secretary of State concerned. Approximately half of these inquiries were concerned with the adequacy of Empire shipping services and harbor development, several were concerned with marine insurance rates, while one dealt with uniform bills of lading and another with the assessment of shipping income taxes within the Empire. Of primary interest to this study, however, are the Committee's inquiries into complaints regarding ocean freight rates and shipping practices.

INQUIRIES OF THE IMPERIAL SHIPPING COMMITTEE[19]

Inquiry No. 8, Freight Rates from Bahamas to United Kingdom, and Inquiry No. 19, Turks and Caicos Islands Freights. In 1921 the Bahamas Chamber of Commerce complained regarding the high rates of freight to the United Kingdom. The Committee replied that the interest of the Empire would best be served in the immediate future by the development of the colony's trade with Canada. Later in the year a similar complaint from the Turks and Caicos Islands received a similar response when the Committee approved the colony's suggestion that the Canadian West Indies service should, if possible, include the Islands in its itinerary.

Inquiries No. 9 and 20, Regarding the Deferred Rebate System. The Australian government brought a complaint against members

---

[19] Based on information contained in the following reports of the Imperial Shipping Committee:

Report on the Work of the Imperial Shipping Committee, June 1926, to May 1930, Cmd. 3646.

ibid., December 1932, Cmd. 4242.

Final Report of the Imperial Shipping Committee on the Deferred Rebate System, Cmd. 1802.

Report on Rates of Freight in the Trade from the United Kingdom to New Zealand (1935).

Report on British Shipping in the Orient (1939).

of the Australian Shipping Conference who, they alleged, granted deferred rebates and refused space to shippers who did not ship exclusively with the conference. The situation was aggravated by the efforts of the government-owned Commonwealth Government Line to enter the trade, and by its statutory inability to pay deferred rebates, which rendered its entrance into conference membership difficult.[20] In 1921 the Committee issued an interim report to give publicity to the fact that the conference lines concerned repudiated any practice of penalizing or threatening to penalize disloyal shippers, and expressed its intention of investigating any such complaint received in the future. (One complaint of discrimination was subsequently submitted and the Committee took action to effect a satisfactory settlement.) In 1923 the Committee issued its final report on the deferred rebate system which had been broadened at the requests of other Empire governments and shippers' associations. The Imperial Shipping Committee agreed that the conference system was necessary and concluded that "conferences must be allowed to exact some such assurance of continuous support from shippers as would limit intermittent and irresponsible competition." The Committee recommended: (1) that individual shippers be given a choice of binding themselves under the deferred rebate system, or by means of an agreement which provided for damages in event of breach by either party; and (2) the formation of associations of shippers to negotiate with the shipping conferences.[21] The result was a modus vivendi between the Australian Conference and the Commonwealth Government Line which was subsequently sold to one of the conference companies. Another result was the impetus given the formation of shippers' associations which have played an increasingly important part in the negotiation of rates and other matters in Australia's trade.[22]

Inquiry No. 12, Rates of Freight in the New Zealand Trade. In 1921 the New Zealand government requested an investigation of the reasonableness of freights charged by lines trading with New Zealand. On the basis of audited information the Committee concluded that under prevailing conditions the freights charged were not un-

---

[20] For a description of the Australian Industries Preservation Act which made it unlawful for the Commonwealth Government Line to pay rebates, see Chapter VI.

[21] The Committee's final report on this subject (Inquiry No. 20) is described more fully in Chapter X on *Tying Arrangements*.

[22] For a description of Australian shippers' associations, see the section on Australia in the following chapter.

reasonable and pointed out that the cost of transport might be reduced if New Zealand could concentrate its shipments at fewer ports.

Inquiry No. 13, St. Helena Freights. The Crown Colony of St. Helena complained in 1921 of high rates on hemp to the United Kingdom. Upon consulting the Union Castle Steamship Company, the Committee was informed that the freights in question had been reduced.

Inquiries No. 14 and 29, East African Freights. During 1920-1921 the Committee received numerous complaints regarding the level of freights on staples from East Africa to the United Kingdom; but the complainants were found to differ so extensively among themselves that the Committee determined that it was useless to proceed further until the shippers formed an association to correlate their demands. An association was formed which negotiated for a time with the shipping conference, but which subsequently lapsed. Late in 1923 the Committee was again requested to examine East African freight rates both to and from the United Kingdom. The Committee again recommended the formation of shippers' associations, with the result that the East African Outward Shippers' Committee was formed in London early in 1925. In East Africa a committee of representatives of the Chambers of Commerce and the Convention of Associations was formed to coordinate freight rates on shipments to the United Kingdom, but subsequently this committee was suspended. The export of sisal was an exception because the trade was controlled in London, and a subsection of the London Chamber of Commerce was formed in 1925 to negotiate with the conference on rates covering this commodity.

Inquiry No. 20, Rates from Trinidad to the United Kingdom. In 1922 the Governor of Trinidad complained that rates to the United Kingdom were high in comparison with rates for similar products from competing countries. The question was taken up with the West Indies Transatlantic Steamship Conference, which replied that the rates on cocoa, sugar, and rubber had been reduced, but since shipments from the West Indies were made in smaller quantities than from ports with which comparisons had been made, reductions could not be expected to equal rates quoted for full cargoes. The Committee accepted the reductions and explanations given as reasonable.

Inquiry No. 25, West Indies Freight on Cacao. In 1923 the Committee was requested to consider freights on cacao from the West Indies to the United Kingdom. The matter was jointly considered by the West India Committee and the West Indies Transatlantic Conference, and certain proposals were then made by the conference which the West India Committee accepted.

Inquiry No. 28, North Atlantic Freights on Canadian Flour. In 1923 the Canadian government objected to the fact that: (a) the rate on Canadian milled flour shipped from United States ports was higher than the rates on United States milled flour shipped from the same ports to the same destinations; and (b) the freight on flour shipped from Canadian ports was higher than that from American ports. The Committee discussed the matter with shipowners and millers in Canada and as a result received assurances from the British flag lines involved that in the future they would quote the same rates on this commodity from U.S. and Canadian ports regardless of the flour's origin.

Inquiry No. 32, Rates on Canadian Cattle. The Canadian government in 1924 requested the Committee to inquire into the rates on store cattle from Canada to the United Kingdom, it being alleged that the existing rates rendered the business so unprofitable to the producers as to check the growth in Canada's export trade in cattle. The Committee ascertained that the costs of handling cattle were high and recommended improvements in the facilities for landing cattle in England, which the British government accepted.

Inquiry No. 39, Rates on Wheat and Flour from Australia. In 1927 the National Association of Flour Importers asked the Committee to investigate a proposal to charge a higher freight for flour than for wheat from Australia to the United Kingdom. After careful consideration, the Committee decided that it could not intervene as it felt that its terms of reference were not intended to cover variations of rates for particular commodities unless there should be prima facie evidence of substantial injustice or exceptional circumstances which it did not find in the present case.

Inquiry No. 55, Rates on Aircraft and Aero Engines. The Society of British Aircraft Constructors, Ltd., in 1930 requested reductions in existing shipping rates for aircraft and aero engines. The Committee made inquiries and consulted with both the Society and shipowners, with the result that appreciable reductions in rates, which the Society allowed were fairly satisfactory, were made on several routes.

Inquiry No. 65, Freight Rates on Fertilizers to South Africa. In March 1932, a complaint was registered regarding a 20 per cent surcharge proposed by the conference lines to South Africa on *all* outward freights. An agreement between the conference and certain Continental shippers of fertilizers guaranteed them the existing rates through 1932. No such agreement had been made with British shippers of fertilizers, who complained that they would suffer a disadvantage for the balance of the year. In view of the representations of the Committee, the conference decided not to levy the proposed surcharge on British fertilizers.

Inquiry re Rates of Freight from the United Kingdom to New Zealand. Following the recommendation of the Imperial Shipping Committee in 1921 in Inquiry No. 12, the New Zealand government created statutory boards to negotiate with shipping companies the rates and services applicable on the extremely important movement of refrigerated cargoes to the United Kingdom. While appreciable reductions were achieved in the rates for refrigerated products, the export rate on wool had not been reduced, and imports from the United Kingdom continued to pay fairly high transportation charges which were often 20 to 30 per cent higher on representative items than the rates from Great Britain to Australia. New Zealand complained of this and in 1935 the Committee published its report. The differences in the two trades which affected both the costs of operation and the alternate sources of revenue were considered, and the Committee concluded that these variables explained and presumably justified the dissimilar rates. There was some difference of opinion regarding whether or not the low rates charged for the carriage of refrigerated products had forced the carriers to maintain high rates on other items moving between the two countries. The Australian and New Zealand members of the Committee insisted that the low rates for refrigerated space were made possible by the rationalization of sailings and cargo movements, and not by undue pressure exerted by the statutory boards as charged by the other members.[23] The Committee recommended the formation of a shippers' organization to rationalize shipments from the United Kingdom to New Zealand and to bargain collectively with the conference.

Inquiry re British Shipping in the Orient. While not primarily concerned with rate or conference matters, no description of the inquiries of the Imperial Shipping Committee would be complete without reference to its excellent study in 1939 of ocean transportation

---

[23] For a description of the manner in which these boards operate, see the section on New Zealand in the following chapter.

in the Orient. The competition faced by British ship operators in this part of the world, especially from the Japanese, and the steps that might be taken to meet this rivalry, are the main theme of this report which also includes some illuminating descriptions of conference activities. Of especial interest are the accounts of the keen competition that occasionally occurs in some of these rings.

The Bombay-Japan Conference was started in 1888 by the Peninsular & Oriental Steam Navigation Co., the Austrian Lloyd, and the Navigazione Generale Italiana. In 1896 the Nippon Yusen Kaisha was admitted as a fourth member, and its share of the business grew steadily and rapidly so that in successive conference agreements it was allotted an increasing percentage of the trade. Strengthened by its connection with the Cotton Spinners Association in Japan (known as Rengokia), the share of the N.Y.K. increased from 18 per cent in 1896 to 28 per cent in 1913, during which year a second Japanese line, the Osaka Shosen Kaisha, entered the route and received an allotment of 12 per cent from the conference. The Austrian and Italian lines subsequently retired, but in 1925 a third Japanese line, the Kokusia Kisen Kaisha, entered the trade. The Japanese lines went after business aggressively and refused to coordinate or restrict their sailings, so that even in the relatively busy season of 1934-1935 little more than half of the available space was filled. The percentage carried by the P. & O. fell from its original allotment of approximately 67 per cent in 1888 to 20 per cent of the trade from Bombay to the Far East, and 15 per cent of the trade in the reverse direction. This fall in percentage participation, however, did not represent a decrease in quantity, since the total volume of business increased so rapidly that the tonnage handled by the British line increased by about 80 per cent between 1897 and 1937. Nevertheless, the Committee found that the P. & O. had lost money on this service, partly because it had been forced to sail with unoccupied space—the Japanese having refused to rationalize their sailings—and partly because of the low freight rate on cotton up to 1937. The Committee observed the curious fact that the conference lines did not fix freight rates by themselves or in negotiations with Japanese importing firms. The rates were fixed annually by contracts between the N.Y.K. and the Rengokia, and were accepted by the other members of the conference and by merchant firms.

The Calcutta-Japan Conference and the Australia-Japan Conference provide additional examples of the aggressive character of Japanese competition and the rapid growth of Japanese participation at the expense of the older British carriers, although in these instances there were no unusual rate-making features. Japanese competition, however, while not entirely unique was, as a result of the close connections before World War II among Japanese financial, shipping, manufacturing, and commercial concerns through a few very powerful money cliques or Zaibatsu, pretty much in a class by itself. This pattern may be of some prognosticative value in considering what might happen if shipping should be nationalized by any important maritime power which also had nationalized its major industries or operated state trading monopolies. In any case it indicates the bitterness which competition in ocean shipping can attain even in situations where conference agreements exist.

Until 1934 the important trade from the Straits Settlements to the Atlantic Coast of North America was carried mainly by six British lines and one American line—all of which were members of the Straits-United States Conference—and one American non-conference line which had an understanding with the conference group. The conference had an exclusive patronage contract with the Rubber Trade Association of London, which represented the Singapore Rubber Association, and an additional charge was made for the carriage of rubber for shippers who had not signed such contracts. An important factor in this trade was one of the Mitsui firms which bought and shipped rubber; and in 1934 the Mitsui Bussan Kaisha and its closely affiliated "K" Line applied to the conference for admission.

The participation of the two Japanese lines grew from 10 per cent after their admission to 15 per cent by April 1935, 25 per cent by July 1935, and 34 per cent by September of that year. The other conference lines proposed limiting the Japanese quota to about 25 per cent; but the rubber dealers intervened and stated that they were not prepared to allow the Japanese lines to carry more than 16 per cent of the traffic, since they had felt increasingly the competition of the Mitsui firm's merchanting department after the introduction of the M.B.K. ships. It was alleged that the Mitsui Line could carry its own rubber at less than the conference rate and that the Mitsuis, as merchants, could then afford to pay local dealers a higher price for their rubber. (This charge, or the similar one that affiliates of "industrial carriers" can sell at a lower price, is frequently levelled against shipping which is allied with industrial or commercial interests. It is based on the assumption that, even if the "industrial car-

81

rier" does charge its affiliates the agreed rates, internal bookkeeping manipulation permits earnings of the transportation venture to underwrite the commercial or industrial operations.)

Beginning early in 1936 the Japanese share declined from the high of 50 per cent it had reached. This decline was attributed in part to lower rates introduced by the other conference lines, but since it continued even after the rates were subsequently increased, it was probably largely due to the strong anti-Japanese sentiment in the important Chinese merchant community in Malaya. By late 1937 the Japanese proportion had fallen to less than 12 per cent and when the "China Incident" created a new and urgent demand for Japanese tonnage they withdrew their vessels from this route.

A somewhat different pattern appeared in the Java-Japan Conference, where the Japanese rapidly increased their participation by waging rate wars. In a new rate war in 1933 the Netherlands Line, with the encouragement of the Netherlands East Indies government, and with the close support of shippers in the Netherlands East Indies and of Dutch firms in Japan, decided to strike back vigorously. In September of that year the N.E.I. government passed a Crisis Import Ordinance which authorized the Director of Economic Affairs to prescribe specific ports of entry for foreign goods. A number of restrictions on Japanese shipping and imports followed, and these led to trade negotiations between the two governments in 1934. The Netherlands East Indies made it known that a solution which assured the Netherlands Line retention of its important place in the trade between the Indies and Japan was essential, with the result that the agreement finally reached assured the Dutch approximately 50 per cent of the business. These negotiations, which were renewed in later years, contributed to the increasing tension between the two countries.

SUMMARY OF IMPERIAL SHIPPING COMMITTEE ATTITUDES

The pattern that emerges from the recommendations of the Imperial Shipping Committee is: (1) an avoidance, whenever possible, of decisions regarding rates; and (2) a reliance on collective bargaining by shippers' associations and conferences of ship operators to settle differences and to neutralize the monopoly power inherent in conferences. The Committee holds "it was not intended that we should intervene unless and until direct settlement of difficulties by frank and friendly discussion between the parties concerned have proved impracticable."[24] In 1927 the Committee felt that it had established an important precedent in Inquiry No. 39, regarding rates on wheat and flour from Australia, when it stated that it was not prepared to hold an inquiry into the rate for a particular commodity unless there was prima facie evidence of substantial injustice or exceptional circumstances.[25] However, in 1921 and again in 1935, acting on complaints made by the New Zealand government, the Committee did investigate the level of freight rates as a whole from New Zealand to the United Kingdom.

In 1923 the Committee, in Inquiry No. 20 regarding deferred rebates, had found tying arrangements of some sort necessary in most trades and suggested that shippers be given "a running option" between deferred rebates and an agreement negotiated by shippers' associations and shipping conferences.[26] The Committee's attitude toward shipping conferences is perhaps best summarized in the statement made in 1939 in its report on British Shipping in the Orient: "It speaks much for the prevalence, on the whole, of fair dealing all round, that a system of such slight internal structure, and so liable to abuse, should have lasted so long, and despite frequent criticism, should produce so few serious disputes."[27] It should be recalled that the earlier reports of both the Departmental Committee on Shipping and Shipbuilding and the Dominions Royal Commission, especially the latter, had been considerably more critical of shipping rings.

[24] *Report of the Work of the Imperial Shipping Committee, June 1926 to May 1930*, p. 7.

[25] *op.cit.*, pp. 7-8.

[26] A committee appointed by the Prime Minister of the United Kingdom in 1924 to inquire into the conditions and prospects of British commerce, issued a report in 1929 wherein, among other things, they mentioned the conference system. The committee endorsed the recommendations of the Imperial Shipping Committee to encourage the formation of shipper associations to bargain collectively with the conferences, and to give shippers an option between deferred rebates and contracts negotiated with the shipping lines by their own associations.

[27] *op.cit.*, p. 78.

CHAPTER VI

ACTION OF BRITISH DOMINIONS AND OTHER COUNTRIES

PREVIOUS CHAPTERS have described investigations of shipping conferences by the United States and Great Britain and the attitude of the governments of these countries to this method of self-regulation. This chapter will consider the activities of shipping conferences in other parts of the world and the reaction to them of other governments.

Contract rates, deferred rebates, or some variety of preferential arrangement are found to be fairly universal, although actual practices vary with the competitive structure of each route. We again find that outbound lines in some trade routes may operate under a conference agreement, while inbound vessels on the same route may operate without a conference, or vice versa. Between Japan and the Netherlands Indies, for example, deferred rebates are offered by the eastbound conference, while in the opposite direction no "shipper tie" has been considered necessary by the westbound conference.

In some countries, copies of conference agreements are not available either to the shippers or to the governments, and in several even tariffs are not available for public examination. A large number of ports throughout the world, and quite a few of the smaller countries, are rarely or ever visited by tramps, except those which may occasionally be chartered by the regular lines to supplement the service their own vessels provide, and which operate therefore subject to conference regulations. This situation is not uncommon in many Central American countries, although it is found elsewhere as well.

Conferences in most of the world's trade routes usually deal with individual shippers, except where trade associations or chambers of commerce are sufficiently interested and powerful to require the conferences to negotiate with them. Chambers of commerce often represent too many interests to be effective bargainers with shipping rings, and frequently even export trade associations are not sufficiently powerful to hold their own with a well-organized conference. As a result the governments of several countries have chosen to assist shippers of important export products in their negotiations with conferences. For example, the Greek government has at times, in an informal manner, taken up with conferences export rates on currants. In Colombia the National Federation of Coffee Producers enlists the cooperation of the government in rate negotiations. Turkey, which required the lines to file copies of their tariffs with the Foreign Trade Department, made no direct attempt to alter conference rates, but a government-owned and operated coastal service exercised an influence through the negotiation of transshipment rates with the European lines. The Peruvian Ministry of Finance and Commerce entered negotiations with shipping companies on the occasion of the opening of new port facilities at Callao in 1935. Since World War II, several hitherto non-maritime nations have promoted their national-flag shipping; and although dissatisfaction with conferences has not been the dominant motive for this development, it has, nevertheless, been cited in some instances as an additional reason.

The investigative and regulatory activities of countries, besides the United States and the United Kingdom, should provide a more accurate conception of the universal nature of many of the problems presented by shipping conferences; so the experience of several other countries is now described. The experience of some of the British Dominions has been particularly illuminating.[1]

CANADA

In 1913, shortly after the Royal Commission on Shipping Rings had reported, the Canadian government instructed Mr. (later Sir) Henry Drayton, chief commissioner of the Board of Railway Commissioners, to discuss with imperial authorities the question of governmental control of ocean freight rates. Drayton was referred to the Dominions Royal Commission, which was currently studying this matter, but to expedite things he submitted independently a tentative report in which he suggested granting the government authority to establish standard maximum rates. In 1923 a Special Select Committee appointed by the Canadian House of Commons to inquire into agricultural conditions once again brought the matter of ocean freights to the surface of official attention. This agricultural committee conducted extensive hearings and collected much evidence with which they documented their reports.[2] The Committee

---

[1] Some of the problems encountered by the Dominions have already been mentioned in Chapter V.

[2] Canada, *Journals of the House of Commons*, Appendix to 60th Volume (1923).

was considerably disturbed by the monopolistic character of shipping lines operating between Canada and the United Kingdom, and by the fact that firm rate quotations for eastbound shipments were not made for longer than a week at a time. The Committee considered this failure of the carriers to quote rates for longer periods of time injurious to Canadian exporters, since shippers of wheat and flour could not ascertain what transportation charges would be a month ahead. An examination of this argument, however, indicates that rates on wheat and flour were quoted only for short periods because tramp competition frequently participated in this movement. The investigation, however, was concerned with more than wheat and flour, so it may be best to let the Committee speak for itself.

The report states, "Your Committee are of the opinion that upon the regular steamship lines trading from Canadian ports the price of transportation service is determined neither by the law of supply and demand, nor on the basis of cost plus a reasonable profit, but that a combine exists . . . known as the North Atlantic and U.K. Conference. . . . The headquarters . . . are at New York and it includes in its membership a very great number, if not all, of the principal steamship companies operating regular lines out of North Atlantic ports. . . . To this North Atlantic Conference belong nearly all, if not all, of the regular steamship lines running from Montreal, including the Canadian Government Merchant Marine. . . . It will be remembered that the Canadian Government Merchant Marine, as well as the Canadian National Railways [which is also owned by the Government], is operated under the control of a Board, and not by a Minister of the Crown. . . . Subsidiary to this Conference there exists a smaller association of steamship men connected with steamship lines trading out of Montreal."[3] It was contended that the Canadian Government Line merely "sat in" with the rest of the steamship lines at their meetings, but that it was not bound in the same manner as the others to maintain rates. "A careful consideration of the evidence," the Committee observed, "hardly supports this contention."[4] The report continues: "It would appear that the shipping combine referred to does not include tramp steamers, which can be chartered from time to time, and among which there exists keen

[3] *ibid.*, pp. viii-ix.
[4] *loc.cit.*

competition. These, however, are only available to those shippers who can load a whole steamer; neither do they take the place of regular lines which are able to effect transportation almost with the regularity of express trains, and which, therefore, offer much greater advantages to those who have to ship perishable articles. . . ."[5] The agricultural committee concluded, "In view of the fact that a very great deal of the shipping coming to Canadian ports is British shipping, concurrent action by the British authorities is respectfully suggested. . . . Meanwhile it would appear wise to recommend that the Government through one of its departments—we suggest the Department of Trade and Commerce—should entertain complaints from shippers of unfair or oppressive treatment by ocean carriers and should hold investigations publicly or privately into such complaints."[6]

The Canadians remained dissatisfied with the structure of ocean freights to the United Kingdom; so in 1925 the government at Ottawa authorized another investigation. This study was made by Mr. W. T. R. Preston, who submitted a report which was highly critical of the North Atlantic Conference and which took a dim view of the effectiveness of the Imperial Shipping Committee.[7] The report states, "The North Atlantic Steamship Combine [conference] is only one section of the steamship combine now endeavoring to control all the great shipping interests of the world."[8] Preston claimed that the North Atlantic Conference threatened to withhold business from a shipbuilding company unless the latter refused to charter ships to a line that proposed to charge steerage passenger fares below those set by the conference.[9] The report continues, "It was only after Sir Henry Drayton was able to secure authentic copies of resolutions that had been adopted at the Steamship Combine meetings, that had been held in various parts of Europe, that the British or Canadian members of the Combine admitted its existence and operation."[10]

Concerning British efforts to improve the situation Preston claimed, "The Imperial Shipping Board [Committee] acts only in an advisory capacity, and has no authority to deal with 'intolerable' practices so frankly condemned by the Royal Commission. The Board is helpless in relation to minor as well as major offenses that

---

[5] op.cit., p. x.   [6] ibid., p. xxi.
[7] Canada, Parliament Sessional Paper 45 (1925).
[8] ibid., p. 3.   [9] ibid., p. 4.   [10] ibid., p. 7.

may be and are committed by this monopolistic Combine [North Atlantic Conference]."[11]

Preston's specific objections concentrated on what he considered to be the excessively high rates charged for moving goods between Canada and the United Kingdom. Rates from Canada to South Africa, and the Continent of Europe, and rates from the United States to both the United Kingdom and the Continent were presumably satisfactory since it was by comparison with these that he concluded that rates from Canada to Great Britain were excessive. He argued that the weakness of market competition was demonstrated by the fact that in 1924 the rates from the United Kingdom were two to four times the rates applicable from the Continent where shipping competition, especially German, was keen. The report also claimed that the conference to the United Kingdom had priced itself out of moving a carload of pianos per week from Canada to Liverpool by asking postwar rates 700 per cent higher than the 1911 charge, and 400 per cent greater than the 1912-1913 tariff; an increase which raised the rate in question from $1.67 per 40 cubic feet in 1911 to $3.15 in 1912-1913, and to $12.00 in 1923-1924.[12] It pointed out that the rates from Canada to the United Kingdom on pianos, agricultural machinery, etc., were higher than the rates charged to carry these commodities to South Africa and the Continent, with the result that many Canadian goods were exported via United States ports. Preston attributed part of the difficulty to the relative absence of tramp competition. "The position of Canada, therefore, is more serious than that of countries where tramp steamers compete freely with the Combine Lines in ocean traffic."[13]

In the same year, 1925, a Special Parliamentary Committee which had been appointed to consider a resolution to give the government of Canada control over certain ocean rates presented its final report in which it concluded that: (1) The discrimination among rates charged for the carriage of different commodities was unduly great. (2) This discrimination was caused by the very low rates charged for the transportation of wheat and flour which was brought about by the presence of tramp competition in the movement of these commodities.[14]

This latter committee, with the cooperation of the lines operating in the North Atlantic route, had an auditor examine their books. This

[11] *ibid.*, p. 10.   [12] *ibid.*, pp. 14-17.   [13] *ibid.*, p. 26.
[14] Canada, *Journals of the House of Commons*, Vol. LXII (1925).

examination concluded that the earnings realized for 1923 and 1924 were not sufficient to pay an adequate return on the capital invested after deducting proper allowances for depreciation. In spite of this finding, the recommendations of the Special Committee went considerably further than the agricultural committee had in 1923. The recommendations of the Special Committee of interest to this study were that:

1. Their auditor should continue his examination of shipping company books (the companies had assented) to determine whether rates currently charged were excessive.

2. All members of conferences trading to Canadian ports should be required to file with the Board of Railway Commissioners all conference agreements, freight rates and such other information as may be desired.

3. The Board of Railway Commissioners be constituted as a tribunal authorized to hear complaints, and to recommend maximum rates. (Publicity, it appears, was to be relied upon to obtain compliance.)

4. Cooperative action among shippers (especially of butter) in scheduling shipments would reduce ocean transport costs by regularizing a movement which was highly seasonal in character.

Despite this series of investigations and the general agreement they displayed in recommending that provisions be made for investigating complaints, no such tribunal was authorized by the Canadian Parliament. Prior to World War II the Canadian government, however, exercised limited authority over ocean shipping rates through subsidy contracts. Except for the important trans-Atlantic and trans-Pacific services operated by the Canadian Pacific Railway, all other recipients of Canadian shipping subsidies had one of two types of rate restrictions written in their contracts. The first type specified that both passengers and cargo were to be carried at rates approved from time to time by the Minister of Trade and Commerce and that subsidy-holders should at all times faithfully abide by all orders and regulations made by the Minister with regard to the performance of steamers subject to the contract. The second type of subsidy contract held that the Minister of Trade and Commerce should at any time have the right to revise the freight and passenger rates charged by the company or to prescribe the maximum rates which might be charged by any steamer performing service under the contract, and such rates were to be available to the public at the offices and agents of the contractors. After freight and passenger rates had been approved by the Minister, they should not be raised by the contractors without previously obtaining his permission. Both of the contracts held by the North Pacific Shipping Co. Ltd., which operated between British Columbia and China and Australia, and between the Pacific Coast of Canada and South Africa, contained a clause forbidding the company to participate in conferences.[15]

UNION OF SOUTH AFRICA

In 1904, before the Union was formed, a conference of delegates from the various South African colonies, which convened in Johannesburg, inquired into ocean freights. They recommended that: (1) the rebate system, preferential rates from the United States or the Continent, and secret concessions to shippers be abolished; (2) shipowners be invited to tender on the above basis and to undertake to carry for the South African governments, for public bodies, and for private traders at uniform rates; (3) the South African governments should (a) guarantee to offer their own cargoes to such carriers and should try to induce public bodies and private traders similarly to support them and (b) penalize by supplementary harbor dues ships contravening the conditions stated in (1) or carrying cargoes below the contract rates on any route, and (c) give preferential dispatch and berthing arrangements to the contractors. The drastic nature of these recommendations might have been due to the shipowners' refusal of invitations to attend the conference. No action was taken, however, for the British government informed the High Commissioner for South Africa that it wished to express its views prior to the passage of legislation on this subject, and because it was felt that legislation passed by the colonies making the rebate system illegal would be ineffectual unless similar legislation was passed by the Imperial Parliament. Two subsequent attempts by the South African colonies to settle the matter failed, and this constituted one of the major reasons for the appointment in 1906 of the Royal Commission on Shipping Rings.

In 1911 the Governor-General of the Union of South Africa was forbidden by the Post Office Administration and Shipping Combinations Discouragement Act from entering into ocean mail contracts

---

[15] A. E. Sanderson, *Control of Ocean Freight Rates in Foreign Trade*, U.S. Department of Commerce, Trade Promotion Series No. 185 (1938), p. 128.

with shipping concerns which he considered to be acting to the detriment of South African trade or industries, or which offered rebates, refunds, or discounts to shippers in consideration for exclusive patronage. The result of this legislation was to force the liner companies trading to South Africa to relinquish the deferred rebate system on cargo carried to or from the Union. Stability was provided by an exclusive patronage contract between the South African Trade Association and the South African Shipping Conference, wherein the former agreed to be loyal in their patronage, and the conference agreed to regular, adequate sailings and to stable rates mutually agreed upon and alike for large and small shippers. Eighteen years later the Shipping Board Act of 1929 created the South African Shipping Board to investigate and report upon matters relating to ocean transportation.[16] The Dominions Royal Commission, it will be remembered, had recommended in 1918 the establishment of shipping boards in all the Dominions for the better protection of the interests of shippers. The Board possessed no rate-making power, although it was authorized to report to the Ministry of the Board of Trade and Industry if inbound rates were so low as to be detrimental to producers in the Union. If the Board of Trade and Industry found the rates so low as to violate the Customs Tariff Excise Duties Amendment Act of 1925, and that it was in the public interest to do so, it could impose a freight dumping duty on goods brought in under such rates.

The Shipping Board was established because it had long been felt that South African interests were not suitably represented in shipping affairs by conferences whose headquarters were overseas

[16] Section 2 of the Shipping Board Act of 1929 defined the functions and duties of the Board in the following words:

"*Function and duty of Board.* It shall be the function and duty of the Board, subject to the provisions of this act and any regulations made thereunder, to investigate and report to the minister upon any matters relating to ocean transport to, from, or between Union ports, including more particularly any question (a) as to whether the rate of freight charged by any shipowner on any particular commodity exported from the Union is prejudicial to Union exporters as compared with their overseas competitors; (b) as to whether the rate of freight charged by any shipowner on any particular commodity imported is unreasonably high having regard to the rate of freight for that particular commodity operating on other ocean routes; (c) as to failure on the part of a shipowner to give reasonable notice of changes in freight classifications or rates; (d) as to the levying by any shipowner of differential freight or other charges as between one shipper and another in respect of the ocean conveyance of goods to, from, or between Union ports; (e) as to differential or unfair treatment by any shipowner of any shipper in respect of the allocation of space accommodation or any other matter. Such reports shall at the request of the Board and with the approval of the minister be laid upon the table of both Houses of Parliament."

and by exporters in London. At the first meeting of the Board the presiding officer stated that it was the intention of the act "to transfer from overseas to South Africa the center of gravity in South African freight matters."[17] The spirit of the act is that protection of the Union's commerce, industry, and agriculture, through supervision of freight rates, should be achieved by friendly representation rather than by coercion.[18]

The Board promptly requested every shipowner to furnish it with a complete and accurate list of all ocean rates and fares for the transportation of goods and passengers carried from, or to, or between ports of the Union of South Africa. It also requested at least twenty-one days' notification prior to any change in these tariffs, although when warranted exceptions to this rule could be granted. In 1937 every shipowner was requested to furnish the Board with a copy of any agreement entered into with other shipowners.

In 1935, in reply to a request from the South African conference lines to permit differential contract rates in view of serious non-conference competition, the Board found such differential rates contrary to the intention of the Post Office Administration and Shipping Combinations Discouragement Act of 1911 and recommended instead the imposition of freight dumping duties. While this decision reflects a dislike for the contract rate system, the use of freight dumping duties was legally possible only because the "disturbing" non-conference carriers were bringing in large quantities of iron and steel at depressed rates to the detriment of Union producers. "The Machinery of the Customs in respect to dumping duties was then inadequate for this purpose, being restricted to the difference between the so-called prevailing rate of freight and the depressed rate, which difference was annulled as soon as the Conference Lines, in self-defense and for the protection of their patrons, adjusted their rates to the level of those of their outside competitors."[19]

The South African government has on several occasions entered into ocean freight agreements with steamship lines. In 1929 a five-year agreement was signed with the Union-Castle Mail Steamship Company, governing the conveyance of cargo between South Africa and the European berth ports of the South African Conference Lines.

[17] Sanderson, op.cit., p. 92.
[18] A letter from Mr. W. A. Horrocks, commercial secretary, Embassy of the Union of South Africa, Washington, D.C.
[19] ibid.

This agreement regulated the transport of government cargo and fixed maximum rates of freight for perishables and other South African products moving to Europe as well as maximum rates for inbound freight. The current agreement with the Union-Castle Company was signed in 1945, and is intended to endure ten years from January 1, 1947. In 1933 the government concluded a five-year agreement with two Italian lines and provided a subsidy of £150,000 per annum, in return for which the lines undertook to maintain certain services to Mediterranean ports and to East and West Africa. Rates to the Mediterranean were not to exceed those charged by other conference lines operating between South Africa and European ports, while rates to East and West Africa were to be fixed by the Ministry of Commerce and Industries. In 1934 the South African government also subsidized Swedish and Norwegian lines to carry its trade at satisfactory rates.

AUSTRALIA

A feature of Australian overseas shipping has been the development of collective bargaining to such an extent that group representation of shippers is not unusual in negotiations with conference lines regarding freight rates, services, and contractual agreements. Although conventional shipping conferences operate in Australian trades with the Far East and North America, the transport of Australia's highly important commerce with Europe is coordinated by an association, a number of whose members are representatives of government-sponsored organizations. This association, known as the Australian Oversea Transport Association, is a voluntary body. The Commonwealth government has no direct representation on the Association, and when the government intervenes it is usually at the Association's invitation.

Freight rates between Australia and Europe since 1929 have been negotiated by the Australian Oversea Transport Association (frequently referred to as A.O.T.A.). This organization resulted from a special conference convened in 1929 by the then Prime Minister of Australia, the Rt. Hon. S. M. Bruce. This conference was prompted by the heavy losses which shipping lines in the European-Australian trade had suffered during the previous several years, and the economic dangers which major Australian exporting interests felt were associated with the lines' proposal to increase rates at a time when

Australian export industries were already severely affected by a loss of markets.

The A.O.T.A. combines in a single formal organization both shipper and shipowner representatives. The constitution of A.O.T.A. provides for a committee of producers, importers, and exporters in each state, called the Exporters Oversea Transport Committee; and a committee of oversea shipowners' representatives in each state known as the Shipowners Oversea Transport Committee. A joint committee comprising representatives of each of the foregoing shippers and shipowners committees exists in each state and is known as the State Joint Transport Committee. Each of these State Joint Transport Committees maintains an executive in Sydney, and is a member of a council of shippers and shipowners representing the whole of Australia, known as the Australian Oversea Transport Association, or A.O.T.A. The purpose of A.O.T.A. is to foster maximum cooperation between Australian exporters, importers, and producers on one hand, and overseas shipowners on the other, to the end of assuring adequate and rationalized shipping services in the general interests of Australian oversea trade. In short, A.O.T.A. coordinates the activities of the State Joint Transport Committees.

A.O.T.A. is responsible for inspecting and approving all contracts for the sea transport of export commodities between Australia and Europe, even though these contracts may have been agreed to by shipowners and sectional interests. These contracts typically specify contract and non-contract rates and such allowances as deferred rebates on freights. Other provisions include penalties for "disloyalty," provisions for altering rates and other conditions, as well as for reviewing or terminating the agreement; and the shipping lines party to the agreement are required to maintain adequate sailings.

At the time A.O.T.A. was established it was hoped that the joint activities of shippers and shipowners would stimulate rationalization in the use of shipping, and that such increased efficiency would permit shipowners to earn satisfactory profits without requiring an increase of freight rates. Accordingly, provisions were included in the original A.O.T.A. contracts for estimating the amount of tonnage Australia would need for its exports, but it was soon found impossible to secure reliable forecasts. At best, this would seem a difficult undertaking, but in the years which followed the Association's formation in 1929 the volume of trade underwent such drastic fluctuation as to render forecasting increasingly difficult.

The Australian Industries Preservation Acts 1905-1937, which in certain respects resembles American anti-trust legislation, made it unlawful as early as 1910 to grant, in Australian outbound trades, rebates, refunds, discounts, or other concessions, privileges, or rewards, deemed to be in the nature of monopolistic or restrictive competitive practices contrary to the public interest.[20] In 1930 the Act was amended to exempt from the provisions dealing with monopolies those agreements between shippers and shipowners which are approved by the Australian Oversea Transport Association.

Shippers who are members of the A.O.T.A. may be fined for noncompliance with these agreements and, furthermore, if they fail to confine their exports to vessels of lines subscribing to the agreement, they are liable to assessment as "liquidated damages" of a sum equal to 10 per cent of the freight paid by such a shipper to all lines parties to the agreement during the twelve months preceding the breach, or from the date of agreement, whichever period is shorter.

It should be mentioned that not only the federal government but certain state governments as well are represented on a number of the statutory authorities which have been established to control the export of various primary products. The powers of these authorities in many instances include the making of contracts covering shipping and insurance. Since the establishment of A.O.T.A., statutory authorities have operated for the whole or portions of the period for wool, wheat, dried fruits, canned fruits, fresh fruits, meat, eggs, and dairy produce. All these interests have been participants in A.O.T.A. activities and agreements. The relationship between A.O.T.A. and the Oversea Shipping Representatives' Association (O.S.R.A.), frequently referred to as "the Conference," is that shipping lines providing shipping services for A.O.T.A. are all members of O.S.R.A., and participate in the Shipowners Oversea Transport Committees.

In 1934, after five years' experience, the Association concluded that it had been a success from the shippers' point of view insofar as the freight rate increases for exports proposed in 1929 had been avoided. From the shipowners' point of view, however, the results were not considered to have achieved the original expectations; but

[20] The Australian Industries Preservation Act of 1906 incorporated suggestions made by a Commission which had been appointed in 1904 to consider the Commonwealth's shipping legislation. The Commission had recommended that rebates be made illegal. The provisions of the 1906 Act regarding rebates were suspended at the request of the Colonial Office pending the investigations of the *Royal Commission on Shipping Rings*.

in light of the course of both world trade and freight rates during the period it is doubtful if the results would have been completely satisfactory to the ship operators in any case. The available information does not indicate whether lines serving the Australian-European trade suffered less than lines in other Australian trades or than shipping lines generally. It is of interest to note, however, that since 1946 there has been strong action, particularly on the part of shipowners, to revive the activities of A.O.T.A. which had lapsed during the war years.

Australia, like the Union of South Africa, also had a freight dumping duty in its customs tariff which became applicable when imports competitive with Australian manufacturers were found to be moving at exceedingly depressed rates. Both Australia and the Union of South Africa, as important raw material producing countries with infant home industries, were interested in regularity of service and stable low outbound rates for their exports, more or less regardless of the cost of providing these services; but in the case of import rates they tried to insist on rates high enough to cover transport operating costs, since low rates were felt to be inimical to their industrial development.

NEW ZEALAND

In New Zealand's trade with Europe, the situation has been somewhat similar to that in the Australian-European trade. The New Zealand Overseas Shipowners' Allotment Committee resembles the Australian Shipowners Oversea Transport Committee. The Overseas Shipowners' Allotment Committee and its London counterpart, the New Zealand Tonnage Committee, deals mainly with statutory agencies (e.g. the New Zealand Meat Board and the New Zealand Dairy Products Marketing Commission) which control the exports of certain of New Zealand's principal products—i.e. butter and cheese, frozen and chilled meats, and apples and pears. Fully 95 per cent of these products are routed via lines which are members of the Overseas Shipowners' Allotment Committee, and before World War II freight contracts covering this movement were negotiated by this committee and the statutory export agencies.

It should be noted that these agencies were concerned with the export of commodities requiring refrigeration. The same vessels that carried the refrigerated cargoes have, with the assistance of perhaps a few non-refrigerated vessels, sufficient uninsulated space to accommodate the major part of New Zealand's exports of wool and other commodities. In 1935, the Imperial Shipping Committee made a study of freight rates in the trade between New Zealand and the United Kingdom and found that considerable and progressive reductions had been made in the freight rates on refrigerated produce, while there had been little or no reduction in the northbound rates on wool and only small and irregular reductions in the rates on imports from the United Kingdom. The majority of the Committee felt that the statutory agencies in New Zealand had exercised considerable pressure to effect these reductions, and pointed to Australia whence rates on similar refrigerated commodities were substantially higher. The New Zealand and Australian members of the Committee, however, contended that the lower rates on refrigerated cargo from New Zealand were not the result of pressure, but had been derived from the substantial economies achieved by rationalizing cargo arrangements and shipping schedules.[21]

The New Zealand government also has the power to control freight rates from New Zealand on vessels carrying mail under subsidy from the government, but this authority had not been exercised. The lines engaged in the United Kingdom trade do not secure mail subsidies.

In 1946, after the Labor government came into office, more direct responsibilities were assumed over the export of primary produce, and the Primary Products Marketing Act of that year gave the Minister of Marketing the sole right to enter contracts for carriage by sea of primary products intended for export; alternatively, he could give approval to the conditions under which contracts may be entered into by other parties, the government thus becoming a party to negotiations for freight contracts.

As recently as 1950, however, there were no contracts covering freight rates such as existed prior to World War II. The bulk of New Zealand's meat, dairy produce, and fruit after the war was sold F.O.B. to the United Kingdom Ministry of Food which is, therefore, the payer of freight. Although the statutory agencies have thus not recently been directly concerned with negotiating freight contracts, they have continued to watch the position closely, as they consider that any increase in freight must ultimately be borne by the producers through a reduction of the prices received for their products from the United Kingdom government.

21 For additional information concerning this report, see Chapter V.

BRAZIL[22]

In June 1933 the Brazilian government issued a decree prohibiting the payments of rebates, commissions, or bounties, in connection with all maritime freights. In December of that year, however, the original decree was amended so as to apply solely to freights on coffee.

In 1936 the São Paulo Chamber of Commerce, which represents the largest shippers in Brazil, reported that while the Chamber was in favor of the rebate system they desired government regulation to prevent abuses. The recommendations of the Chamber are of interest as they indicate the nature of the abuses which they had in mind. It was recommended that: (1) all rates and rebates should be published; (2) the length of time during which rebates could be held by shipping companies should be limited, and 120 days was suggested as an appropriate period; (3) in return for exclusive patronage contracts the shipping companies should agree not to alter their rates for some specified period of time; (4) exporters should be allowed the privilege of shipping in any vessels whenever the conference lines did not have adequate facilities available; and (5) shippers should be permitted to ship in Brazilian vessels not belonging to the conference without being subjected to any penalty. (Discriminatory efforts to foster Brazilian flag shipping have not been uncommon in that country.)

The recommendations of the São Paulo Chamber of Commerce were followed in February 1937 by a new act (Law No. 388) to regulate foreign maritime freights. The principal features of this legislation provided that, subject to conditions specified below, shipping concerns maintaining regular lines between Brazilian and foreign ports would be allowed to enter contracts with exporters permitting shipowners to concede special advantages to exporters in consideration for their preference in the routing of cargoes. These special advantages could consist of a reduction in rates, preferential treatment in the allocation of space, or a refund of guarantees deposited in the Caixas Economicas of Brazil or in the Bank of Brazil. Shipping concerns as well as exporters were required to make such deposits, which were to constitute a reciprocal guarantee regarding the availability of space on the one hand, and the provision of cargo

[22] Sanderson, *op.cit.*, pp. 118-123.

for shipment on the other hand. Penalties were provided for contract violations by either party.

Another condition which the law provided was that such contracts would be valid only when they stipulated freight rates approved by the Minister of Finance after the same have been submitted to the Federal Foreign Trade Council for examination and opinion. Subsequent changes of rates would not be permitted without this formality and without a hearing of the interested parties. Additional power to enforce these provisions was provided by another article in the law which stipulated that export permits would be issued only on production of proof that the necessary ocean transportation has been arranged at freight rates validated by the Ministry of Finance. Difficulties inherent in unilateral regulation of rates in foreign commerce have retarded the application of this aspect of the law.

PORTUGAL[23]

Portugal established the Councils on Tariffs in 1934 to regulate freight and passenger tariffs of national-flag shipping companies trading with Portugal's African colonies and Northern Europe. The Portuguese lines in these trades were members of conferences which fixed rates and pooled cargoes, so whatever regulatory authority the Councils on Tariffs exercised presumably must have influenced the conferences. In addition to the conference lines, however, there was also non-conference competition so the effect of government regulation was probably slight. In 1939 the Portuguese government issued a decree which grouped all Portuguese shipowners and charterers within one corporate organization known as the National Board of the Mercantile Marine (Junta Nacional da Marinha Mercante). This Board assumed the powers previously given to the Councils on Tariffs.

SPAIN[24]

Spain, prior to the Civil War, subsidized a number of important Spanish lines and required them, among other things, to submit their tariffs to the Minister of Marine for approval, which was granted only after a public hearing of interested shippers. The Commanding General of the Canary Islands in 1937 issued a decree which

---

[23] A. E. Sanderson, *Wartime Control of Ocean Freight Rates in Foreign Trade*, U.S. Department of Commerce, Trade Promotion Series No. 212 (1940), pp. 36-37.
[24] Sanderson, *Control of Ocean Freight Rates in Foreign Trade*, op.cit., p. 189.

99

established maximum freight rates and other conditions for obtaining shipping contracts in the banana trade to all important European destinations, foreign as well as Spanish.

JAPAN

Japan for many years required its subsidized vessels to obtain government approval of maximum rates for the carriage of merchandise and passengers. During the first World War such control restrained some carriers from taking full advantage of the large wartime increase in rates.[25] In 1936 the Japanese Shipping Routes Control Law was passed to prevent excessive competition. It applied only to Japanese tonnage and called for the provision of government advice when inordinate competition jeopardized the sound development of the industry. When such advice was not efficacious, the government could order the formation of a conference, and if this failed the government could prohibit or control the operation of the route.[26]

In 1937, as the war with China developed, control over tramp rates was found necessary. This control was originally exercised through the Japanese government's power to grant or refuse permission to remit funds abroad covering the charter of foreign vessels. While this ostensibly applied only to tramps, it is easy to see how under certain market conditions exchange control might be used to influence liner rates. Now that exchange control has become so widely employed throughout the world, this precedent may assume greater importance.

ITALY[27]

Italy's interest in freight rates was influenced before the war by her development as a corporate state. Trade organizations representing shipper groups met from time to time with the shipping conferences to negotiate rates. The principal group, the National Fascist Institute for Foreign Trade, was a semi-governmental body directed by leading businessmen with the assistance of government departments. This group acted as an advisory and consulting body to the government on all matters affecting Italian foreign trade. The Institute had several divisions and one of these was concerned with

[25] Abraham Berglund, "The War and Trans-Pacific Shipping," *American Economic Review*, September 1917.
[26] Imperial Shipping Committee, *British Shipping in the Orient*, *op.cit.*, pp. 131-132.
[27] Sanderson, *op.cit.*, p. 144.

maritime rates and facilities. Whenever exporters considered rate adjustments necessary, the Institute stood willing to request the shipping conference concerned, either directly or through the Ministry of Corporations, to make the requested alterations. Such requests, however, were merely in the form of a petition and did not have legal force, because the Italian government did not exercise any formal authority over rates beyond requiring Italian lines not to charge more than competing foreign carriers.

GERMANY[28]

Germany before World War II did not exercise any regular authority over rates, but was in a position to bring its influence to bear through the government's controlling interest in the North German Lloyd and Hamburg-American Lines. Furthermore, through the use of export subsidies, preferential rail rates, and exchange control, the German government was in a position to favor German export industries and shippers without interfering with the usual ocean rate-making practices.

U.S.S.R.[29]

The Union of Soviet Socialist Republics does not participate in international shipping conferences, but at the same time Soviet vessels have not practiced a policy of undercutting rates. Whenever foreign ships are necessary to supplement the Soviet merchant marine in the carrying of Soviet commerce, vessels are chartered by the All-Union Combine for the Chartering of Foreign Ships.

CEYLON

In Ceylon relations between shippers and conferences were marred in the inter-war period by controversies over deferred rebates. The government appointed a special commission to investigate this practice, but in its report submitted in 1934 the commission's members were evenly divided, with the result that the situation remained unchanged.[30] In 1937 a group of coconut exporters passed a resolution requesting the government: to make deferred and secret rebates in relation to shipping freights illegal; to require new shipping conferences to obtain the consent of the Governor; to establish shipping freights by agreement between liner conferences

[28] ibid., pp. 137-138.   [29] ibid., pp. 124-125.
[30] Ceylon Sessional Paper XI, 1934.

and a board consisting of representatives of producers, exporters, and relevant trade associations or assemblies (but when agreement could not thus be reached a conciliation tribunal of three persons appointed by the Governor was to be empowered to fix rates).

In 1940 the Director of Commerce and Industries for Ceylon conducted another investigation.[31] He reported the conference operating from Ceylon to the United Kingdom to have been autocratic, and to have charged rates which were too high and unduly discriminatory against Ceylon. By way of contrast, the report mentioned that shipping rates and service to the United States, where no deferred rebates were allowed, appeared to be satisfactory. It was observed that shippers in Ceylon could not form an association of their own to bargain collectively with the conferences, and this failure the report explained by the fact that several important shippers were also agents for the shipping lines. The report agreed that conferences appeared to be necessary, but since shippers' associations were unable to function in Ceylon, it was suggested that the government consider subsidizing a non-conference service if conference carriers "do not fall into line."[32] In other respects the recommendations of the Director's report were similar to the resolutions passed by the coconut exporters. It was recommended again that conferences should be required to obtain government approval, deferred and secret rebates should be illegal, and the refusal of space by a carrier should also be made illegal. It was also suggested that an agreement to provide adequate sailings should be required. The report further recommended that all rates and changes of rates should be agreed upon by the shipowners and a board representing the shippers, but when agreement between these groups was impossible the question should be referred to a government conciliation board. The report concluded that the colonies should not be required to subsidize British shipping, and referred to the experience at Singapore to show that Ceylon was not the sole sufferer.

INDIA[33]

Indian tea shippers found deferred rebates so objectionable that they assisted at one time in maintaining an independent line in competition with conference carriers. Consequently the conference lines

[31] Ceylon Sessional Paper V, 1940.
[32] *ibid.*, p. 16.
[33] Sanderson, *op.cit.*, p. 142.

offered a discount effective at the time when freight monies were paid in place of a deferred rebate on tea shipments. The hostile feeling against the deferred rebate system was not confined to tea, with the result that the Calcutta Liners Conference agreed to pay a deferred commission of 10 per cent on general cargo three months after the end of each quarter for which shippers had fulfilled the requirements. This, in effect, tied up shippers for only half as long as the previous deferred rebate contract.

PHILIPPINES

Early in 1952 a maritime bill was drafted by members of the Philippine government which among other things would have outlawed rate-making bodies such as conferences. The allegation that conference rate-making was monopolistic and detrimental to the archipelago's commerce might have been exacerbated by the unusual breadth of control of the Associated Steamship Lines of Manila, a "super-conference" whose various sections covered trade from the islands to almost all parts of the world. Presumably as a result of comments received from the United States, British, and Norwegian governments, President Quirino requested the assistance of an American technical committee to redraft the bill so as to establish a regulatory maritime commission to supervise conference practices.

SUMMARY

The foregoing accounts of various countries may not be absolutely complete and up-to-date. They should suffice, however, to indicate worldwide recognition of the problems of regulating ocean transport. (In addition to the unilateral activity described in this chapter, several nations, notably India, Colombia, Ecuador, El Salvador, Haiti, Panama, and Venezuela, have complained of shipping conference practices to international agencies. International action is considered in Chapter XIII).

The dominant pattern which emerges from the individual actions of nations is the widespread acknowledgment of the constructive functions performed by shipping conferences and of their discriminatory and abusive practices. On this is embroidered a variety of regulatory procedures, such as supervisory agencies, shippers' associations, general restrictions imposed by statute or decree, and specific restrictions for subsidized carriers. Of course, it should also be recalled that numerous countries, e.g. the United Kingdom, Belgium,

France, Norway, Sweden, the Netherlands, and many others, have not seen fit to impose any special form of restraint on shipping rings. A description of unilateral regulation of shipping is seriously incomplete, however, without a consideration of the practices of the United States. This is the subject of the next chapter.

CHAPTER VII
U.S. REGULATION OF OVERSEAS SHIPPING

WHILE SEVERAL agencies of the United States government have regulatory authority over various phases of the shipping industry—safety and certain technical matters, for example, are handled by the Bureau of Steamboat Inspection and Navigation and by the Coast Guard—the regulation of rates and commercial practices has been under the jurisdiction of the United States Shipping Board and its successors.

In 1933 the United States Shipping Board Bureau of the Department of Commerce was created and assumed the regulatory responsibilities of the previously independent Board, only to lose them in 1936 to a new and independent agency, the United States Maritime Commission. Each of these agencies in turn received new powers of its own, as well as the authority previously vested in its predecessor. The Commission was abolished in its turn, and in 1950 the regulatory functions were once again transferred to the Department of Commerce, this time to the newly organized Federal Maritime Board. Although a desire to separate judicial from operational and promotional activities did play a role in the last transfer of authority —a Maritime Administration was also established in 1950 to assume the latter responsibilities—the transfer of the regulatory functions of principal interest here constituted only a small part of the motivation underlying the change. Since the regulatory activities, therefore, had relatively little to do with these administrative alterations, they will not be dwelt on, and have been mentioned primarily to facilitate an understanding of American regulatory experience as first one and then another of these agencies is mentioned.

REGULATORY LEGISLATION

The earliest legislation directly regulating the rates and practices of water carriers as such was the Shipping Act of 1916, which provides for the supervision of common carriers operating on regular routes on the high seas and Great Lakes (1) in the foreign trade of the United States (except ferry boats) and (2) in both interstate and

105

non-contiguous domestic trade.[1] Supervision was also provided for other persons carrying on the business of forwarding or furnishing wharfage, dock, warehouse, or other terminal facilities in connection with a common carrier by water on the high seas or Great Lakes.[2] Since this volume is concerned with overseas shipping rather than domestic shipping, the following paragraphs describe the provisions of American legislation applicable to carriers engaged in the international trades.[3]

The Act prohibits: (1) deferred rebates, (2) "fighting ships,"[4] (3) retaliation or discrimination against any shipper, and (4) unfair or unjustly discriminatory contracts with any shipper. A fine of not more than $25,000 for each offense is provided as the penalty for a breach of these provisions.[5] If water carriers—other than citizens of the United States—violate the foregoing provisions or deny an American common carrier admission to a conference on equal terms with all other parties, the Secretary of Commerce, upon certification by the Board, is empowered to bar vessels of the offending parties from United States ports.[6]

All agreements, understandings, conferences, or other arrangements between parties subject to the act which affect competition in any way, or changes in earlier agreements, must, according to Section 15 of the 1916 act, be filed with the Board. The Board, furthermore, may disapprove, cancel, or modify any such agreement or modification thereof deemed to operate to the detriment of United States commerce, to be in violation of the act or to be "unjustly discriminatory or unfair" between carriers, shippers, exporters, importers, or ports, or between exporters from the United States and their foreign competitors. Approved agreements are exempted from the anti-trust laws. Violators are subject to a fine of $1,000 for each day of the offense.[7]

---

[1] 39 Stat. 728 (1917), 40 Stat. 900 (1919), 46 U.S.C. §801 (1940). Authority over interstate carriers by water was transferred to the Interstate Commerce Commission by the Transportation Act of 1940, 54 Stat. 933 (1941), 49 U.S.C. §904 (1940).

[2] *ibid.*

[3] At the very least the same or similar restrictions apply to common carriers by water in the more rigorously regulated domestic trades. For example, domestic common carriers are subject to maximum and minimum rate control.

[4] A "fighting ship" is a vessel, placed on berth by one or more established lines, which quotes lower rates than its sponsors in order to render entry of a newcomer to the route difficult.

[5] 39 Stat. 733 (1917), 41 Stat. 996 (1921), 46 U.S.C. §812 (1940).

[6] 39 Stat. 733 (1917), 41 Stat. 996 (1921), 46 U.S.C. §813 (1940).

[7] 39 Stat. 733 (1917), 46 U.S.C. §814 (1940).

It is unlawful: (1) to give unreasonable preference to any person, locality, or description of traffic, or to subject any of the foregoing to undue disadvantage; (2) to permit by false billing, weighing, etc., transportation at less than regular rates; (3) to influence insurance companies to discriminate against a competitor; and (4) to disclose information detrimental to shippers or consignees.[8] It is also unlawful for any shipper, consignor, or consignee to obtain or attempt to obtain by false billing, false weighing, etc., rates less than otherwise applicable. A fine of not more than $5,000 is provided for each offense.[9]

The charging of rates or fares that are "unjustly discriminatory" between shippers or ports, or "unjustly prejudicial" to United States exporters compared to their foreign competitors, is prohibited, and the Commission is empowered to alter rates which are in violation of this section. Reasonable regulations covering practices relating to receiving, handling, storing, or delivery of property must be observed,[10] and the Board has authority to require the filing of reports, records, etc., of any person subject to the Act.[11] The Board is also authorized to investigate any violation of the act on its own volition, or upon the filing of a complaint. In the latter case full reparation for injury may be awarded if the complaint is filed within two years of the cause of action.[12]

The main provisions of the Merchant Marine Act of 1920 were concerned with the continued operation of war-built American vessels by the Shipping Board and their ultimate sale to private operators. Section 19 of the act, however, authorizes the Commission to make such rules and regulations affecting shipping in foreign trade as are necessary to meet unfavorable conditions resulting from foreign rules or laws or from competitive methods of foreign ship operators or their agents.[13]

The principal purpose of the Merchant Marine Act of 1936 was promotional, but in addition to transferring to the Maritime Commission the regulatory powers described above, the 1936 act contained two new regulatory provisions. The act made it unlawful for a common carrier by water to prevent or attempt to prevent any

[8] 39 Stat. 735 (1917), 46 U.S.C. §819 (1940) and 39 Stat. 734 (1917), 46 U.S.C. §815 (1940).
[9] *ibid.*   [10] 39 Stat. 734 (1917), 46 U.S.C. §816 (1940).
[11] 39 Stat. 736 (1917), 46 U.S.C. §820 (1940).
[12] 39 Stat. 736 (1917), 46 U.S.C. §821 (1940).
[13] 41 Stat. 995 (1921), 46 U.S.C. §876 (1940).

other such carrier from serving a port within the continental limits of the United States, designed for the accommodation of ocean-going vessels, when an improvement project for such port had been authorized by Congress.[14] (This example of local favoritism had been engineered by a few recently-developed outports seeking to assure themselves of direct water service at terminal rates, regardless of whether or not it was an economical operation for the vessel.) The 1936 act also authorized the Commission to investigate discriminatory rates and practices whereby American exporters were required to pay a common carrier in the foreign trade of the United States a higher rate to a foreign port than the rate charged by such carrier on similar cargo from the foreign port to such United States port.[15] Pursuant to this authority, a study was made by the Maritime Commission in its first year, coming to the conclusion that services and conditions in the import and export trade are so different that no decision regarding discrimination could be drawn.[16]

REGULATORY PROCEDURE[17]

The Shipping Board and its successors borrowed heavily from the Interstate Commerce Commission in the administration of their regulatory authority. Therefore, many of both the strengths and the weaknesses of Interstate Commerce Commission procedures can also be found in the regulation of ocean carriers. By and large, however, the system has worked well, and such shortcomings as are at times alleged to exist can be attributed to the interpretation given the statutes by the regulatory agency, or to occasional lack of zeal, rather than to the administrative procedures.

Formal Docket. The procedure in the case of formal dockets is quite similar to that before a United States district court sitting as a court of equity. Formal complaints are filed and served on the respondent, and an opportunity is afforded him to reply to the complaint. An examiner, whose duties are similar to those of a master in chancery, is appointed by the Commission to hear evidence and report his findings. Exceptions, if any, to the findings of the examiner

---

[14] 49 Stat. 1987 (1936), 46 U.S.C. §1115 (1940).
[15] 49 Stat. 1990 (1936), 46 U.S.C. §1122 (1940).
[16] *Rept. U.S. Maritime Commission 1937*, p. 17.
[17] This section was written just before the transfer of authority from the Maritime Commission to the Federal Maritime Board; and since no changes in procedure have come to the writer's attention "Commission" can be read in this section to mean "Board" and "Commissioners" can be read as "members of the Board."

are then heard by the Commission. Finally, the Commission considers the record of the case and issues a report containing its findings, and if necessary issues a formal order. Even in investigations initiated by the Commission there is an element of an adversary nature; one section of the Commission's legal staff prosecutes the case, while another section of the staff advises the Commissioners as to the merits of the case and its proper disposition. The same counsel who conducts the case for the government does not advise the Commission. As a result of such hearings, orders are issued: (1) to cease and desist from an unlawful practice; (2) to fix a rule governing future practices of respondent and other carriers; and (3) to pay reparation for injury caused by unlawful acts or practices.[18] These orders may be reviewed in the federal courts. During the fiscal year 1941 a shortened procedure was introduced, whereby complaints may be disposed of upon the submission of evidence under oath by memoranda, thereby avoiding the need of a hearing.

Informal and Special Dockets. An informal docket is also maintained to assist shippers, carriers, and other persons in the adjustment of controversies which arise in regard to rates, fares, and other charges. Informal complaints are handled by correspondence or adjusted through informal conference, thereby avoiding the delay and expense incident to formal procedure.

A special docket is also maintained, but rarely used in the foreign trade, which permits reparations to shippers when carriers believe that the charges they have collected for transportation are unlawful. Applications for such authorization must admit that the rate charged was unreasonable, and are considered the equivalent of informal complaints. Careful consideration is given them in order to avoid the possibility of granting rebates to favored shippers.

Section 15 Agreements. Under Section 15 of the Shipping Act of 1916, common carriers by water and other persons subject to the act are required to file for approval a true copy (or, if oral, a true and complete memorandum) of every agreement with any other such carrier or such person to which it may be a party, fixing or regulating rates; or controlling, regulating, preventing or destroying competition; or allocating ports or restricting or otherwise regulating sailings; or in any manner providing for a cooperative working arrangement. In 1950 there were almost six hundred such agreements on file, of

---

[18] Cunningham, *The U.S. Maritime Commission—A Study in Administrative Law* (Unpublished thesis in Harvard Law School Library, 1939), pp. 70-78.

which one hundred and twenty-seven were conference agreements of the type in which this volume is primarily interested. The number of conference agreements has shown remarkable constancy, the number on file now being approximately the same as prewar. All such agreements, modifications, or cancellations are subjected to analysis and, if found to be unexceptionable, are approved as a routine matter.[19] (Great care is taken to assure the accurate expression of intent of the parties filing the agreement. Thus, the Commission combines regulatory and service functions.) If the Commission has changes to suggest, or if a protest against approval of an agreement is received, an effort is always made to reach informally a solution satisfactory to all. If a proper solution cannot be achieved in this manner, a formal hearing is scheduled.

The requirement to file *every* agreement and all modifications and cancellations thereof necessitated administrative clarification, since the conferences claimed in an ex parte investigation in 1927 that the inclusion of "routine operations relating to current rate changes and other day-to-day transactions . . . would result in delays and inconveniences to both carriers and shippers."[20] The Shipping Board in a rather vaguely worded decision held that the 1916 act had been very specific regarding the matters affecting competition that must be reported, and stated that the usual though not invariable practice of conferences of submitting copies of their minutes, etc., which contain only routine arrangements not covered by Section 15, was not to be regarded as filing under this section, but rather as voluntarily furnished information on conference activities.[21]

The Commission decided in 1938 that an agreement covering the transshipment at Panama of goods from South America destined to the United States was subject to filing under Section 15,[22] and in 1940 held that the sale of goodwill accompanied by an agreement in

[19] A provision introduced in 1950 required for the first time that a synopsis of agreements must be published in the Federal Register prior to approval, unless special circumstances made such a course unnecessary.

[20] Section 15 Inquiry, 1 U.S.S.B. 121 (1927). (In this chapter reports of the United States Shipping Board will be designated by the letters U.S.S.B.; reports of the United States Shipping Board Bureau of the Department of Commerce will be indicated by U.S.S.B.B.; and reports of the United States Maritime Commission will be designated by U.S.M.C. In the text, the United States Shipping Board will be referred to as the Board; the United States Shipping Board Bureau of the Department of Commerce will be called the Bureau; and the United States Maritime Commission will be designated as the Commission.)

[21] *loc.cit.*

[22] Commonwealth of Massachusetts *v.* Colombian S.S. Co., Inc.; 1 U.S.M.C. 711 (1938).

which the seller covenants not to compete with the buyer is one which affects competition and, therefore, is subject to this section.[23] In 1946 the Commission found the "rules and regulations" of one conference so closely related to the conference agreement that it held them subject to filing and review under Section 15.[24]

Filing of Tariffs. The Commission requires all conferences to file their tariffs as an administrative matter in its supervision of Section 15 agreements. However, as not all common carriers by water are members of shipping conferences, it has been necessary to supplement this requirement. Rate cutting by non-conference lines during the early 1930's created considerable rate instability on several of the principal routes in United States foreign commerce and, as this competition increased, disaffection of conference members threatened further disruption. Therefore, in 1935 the Shipping Board Bureau issued a regulation requiring all common carriers by water engaged in the nation's foreign commerce to file all tariffs covering the transportation of property, except bulk cargoes loaded and carried without mark or count, from the continental United States to foreign ports.[25] Such tariffs have to be filed within thirty days of their effective date. In 1943 the Maritime Commission held that common carrier status did not necessarily depend on a regular sailing schedule or on regularity of calls at ports, but that service offered on a regular route would be a sufficient condition; and that such a carrier was required to file its export rates on all commodities except bulk cargoes.[26] Bill-of-lading forms are also filed under regulations prescribed by the Commission.

Pursuant to an order issued by the Commission on January 26, 1939, common carriers are required to file their rates and charges on cargo, other than bulk cargo, transported from the East Coast of South America to the Pacific Coast of the United States;[27] and, in 1943, joint through rates on cargo from South America transshipped at Panama for the United States were held to require filing and approval.[28] Rate filings by carriers in foreign commerce totaled over 19,000 in the fiscal year which ended June 30, 1950.

[23] N.Y. and P.R.S.S. Co.—Waterman S.S. Corp., Agreement 2 U.S.M.C. 453 (1940).
[24] Pacific Westbound Conference Agreement, 2 U.S.M.C. 775 (1946).
[25] Investigation of Sec. 19 of Merchant Marine Act of 1920, 1 U.S.S.B.B. 470 at 502-503 (1935), Isbrandtsen-Moller Co. *v.* United States, 300 U.S. 139 (1937).
[26] Rates of General Atlantic S. S. Corp. 2 U.S.M.C. 681 (1943).
[27] Rates, Charges, and Practices of Yamashita and O.S.K., 2 U.S.M.C. 14 (1939).
[28] Restrictions on transshipments at Canal Zone, 2 U.S.M.C. 675 (1943).

REPORTS

The decisions, or reports as they are called, of the agencies which have regulated the commercial practices of shipping in the foreign trade routes of the United States provide a revealing insight both into some of the problems and practices of common carriers operating on the high seas and into the regulatory principles of the Maritime Commission and its predecessors. Some of these reports apply to complaints or investigations concerning the practices of an individual carrier, but a large number involve activities of carriers operating in concert through a conference agreement. The entire character of the industry and the nature of the regulatory problem is affected by the presence of the conference system through which the industry practices, for better or worse, considerable self-regulation; and, therefore, the cases involving conferences are of paramount importance.

The general policy of the Maritime Commission and its predecessors has been to persuade the industry to regulate itself through conferences, and to subject carriers in the foreign trade to as few restrictions as possible with respect to rates and practices. The result has been that regulatory control has been exercised for the most part only when it was thought that the public welfare required it, with general supervision being maintained for the purpose of checking abuses and correcting unfair practices in so far as is possible. Nevertheless, in spite of some limitations, the regulatory experience which has been acquired by the United States sheds considerable light on the nature of shipping conferences.

American experience with the regulation of domestic ocean trade, over which the government has maximum and minimum rate control, is more complete than that with shipping in foreign trade. Nonetheless, a considerable body of cases concerned with carriers operating in the foreign trades is available. Furthermore, many of the Commission's powers are applicable to carriers in both the foreign and domestic trades; therefore, cases involving domestic carriers occasionally evolve principles apposite to carriers in the foreign trades. The narrowness of the Commission's legal authority implicitly limited its regulatory decisions. The Commission possessed no mandate to consider the broader social and economic consequences of its actions[29] or the impact of its decisions on international economic and

[29] But see Ames Harris Neville v. American-Hawaiian Steamship Co., 1 U.S.M.C. 765 (1938), (anti-monopoly policy invoked), discussed *infra* at p. 117, and see dis-

political relations. In addition, the Commission's primary function was the promotion of American-flag shipping; and although it appears to have succeeded rather well in keeping its judicial and operational responsibilities separate, one cannot help suspecting that promotional activities were generally of more absorbing interest to the Commissioners.

The Commission's policy was to base decisions on the facts of record in each case, and it maintained that findings in connection with similar practices do not have the force of law in subsequent proceedings involving different carriers, different trades, different competitive conditions, or different statutory provisions.[30] Despite this alleged policy of considering each case *in vacuo*, certain general principles can be traced, although they should not be regarded as established precedents possessing the force of law.

Standards of Reasonableness.[31] The Commission's predecessors devoted considerable attention to evaluating general factors pertinent to the reasonableness of rates and practices. But, since the regulatory agencies had no specific authority over the reasonableness of rates in the foreign trade, almost all the cases concerned with this problem are found in the domestic trades. Nevertheless foreign rates that are patently unreasonable can be considered detrimental to the nation's commerce and therefore subject to regulatory criticism. While it should be kept in mind that concepts of reasonableness in the domestic trades are not directly translatable to foreign rates,[32] a few domestic cases, decided prior to 1933, when the Bureau received the authority to supervise minimum as well as maximum domestic rates, are presented to give the flavor of the thought on this subject.

Value of service was early recognized as a factor to be considered in rate determination,[33] although not conclusive when considered alone.[34] Cost of service was also recognized as an important criterion, so that a justifiable rate for a cheap article might be greater

---

cussion of the Commission's assumption of authority to consider the reasonableness of conference rates *infra* at pp. 119-120.

[30] Los Angeles By-Products Co. *v.* Barber Steamship Lines, 2 U.S.M.C. 106 at 115 (1939).

[31] Several of the cases discussed under this heading also involve considerations of undue preference and prejudice.

[32] Cf. Sec. 17 of the Shipping Act of 1916 (39 Stat. 734) applicable to foreign trade with Sec. 18 (39 Stat. 735) applicable to interstate transportation.

[33] Judson L. Thomson Manufacturing Co. *v.* Eastern Steamship Lines, 1 U.S.S.B. 58 (1924).

[34] Dobler & Mudge *v.* Panama Railroad Steamship Line, 1 U.S.S.B. 130 (1927).

in proportion to its value than the rate for a high-priced article.[35] But a carrier was held not justified in burdening a port with a differential for the sole reason that the cost of operation from that port is greater than from some other port; such elements as volume of traffic, competition, distance, advantages of location, character of traffic, frequency of service, and others were deemed to merit consideration.[36] However, reasonableness of rates is not to be gauged by the ability of shippers to market their products with profit.[37]

The reasonableness of passenger fares has been considered in only one case. In 1934, the Bureau held that classification of passenger fares should depend not only on location and type of space but also on service, freedom of the ship, and age, size, speed, and itinerary of the vessel.[38]

The rates of other carriers and services are not determinative of the reasonableness of water carrier rates. In the foreign trade, export rates higher than import rates have been held not unreasonable, i.e. not detrimental to the nation's commerce, if the import volume is far greater and there is no proof that reduced export rates would produce a comparable volume.[39] In 1936 the Bureau commented that whatever their immediate effects, unremunerative or noncompensatory rates were detrimental to commerce in the long run, since commerce embraces not only the cargo moving but the instrumentalities employed in moving it. Nevertheless, the Bureau held that the statute did not prohibit the reduction of rates to an unremunerative level.[40] However, a year earlier, the Bureau had held, "An unreasonably high rate is clearly detrimental to the commerce of the United States, and upon a showing that a conference rate in foreign commerce is unreasonably high the Department [of Commerce] will require its reduction to a proper level. If necessary, approval of the conference agreement will be withdrawn."[41] The regulatory agency's attitude toward unreasonably high rates was obviously sterner than its attitude toward unremunerative rates, despite the fact that it deplored

[35] Atlas Waste Manufacturing Co. v. The New York & Puerto Rico Steamship Co., 1 U.S.S.B. 195 (1931).
[36] Port Utilities Commission of Charleston, S. C. v. The Carolina Co., 1 U.S.S.B. 61 at 71-72 (1925).
[37] See note 33 supra.
[38] Passenger Classifications and Fares, American Line Steamship Corp., 1 U.S.S.B.B. 294 at 302-305 (1934).
[39] Edmond Weil v. Italian Line, 1 U.S.S.B.B. 395 (1935).
[40] Seas Shipping Co. v. American South African Line, 1 U.S.S.B.B. 568 (1936).
[41] 1 U.S.S.B.B. 395 op.cit., at 398.

114

both. This attitude is consistent with the customary Congressional practice of providing maximum rate regulation long before granting minimum rate control. In 1939, the Commission held that joint through rates greater than a combination of locals and transfer charges did not violate the act, since the conference controlling the through rates did not control the local rates.[42] However, in 1943 the Commission found the existing division of joint through rates to be unfair between carriers and suggested an acceptable basis for division in the future.[43]

Questions of services which ocean carriers should perform without charge, and of what constitutes reasonable charges for services that need not be included in the transportation rate, have been adjudicated frequently. The Bureau inclined to the view that the published rate must be all inclusive. In 1935, in *Re Assembling and Distributing Charge*,[44] it held that the carriers' undertaking was not only to transport cargo but also to present it in a deliverable state, and, therefore, carriers cannot charge for assembling and distributing services at one port when they customarily provide such services without additional compensation elsewhere. Similarly, it was held that no charge could be made for the issuance of bills of lading because this was part of common carrier service.[45] The Commission, after a decision that carriers are obliged to mail arrival notices without charge,[46] came to the conclusion that nothing in the Shipping Acts prohibits carriers from dividing their rates for different services performed, or requires them to publish their charges in single amounts.[47] Following a 1939 rehearing of the *Assembling and Distributing* case, the Commission overruled its predecessor and held that a carrier is entitled to compensation for any transportation services rendered.[48] The fact that all parties were benefited by the delivery and receipt of general cargo at place of rest on dock instead of at end of ship's tackle could not operate to prohibit carriers from charging for services actually rendered in performing the handling beyond ship's tackle, when, as here, it was not shown that the published tackle-to-

[42] Neuss, Hesslin v. Grace Line, 2 U.S.M.C. 3 (1939).
[43] Restrictions on Transshipments at Canal Zone, 2 U.S.M.C. 675 (1943).
[44] 1 U.S.S.B.B. 380, *op.cit.*
[45] *In re* Gulf Brokerage and Forwarding Agreements, 1 U.S.S.B.B. 533 (1936).
[46] Intercoastal Segregation Rules, 1 U.S.M.C. 725 at 733 (1937).
[47] Los Angeles By-Products Co. v. Barber Steamship Lines, 2 U.S.M.C. 106 at 114 (1939).
[48] J. G. Boswell Co. v. American-Hawaiian Steamship Co., 2 U.S.M.C. 95 (1939); Los Angeles By-Products Co. v. Barber Steamship Lines, 2 U.S.M.C. 106 (1939).

tackle rates included compensation for further services or were in excess of fair and reasonable rates for the tackle-to-tackle service actually rendered. In 1940, the Supreme Court sustained the Commission's view that the separation of charges by water carriers to show costs beyond ship's tackle is lawful.[49] In 1950 the Commission approved absorption of excess cargo insurance premiums arising from the use of inferior vessels having a "disability" rating with insurance companies.[50]

To grant excessive free-time storage has been held unlawful, the Commission stating that only such free time should be allowed as may be reasonably required for the removal of property, the criterion of reasonableness being transportation necessity and not commercial convenience.[51] Subsequently, nominal charges on coffee were held in violation of the foregoing decision, as coffee did not share the proper burden of preventing pier congestion.[52]

During World War II the Commission was granted temporary authority to control ocean freight rates, but since this power has terminated it is not strictly relevant to the peacetime supervision of conferences. Suffice it to say here that the cooperation of the conferences was enlisted to provide information regarding costs of operation, port facilities in different parts of the world, etc. The Commission endeavored to base rate increases, which they allowed in the form of surcharges, on increased costs. These surcharges were fixed to reflect the actual extra costs of war risk insurance, war risk crew bonuses, the increased length of voyage, etc. Insofar as possible, the basic peacetime rate levels were preserved, and the surcharges adjusted as "war costs" rose or fell.

Undue Prejudice, Preference and Discrimination. In addition to cases involving the reasonableness of rates, questions of undue prejudice, preference, and discrimination were among the earliest problems requiring the Board's attention. In 1936, the Bureau indicated its general philosophy when it stated that the existence of unjust discrimination and undue prejudice and preference is a question of fact which must be clearly demonstrated by substantial proof,[53] the bur-

---

[49] Sun-Maid Raisin Growers Association v. United States, 33 F. Supp. 959 (N. D. Cal. 1940), *aff'd* 312 U.S. 667 (1941).

[50] Absorption of Insurance Premiums, 3 U.S.M.C. 201 (1950).

[51] Storage of Import Property, 1 U.S.M.C. 676 at 682 (1937).

[52] Storage Charges Under Agreements 6205 and 6215, 2 U.S.M.C. 48 (1939).

[53] Philadelphia Ocean Traffic Bureau v. The Export Steamship Corp., 1 U.S.S.B.B. 538 (1936).

den of which in the foreign trades rests on the complainant.[54] Acceptable evidence from which to infer the unreasonably prejudicial nature of rates may include showing a differential not justified by cost, value of service, or other transportation conditions.[55] However, the acts do not afford relief from disadvantages inherent in geography.[56] Different port conditions and facilities, warranting different methods of handling cargo, may justify differential charges.[57] The advantage which comes to a shipper merely from the location of his plant does not constitute an illegal preference.[58] Accordingly, rates to Hawaii from Gulf and Atlantic ports, higher than those from Pacific ports, have been held lawful.[59]

In 1936, the Bureau held that prejudice to one shipper, to be undue, must ordinarily be such that it shall be a source of positive advantage to another shipper.[60] This principle received specific illustration in several cases involving minimum weights. For example, rates based on minimum weights so large as to be available to only one shipper constitute undue and unreasonable preference;[61] and quantity discount rules in the intercoastal trade are unjustly discriminatory.[62] Moreover, where the prevailing shipping quantity is small, even though carload lots are offered by some shippers, any-quantity rates are lawful since they protect small shippers, and thereby are consonant with general anti-monopoly policy.[63]

Underquoting any rate which other carriers quote, and the use of rate cutting as a club to compel other carriers to adopt pooling agreements, rate differentials, or other measures have been held unfair practices and detrimental to American commerce.[64] In 1940 the Commission elaborated this point when it stated that while there is nothing unlawful per se for a carrier to charge a rate different from that of another, the practice of making rates lower by a fixed percentage from those of other carriers destroys stability and is detri-

---

[54] U.S.M.C. General Order No. 41, Revised, Sec. 201.122.

[55] Atlantic Refining Co. v. Ellerman & Bucknall, 1 U.S.S.B. 242, 250 (1932).

[56] Sharp Paper & Specialty Co. v. Dollar Steamship Lines, 2 U.S.M.C. 91 (1939).

[57] Foreign Trade Bureau New Orleans Association of Commerce v. Bank Line, 1 U.S.S.B. 177 at 185-186 (1930).

[58] 1 U.S.S.B. 242, op.cit., at 251.   [59] 1 U.S.S.B. 177, op.cit.

[60] California Packing Co. v. American-Hawaiian Steamship Co., 1 U.S.S.B.B. 543 (1936).

[61] Intercoastal Rates of American-Hawaiian Steamship Co., 1 U.S.S.B.B. 349 (1934).

[62] Transportation of Lumber Through Panama Canal, 1 U.S.M.C. 646 (1937).

[63] Ames Harris Neville Co. v. American-Hawaiian Steamship Co., 1 U.S.M.C. 765 (1938).

[64] Section 19 Investigation, 1935, 1 U.S.S.B.B. 470 at 498 (1935).

mental to the nation's commerce.[65] The payment of a commission to a consignee on his own cargo in addition to a fee for handling the ship was held to give undue preference;[66] and "brokerage" payments to shippers were held to be unlawful methods of reducing freight rates.[67] An interesting feature of the cases in this paragraph is that they all apply to non-conference carriers, thereby demonstrating, if demonstration is required, that discriminatory practices may be employed by others than conferences.[68]

Members of conferences, however, also engage at times in unlawful practices. The refusal of conference lines to accept cargo from a certain shipper when space was available was discriminatory and in violation of the law.[69] (Eventually a reparation of over $25,000, one of the largest amounts ever involved in a Commission reparation case, was awarded.)[70] In 1940, the Commission, on its own initiative, instituted investigations into false billing and misdescriptions of cargo. Nine of fourteen respondent carriers were found to have permitted shippers to obtain transportation from Japan to the United States at less than regular rates by means of false billing;[71] nine shippers and six carriers were found to have violated the Shipping Acts by misdescribing shipments from New York to the Philippine Islands.[72] The Department of Justice is responsible for the prosecution of such violations.

Agreements. Problems involved in the administration of the requirements concerning the filing of conference agreements and rates has been described in a previous section of this chapter.[73] There were several other aspects of conference agreements with which the Commission concerned itself.

In 1938 the Commission considered the agreement between the Matson Navigation Company and the Dollar Steamship Lines,[74]

[65] Cargo to Adriatic, Black Sea, and Levant Ports, 2 U.S.M.C. 342 (1940).
[66] *loc.cit.*
[67] Rates, Charges, and Practices of L. A. Garcia & Co., 2 U.S.M.C. 615 (1941).
[68] Also see Rates of General Atlantic S. S. Corp., 2 U.S.M.C. 681 (1943).
[69] Roberto Hernandez, Inc. *v.* Arnold Bernstein Schiffahrtsgesellschaft, M.B.H., 1 U.S.M.C. 686 (1937).
[70] Roberto Hernandez, Inc. *v.* Arnold Bernstein Schiffahrtsgesellschaft, M.B.H., 2 U.S.M.C. 62 (1939), *rev'd on other grounds,* 31 F Supp. 76 (S.D.N.Y. 1940), *rev'd on other grounds,* 116 F (2d) 849 (C.C.A. 2d, 1941), *cert. denied sub nom.* Compania Espanola de Navegacion Maritima *v.* Robert Hernandez, 313 U.S. 582 (1941).
[71] Rates from Japan to United States, 2 U.S.M.C. 426 (1940).
[72] Rates from United States to Philippine Islands, 2 U.S.M.C. 535 (1941).
[73] *supra,* pp. 109-111.
[74] In the matter of Dollar-Matson Agreements, 1 U.S.M.C. 750 (1938), *aff'd on rehearing,* 2 U.S.M.C. 387 (1940).

whereby Matson agreed not to operate to the Far East in return for Dollar's agreement not to solicit traffic between the Pacific Coast and the Hawaiian Islands and to pay Matson 50 per cent of any such business Dollar happened to carry. The Commission held, over the dissent of two Commissioners, that agreements restricting competition should be of definite duration and for reasonably short periods, so that the parties concerned and the Commission would have an opportunity to consider changed conditions. The Commission continued that the exemption from the anti-trust laws granted by Section 15 is intended to permit water carriers to regulate competition so as to eliminate rate-cutting and other abuses injurious to shipper and carrier alike, but is not intended to foster monopoly. In a subsequent case, the Commission held that the advantages of group rate action and exemption from the anti-trust laws require conferences to consider shipper needs and to provide an opportunity for an exchange of views with their customers.[75]

Pooling. In 1939, the Commission upheld an agreement to pool earnings in the United States North Atlantic-Germany run, because the result of the agreement was effective control of destructive competition without introducing unfair discrimination or being detrimental to American commerce.[76] However, in 1940, changed circumstances brought about by the war, which resulted in unfair discrimination between signatories, was considered ground for disapproving another pooling agreement which had previously been approved.[77] In 1951, the Federal Maritime Board approved a new pooling agreement in this trade.[78]

Conference Rates. Although there is no specific statutory provision in peacetime authorizing the Commission to pass upon the reasonableness of rates established by conferences in the foreign trade, the Commission found an opportunity to influence such rates in its power to disapprove conference agreements. If the Commission disapproves the agreement, the parties thereto are compelled to operate individually, since they would no longer be exempt from anti-trust statutes, and thereby lose the advantages of the conference system. This meth-

[75] Pacific Coast-European Rates & Practices, 2 U.S.M.C. 58 (1939).

[76] Agreements 1438 and 5260-4, 2 U.S.M.C. 228 (1939). For additional discussion of this case and of pools in general see Chapter VIII.

[77] Pooling Agreement No. 5893, 2 U.S.M.C. 372 (1940). Commissioner Truitt dissented on the grounds that he was not satisfied that unfairness existed, and that the Commission should have left such interpretation of a contract to the courts.

[78] West Coast Line v. Grace Line Inc. (decided May 14, 1951). See Chapter VIII.

od of influencing rates was first employed by the *Bureau* in 1935, when it held that upon a showing that a conference rate in foreign commerce is so unreasonably high as to be detrimental to the country's commerce, then its reduction to a proper level will be required; and, if necessary, approval of the conference agreement will be withdrawn.[79] This was a considerable departure from the earlier attitude that in Section 15 Congress had given sanction and encouragement to conferences, as the benefits from them to shippers are often as great as the benefits accruing to the carrier members, and, therefore, it was the *Board's* function to afford relief only from actual and not from theoretical wrongs arising from such agreements.[80]

Contract Rates. As "fighting ships" and deferred rebates were prohibited by the 1916 act, contract rates came to be widely used in United States foreign trades.[81] In 1922, the Board decided that contract rates were in violation of the 1916 act, where a single line operated in the trade;[82] but in 1933 it upheld the practice where more than one line quoted the contract rates and new lines could join the conference if they so desired.[83] By the outbreak of World War II, sixty-eight conferences in the foreign trade of this country were employing the contract rate system.[84]

Since these contracts are generally exclusive patronage agreements, which require the shipper to agree to tender to the members of the conference all his business moving on the particular route covered by the conference agreement, they have been criticized by some non-conference operators and attacked by the United States Department of Justice as monopolistic. The conferences and the Maritime Commission have defended them as necessary on some routes to assure stability and to avoid the chaos of cutthroat competition. A subsequent chapter on Tying Arrangements discusses the problem of exclusive patronage contracts in some detail; but it is relevant to the

[79] 1 U.S.S.B.B. 395 *op.cit.*

[80] *In re* Rates in Canadian Currency, 1 U.S.S.B. 264 at 281 (1933).

[81] Contract rates grant shippers, who agree to patronize conference lines exclusively for a stipulated period of time, lower rates than shippers who do not enter such an agreement. This differs from the deferred rebate system, which is widely used abroad, in that the latter arrangement requires the shipper to give the contract carriers his business during a period of deferment as well. Both of these devices are discussed in more detail in Chapter X.

[82] Eden Mining Co. *v.* Bluefields Fruit & Steamship Co., 1 U.S.S.B. 41 (1922).

[83] Rawleigh *v.* Stoomvart, 1 U.S.S.B. 285 (1933).

[84] *Inter-American Maritime Conference* (Washington: Government Printing Office, 1941), p. 176.

present discussion to summarize two decisions in which the Commission defined its holdings regarding contract rates.

After World War II the Commission conducted a highly significant investigation of the Pacific Coast European Conference in which several important precedents were established. One of the most important was the holding in regard to the contract rate system. The Commission upheld the legality of the practice by arguing that since these contracts were subject to its supervision under Section 15 of the 1916 act, they were removed from the application of the antitrust statutes, if they had been accorded the Commission's approval.[85] The Commission, however, objected to the inclusion in the contract of a "penalty clause" of any nature; especially in the instant case to three provisions which: (1) gave the carrier an option as to whether or not to assess damages; (2) might prevent shippers from securing a contract in the future; and (3) established damages on a retroactive basis by making shipments transported by conference members prior to the disaffection liable to the payments of additional freight. The Commission suggested that the liquidated damages clause specifically fix the amount of damages by a definite formula which had no retroactive feature.[86] As recently as 1950, the Federal Maritime Board again reaffirmed the propriety of the exclusive patronage dual rate system,[87] although at the time of writing its legality is being contested.

In a case involving the right of lines operating from United States North Atlantic ports to the European range to prevent contract shippers located in the interior of this country from patronizing vessels which called directly at Great Lakes ports, the Commission pointed out that the contract rate system in foreign commerce is not unlawful per se, but is condemned where it operates solely to effect a monopoly. Since the North Atlantic lines carried more than 80 per cent of the traffic originating in the Great Lakes areas, it was held that they had a practical monopoly and that a difference in rates for identical services based solely upon whether the carriers secure the shippers' entire patronage was, prima facie, discriminatory.[88] In the instant case, the discrimination was held to be undue and unreasonable, since the flow of traffic was not naturally tributary to the North At-

[85] Pacific Coast European Conference 3 U.S.M.C. 11 (1948).
[86] *ibid.*
[87] Isbrandtsen Co. *v.* N. Atlantic Continental Frt. Conf. *et al.* 3 Federal Maritime Board 235 (1950).
[88] Note influence of Swayne & Hoyt, Ltd. *v.* United States, 300 U.S. 297 (1937).

lantic lines, and the same shippers were permitted to use the Gulf routes to Europe without jeopardizing their contracts.[89]

Membership. Whether or not a line can join a conference already in existence is often crucial in determining the degree of monopoly which the conference may enjoy. This matter, which affects the freedom of entry of new capital to a trade route, assumes especial significance when the conference is employing exclusive patronage contracts or some other effective tying arrangement that renders competition from non-members extremely difficult. The exclusion of applicants from conference membership has posed a series of questions. The Commission stated in 1940 that its policy was to require, in all conference agreements, a clause permitting the admission as a conference member of any line seeking admission on *equal terms*, but that this does not mean that a ship operator can become a member merely by requesting admission.[90] Since this policy applied to vessels of all nations regardless of flag, it represented an extension of Section 14a of the 1916 act, which makes it unlawful to exclude from membership, upon equal terms with all other parties thereto, a United States flag common carrier which has applied for such admission.[91] The early decisions on membership, however, do not seem to indicate a consistent regulatory philosophy so much as a response to expediency, particularly where contract rates or war conditions enter the picture.

Exclusion of an applicant who would charge 10 per cent less than conference rates has been sustained where there was no proof that a differential was justified and the existing members did not have a monopoly;[92] and where previous contract commitments obligated the applicant to charge lower than conference rates, the admission sought was held not to be on equal terms, so exclusion by the conference was also permitted.[93]

Refusal of membership on the grounds that the applicant was not a common carrier actually operating in the trade has also been held not to result in discrimination, undue prejudice, or detriment to the commerce of the United States,[94] even where the applicant did not

[89] Contract Routing Restrictions, 2 U.S.M.C. 220 at 225-226 (1939).
[90] Inter-American Maritime Conference *op.cit.* at 175.
[91] 39 Stat. 733; 41 Stat. 966; U.S.C. Title 46, §813.
[92] Wessel, Duval & Co. *v.* Columbia Steamship Co., 1 U.S.S.B.B. 390 (1935).
[93] Application of G. B. Thorden for Conference Membership, 2 U.S.M.C. 77 (1939).
[94] Hind, Rolph & Co. *v.* French Line, 2 U.S.M.C. 138 (1939).

at the time operate in the trade because contract rates prevented operation except at a substantial loss.[95]

However, the Commission moved toward a more liberal attitude by rejecting voting provisions which permitted inactive members of a conference to exclude a new member who would operate actively in the trade;[96] and by holding that conference membership cannot be denied because of the adequacy of existing services, for carriers in the trade could thereby perpetuate a monopoly by continuing to maintain adequate service.[97] The Commission maintained that the test for admittance to conference membership cannot be the same as that for a certificate of public convenience and necessity because: (1) the Commission has no such express power; and (2) it would be illogical to imply such power after a Federal District Court had denied the Commission the right to prevent abandonment of service.[98]

In 1940, the Commission completely altered the stand it had taken in Hind, Rolph & Co. v. French Line when it stated that the announcement of a proposed service, the publication of sailing schedules, and the solicitation of cargoes resulting in common carrier commitments are sufficient to qualify a line to submit an application for membership in a conference.[99] But in 1945 it was held that an agent who avoids all the obligations of a common carrier may be denied membership.[100] After World War II some carriers showed a desire to enter trades they had not formerly served, and this created several disputes regarding the admission of new members. In 1946 the Commission explained that, "While all conference agreements provide that no line shall be denied membership except for just or reasonable cause, it has been found that conferences will frequently resist admission of a new line because (1) it is not regularly engaged in the trade, (2) does not propose to participate in the trade on an equal basis, (3) is not a common carrier by water, (4) the trade is adequately tonnaged, and for other reasons."[101] In an important decision the Commission held that it was discriminatory and unfair to require the applicant to place ships in operation as a prerequisite to conference membership; and concluded that the test should be the proven

---

[95] In the Matter of Gulf Intercoastal Conference Agreement, 1 U.S.S.B.B. 322 (1934).

[96] Sprague S. S. Agency, Inc. v. A/S Ivarans Rederi, 2 U.S.M.C. 72 (1939).

[97] Waterman Steamship Corp. v. Arnold Bernstein Line, 2 U.S.M.C. 238 (1939).

[98] McCormick Steamship Co. v. United States, 16 F. Supp. 45 (N.D. Cal. 1936).

[99] Cosmopolitan Line v. Black Diamond Lines, 2 U.S.M.C. 321 at 328 (1940).

[100] Agreement No. 7620, 2 U.S.M.C. 749 (1945).

[101] Rept. U. S. Mar. Com. 1946, p. 20.

ability and intention of a carrier to operate a regular service.[102] Applications, however, were not approved where it was clearly demonstrated that the applicant's interest in a trade is dissimilar to that of regularly established lines, and that the apparent purpose of the concern applying for membership is to "skim the cream" from the trade without accepting the obligations of regular service.[103] The Commission has continued to insist that conferences provide for the admission of qualified common carriers and that no applicant be denied admission without just and reasonable cause, and furthermore has stated that it considered the danger of overtonnaging a trade to be of lesser consequence than the possible perpetuation of a monopoly in the hands of existing conference carriers.[104] In 1947, in reply to a conference which claimed that since it did not employ the contract rate system an applicant was not prejudiced by not being admitted, the Commission agreed with the applicant that "shippers always have contracts in mind and ordinarily will not patronize non-conference lines because they [the shippers] desire stability in the trade."[105] Accordingly, the Commission threatened to disapprove the conference agreement unless the applicant was admitted; for this was the method usually employed by the Commission to enforce its decisions in such matters. And in 1948 the Commission disapproved a proposal of one conference to increase its admission fee from $250 to $5,000 on the grounds that the increase was unnecessary, unduly discriminatory, and might, by reducing potential competition, be detrimental to the nation's commerce.[106]

(In 1920 Congress demonstrated that it favored a membership policy that would require conferences throughout the world to admit American flag applicants. In an amendment to the 1916 act, Congress provided that if a foreign carrier excluded an American carrier from admission on equal terms to any agreement, the Shipping Board or its successors should certify such fact to the Secretary of Commerce who should thereafter refuse to permit ships owned or operated by such an offending party the right to enter United States ports.[107] Although complaints have been brought under this section, disputes

---

[102] Black Diamond S. S. Corp. v. Cie Maritime Belge (Lloyd R.) S. A. 2 U.S.M.C. 755 (1946).
[103] *Rept. U. S. Mar. Com. 1946*, p. 21. Also see footnote 100.
[104] *Rept. U. S. Mar. Com. 1947*, p. 11.
[105] The East Asiatic Co. Ltd., v. Swedish American Line, 3 U.S.M.C. 1 (1947).
[106] Pacific Coast European Conference, 3 U.S.M.C. 11 (1948).
[107] 39 Stat. 733; 41 Stat. 966; U.S.C. Title 46, § 813.

have hitherto been settled in such a way that the Board or Commission has not been required to certify the matter to the Secretary of Commerce.[108] In this fashion the Secretary of Commerce has been spared the embarrassing necessity of taking an action which undoubtedly would have been termed a violation of the treaties of commerce and navigation the United States has with most foreign countries.)

Voting. There have been several interesting decisions concerning the voting procedures of conferences. Voting provisions have been rejected which gave a conference control of traffic moving over routes in which none of its members participated;[109] and, as has been noted previously, provisions which permitted inactive members of a conference to vote to exclude a new active member were also held invalid.[110]

As early as 1925, the Board held an agreement among three separate conferences unfair to the member carriers and detrimental to American commerce, because unanimous consent was required to change a rule or rate.[111] The regulatory agency's attitude toward the unanimous voting rule was different when it applied to a single conference; and in a postwar case the Commission held that conferences may have the unanimous, two-thirds, three-fourths, or majority voting rules; no one of these can be disapproved as an organizational procedure. The lawfulness of any of them, it was contended, must be based upon evidence, as to their working in practice, introduced in a public hearing. Tests of lawfulness, the Commission continued, are found in actions or courses of conduct, not in organizational procedure.[112]

An interesting case arose in the trade from the United States to the Orient where the members of the Pacific Westbound Conference compete with lines sailing from the Atlantic and Gulf for some cargo

[108] In 1932 the Dollar Steamship Lines complained that it had been denied membership by the Japan China Straits-Bombay Conference whose membership was composed of British and Japanese lines; but in 1933 the American carrier was admitted and the Shipping Board discontinued its investigation. Dollar S. S. Lines v. P. & O. Steam Nav. *et al.*, 1 U.S.S.B. 262. In 1950 the Straits-Bombay Conference, which the American flag Pacific Far East Lines accused of denying it membership, dissolved and petitioned the Maritime Board to dismiss the complaint. The dissolution followed the withdrawal of the American President Lines from the Conference because of the denial of the P.F.E.L. application.

[109] Commonwealth of Mass. v. Colombian S. S. Co., 1 U.S.M.C. 711 (1938).

[110] 2 U.S.M.C. 72 *op.cit.*

[111] Port Differential Investigation, 1 U.S.S.B. 61 (1925).

[112] Pacific Coast European Conference, 3 U.S.M.C. 11 (1948).

originating in the interior of the North American continent. In addition, some lines whose services originated at Atlantic or Gulf ports "topped off" at California ports en route to the Far East. The Pacific Westbound Conference, therefore, devised two types of membership: regular members were those whose service originated on the Pacific Coast, and associate memberships were available for lines which came from the Atlantic or Gulf. Associate members did not vote, pay an admission fee, put up a performance bond, or pay part of the conference expenses; but they were kept advised of all conference proceedings, and participated in exclusive patronage contracts on an equal basis with regular members. In reply to a request from an associate member to be admitted to regular membership with its voting rights, the Commission decided that while the petitioner's desire to have a voice in fixing its rates was natural and had merit, it could not overlook the interest of the regular members which was preponderantly in the direct traffic from the Pacific to the Orient, and, therefore, did not believe the existing situation contrary to the public interest.[113]

"OTHER PERSONS SUBJECT TO THE (1916) ACT"

In addition to common carriers by water, the Shipping Act of 1916 also applied to persons "carrying on the business of forwarding or furnishing wharfage, dock, warehouse, or other terminal facilities in connection with a common carrier by water."[114] After the Commission's regulatory jurisdiction over carriers by water in interstate commerce had been transferred to the Interstate Commerce Commission by the Transportation Act of 1940, the Maritime Commission appears to have become more interested than previously in the activities of other persons subject to the 1916 act. The regulation of these "other persons" is quite different from the regulation of shipping conferences, since the former are under the exclusive jurisdiction of one country. The Maritime Commission could regulate without international jurisdictional dispute the terminals situated in the United States, but it had no authority over terminals in other countries. Therefore, despite the fact that these "other persons" provide the nexus between ship and shore or between shipper and ship operator, their regulation will not be considered in this volume. However, on

---

[113] Agreement No. 7790 2 U.S.M.C. 775 (1946).
[114] 39 Stat. 728 (1917), 40 Stat. 900 (1919), 46 U.S.C. § 801 (1940).

the basis of a new enactment, the Bland Forwarding Act,[115] two decisions involving shipping conferences were made. The Bland Forwarding Act charges the Commission with preserving forwarding facilities and coordinating their functions for the restoration and development of foreign commerce. The Commission has held that conference provisions prohibiting the payment of brokerage fees to freight forwarders were detrimental to the commerce of the United States and in violation of the Bland Act,[116] and Section 15 of the 1916 act.

SOME COMMENTS ON THE GENERAL POLICY OF THE REGULATORY AGENCIES

Besides furnishing additional evidence of the need for some regulation, the foregoing section of this chapter has demonstrated both the success and limitations of American regulatory activity. The Maritime Commission and its predecessors have been successful in correcting unreasonable discrimination and some other similar abuses, and in restricting the growth of monopoly power—especially by requiring conferences to maintain an open membership policy. However, the regulatory agencies have sanctioned exclusive patronage contracts and pooling agreements, both of which tend to enhance the monopolistic authority of the lines employing them. The implications of these practices are examined more fully in subsequent chapters. The antecedent section also indicates that the limitations of unilateral regulation of international shipping are most apt to be found in connection with the control of rates, especially the general rate structure or level of rates.

Before concluding this chapter let us review the background of the American regulatory effort and examine some problems that have beset its development.

The Shipping Act of 1916 was based directly on recommendations the Alexander Committee had submitted to the Congress two years earlier. The only significant change from the Committee's suggestions was the vesting of regulatory control in the newly created United States Shipping Board instead of adding these powers to those of the Interstate Commerce Commission. The Shipping Board was also charged with encouraging and creating a merchant marine to meet

[115] 56 Stat. 171. Upheld in 327 U.S. 437.

[116] Agreement No. 7790, 2 U.S.M.C. 775 (1946); and Agreements and Practices Re Brokerage, 3 U.S.M.C. 170 (1949).

the commercial and naval requirements of the nation. World War I, and the subsequent participation of the United States in it, not only emphasized these latter responsibilities, but postponed implementation of the Board's regulatory powers until after the termination of hostilities. The conclusions of the Alexander Committee regarding the desirability of adequately regulated shipping conferences naturally reflected itself in the 1916 act and in the attitude of the Shipping Board and its successors, the Shipping Board Bureau of the Department of Commerce 1933-1936, and the Maritime Commission 1936-1950. Conceptions of what constitutes adequate regulation has shifted slightly with the passage of time from the rather lenient attitude of the *Board* to the somewhat less lenient attitudes of the *Bureau* and the *Commission*.[117] Although both of the latter agencies were contemporaneous with the New Deal and were doubtless somewhat affected by the predominant social philosophy of the era, they cannot be charged with pursuing their regulatory responsibilities with crusading zeal. Their deliberations and decisions in regulatory cases were judicial in nature. They adjudicated within the framework of a law; they did not freely interpret existing legislation, nor, in the case of foreign commerce, recommend changes in existing statutes. Nevertheless, policies emerged and developed, though their course is sometimes obscure, the view at times being lost, one suspects, in the fog of expediency.

The Shipping Board's earliest contact with conferences was as a member of them. After World War I the Board undertook to establish numerous regular, permanent American-flag shipping services.

[117] An extenuating circumstance helps explain the leniency of the Board. Mr. S. S. Sandberg, vice chairman of the Shipping Board, stated, "Similarly, as was the experience of the Interstate Commerce Commission in its early days, has been the experience of the Board in defending its jurisdiction over subject carriers . . . it was seriously contended until the latter part of 1929, that the Board had no authority under the shipping act over carriers in foreign commerce of the United States, unless such carriers were American-flag carriers, and particularly that the Board's regulatory authority did not extend to rate and practice controversies when the contracts of affreightment were made in a foreign country." *Proceedings of the Sixth National Conference on the Merchant Marine* (Washington: U.S. Government Printing Office, 1933), pp. 77-78. The Supreme Court in 1929 upheld the decision of the Circuit Court of Appeals that the Board's authority was as applicable to foreign-flag carriers engaged in United States commerce as it was to American-flag vessels, and the place where the contracts of affreightment were made was immaterial. Comp. Générale Transatlantique v. American Tobacco Co., 280 U.S. Reports 555 (1929); 31 F. (2d) 487; 1 U.S.S.B. 97 (1925); 1 U.S.S.B. 53 (1923). The reparation of $78,000, which the Board ordered the French Line to pay for the unjust discrimination it had been found to have practiced for six years, is the largest payment of this kind requested by the Board or its successors.

The prevailing disturbed rate situation caused financial losses and contributed to the difficulty of transferring the United States Merchant Marine to private ownership. Consequently, the Board, through its operating agency, the Emergency Fleet Corporation (later the Merchant Fleet Corporation), turned to the conference system of rate making and held active memberships in most of the important conferences in the foreign trade of the United States, as well as in others throughout the world. Some of the conferences engaged in practices that would have been illegal in the United States' trades.[118]

After the passage of the Merchant Marine Act of 1928, as more and more government lines were sold to private operators, the government's direct influence on conferences, which it had exercised through its own lines, naturally decreased. Consequently, more attention was directed to the Board's regulatory powers and the indirect supervision of conferences. As a result of the unusually severe depression of the 1930's, the conference system, like many other economic institutions, failed to function as expected and serious rate-cutting developed in some trades. To avert the result of this destructive competition, the Shipping Board Bureau undertook an investigation at which exporters and importers testified to the necessity of stable rates and regular service. As a result, regulations were issued, as previously noted, requiring *all* common carriers in the foreign trade of the United States to file with the Bureau, within thirty days of the effective date, their *export* rates on all cargo, except that moving in bulk without mark or count.[119] Prior to this, only conference carriers had filed their rates with the government. This decision was upheld by the Supreme Court in 1937 when it sustained the regulatory agency's right to require the filing of export rates as long as compliance with this requirement did not preclude subsequent deviations from the rates filed.[120] In 1939, as a result of a bad case of rate-cutting by Japanese lines in the route between the East Coast of South America and the Pacific Coast of the United States, the Maritime Commission required common carriers in this trade to file their *im-*

---

[118] According to D. H. Robertson: "In April, 1920, the representatives of the United States Shipping Board began to take part in the British North Atlantic Conferences, and in the autumn of 1920, after swallowing their scruples about the system of deferred rebates, were admitted to the European Far Eastern Conference," *Economic Fragments* (London: P. S. King & Sons, Ltd., 1931), pp. 114-115.

[119] 1 U.S.S.B.B. 470, *op.cit.*

[120] Isbrandtsen-Moller *v.* United States 300 U. S. 139 (1937).

port rates within thirty days, except for cargo shipped without mark or count.[121] Many carriers on other routes voluntarily filed their import rates, but they are not required to do so.

The Maritime Commission aimed to secure through the conference system the maximum of industry self-regulation, with only such supervision as proved necessary to assure that the powers inherent in these agreements were not abused. Nevertheless in 1940, after being relieved of the considerable burden of regulating water carriers in the domestic trade through the transfer of this responsibility to the Interstate Commerce Commission, the Maritime Commission appears to have become more active in supervising the foreign carrying trade. Regulation of terminal practices also occupied much of its attention; and several investigations into false billing and the misdescription of cargo were begun at this time. (Before the Second World War, the Commission frequently had a representative of its Division of Operation and Traffic—not the Commission's Division of Regulation which was charged with supervision of conferences—attend conference meetings where subsidized American operators were members. These representatives were probably more concerned with promotional than regulatory problems.) After the war, the Commission stated that a most rapid and effective method of aiding the transition from government control to private operation would be the reactivation of conferences; and that the conference method was the most feasible method of providing supervision over carriers in the nation's foreign commerce.[122] The Commission felt that the ability to adjust rates quickly to meet rapidly changing conditions is requisite to the successful conduct of international trade; and that stability, achieved at the expense of flexibility, would be obtained at too high a price. The Commission believed that properly functioning shipping conferences provide stability without sacrificing flexibility.[123]

There are special problems involved in controlling rates and practices in the foreign trades. No specific minimum or maximum rate power was granted to the Commission or its predecessors; and, it is very doubtful if unilateral action could have successfully established specific rates on international routes. Consequently, the Commission considered the regulation of rates in the foreign trade to be one of

[121] 2 U.S.M.C. 14, *op.cit.*
[122] *Rept. U. S. Mar. Com. 1946*, pp. 17-18.
[123] *Inter-American Maritime Conference, op.cit.*, pp. 180-181.

its most difficult problems. However, the Commission believed that regulation was facilitated by: (1) the community of interest that existed between the shipper and the shipowner; (2) the fact that the ocean is free and no agreement among operators can banish all competitors forever; and (3) because there are frequently alternate sources of supply, so that if lines on one route charge rates that are unduly high, the traffic may be diverted to another route.[124] However, since these forces by themselves would not always assure equitable charges, the Commission, and its predecessors, found it necessary to participate occasionally in the control of rates and practices of common carriers in the nation's foreign trade insofar as their authority permitted. When it was considered necessary, the Commission threatened to exercise its power to disband a conference by withdrawing from the conference agreement the Commission's approval which is necessary to exempt that arrangement from the anti-trust laws. The Commission acknowledged that although there was no specific statutory provision giving it the right to pass upon the reasonableness of rates established by a conference; it claimed nevertheless to possess certain power in this respect through its right to disapprove the conference agreement.[125] In addition to such authority being round-about this procedure had two fairly serious shortcomings. In the first place, carriers who were not members of a conference were not subject to the same pressure, with the result that it was difficult to prevent discrimination in cases where non-conference lines operated. In the second place, although conferences were generally created to prevent cutthroat competition, they proved to be rather fragile instruments in the Great Depression of the 1930's. It might also be pointed out that the action of conferences in 1941, when the Commission was attempting to prevent rates from rising too rapidly, was frequently disappointing, although the Commission certainly enjoyed far more cooperation from conference lines in holding rates down than it did from non-conference carriers and tramps.

In short, the Commission's policy has been to subject carriers in the foreign trade of the United States to as few restrictions as possible with respect to their freight rates and shipping practices. Active and specific regulatory control has been established only when the public welfare has, in the eyes of the Commission, seemed to require it, although general supervision has been maintained for the

---

[124] *ibid.*, p. 151.
[125] *ibid.*, p. 175.

purpose of checking and correcting patently unfair practices so far as possible. The Commission's authority extends only to common carriers in the foreign trade, and its influence over common carriers who are members of a conference is greater than over non-members.

"In general, Federal Government interest in the broad field of transportation is based upon the assumption that this service is so inextricably interwoven into the social and economic fabric of the country that all activities which are designed on the one hand to guarantee the efficient and nondiscriminatory management of the business constitute, in the language of the Supreme Court, 'functions of the State.' In short, the general assumption exists that the business of transportation is one 'affected with a public interest.' "[126]

Although this statement describes fairly accurately the philosophy behind both the regulatory portions of the Shipping Act of 1916 and their administration, it is important to keep clearly in mind the limited terms of reference of this legislation, especially in its application to shipping in the nation's foreign trade. It was neither the intent of the 1916 act, nor has it been the policy of its administrators, to be concerned with the effects of ocean freight rates on the utilization of resources, the location of industrial, commercial, or agricultural activity, the volume of employment, or the distribution of the national income. The agencies charged with regulating shipping in the foreign trades tried to protect: (1) shippers; (2) shipowners (in order to promote water transportation); and (3) the nation's foreign commerce. In spite of the community of interests that frequently exists between shippers, carriers, and the national concern with overseas commerce, this coincidence does not preclude the possibility of conflict in numerous instances. Whereas certain regulatory principles seem to have emerged gradually from the regulatory decisions, a careful study of these reports impresses the reader with the feeling that expediency is frequently an important determinant. Perhaps a policy of regulation which appears to be based, in part, on expediency is inevitable and to a certain extent desirable where equity is stressed (and it is quite proper that equity should be stressed in these cases), and where the dynamic nature of the industry causes the situation to change frequently. Furthermore, it must be remembered, the regulatory mandate provided by Congress did not include specific authority to consider broader social and eco-

[126] U.S. Senate, 75th Congress, 1st session, Report 1275, Part 12. *Report on the Government Activities in the Field of Transportation*, pp. ix-x (1937).

nomic objectives. It was not this limitation, however, but rather the much less extensive authority over rates which distinguishes the regulation of ocean carriers in the foreign trades from that provided to control railroads and ocean carriers operating domestic services. Since confusion on this score should be avoided, the major differences between foreign and domestic rate regulation will be briefly examined.

Unlike its omission of the power to regulate rates in the foreign trades, the Shipping Act of 1916 as originally enacted gave the Shipping Board the authority to prescribe reasonable maximum rates in the domestic trades. In consequence of the Great Depression a series of enactments extended minimum as well as maximum rate regulation to domestic common carriers by water; and in 1940 rate authority over domestic common and contract water carriers was transferred to the Interstate Commerce Commission.[127] Domestic ocean transportation during the inter-war period was characterized by frequent and bitter rate wars, a condition which was not nearly so prevalent on most foreign routes. However, since the domestic trade is not only restricted by definition to United States ports but is restricted by the Coastwise laws to United States flag vessels as well, it is unqualifiedly subject to the sole jurisdiction of the United States government, and serious efforts were made to control domestic ocean rates, especially in the intercoastal trade.

Furthermore, the domestic regulatory problem involves not only the control of competition among the water carriers themselves, but the coordination of shipping with competitive forms of land transport—railroads and, to a lesser extent, trucks; while the essence of the foreign regulatory problem is the control of nationally differentiated competitors all of whom operate the same form of transport —ships. It is also important to bear in mind the crucial differences between the shipping industry and railroading, for entirely erroneous conclusions are sometimes reached by applying concepts of regulation suitable to one to the other. The ocean is not only a highway, free to all persons, which does not require investment in right-of-way; but it is also relatively easy to shift a vessel from one part of the world to another. The results are that in shipping far less capital is required than in railroading and the investment is far more mobile; with the consequence that competition from tramps as well as from

[127] Except in wartime, there has been no legislation providing for the control of charges of tramp vessels in either the domestic or foreign trade of the United States.

other liner services can appear quite rapidly in shipping whenever a route appears to offer profitable opportunities and can be withdrawn relatively easily when prospects worsen. Trucking may at times provide railroads with this sort of competition, but new competitive railroad lines do not frequently enter the picture.

Another great limitation on the ability of a government agency to regulate ocean shipping rates in the foreign trades is imposed by the existence of tramp vessels. Worldwide business conditions decide the general level of tramp and charter rates, and, therefore, any attempt on the part of one country to control them is almost certain to prove futile. Since tramp and charter rates are not amenable to unilateral government regulation, the control by a government of rates for liner services could so restrict the ability of liner operators, in many instances, to obtain certain types of cargo, as to prove disastrous to the liners. Coordinated control by the governments of the world of the tramp and charter markets could conceivably insulate them from some market forces. But the world market, which has generally been free, has provided a highly efficient method of pricing and allocating irregular transportation which is so well suited to the carriage of many bulk shipments, and which is also occasionally so very useful in the transportation of other types of cargo. Except during wartime and its immediate aftermath, and for assistance to a pooling arrangement during the latter part of the Great Depression, governments have not in recent years tried to control tramp and charter rates. Such rates have been quite free to affect, through their competition, some liner rates and practices, and thereby to complicate the problem of regulation. The extent to which tramp competition generally affects liner operations will be considered in Chapter XI.

Related to the problem of tramp competition is the matter of rate flexibility. The ability to adjust rates quickly to meet changing world conditions is requisite to the successful conduct of international trade. Properly functioning steamship conferences provide stable rates without sacrificing flexibility; but competition is the best spur to the proper functioning of conferences, since by its nature government regulation is not conducive to flexibility. Rate regulation can be concerned with the reasonableness of individual rates or the reasonableness of the rate structure. Government regulation, such as provided by the Shipping Act of 1916, can be helpful in preventing individual rates from being discriminatory; but this legislation is not well designed to control the reasonableness of the structure of rates. It was felt, at the time this legislation was drafted, that actual or potential competition was sufficient to keep the rate level in line; and since tramp competition affects bulk items primarily, the actual or potential presence of competition from vessels being placed on berth to carry general cargo was apparently contemplated. If the influence of such berth competition is to be felt, conference policies regarding the admission of new members and the use of exclusive patronage contracts or other tying arrangements have demonstrated that they often require supervision by an outside agency. The American regulatory agencies have only recently taken a firm stand in regard to conference membership policy and to some abusive features of the exclusive patronage contract.

The reluctance of American regulation to interfere with pooling agreements and the exclusive patronage contract system, which are claimed to be necessary in some trades to assure rate stability, may be partially explained by inertia; but a far more likely reason is to be found in the international nature of ocean shipping. Except as a temporary emergency measure, the unilateral control by one government of rates in a trade subject to the jurisdiction of two or more sovereign governments has not been considered advisable by the American agencies responsible for administering the 1916 legislation. Congress has considered many proposals to provide authority to regulate rates in the foreign trade. The Maritime Commission reports, "With few exceptions exporters and importers and shipowners and operators have opposed such legislation on the grounds that the fixing of hard-and-fast rules for the naming of rates for overseas transportation is impractical and would be harmful to trade."[128] Furthermore, it is believed that such government control would not be in harmony with treaties of commerce, navigation, and friendship which the United States has entered with most other countries and under which the signatories are granted freedom of access to each other's ports.[129] It must also be remembered that vessels are not fixtures in any trade; and, therefore, it is not unlikely that the imposition of conditions which made a trade less attractive than others not similarly controlled would, in periods when tonnage was scarce and rates high or rising, cause vessels to be shifted to routes where their activities were not restricted. In times of tonnage scarcity shippers

[128] *Inter-American Maritime Conference, op.cit.*, p. 178.
[129] *ibid.*, pp. 181-182.

frequently approach carriers with an offer of higher rates in an effort to obtain space. If rates were unilaterally controlled, there might not be sufficient flexibility in the control procedure to permit a shipper to protect his requirements by such means. As a result of these considerations, the regulatory policy of the United States, according to the Maritime Commission, has been to encourage self-regulation of the industry through the medium of conferences and pools, which are then subjected to general supervision in order to make certain that the powers conferred by these agreements are not abused.[130] In this manner ship operators of many nationalities are permitted to take joint action to stabilize rates and regularize practices and charges.

Except for strong disagreement with the Maritime Commission's policy concerning exclusive patronage contracts, there has been little criticism of the regulation of ocean shipping under the Shipping Act of 1916. Because of the exceedingly slow start made by the original Shipping Board in regulatory affairs our experience with such matters is largely limited to the period from 1933 until 1941 and from 1946 to date. The record seems to indicate that relatively few conferences have been guilty of very serious abuses, unless exclusive patronage contracts and pooling arrangements approved by the Commission are so condemned.[131] The record indicates, furthermore, that the regulatory agencies have been reasonably successful in achieving their limited objectives. Nevertheless, as the reports show, abuses have existed, and undoubtedly others will continue to develop from time to time, to a sufficient extent to justify the active supervision and regulation of the conference system. One may hope that the more energetic policy of regulation of shipping in the foreign trade, which the Maritime Commission began in 1940, upon being relieved of the responsibility of regulating domestic shipping, and which the Commission apparently resumed after the termination of hostilities, will be continued by the newly created Federal Maritime Board.

[130] *ibid.*, p. 178.
[131] Exclusive patronage contracts are discussed in detail in Chapter X; and pooling arrangements are described in Chapter VIII.

CHAPTER VIII
SHIPPING AGREEMENTS IN U.S. FOREIGN TRADE

AGREEMENTS AMONG shipping lines assume a variety of forms, and in the foreign trade of the United States may be classified as conference agreements, inter-conference agreements, pooling agreements, transshipment agreements, and joint service agreements. In January 1950 there were in effect in the foreign trade of the United States 109 conferences,[1] 11 inter-conference agreements, 2 pooling arrangements, and approximately 150 transshipment and 50 joint service agreements. Each of these methods of cooperation will be considered in turn.

A shipping conference, as previously noted, is an agreement reached by shipping companies operating liner services for the purpose of regulating or restricting competition. These conferences are actually what their name implies, meetings of independent and competing shipping lines, and not incorporated bodies. There is nothing in common between such a conference and a combine of shipping companies linked by share holdings or common ownership of assets. Moreover, the majority of shipping conferences are international, in the sense that they consist of companies under various national flags. Most conferences confine their activities to traffic between two geographic areas or ranges, although a few cover two or more trades and in such cases are apt to be divided into sections or sub-conferences. Inbound and outbound segments of the trade between two given ranges are generally considered as separate trades; and therefore separate conferences are usually formed to cover outward and inward operations, although some conferences cover traffic moving in both directions.[2] In a few situations a route is subject to a con-

[1] Five additional effective conference agreements on file at this date covered operations between the United States and its non-contiguous territories; but we do not consider them here, since the regulation of carriers on these routes, all of which are restricted to American-flag vessels, does not present the same multi-jurisdictional problems as operations in the nation's foreign commerce.

[2] The main reasons for the separation of inbound and outbound trades into separate conferences arise from the differences in the nature of the commodities shipped, the different shipper interests involved, and from the fact that the lines in the outbound and homebound trades may not be identical. There is a large amount of flexibility in liner operation, and a line does not always return its ships to a terminus by the most

ference understanding in only one direction, and the return voyage is not controlled. A steamship company may be a member of one or more conferences, and generally a company will belong to a conference for each route on which it operates a liner service, although in a few instances shipping concerns may participate in conference organizations on only some of their routes.

Of the 109 conferences in effect in January 1950 in the United States foreign trade, 100 were concerned with freight traffic and 5 with passengers. Of the 100 conferences concerned with freight, 42 covered outbound movements, 45 covered inbound movements, and 11 covered both exports from and imports to the United States. Two others coordinate the administrative activities of two groups of member conferences. The remaining four agreements set up committees which are concerned with the local activities of conference lines in one port or country. Two of them are in New York, and two are in England.

A small number of these agreements covered more than trade with the continental United States. The Associated Steamship Lines (Manila) Conference, for example, covers freight traffic shipped from the Philippine Islands directly, or via most Oriental ports, to North America, South America, Central America, Caribbean, and Australasian destinations. In fact, its activities are divided into seven geographical groups and the member lines, depending on the areas served, belong to one or more of these sections. Another example is the Association of West India Trans-Atlantic Steamship Lines which covers freight traffic between European ports and Puerto Rican and Virgin Island ports. Whereas the passenger conferences have from 4 to 17 members and the freight conferences have from 2 to 29 members, the number of "sellers" is neither so large nor so small as appears at first glance. For passengers, either product differentiation between ships of the same line, not to mention differences between lines, is apt to be so great that the actual number of sellers is of relatively small importance, or the date of sailing is of paramount importance. In the case of freight conferences many of them with a small number of members—5 or less, of which there were 29—generally operate on routes where the volume of traffic could not sup-

---

direct route, but may engage in a triangular or even more circuitous service. (Witness the round-the-world services.) In a few instances an operator may provide common carrier liner service in one direction only, and return as a contract carrier or with a load belonging in its entirety to a subsidiary or parent concern.

port a large number of concerns. On the other hand freight conferences with a large number of members—16 or more, of which there were 22—are very apt to include a few inactive members, and to cover a rather broad territory, with the result that not all the lines compete with each other, each tending to concentrate its activities at certain ports of call. (Port specialization is also practiced at times by members of the smaller conferences, where it is even more likely to produce a monopoly. Since, in these cases, the volume of traffic is frequently too small to warrant the entrance of additional concerns, monopoly or duopoly is often inevitable.)

Examples of conferences with small membership operating in trades of limited traffic are the Norway-North Atlantic Conference, covering freight from Norway to U.S. North Atlantic ports, which has 3 members; and the Hawaiian Islands-Australasia Conference covering freight from Hawaii to the Fiji Islands, Australia, and New Zealand, which has 2 members. The following are examples of large conferences where the individual members do not operate from or to all of the ports of origin or destination covered by the agreements: the Trans-Pacific Freight Conference of North China with 17 members, covering traffic from Shanghai, Formosa, and North China ports to Hawaii and to U.S. and Canadian Pacific ports; and the Pacific Coast-European Conference, with 23 members, covering freight from U.S. Pacific Coast ports to Great Britain, Irish Free State, Continental Europe, Baltic destinations, and Scandinavia, as well as to certain Mediterranean ports, and which also includes transshipment to Adriatic, Black Sea, African, and Indian ports. Furthermore, there are conferences such as the Pacific Westbound Conference, covering freight from Pacific Coast ports in North America to the Far East from Siberia to Indo-China, which has, in addition to 19 regular members, 8 associate members. The United Kingdom-United States Pacific Freight Association, covering traffic from the United Kingdom to United States Pacific ports and transshipment to Honolulu has, in addition to 4 regular members, 2 associate members, and 2 associated lines. An associate member is a line, usually without full voting rights, which operates a service parallel to that of the conference members for all or part of the route, and which agrees to observe conference rates, rules, regulations, and conditions on traffic which it handles in the trade covered by the conference agreement. An associated line is one which operates a service between a port or ports from or to which the conference agreement applies and some other port, and which agrees to observe conference rates, rules, regulations, and conditions on *through* traffic in the movement in which it participates. Thirteen conferences in the American foreign trades have one or more associate members, and sixteen of the conferences have one or more associated lines affiliating themselves with the basic group for transshipments.[3]

The outbound freight conferences and conferences covering freight traffic moving in both directions all have their headquarters in one of the major port cities of the United States; while most of the conferences concerned with inbound shipments have their headquarters at some principal port overseas. Nevertheless, approximately one-third of the inbound conferences maintain their offices in the United States; these conferences all cover trade from areas which do not include ship operating countries, such as Africa, South and Central America, and Australasia. Most freight conferences covering both inbound and outbound traffic are concerned with business in the Caribbean area. The location of a conference's headquarters, while not of major importance, is not without significance, because it is at times more difficult for an American regulatory agency to obtain information from, and to exert influence on, an organization whose situs is under the jurisdiction of another nation where practices unlawful under the Shipping Act are entirely legal.

The foregoing indicates the existence of considerable variety in the size and organization of conferences; and when one takes into account the nature of the traffic, the competition from other sources of supply or markets, and the possible existence of inter-conference agreements to control such competition one begins to visualize the difficulty of making sweeping generalizations concerning the effects of this form of industrial self-regulation.

Passenger conferences, in view of the differences in the problems confronting them, display some unique characteristics which will be described in more detail in the following section of this chapter, but in general they closely resemble the freight conferences. The passenger conferences, with one exception, cover traffic moving in both directions, and they apply to a greater range of territory than all but a few freight conferences.

[3] These transshipment arrangements by which an on-carrying line associates itself with a conference are specifically covered by transshipment agreements which are described more fully below.

Conference agreements are usually treated with great secrecy, so very little information is available regarding current understandings except for conferences operating in United States trades which must file their agreements with the Federal Maritime Board. The rulings of the Board's predecessors have probably brought about some standardization, and the restrictions of the Shipping Act of 1916 may well have had an influence which renders agreements in American trades unrepresentative of those for other parts of the world. Nonetheless, considerable variety persists in agreements filed with the Board, and when a comparison is made with agreements described by early investigations there is reason to believe that a description of conference contracts currently on file will not misrepresent too badly the more general features of agreements covering trade elsewhere.[4] A limitation which is probably far more serious is the unavailability of information concerning the actual negotiations among members at meetings—both meetings during which the agreement is first negotiated and those later ones when the contract is in operation and decisions are made regarding the admission of new members, the establishment and changing of rates, classifications, practices, allowances, etc. These matters are carefully kept business secrets in most instances, and we are forced, therefore, to let our imagination bridge the gap between the introduction of an issue and those final decisions of which we have knowledge. The external forms of political and business institutions frequently fail to reveal the processes by which decisions are actually reached and the hands in which power really lies.

Despite their great variety, conference agreements in American trades have a number of features in common. They invariably start with a delineation of the geographical areas to or from or between which they have been formed "to promote commerce."[5] The nature of the business to be controlled is then specified; that is, whether passenger or freight traffic is intended, and if there are any commodities excepted from the agreement. (Bulk commodities and others moving in great volume as well as those requiring special facilities

[4] See reports of the Royal Commission on Shipping Rings and of the Alexander Committee, *op.cit.* The anti-trust laws of the United States undoubtedly influenced the nature of written commitments of American conferences even prior to 1916.

[5] Some conferences are divided into sections or sub-conferences covering trade to different regions. A line may belong to one, several, or all of the sub-groups. A notable example is the Associated Steamship Lines (Manila).

are frequently among the exceptions.) The agreements customarily cover the establishment, regulation, and maintenance of rates, and other charges and practices.[6] Most conferences agree on the actual rates to be charged, although a few agree only on minimum rates. Such minimum rates are usually the actual rates charged, but in a favorable market the members are free to charge what they can get.[7] When conferences cover both inbound and outbound shipments the participants bind themselves to observe the agreed rates and practices on traffic moving in both directions. A few agreements specifically provide for the quotation of through water and rail rates for goods originating in or destined to inland points. Some agreements provide for creating "open" rates on items which become subject to tramp or other non-conference competition, which is equivalent to exempting such goods from the agreement, although these conferences generally provide for returning commodities from an "open" to a "closed" rate status when the competitive situation changes. Some agreements specify the currency in which bills must be paid.[8] The control of practices and of charges other than the actual ocean transportation rate is also extremely important, because of the great amount of discrimination that might develop without accord concerning these matters. This can be readily illustrated by quoting from one rather typical conference contract.

"All freight and other charges for and in connection with such transportation shall be charged and collected by the parties hereto based on actual gross weight or measurement of the cargo or per package according to tariff, and strictly in accordance with the rates, charges, classifications, rules, and/or regulations adopted by the parties. There shall be no undue preferences or disadvantages, nor unjust nor unreasonable discrimination, or unfair practices against any consignor or consignee by any of the parties hereto.

"Each of the parties hereto agrees that neither it nor its principals

[6] As a cooperative method of rate-making, conferences resemble the rate bureaus of the American railroads.

[7] An interesting deviation from the usual pattern is exemplified by the Outward Continental North Pacific Freight Conference which grants members the right to fight outside competition by following or underquoting rates offered by that competition, provided the members availing themselves of this privilege keep other members of the conference fully informed.

[8] In periods of devaluation the currency or currencies in which freight bills can be paid assumes great importance. See *Rates in Canadian Currency*, 1 U.S.S.B., 265 (1933). A similar problem arises when convertibility of currencies is difficult. Since World War II some South American countries have demanded that freight on imports be payable in their national monies, instead of dollars.

nor associated nor affiliated companies of any of them shall give or promise, either directly or indirectly, to any shipper, or consignee or broker, or prospective shipper or consignee or broker, or to any officer, employee, agent or representative of any such shipper or consignee or broker, or prospective shipper, or consignee or broker, or to any member of the family of any of the aforesaid, in any manner, any return, commission, compensation, concession, free or reduced storage, free or reduced passenger rates, any bribe, gratuity, gift of substantial value or other payment or remuneration through any device whatsoever, or render to any of the foregoing any service outside or beyond that called for in the contracts of affreightment or tariffs.

"NOTE: Free or reduced rate ocean passages. Personal Grounds—Principals of Member Companies may grant free or reduced rate passages on personal grounds, but in no instance shall free or reduced rate passages be granted in conflict with the above or in violation of Section 16 of the Shipping Act, 1916.

"The parties hereto and each of them further agree that they shall not enter into any agreement of any nature, with any party or parties, which would in any way affect the integrity of this agreement, or any agreements, rates, rules or regulations made pursuant hereto."[9]

To protect shippers from unjust discrimination and to make certain that the carriers get the proper rates, some conferences in the trans-Pacific trades now employ inspectors to make spot checks to ascertain if shipments are properly described and accurately billed.[10] Several agreements stipulate that a conference member shall not employ more than one agency at any one port.

Agreements often require the appointment of a chairman, who shall not be interested in or employed by, or in any way connected with, any member of the conference. Sometimes provision is made for meetings at weekly or less frequent regular intervals, while in other cases no regular meetings are scheduled, but they can be called whenever it is necessary. Expenses are customarily pro-rated, and sometimes an admission fee is required. In the United States trades this fee is nominal when it exists, because the Commission has required that it be kept low.[11] Rules for voting and quorums seem to

[9] Pacific Coast European Conference, Article 3.
[10] cf. Rates from United States to Philippine Islands, 2 U.S.M.C. 535 (1941).
[11] Pacific Coast European Conference, 3 U.S.M.C. 11 (1948).

vary widely. Some conferences require a unanimous vote on all issues, while others require unanimity only on particularly crucial matters, and other conferences are satisfied whenever the majority, two-thirds, or three-fourths of all the members agree.[12] Some agreements provide that the right to vote will be lost by any member who fails over a specified period to have a sailing in the trade. Some conferences impose fines for violations of the agreement; and the Pacific Coast European Conference, for example, requires the payment of a penalty of $12,500 whenever a member fails to maintain a minimum of eight sailings per year. Other conferences require the posting of bonds in the form of cash or government securities (e.g. $25,000) to secure payment of penalties levied for violation of the agreement. Most conferences provide that disputed matters, of which the levying of penalties may be taken as an example, shall be submitted to arbitration. Provisions covering voluntary withdrawals and the expulsion of existing members are customarily provided; and arrangements for the admission of new members is also usually described. Conference admission policy in United States trades has been liberalized by Maritime Commission decisions.[13]

In addition to the regular freight conferences there are five associations or committees—two in New York, one in San Francisco, and two in England—whose function it is to make rules and regulations covering the loading or discharging and delivery of cargoes. These organizations do not have rate-making authority, although they may make recommendations to the conferences regarding the traffic with which they are concerned. In short, they supplement the supervision of the freight conferences, which are themselves in one of the leading ports of origin, by providing supervision in the area to which the cargo is consigned,[14] and they are in a position to help to coordinate the policies of the several conferences whose loading or discharging operations they supervise. The Atlantic-Eastbound Freight Association in Liverpool is concerned with problems arising

[12] Although a majority or two-thirds voting rule may appear to provide more flexibility than a three-fourths or unanimous vote requirement, it should be noted that for basic policy decisions all major lines must be satisfied or else there is great danger that the conference will break up. For less important decisions a majority rule is probably less rigid, and a few conferences do have different voting requirements for problems of different importance.

[13] *supra*, Chapter VII, pp. 122-125.

[14] The Trans-Atlantic Freight Conference (New York) is an exception in that it is located in the port of origin along with the headquarters of the associated conferences. See below.

at ports in Great Britain in connection with freight from Canadian Atlantic and U.S. Atlantic and Gulf ports. The Pacific Coast East-bound United Kingdom Conference Association, with headquarters in London, does the same for traffic originating on the Pacific Coast of North America.

The New York Committee of Inward Far East Lines coordinates local questions arising from the discharge and delivery of Far East-ern cargo at U. S. Atlantic and Gulf ports. Its operations are divided into six sections: Straits Settlement section, Netherlands-Indies sec-tion, Colombo section, Philippine section, China section, and Japan section. The individual member lines belong to from one to all six sections, depending upon the scope of their activities. The Pacific Coast Committee of Inward Trans-Pacific Steamship Lines performs similarly at Pacific Coast ports, and in March 1950, when this agree-ment received the approval of the Maritime Commission, consisted of the following four subcommittees: (a) Japan, Korea, and China; (b) Philippine Islands; (c) French Indo-China, Siam, Indonesia, and Malaya; and (d) India, Pakistan, and Persian Gulf. The fifth agreement of this type concerns itself with matters of local port in-terest in the loading at New York of cargo for Europe, and is known as the Trans-Atlantic Freight Conference (New York) Agreement. Besides problems of local interest, this agreement provides for deal-ing with questions of general interest to the North Atlantic trade through its representatives on the executive committee of the Trans-Atlantic Associated Freight Conferences, which is an inter-conference agreement among seven of the nine conferences covering the trans-portation of cargo from American North Atlantic ports to the Euro-pean Continent.[15] None of these five agreements has any direct au-thority over ocean freight rates, although they all are in an excellent position to make recommendations on this subject.

Passenger conferences, because of the great differences that dis-tinguish the transporting of people from the carrying of cargo, are confronted with somewhat different problems. In the first place, pas-senger accommodations are divided into classes, and even within any one class there is considerable variety on any given ship, not to mention the still greater differences that exist between vessels and between lines. In the second place the traveling public is far more numerous than the number of shippers of freight; and the prospec-tive traveler wants to have some idea of the space he is to occupy,

[15] See section of this chapter entitled "Inter-Conference Agreements."

145

with the result that a large number of agents and sub-agents throughout the world seek to deal directly with the voyager. Finally, no tying arrangements would be effective, even if legal, in the case of passengers, since relatively few of them travel the same route often enough to provide such measures with any influence on the purchaser of passenger transportation. As a result, passenger conferences go into great detail concerning the supervision of agents, sub-agents, and advertising. Both the purpose and result of this supervision are to protect the traveling public from crooked, fly-by-night ticket sellers, as well as to protect the lines themselves against dishonest agents and unbridled competition. Agencies and sub-agencies authorized to sell tickets are under strict contracts which: carefully control the handling of tickets and funds; regulate commissions and prohibit sharing them with purchasers; prohibit advertising which makes unfavorable comparisons between any of the member lines or their steamers, or is in any way misleading, or does not conform to truth and good taste. Penalties for violation of these agency contracts are severe and not only may involve fines but also may bring about the offenders' "disbarment" by all members of the conference.

In the important trans-Atlantic trade, close cooperation exists between the Atlantic Conference with headquarters in London and the Trans-Atlantic Passenger Conference with headquarters in New York, since the former explicitly relies upon the latter for enforcement of the London agreement in the United States and Canada. The London agreement provides that, "The basic minimum rates for all ships, all classes, shall be established by unanimous agreement of the Member Lines according to the factors of age, size and speed. A Member Line may quote rates higher than those agreed upon, but no lower rates may be applied except by agreement."

The other passenger conferences do not exercise direct control over fares, but provide that each member company shall determine and fix its own rates. However, these conferences require their members to notify the conference secretary thirty or more days in advance of any decrease in their fares or changes in their classifications of accommodations. The conference must also be provided with the plans and proposed fares for any new vessel that a member intends to place in the trade. The granting of reduced or free fares and the payment of commissions are carefully regulated by all these conferences. Associate membership is generally provided by passenger conferences for operators of freighters with limited accommodations for passengers, and thereby fares on these vessels are controlled and co-ordinated with the fares charged by passenger and combination liners. The Western Hemisphere Passenger Conference also provides for "cruise service members." The North Pacific Coast-Europe Passenger Conference provides for interchanging round-trip tickets among its members, although the agreement itself does not apply to passages from Europe to North America. A detailed provision in the agreement of the Trans-Pacific Passenger Conference concerning entertainment reveals the extent to which it has seemed advisable to the carriers to control competition. Paid theatrical entertainment and variety shows are not to be provided aboard ship, and cinemas provided by member companies "shall be on a limited and modest scale."

While all conferences, both freight and passenger, traditionally treat conference deliberations as strictly confidential, the passenger agreements all provide specifically that no information of conference proceedings shall be given to outsiders. Press announcements of conference activities usually require unanimous consent. This tradition is perhaps best expressed by the Trans-Atlantic Freight Conference (New York), which was formed in 1896 and re-established in 1909 by an agreement which is still in force. It provides that "Each member undertakes, on his honor, to consider and maintain all questions and actions that may be considered or adopted in connection herewith, as sacred and confidential in the highest degree."

Since conference actions are generally shrouded in secrecy, there is not much information available regarding their procedures. While the members of many conferences may live amicably with each other, there is abundant evidence that this is not universally the case. Symptoms of internal struggling occasionally break the apparent surface calm. This is especially apt to come to public attention during rate wars or when the traffic is divided by a pooling arrangement, since changes in the shares assigned to each line may become known. One of the most spectacular occurrences of this type in recent years was the dispute which erupted with volcanic fury in 1949 between the British and Dutch members of conferences regulating trade between Northern European ports and India, Pakistan, and Ceylon. During the hostilities, which is the most appropriate word to describe the intensity with which the Dutch lines raided British ports for traffic and the bitterness with which rates were cut by all parties, the actual cost of ocean transportation fell by 90 per cent to 10 per cent of the conference rates applicable before the dispute. The contest, which lasted for about six weeks, was reported to have been caused by a difference of opinion regarding the division of the carriage of German trade, which prior to the War had been hauled by German lines; but the terms of the settlement remain unknown to the public. Rates, it was reported, were restored to the level which prevailed prior to the "misunderstanding."

Except in cases where the conference mechanism breaks down, such internal competition avoids the price mechanism, and relies instead on service competition, reciprocal arrangements with some shippers, competition for advantageous berth assignments, and all manner of political maneuvering within the conference.[16]

It should be remembered that conferences are in a very real sense political organizations. The Imperial Shipping Committee has stated, "A shipping conference is a meeting in which the competitors face one another with the object of achieving that minimum of co-operation which will suffice to prevent such chaotic competition as might render impracticable the liner system of working ships. Each member of a conference is seeking the minimum surrender of his competitive freedom which is compatible with this object; his attitude in debate is determined by the sources of strength which lie behind his diplomacy."[17] Conferences may be dominated by a large concern, which exerts its influence in the manner traditional to price leaders, or they may be more democratically run, in which event, the customary methods of logrolling are apt to be found. It is perhaps more accurate to describe conferences, even in the absence of price leadership, as plutocratic rather than democratic; for a line with strong financial or government backing is considerably more influential than a financially weak line, and vastly more so than a company hovering on the brink of bankruptcy. Similarly, low-cost operators are in a position to exert more influence than a high-cost operator, unless the latter is being profligately subsidized. Unlike associations with a very large number of members, such as labor unions, shipping conferences do not as a rule assume an independent political existence, nor do

---

[16] For an example of a keen internal struggle, see North Atlantic Continental Freight Conference Agreement, 1 U.S.S.B.B. 562 (1936).

[17] British Shipping in the Orient, op.cit., p. 51. If the word "sovereignty" is substituted for the phrase "competitive freedom," and a corresponding adjustment is made in defining the objective, then the similarity with unions of sovereign states appears even more strikingly.

148

conference officials ordinarily gain a position of power independent of and superior to the members.

The relations of conferences with shippers, however, are not only of considerable importance but also hard to keep obscure; and, therefore, some interesting information is available on this subject.[18] When making rate changes the conference may, but need not, consult with shippers or shipper organizations beforehand. Some conferences make it a practice to notify all shippers well in advance of the date of proposed changes, while other conferences only protect exclusive patronage contract shippers from unannounced rate increases, and other conferences have not even recognized the obligation to notify these contract shippers. Some conferences provide that although rates are subject to change without notice, options may be granted for a few days at firm rates for specific quantities of stated commodities; and others permit cargo to be booked firm for a specified advance period. In periods of great demand for tonnage some conference lines, according to the Maritime Commission, have gone into the prevailing high charter market to secure extra vessels necessary to accommodate their customers, even though the operation of these chartered vessels at conference freight rates may yield little if any profit.[19] There does not seem to have been any difference between conferences employing the exclusive patronage system and conferences not using this system so far as giving advance notice of rate changes. Some contract-using conferences and some non-users make it a practice to give advance notice, while others—users and non-users alike—do not.

Rate changes are not always made without the knowledge of shippers, and individual merchants or trade associations may negotiate directly with individual lines or with conferences for rate adjustments. (In addition to such direct negotiation, shippers in United States trades have recourse to the Federal Maritime Board whenever they can establish that rates are unduly discriminatory or detrimental to the nation's commerce.) The majority of United States conferences now provide special forms to assist shippers in furnishing pertinent and adequate information for conference use in appraising applications for rate adjustments. Most of these conferences accord

---

[18] Some information on this subject has been made available by the U.S. Bureau of Foreign and Domestic Commerce. See E. S. Gregg, *Rate Procedure of Steamship Conferences*, Trade Information Bulletin 221, 1924; and A. E. Sanderson, *Control of Ocean Freight Rates in Foreign Trade*, Trade Promotion Series 185 (1938), pp. 18-28.

[19] Inter-American Maritime Conference, *op.cit.*, p. 171.

applicants the opportunity of appearing in person to present their views to the full membership, or to a rate committee when one exists; but as a general rule conferences do not permit shippers to be present when their applications are being acted upon. Industries which ship in large volume are often represented before the conferences by trade associations, and these associations have at times been very effective in helping the industry to negotiate more favorable rates and contract terms. Local chambers of commerce and port authorities occasionally appear before conferences to present their views on the service and rates needed by their localities. Conference tariffs are often regarded as highly confidential, and even in the United States trades, where all outbound and some inbound tariffs must be filed within thirty days of their effective date, some shipping rings will not circulate their rates. Ship operators argue that ocean rates must be very flexible, and therefore published tariffs might be misleading. Conference rates are rarely altered as frequently as every thirty days, so rates filed with the government are usually the applicable rates; and information services exist which, for a fee, will furnish clients with copies of specific conference rates, or the entire conference tariff. In most other countries conference tariffs are not available to the public, although freight forwarders and shippers learn very rapidly what alterations, if any, have been made in the rates in which they are interested.[20]

Conference rates are not always the same for a given commodity. A few conferences provide for differential rates on some items; while others provide contract rates that are generally 10 to 20 per cent below those charged shippers who have not signed an exclusive patronage agreement. Differential rates are sometimes allowed when the quality of service offered by members of the conference is distinctly different. For example, if one or two member lines operate much slower ships and provide much less frequent sailings than the other member or members, then it is not unusual for lower rates to be quoted, especially for low value cargo which does not require the better service, for shipment via the inferior service. The contract rate system is widely used in the United States trades where the traditional deferred rebate method of tying shippers to a conference is illegal, and in 1950 seventy-eight of the ninety-six freight conferences

---

[20] The secrecy surrounding rates has resulted in a shipper being unaware, for a period of time, of the appropriate classification and rate applicable to his merchandise. See Lesem Back v. International Mercantile Marine Co., 1 U.S.S.B. 232 (1932).

(about 81 per cent) in the foreign commerce of the United States employed exclusive patronage contracts.[21]

INTER-CONFERENCE AGREEMENTS

Since competition frequently arises not only from lines operating on the same route, but also between lines which serve alternate sources of supply, or which provide an alternate means of routing by running from alternate gateways or via transshipment, a series of agreements among conferences have been formed. In the foreign commerce of the United States these inter-conference agreements are of three types.

The first type consists of two associations, one with headquarters in New York and the other in New Orleans, whose purpose it is to coordinate the activities of the several conferences controlling the movement of freight from American and Canadian North Atlantic ports and from United States Gulf ports, respectively, to European, Near East, and African destinations. The Trans-Atlantic Associated Freight Conferences claims to provide administrative organization for and to coordinate what it describes as the non-competitive activities of the following seven conferences: North Atlantic Continental Freight Conference, Morocco Algeria Tunisia North Atlantic Westbound Freight Conference,[22] North Atlantic United Kingdom Freight Conference, North Atlantic Red Sea & Gulf of Aden Freight Conference, North Atlantic French Atlantic Freight Conference and the North Atlantic Mediterranean Freight Conference. Provision is made for the organization of affiliated port conferences at Montreal and such American ports as may be necessary to simplify the work of the Associated Conferences. While the Gulf Associated Freight Conferences is not authorized to make rates, it may arrange joint meetings of two or more of its member conferences "for the purpose of considering and acting upon matters of common interest." The associated conferences are: Gulf-United Kingdom Conference, Gulf-French Atlantic Hamburg Range Freight Conference, Gulf-Scandinavian and Baltic Sea Ports Conference, and Gulf-South and East African Conference. Cooperation is not handicapped, one may presume, by the fact that the person who is chairman of the Trans-At-

[21] A few of the seventy-eight conferences had been temporarily enjoined from using exclusive patronage contracts pending determination of the legality of this device. See Chapter X.

[22] This conference, unlike the other six members of the "Associated Conferences," is concerned with westbound traffic.

lantic Association is also chairman of its seven affiliated conferences; and the Gulf Association and its five affiliated conferences are similarly all headed by one individual.

Two of the conferences regulating freight traffic from Gulf ports to Europe carry cooperation still further by a second type of inter-conference understanding which provides for the Gulf-French Atlantic Hamburg Range Conference and the Gulf-United Kingdom Conference to offer patronage contracts collectively, and to observe each other's rates on transshipped cargo. A similar agreement between the Havana Steamship Conference (U.S. North Atlantic ports to Havana) and the Gulf and South Atlantic Havana Steamship Conference provides for exclusive patronage contracts which bind shippers dispatching cargo from North Atlantic, South Atlantic and Gulf ports to members of the two aforementioned conferences.

A third type of inter-conference agreement provides for the subscribing parties "to protect each other's rates." Such an understanding exists between the Continental North Atlantic Westbound Freight Conference and the French North Atlantic Westbound Freight Conference. Another agreement of this type provides that shipments from Shanghai and other North China ports to United States Atlantic and Gulf ports will move at the same rates, whether they are shipped direct or are transshipped at Pacific Coast ports. A similar agreement covers goods from Hong Kong and other Southern Chinese ports. An agreement between the North Atlantic Spanish Conference and the North Atlantic United Kingdom Conference provides for the maintenance of the same rates to Spain on direct shipments as for cargo transshipped at United Kingdom ports. An interesting series of three agreements provides for the same through rates to be quoted on Swiss exports to United States North Atlantic ports whether they move via Italian, French Mediterranean, French Atlantic, or other Continental ports. Inland transportation charges are equalized on the basis of the lowest official rate to any of the European ports of exit covered. The Pacific Westbound Conference and the Far East Conference represent lines which have at times competed with considerable intensity for the carriage of goods originating in the interior of the United States and destined to the Orient. An early agreement to cooperate and to take joint action on rates and related matters was terminated in 1930. However, in 1950 a new agreement to cooperate was signed by the members of these two conferences.

All three types of inter-conference agreements—the association of conferences, the collective patronage contract, and the mutual protection of rates—are designed to regulate, control, or eliminate the indirect competition of conference lines operating from or to alternate gateways, or providing alternate routing via transshipment. The extent to which such activities are in the public interest is, of course, arguable. Some cooperation among the seven conferences which regulate the carrying of freight from American North Atlantic ports to various segments of the European Continent are in all probability necessary if cutthroat competition is to be avoided. Many interior points both in America and Europe can be reached via different ports of entry; and furthermore the ports themselves are often made competitive by coastal carriers, so that cargo discharged at London, for example, may be readily transshipped to most continental ports.

An alternative would be the formation of one conference covering all trade from American North Atlantic gateways to all European destinations; but this would, depending on the voting procedures adopted, either have the disadvantage of giving lines operating in one section of the trade a direct voice in the determination of rates and other matters on business in which they do not participate, or it would enhance the powers of the few very large lines. Similar considerations apply to the second and third types of inter-conference understandings. Although the collective use of patronage contracts cannot fail to arouse suspicions, the essence of the matter is the same as that involved in the use of this tying arrangement by a single conference; since the conferences, which choose to employ this device jointly, could accomplish the same result by merging into one conference before entering into patronage contracts. Therefore, further consideration of this problem will be deferred until Chapter X.

In short, these agreements among conferences can be highly effective devices for extending the area over which competition is controlled. They are, therefore, an alternate to an enlargement of the participating conferences to a size which might make agreement more difficult of attainment, or which might require it to be achieved more by force, than is probably the case at present. The important point, however, is that agreements covering large areas are necessary, by one means or another, if indirect competition without them is sufficiently severe to cause rate wars. Yet by the same token, the control of indirect competition removes another of the forces which tend to keep conferences from achieving that degree of monopoly power which tempts them to abuse the privilege of being exempted from the anti-trust laws. A final answer will depend on the behavior of the conference or conferences, and their behavior will be substantially affected by the amount of competition that remains outside of their control. For example, if complete agreement is reached by the two conferences controlling freight traffic from all American ports to the Far East, does the competition from alternate sources of supply, e.g. Europe, and the actual and potential presence of tramps and non-conference lines from America on their own trade routes, combined with the possibility of new applicants for conference membership, provide sufficient restraint to keep the two conferences in line? The answers are not simple, and precise answers require careful periodic study of the situation on each major trade route; but deduction and common sense clearly indicate that the elimination of important sources of indirect competition, either by enlarged conferences or by inter-conference understandings, requires careful and continual scrutiny by some outside agency, if abuses are to be prevented from occurring and promptly eliminated if they do occur.

TRANSSHIPMENT AGREEMENTS

Agreements covering the transshipment of goods or passengers originating at or destined to ports under the jurisdiction of the United States must also be filed with the Maritime Board.[23] Most of these agreements cover transshipment at mainland American ports of goods coming from or destined to the non-contiguous territories of the United States.[24] Whereas the actual through rates, which may be either a combination of locals or a special joint through rate, are generally filed separately, the agreements indicate the basis for the division of the through charges and which carrier will pay the transshipping expenses. These agreements also customarily specify that if a conference covers the route from the port of origin to the port of

[23] The general counsel of the Board has recently (1950) expressed the opinion that all agreements for transshipments taking place at United States ports should be filed regardless of whether the port of origin or destination is under United States jurisdiction, since both of the carriers involved are subject to the Shipping Acts.

[24] When a party to the transshipment agreement operated in the domestic coastwise or intercoastal routes, the transshipment agreement has, since implementation of the Transportation Act of 1940, been filed with the Interstate Commerce Commission.

ultimate destination then the transshipment rates will correspond with the rates filed by that conference. Thus, the rates charged are the same, for example, on shipments from most European and Asiatic ports to Puerto Rico, whether the shipment has been direct or has been transshipped en route at a mainland American port. Although these agreements have the advantage of providing for the through billing of shipments (which would otherwise often require slower and more complicated handling), they do nevertheless extend the influence of conferences in numerous instances, by equating the rates quoted for direct and indirect routing. There were approximately 150 transshipment agreements in effect in 1950.

JOINT SERVICE AGREEMENTS

Another form of agreement which must be filed is the joint service agreement. These are agreements between independent shipping companies to cooperate in furnishing a liner service, or they may be agreements between owners of individual vessels to have their ships operated as a line by an operating agent. An example of the former is the "De La Rama Lines" which provides cargo and limited passenger service between ports on the Atlantic, Gulf, and Pacific Coasts of the United States and the ports of Japan, Korea, Formosa, Siberia, Manchuria, China, Hong Kong, Indo-China, and the Philippines. Members of the agreement are the De La Rama Steamship Co., Swedish East Asia Co., Ocean Steamship Company, China Mutual Steam Navigation Co., and the Nederlandsche Stoomvart Maatschappij "Ocean" N.V. In agreements of this type the voting strength and contribution to joint expenses are generally proportional to each member's contribution to the enterprise. Profits and liability in this agreement, however, are for the account of the individual vessel, and tickets and bills of lading must clearly show which of the participating companies is the actual carrier. Other agreements provide for a pooling of profits or losses on some basis such as deadweight ton days contributed to the joint enterprise. Provisions for terminating the agreement provide for advance notice.

The second type of joint service agreement, whereby separate shipowners have their vessels operated as a line by a managing operator, is particularly common in Norway where an important outlet for investment funds is ships. Investors may own one vessel or part of a vessel. These may be operated as tramps, or, by joining forces, several of these ships may place themselves under a managing agent and form a line. An example is the Pacific Orient Express Line which operates four vessels under a managing operator who handles, among other things, the pooling of earnings and expenses.

The significance of these agreements is that they provide a method by which relatively small shipowning interests can pool their resources and organize a liner service that can effectively maintain its position vis-à-vis the largest owner-operators. So long as vessels suitable to the trade are available, a new line can be formed, even if the owners and their vessels are of different nationality. This obviously tends to narrow the distance between potential and actual competition. It is interesting to note the several nationalities represented in the "De La Rama Lines," and the fact that the overseas agents representing the Pacific Orient Express Line were Swedish and American. There were approximately 50 joint service agreements in effect in 1950.

POOLING AGREEMENTS

Agreements to pool revenue or traffic, though far less numerous than ordinary conference agreements, are not uncommon and frequently supplement regular conference understandings. In 1950 only two pools were operating in United States trades—one from Gulf ports to Liverpool and Manchester,[25] and another covering passenger traffic on Puget Sound ferries running between American and Canadian ports—but Maritime Board approval had been requested for three additional pools; two covering cargo moving between the United States and Chile, and one covering coffee from Colombia. On October 1, 1940, however, twenty-eight pooling agreements had been on file with the Maritime Commission.[26] These included, among others, cargo movements on the following United States routes: At-

[25] This agreement divided pooled revenue evenly between the British-flag Harrison Line and the American-flag Lykes U.K. Line. State buying of several of the most important commodities moving in this trade, which gave control of the routing to His Majesty's Government and American statutory requirements that 50 per cent of exports purchased with funds provided by the United States government must be carried, if possible, by American vessels, raises the interesting question of whether this pooling agreement altered appreciably the distribution of revenues that would have prevailed if the pool had not existed.

[26] U.S. Maritime Commission *Annual Report*, 1941, p. 32. Additional pooling agreements or other private arrangements between foreign carriers might have existed, and might still exist, unbeknownst to the Commission, and the Board. It is doubtful, however, if any United States flag carriers would take the risk of engaging in such practices illegally, since their actions are much more apt to come to the government's attention, and the Commission's approval was not difficult to obtain.

lantic Coast ports to Southwest, South and East Africa; Atlantic Coast ports to Poland; Atlantic Coast ports to the West Coast of South America; Atlantic Coast ports to and from Colombian ports; New York to and from Bremen; and coffee from Central America to Pacific Coast ports.

The pool may cover only one commodity, several commodities, or it may cover all commodities except for a few specifically exempted items. Revenue pools are the more usual, and generally divide the net revenue earned on the commodities covered by the agreement on the basis of past performance. Net revenue is usually computed by allowing specific deductions of so much per ton to cover out-of-pocket expense, though an additional allowance is granted by some pools for calls at outports. These agreements customarily specify the number of sailings each participant is to make within the pooling period, or provide for a rotation of sailings, or require each member to provide a stipulated share of carrying capacity. If a line fails to maintain the specified number of sailings or carrying capacity, its allotted percentage is usually reduced. Some pools penalize a participant who fails to carry a stipulated minimum volume of traffic. For example, the pool which before the war covered most commodities moving from New York, Boston and Philadelphia to or through Gdynia and Danzig and which provided that each of the two participants should receive 50 per cent of the pooled revenue, also specified:

"If, according to the complete yearly statistics of cargo carried under this agreement either line has carried less than 45 per cent as its share, then the difference between 45 per cent and any lower percentage carried will be added to the 50 per cent of the freight revenue due to the line carrying the surplus. For example, on annual carryings showing, say, a proportion of 40 per cent and 60 per cent respectively for the two lines, the line carrying the surplus will receive an additional 5 per cent of the pooled freight revenue." Some agreements provide for a pro rata increase or decrease in the total number of sailings if sudden and substantial changes occur in the volume of business. The pool members often obligate themselves to accept all cargo, whether favorable or unfavorable for carriage, as it comes along, and they may also cooperate in other ways which are of benefit to the shippers. Agreements of this type almost invariably require the participants to observe rates, practices and allowances which have been mutually agreed upon; or, if a conference covers the route, then the members of the pool agree to observe the conference tariff.[27] Pool agreements generally arise out of conference agreements whose efforts at self-regulation the pools are designed to supplement. The pooling agreements also generally provide that disputes among participants, which they are unable to resolve by themselves, should be submitted to arbitration. Copies of ships' manifests are customarily deposited with a pool secretary, who submits accounts promptly to the members, on the basis of which a settlement is made at specified intervals—usually annually, semi-annually, or quarterly. Whereas pools usually include all lines regularly operating on the route covered, this is not invariably so, and the prewar agreement for pooling revenues in the outbound South African route between five British lines and one German line did not include the American-flag carrier operating in this service.

What are perhaps the most interesting pooling arrangements to have occurred in United States trades in recent years was the series of agreements which covered the trade between the Atlantic Coast of the United States and the ports of Rotterdam, Antwerp, Hamburg, and Bremen. Both eastbound and westbound competition had been extremely severe; since there was not only intense rivalry among the carriers but among the ports as well, especially for traffic originating in or destined to the interior of Germany, Czechoslovakia, Austria, Switzerland, and Roumania. As early as 1894 a westbound pool was formed on this route by German, Dutch, and Belgian lines, and this continued in effect until the outbreak of war in 1914. At that time the Northern or German lines received 61½ per cent of the pooled funds and the Western or Belgian and Dutch lines' share was 38½ per cent. With the return of peace and the restoration of the German merchant marine, competition once again became bitter, and as a result the North Atlantic Continental Freight Conference (eastbound), and the Continental North Atlantic Westbound Freight Conference did not succeed in preventing rate wars, unequal treatment of shippers, and other undesirable practices. In 1928 some of the carriers operating westbound from Rotterdam and Antwerp again formed a pool which relieved the situation to some extent. Within a few years this was followed by the formation of separate pools covering the westbound traffic from the German ports, a pooling agreement between the westbound groups, and an eastbound

[27] For a partial exception to this, see the pooling agreements with the U. S. Navigation Co. described below.

pool covering traffic from New York to Hamburg.[28] This time an American-flag line participated in the various arrangements, and the pooled revenue was divided between the westbound groups so that 52 per cent went to the Northern Group and 48 per cent to the Western Group. All of these agreements were terminated during World War II.

An unusual feature of these agreements was the inclusion of a non-conference operator in two of them.[29] The eastbound pool, formed in 1930 to cover traffic from New York to Hamburg, gave 86½ per cent of the pool revenue to the two conference lines—the United States Lines and the Hamburg American Line—and 13½ per cent to the non-conference U.S. Navigation Co.[30] Although the latter concern did not agree to charge conference rates, it did agree to provide not less than twelve nor more than twenty-four sailings each year, and it agreed furthermore not to extend its service to other American and Continental ports without the sanction of the other lines. In 1933 a westbound pooling agreement was negotiated covering traffic from Hamburg and Bremen to New York. In addition to the three signatories of the New York-to-Hamburg pool this latter agreement included the North German Lloyd. The U.S. Navigation Co. obligated itself to sailing requirements and port restrictions similar to those it had agreed to in the New York to Hamburg agreement, for which it was to receive 8½ per cent of the pooled westbound revenue, part of which was later furnished by carriers running from Rotterdam and Antwerp.[31]

The U.S. Navigation Co. had, for a number of years, operated slower cargo vessels than those generally operated by the conference lines, and it had attracted mainly low-grade commodities (e.g. flour, rags, asphalt, lubricating oil, grain, potash, wood pulp, scrap metal, and scrap rubber) by charging lower rates than the conference car-

[28] In 1933, an additional eastbound revenue pool, covering the movement of unboxed automobiles, trucks, tractors, and airplanes to Belgium and Holland was formed.

[29] For a description of other methods used to throttle the non-conference competition of the U.S. Navigation Co., see U.S. Nav. Co. v. Cunard S. S. Co. et al., 284 U.S. 474 (1932).

[30] These percentages were actually 86.446892 and 13.553108 and were based on the respective percentage of cargo earnings during the previous three years. For 1938 the distribution was altered to 88 per cent and 12 per cent.

[31] Effective in 1938, the U. S. Navigation Co. share was reduced to 6.375 per cent. In 1936 a pooling arrangement between the lines sailing westbound from the German ports and those sailing from Holland and Belgium came into operation. There were also provisions which connected the westbound pools and the eastbound pool so that in effect they formed an interrelated structure.

riers. Immediately after the pooling agreements were consummated the U.S. Navigation Co. reduced its sailings in the Hamburg trade from 24 to 12 per annum. As a result it was always an undercarrier in both pools, and from 1931 through 1938 collected from them almost one and three quarter millions of dollars. The arrangements were apparently satisfactory to all parties to the agreements, since at hearings on the matter held by the Maritime Commission in 1939 they all were in accord in desiring their continuance. The U.S. Navigation Co. continued to charge lower rates than the conference lines, although the agreements made it unnecessary to engage in arbitrary rate-cutting; and furthermore, it shared handsomely in the pooled revenues. The conference carriers, on the other hand, also fared well. In return for the payments made to the U.S. Navigation Co. they benefited by the decreased competition from this concern and from the increased stability of conference rates. In fact, the conference increased some rates after the pooling agreements became effective, but the Maritime Commission found no evidence that these increases "were the direct results of the agreement."[32] Furthermore, the continued service of the U.S. Navigation Co. at less than conference rates provided the conference members some protection against competition from tramps and other potential non-conference lines.

One cannot help wondering about the effect of these arrangements on the general public. In one of the few cases concerned with pools the Commission held that the pools in the North Atlantic trades described above were not detrimental to the commerce of the United States, nor unfair or unjustly discriminatory to the carriers involved, and went on to state, "There have been no complaints from shippers against the agreements, and there is no evidence that the agreements have operated to deprive shippers of adequate facilities for the movement of their goods."[33] There is no comment regarding the fairness of the rate level before or after the agreements came into effect, but rates were more stable after the agreements than before. Shippers (or consignees) were probably able to pass on to their customers or suppliers most of the rate increases that did occur; so it is not astonishing that there were no complaints from shippers. The final incidence of the rate increases is impossible to ascertain, but it is unlikely that the impact on the final consumers was large even if all the

[32] Agreements 1438 and 5260-5264, 2 U.S.M.C. 228 (1939).
[33] ibid.

increase, plus any pyramiding effect,[34] was passed along to them, because during this period of depression freight rates were high in only one year—1937.

Nonetheless arrangements of this type cannot be regarded with complacency, and their effect on the general public in periods when ship operators are in a better position to exploit more completely the advantage thus provided cannot be dismissed without much closer investigation than the Maritime Commission and its predecessors gave them. While it is true that pooling may at times help to stabilize rates, to improve vessel utilization, to eliminate some other wasteful and discriminatory practices, and to reduce competition, it seems that the Commission may have taken too tolerant a view of them. The Commission has probably been correct in stressing their usefulness in regulating and spacing sailings and in allocating ports. These activities may very well assist in providing shippers with more convenient schedules and in the avoidance of the expensive and wasteful practice of having all lines attempt to serve all ports.[35] But the Commission, in explaining pooling agreements to our Good Neighbors at an Inter-American Maritime Conference in 1940, also employed some rather dubious arguments. In stating that "Pool agreements also tend to remove the temptation for carriers to employ unfair and dishonest methods of competition in securing traffic, . . ."[36] the Commission seemed to be acknowledging either its dereliction in failing to prevent such practices or its inability to do so; for the ability, if not the temptation, to do such things should have been removed by the Shipping Act of 1916. Furthermore, the Commission's contention that an advantage of pools is that they protect weaker lines by assuring them an allotment which may be somewhat higher than the circumstances would otherwise warrant[37] is an argument in favor of having efficient operators subsidize the inefficient. The Colombian delegation inquired if a monopoly did not exist when: (1) owing to the gradual elimination of competition only two shipping companies remained to serve a trade route, and they had in turn eliminated rate competition by forming a conference; (2) the two conference lines employed exclusive patronage contracts; and (3) in addition to the

---

[34] "Pyramiding effect" refers to the practice of adding a percentage mark-up to the cost of merchandise to determine the price at which it will be offered for sale. To the extent to which such pricing is practiced an increase in cost at an early stage of distribution causes a more substantial increase in later stages.

[35] Inter-American Maritime Conference, *op.cit.*, pp. 263-265.

[36] *loc.cit.*   [37] *loc.cit.*

161

foregoing the two companies had signed a pooling agreement under which they distributed equally the freight revenues.[38] It is not surprising that the Colombian delegation was not satisfied with the Commission's explanation.

Despite the internal struggles between pool members, which occur when an aggressive line attempts to improve its participation in the shared revenue, pooling appears to be an excellent means of arresting competition and thereby of retarding development and preserving the *status quo*. It is doubtful if there are many instances when legitimate and constructive objectives cannot be achieved by a conference without resorting to the device of pooling which by increasing the monopoly characteristics and power of the participants tends either to invite abuses or to encourage the extension of such malpractices as may already exist. In the future the Federal Maritime Board should scrutinize pooling agreements with great care and with more concern for their economic implications than seems to have been accorded them in the past. The Board should remember that absence of shipper protests may not be a significant indication of harmlessness or merit, and that they can give a broad and economically sophisticated interpretation to the consideration of what is "detrimental to the commerce of the United States" as well as a narrowly legalistic content.

Since the foregoing was written, the Federal Maritime Board has approved two pooling agreements covering trade between the United States and Chile. One pool covers freighting operations of the American-flag Grace Line and the Chilean-flag Compania Sud Americana de Vapores (C.S.A.V.) on all southbound cargo, with specified minor exceptions,[39] shipped from the Atlantic Coast of the United States to Chile, and on all northbound copper metal from Chile to United States Atlantic ports. The second pool covers the southbound freighting operations only of the American-flag Gulf & South American Line and C.S.A.V. on shipments from American Gulf ports to Chile.[40] Both pools provide for minimum sailing requirements and for an arbitrary division of the pooled net revenues. The members of the pools are also members of the Atlantic & Gulf-West Coast of South America Conference and of the West Coast South America North-

---

[38] *ibid.*, p. 144.

[39] Cargo originating in Europe or Canada, and cargo destined to Bolivia is excluded from the arrangement, as are mail and passengers' baggage including passengers' automobiles.

[40] The Grace Line has a 50 per cent interest in the Gulf & South American Line.

bound Conference which regulates respectively the southbound and northbound freight movements between the American Atlantic and Gulf coasts and Chilean ports. A complaint was filed by the West Coast line, an operator of Danish-flag vessels. The West Coast Line, also a member of both conferences, alleged that it had requested membership in both pools, but had been refused; and that therefore the operation of these agreements, in combination with the Chilean government's import control system which provided that 50 per cent of Chilean imports had to move on Chilean vessels, would permit the members of these pools to effect a complete monopoly of the trade. This transport requirement had already been protested by the governments of the United States, United Kingdom, Norway, Sweden, the Netherlands, and Denmark. The even greater discriminatory features implicit in adding these pooling agreements to the Chilean import license restrictions was evident, and led the Danish government to submit a protest to the State Department in Washington. After the signing of the proposed pooling agreements, but prior to their approval by the Federal Maritime Board, the Chilean import permit system was amended so that the 50 per cent restriction was made applicable to shipments on "national or associated" vessels instead of exclusively "national" vessels as formerly. (This may have been in response to the protests of other governments.) Under the terms of the amended regulation, members of the pools were considered "associated" carriers, and therefore Grace was an "associated" carrier on the North Atlantic Run, and Gulf & South American became an "associated" carrier on the Gulf route. Furthermore, Chile announced, very shortly thereafter, the establishment of a free list (i.e. cargo not subject to import licensing), which included approximately one-half of the complainant's (the West Coast Line's) southbound carryings.

The Federal Maritime Board rendered its decision in 1951, and held that "an agreement to pool earnings by two or more carriers in a particular trade is not per se unlawfully discriminatory or a violation of the Shipping Act, 1916, as amended. Nor does the refusal by members of a pool to admit an additional applicant necessarily render the continued operation of the pool unjustly discriminatory. . . ."[41] The Board pointed out that it "is only able to decide cases on the evidence of existing facts and the reasonable deductions to be

[41] West Coast Line v. Grace Line, et al., Federal Maritime Board Docket No. 705, decided May 1951.

drawn therefrom. It is not authorized to base decisions on speculative possibilities." "However," the Board continued, "a finding at this time that the operations of the pooling agreements in question do not today result in unfair discrimination, does not close the door to a re-examination of the same pooling agreements at a future date if changed conditions bring changed results."[42]

The complainant's brief estimated that if the agreement had been in effect in 1950 the Grace Line would have had to pay C.S.A.V. approximately $300,000. What advantages were expected in return for such an appreciable outlay? The evidence indicates that there were a number of factors contributing to the Grace Line's willingness to become a party to this arrangement, but the Federal Maritime Board concluded that "the Chilean [import] regulations were clearly dominant."[43] In light of this complaint it is interesting to note that in July 1951 the Board decided to investigate the effects of pooling on American subsidized carriers and on the competitive structure of the routes they serve.

CONFERENCES IN WARTIME

In the early years of World War II, before the United States became a belligerent, members of shipping conferences in United States trades made every effort to maintain the conference system by permitting lines which had been forced to suspend or withdraw their services to remain as inactive members. The Maritime Commission, in an effort to prevent an unwarranted increase in rates such as had occurred in the First World War, closely scrutinized, after September 1939, the rates filed by freight conferences and by individual lines. In February 1941, as the supply of tonnage became tighter, the Commission directed the various freight conferences to notify it in advance of any contemplated rate increases and to accompany the notice with a statement supporting the necessity for the proposed changes. While these instructions tended to restrict rate increases, they did not prevent a general rise in the level of rates. By May 1, 1941, the Commission considered that transportation charges had reached the maximum justifiable under existing conditions; and accordingly gave notice to this effect to United States vessel owners and to freight conferences operating outside of the European war zone.

A few days later, on May 20, a second notice called upon these

[42] *loc.cit.* [43] *loc.cit.*

same carriers and conferences to cancel immediately any increases which might have been made after May 1. Provision was made for allowing increases on specific commodities where the facts warranted them; but the general intent was to freeze rates at the level which existed on April 30, 1941.

Although the Commission was in a position to "influence" the actions of subsidized United States operators, and could threaten to disapprove conference agreements, this program was essentially voluntary, since the Commission could not bring any legal sanctions to bear on either American or foreign operators.

The Commission's authority to control rates in the country's foreign commerce was very weak, consisting solely of its right to disband conferences. In a period when ship tonnage is scarce, such as during a war, the lines have little need for conferences; since they can operate alone without fear of cutthroat competition. While a majority of the conferences and carriers showed a willingness to comply, their efforts were soon nullified by those who took advantage of the situation. Charter rates were not controlled in any way, with the result that shipowners who wished to avoid the Commission's strictures could, along with all others who had vessels available, charter their ships at any rate that the market would support. The Commission ruefully observed that "because of the interdependence between charter rates and berth rates, it is practically impossible to control the level of one without a control of the level of the other."[44]

To meet this situation, the Ship Warrants Act was passed by Congress, and became effective July 14, 1941. This legislation not only gave a measure of control over charter rates but also strengthened the Commission's authority over berth rates. A further extension of wartime rate control took place under the newly formed War Shipping Administration after American entry into the war, but sheds no light on the activities of conferences whose rate-making function lapsed for the duration. Nevertheless, most conferences in American trades maintained their organizations in skeleton form after eliminating, on the Commission's orders, alien memberships. The Commission continued to utilize these skeleton organizations to publish and file tariffs, and to provide information on operating costs, practices and conditions prevailing in foreign ports, and for other such purposes. Although the action of conferences in helping to keep rates

[44] U.S. Mar. Com. *Annual Report*, 1942, p. 42.

from rising inordinately was frequently disappointing, the Commission certainly received far more cooperation from conference lines in holding rates down than it did from non-conference carriers and tramps.[45] The end of the war brought about a marked increase in conference activities as new conferences were organized and as old conferences were revived and extended.[46] As soon as vessels were returned to regular commercial operation the conference system resumed its activities, for the most part, pretty much where it had left off.

A comparison of the conference agreements described by the Alexander Committee in its report to Congress in 1914 with agreements filed with the Shipping Board after the First World War indicates that the conference system also came through that war essentially intact.

[45] Hobart S. Perry, "Ocean Rate Regulation, World War II," *Harvard Business Review*, xxi (Winter 1943), pp. 244-245.

[46] U.S. Mar. Com. *Annual Report*, 1945, pp. 16-17.

CHAPTER IX
CONFERENCE AND NON-CONFERENCE COMPETITION
IN U.S. FOREIGN TRADE

In the summary of its report, the Alexander Committee, in 1914, observed that "The foregoing chapters contain a description of 80 steamship agreements and conference arrangements, which, when considered collectively, show that as regards nearly every foreign trade route practically all the established lines operating to and from American ports work in harmonious cooperation, either through written or oral agreements, conference arrangements, or gentlemen's understandings." The current situation is not appreciably different. The requirement to file all such agreements with the Maritime Board, or its predecessors, has presumably converted all oral understandings to written commitments, and this accounts for some of the larger number of agreements—109—now on file.[1] Most of the additional conference agreements are accounted for by the introduction, after World War I, of liner services on American trade routes not previously provided with regular, direct scheduled sailings. A detailed comparison of the present geographical distribution of conferences with that reported in 1914 provides little of interest, but it is perhaps not without significance that the pattern is still substantially the same, after allowing for the new post World War I liner services.

Conferences generally control traffic from one group of ports to another group of ports, or from one coastal area known as a *range* to another, although some conferences cover more than one range while others apply to but a single port. The coastal frontage of the United States is divided into four major ranges: (1) *The North Atlantic Range* runs from Portland, Maine, to Hampton Roads, Virginia, and includes, in addition to these ports, Boston, New York, Philadelphia, and Baltimore; (2) *The South Atlantic Range* extends from Wilmington, North Carolina, to Jacksonville, Florida, and in-

[1] Unless otherwise indicated, all statements regarding conferences or conference membership in this chapter describe the situation as of January 18, 1950, according to Maritime Commission records. Only a few relatively minor changes occurred in the following two years.

167

cludes Savannah and Charleston; (3) *The Gulf Range* runs from Tampa, Florida, to Brownsville, Texas, and includes Mobile, New Orleans, Galveston, and Houston; (4) *The Pacific Range* covers the entire Pacific Coast of the United States including, among other ports, Seattle, Portland, Oregon, San Francisco, and Los Angeles. Canadian ports are included by some conferences operating in the United States trades; but even when Canadian commerce is covered by a separate agreement the rates and other conditions of shipment are frequently the same as those applicable to the United States, except that payment in Canadian dollars is permitted.[2]

FREIGHT CONFERENCES IN THE EUROPEAN TRADES

The trade routes between America and Europe are extremely important to both continents, and the conferences in these trades are among the oldest in American commerce. The relationships of these conferences provide a comprehensive view of some of the more highly developed conference structures in American ocean transportation. For this reason the conferences regulating freight traffic between North America and Europe will be examined in some detail.

Freight traffic from the United States to Europe and the Near East is regulated by a large number of conferences. Cargo from North Atlantic ports comes under the jurisdiction of eight conferences, two inter-conference agreements, and two associations concerned with port matters—one in New York and one in Liverpool. Six conferences are affiliated with the Trans-Atlantic Associated Freight Conferences which describes its purpose to be the coordination of activities in respect to non-competitive matters and the provision of administrative organization and clerical work for the member conferences.[3] These conferences are: North Atlantic Continental Freight Conference; North Atlantic French Atlantic Freight Conference; North Atlantic Baltic Freight Conference; North Atlantic United Kingdom Freight Conference; North Atlantic Mediterranean Freight Conference; and North Atlantic Red Sea and Gulf of Aden Freight Conference.[4] All six of these conferences as well as the coordinating con-

---

[2] When the Canadian dollar has been at an appreciable discount for more than a few weeks the general practice has been to raise rates to and from Canada by a percentage approximating the discount.

[3] The Morocco, Algeria, Tunisia-North Atlantic Westbound Freight Conference covering goods shipped to America is also affiliated with the Associated Conferences. For additional information, see Chapter VIII.

[4] The names of conferences are generally descriptive of the areas covered, but their titles are not always completely unambiguous. For example, take the destinations

ference have the same chairman. The Trans-Atlantic Freight Conference (New York), also under the same chairman, is likewise affiliated with this parent conference and deals with local matters at New York in connection with the transportation of freight from that port to European destinations.

Two conferences operating in this area, the North Atlantic Portuguese Freight Conference and the North Atlantic Spanish Conference, are not affiliated with the Trans-Atlantic Associated Freight Conferences. However, the Spanish conference has an agreement with the North Atlantic United Kingdom Freight Conference regulating competition between cargo transshipped at England and cargo shipped directly to Spain. Furthermore, the conference controlling traffic to the United Kingdom is informally affiliated with the Atlantic Eastbound Freight Association at Liverpool which deals with problems arising at British ports in connection with freight from Canadian Atlantic and United States Atlantic and Gulf ports.

A separate conference known as the South Atlantic Steamship Conference regulates traffic from South Atlantic ports to practically all of the destinations covered by the eight conferences from United States North Atlantic ports. Three of the five lines belonging to the South Atlantic Steamship Conference are also members of the Trans-Atlantic Associated Freight Conferences and of several of the affiliated rings.

From the Gulf, freight traffic to Europe is supervised by four conferences, two inter-conference agreements, and one port association. The Gulf Associated Freight Conferences, which deals with administrative matters, includes as its affiliates the Gulf Scandinavian and Baltic Sea Ports Conference, Gulf Mediterranean Ports Confer-

---

covered by the conferences mentioned in the text. The North Atlantic Continental Freight Conference covers freight traffic loaded anywhere from Portland, Me., to Hampton Roads, Va., that is destined to ports in Belgium, Holland, and Germany (except German Baltic ports). The Baltic Conference covers direct and transshipment traffic to Denmark, Finland, Iceland, Norway, Poland, Sweden, as well as to all Continental and Russian ports served via the Baltic. The French Atlantic Conference covers freight to French Atlantic ports in the Dunkirk-Bordeaux range; the Mediterranean Conference covers both direct and transshipment traffic to all ports (except Spanish Mediterranean ports) served on the Mediterranean Sea from Gibraltar to Port Said including Adriatic and Black Sea ports and from Casablanca to Port Said inclusive. The Spanish Conference covers the Spanish destinations on both the Atlantic and Mediterranean, while the Portuguese Conference covers that country. The United Kingdom Conference applies to traffic moving to the Irish Free State as well as to cargo for England, Scotland, Wales, and Northern Ireland. It should be noted that conferences delineate their territories so as not to overlap, and so as to leave no ports uncovered.

169

ence, Gulf United Kingdom Conference, Gulf French Atlantic Hamburg Range Freight Conference.[5] The latter two have an agreement between themselves covering contracts with exporters and the observance by each of rates on transshipment cargo. The Gulf United Kingdom Conference is also affiliated with the Atlantic Eastbound Freight Association at Liverpool.

A separate conference known as the Pacific Coast European Conference covers direct traffic from United States Pacific Coast ports to all European destinations as well as transshipments to several other parts of the world. The Pacific Coast Eastbound United Kingdom Conference Association at London coordinates the action of parties to the foregoing agreement at ports in the British Isles.

In addition to these conferences from the North Atlantic, South Atlantic, Gulf, and Pacific Coast, two shipping lines form the Great Lakes London and Bordeaux-Hamburg Range Eastbound Conference which covers freight traffic from United States and Canadian Great Lakes ports as well as from the St. Lawrence River, Nova Scotia, New Brunswick, and Newfoundland.

In January 1950, eighty-five companies were recorded as members of one or more of the freight conferences supervising traffic from the United States to European and Near Eastern destinations. Some of these companies operated more than one line or service from America to Europe. Nonetheless, one should not conclude that this total necessarily implies a highly competitive situation. In the first place, an account of inter-corporate relationships, if it could be made, would reduce the number of independent units somewhat.[6] Secondly, some conference members may be inactive, but have retained their membership for possible future use.[7] Finally, not all the lines operate

[5] The Gulf-South and East African Conference is also affiliated with the Gulf Associated Freight Conferences.

[6] Adjustment for wholly owned subsidiaries of publicly owned shipping corporations is not difficult, but only reduces the total number of companies by five or six. Most of the eighty-five companies are privately owned, and information regarding their subsidiaries, and inter-company relationships is not available.

[7] Prior to 1946, when the Maritime Commission held, in a clear and strong decision, that bona fide liner operators applying for conference membership must be admitted (see Chapter VII), it was customary for a steamship company which discontinued common carrier service on a particular route to retain its conference membership in order to provide for its possible future return. The "dead hand" or voice of these inactive members was sometimes used to exclude from membership a new active line seeking admittance, but recent rulings of the Commission have discouraged this; so that at present many conferences provide that a member which has not operated for a specific period of time loses the right to vote until active service is resumed.

between the same terminals. There is also a good deal of overlapping in the membership of the various conferences, which cannot help but influence the amount of competition among them.

Some of these relationships may appear more clearly from an examination of the conferences regulating traffic from American North Atlantic ports to Europe, graphic representation of which is provided in the accompanying chart. The Trans-Atlantic Associated Freight Conferences, for example, had 51 members in January 1950. (It is customary for all members of the six affiliated conferences to belong to the Trans-Atlantic Associated Freight Conferences.) All 47 members of the Trans-Atlantic Freight Conference (New York) belonged to the Associated Conferences.[8] All seven members of the North Atlantic French Atlantic Conference are among the eleven members of the North Atlantic Continental Conference. Seven of the seventeen members of the North Atlantic Baltic Conference also belong to the North Atlantic Continental Freight Conference. Of the thirteen members of the North Atlantic United Kingdom Conference four belong to the Baltic Conference, four to the French Atlantic Conference, six to the Continental Conference, and two to the North Atlantic Spanish Conference.

Such overlapping is common, and several of the larger shipping companies belong not only to several conferences from North Atlantic ports to Europe but also to conferences from the Gulf and Pacific Coast. The Holland-America Line, for example, belongs to four conferences from the North Atlantic to Europe, as well as to three conferences running from the Gulf to European destinations, and in addition is a member of the Pacific Coast European Conference. The United States Lines belongs to four conferences from North Atlantic ports to Europe; while the Waterman Steamship Corporation belongs to four conferences from the North Atlantic to Europe, three from the Gulf to Europe, as well as to the South Atlantic Steamship Conference, and the Pacific Coast European Conference. Cunard White Star Limited belongs to five conferences from the North Atlantic to Europe; and the French Line belongs to a similar number in addition to holding memberships in one conference from the Gulf and in the Pacific European conference. The Ellerman and Bucknall interests are also widely represented in con-

[8] The four members of the Associated Conferences which are not also members of the Port Association at New York do not operate from that port to Europe.

171

FREIGHT CONFERENCES REGULATING TRAFFIC FROM THE U.S. N. ATLANTIC RANGE TO EUROPE AND THE NEAR EAST

(AS OF JANUARY 1950)

10—— NUMBER OF MEMBERS BELONGING TO THE TWO CONFERENCES CONNECTED BY THIS LINE

TRANS-ATLANTIC FREIGHT CONFERENCE (NEW YORK)
47 MEMBERS
C. R. ANDREWS, CHAIRMAN

TRANS-ATLANTIC ASSOCIATED FREIGHT CONFERENCES
51 MEMBERS
C. R. ANDREWS, CHAIRMAN

N. ATLANTIC UNITED KINGDOM FREIGHT CONFERENCE
13 MEMBERS
C. R. ANDREWS, CHAIRMAN

AGREEMENT BETWEEN N. ATLANTIC UNITED KINGDOM AND NORTH ATLANTIC SPANISH CONFERENCES
16 MEMBERS

NORTH ATLANTIC BALTIC FREIGHT CONFERENCE
17 MEMBERS
C. R. ANDREWS, CHAIRMAN

N. ATLANTIC-FRENCH ATLANTIC FREIGHT CONFERENCE
7 MEMBERS
C. R. ANDREWS, CHAIRMAN

NORTH-ATLANTIC CONTINENTAL FREIGHT CONFERENCE
11 MEMBERS
C. R. ANDREWS, CHAIRMAN

ATLANTIC EASTBOUND FREIGHT ASSOCIATION
17 MEMBERS
(LIVERPOOL)

NORTH ATLANTIC SPANISH CONFERENCE
3 MEMBERS
F. ROTHE. CHAIRMAN

N. ATLANTIC PORTUGUESE FREIGHT CONFERENCE
15 MEMBERS
E.A. McDONALD, CHAIRMAN

N. ATLANTIC MEDITERRANEAN FREIGHT CONFERENCE
29 MEMBERS
C. R. ANDREWS, CHAIRMAN

NORTH ATLANTIC, RED SEA, AND GULF OF ADEN FREIGHT CONFERENCE
7 MEMBERS
C. R. ANDREWS, CHAIRMAN

ferences in these trades.[9] All of the foregoing figures of conference membership are exclusive of memberships in the Trans-Atlantic Associated Freight Conferences and the Trans-Atlantic Freight Conference (New York) to which these lines also belong. Before World War II a series of pooling arrangements also influenced competition on the trans-Atlantic route.[10]

Unlike traffic moving to the Far East, Pacific Coast lines do not customarily compete with carriers from Atlantic and Gulf ports for business moving to Europe. However, there is some rivalry among North Atlantic, South Atlantic, and Gulf ports for traffic originating in the interior of the country, and in 1920 the conferences controlling trade from these three ranges entered an agreement establishing differential rates on some commodities lower from North Atlantic ports than from South Atlantic gateways, and the latter in turn were lower than for shipments via Gulf ports. This agreement was disapproved by the Shipping Board in 1925.[11] In the latter part of the interwar period additional competition for traffic originating in the Middle West appeared, during the season of open navigation, when direct liner service was inaugurated from Great Lakes ports to Europe. Keen competition also exists among the various ports on any given range. This competition between ports on the North Atlantic range and between the railroads serving them has been so intense that a system of port differential rail rates was developed. Since these are railroad rates, and not ocean rates, they are under the jurisdiction of the Interstate Commerce Commission, and not a matter over which shipping conferences have any control.[12]

In addition to ships operated by conference members, tramp shipping has appeared whenever the volume of bulk shipments has been sufficiently large, and this occurred frequently in the postwar period as large quantities of American food, feed, fertilizer, and coal were shipped to the war-devastated European Continent. There has also

[9] Several of the larger shipping organizations belonged to more than thirty conferences and associations controlling American commerce with various parts of the world.

[10] *supra*. Chapter VIII.

[11] See Port Differential Investigation, 1 U.S.S.B. 61 (1925).

[12] These differential railroad freight rates are available on export commodities moving in carload lots from points in the Middle West to ports on the Atlantic seaboard. They provide similar rates to New York and Boston, but slightly lower rates on cargo moving through Philadelphia, and still lower rates on shipments via Baltimore or Norfolk. These port differential rail rates do not apply only to Europe, but are applicable to all export shipments. They were severely criticized by the U.S. Supreme Court late in 1951.

been substantial independent liner competition offered by non-conference carriers. The amount of non-conference competition is somewhat greater at the time this is written (1950) than before World War II. This has resulted from a concatenation of events, of which the more important probably are: (1) the disruption of normal trading and shipping connections during the war; (2) the very greatly reduced participation of Axis shipping; (3) the opportunity offered to concerns which previously operated in the tramp and charter market to enter the liner business by purchasing vessels suitable for liner operation from the government's war-built fleet; (4) the abundant volume of traffic; (5) the great importance of shipments by the United States government; and (6) the absence, for several years, of the exclusive patronage contract system, which was probably due at first to the abundance of business and the legal inability of the United States government to participate in such schemes, and finally to the restraining order prohibiting their use that was issued by a federal court at the request of one of the independent lines. Since these matters are developed in some detail later in this chapter, they will not be described more fully at this point. Suffice it to say that in November and December 1950 there were four non-conference lines operating between North Atlantic United States ports and European Atlantic ports; and there were four other independent services between North Atlantic America and the Mediterranean. Two additional independent lines ran between the Gulf and European Atlantic ports, and another connected the Gulf with the Mediterranean.

Freight moving westward from Europe and the Near East to the United States is controlled by fifteen conferences and four interconference agreements. The North Atlantic Westbound Freight Association covers traffic from Great Britain and Ireland to United States North Atlantic, South Atlantic, and Gulf ports. In addition, the following nine conferences regulate cargo moving to the American North Atlantic range: Norway-North Atlantic Conference; Spain-Portugal North Atlantic Range Conference; French North Atlantic Westbound Freight Conference; Marseilles-North Atlantic U. S. A. Freight Conference, Continental North Atlantic Westbound Freight Conference; The West Coast of Italy, Sicilian, and Adriatic Ports-North Atlantic Range Conference; Swiss-North Atlantic Freight Conference; Middle East Mediterranean Westbound Freight Conference; and Morocco, Algeria, Tunisia-North Atlantic Westbound Freight

Conference. As in the case of the eastbound conferences there is considerable duplication of membership since some companies belong to two or more of these rings. Furthermore, members of the Continental and French North Atlantic conferences are parties to an agreement to protect each others' rates. And the members of these two conferences together with members of the Marseilles and Italian conferences are all parties to an agreement providing for "the stabilization of Ocean Freight Rates, and, insofar as possible, parity of such rates" on cargo (other than cargo within the scope of the Swiss-North Atlantic Freight Conference) which is common to the European territory served by two or more of the conferences and moves to U.S. North Atlantic ports. The Swiss-North Atlantic Freight Conference covers freight originating in Switzerland and upper Alsace shipped via ports served by members of the Continental and French North Atlantic Conferences. The Swiss Conference has separate agreements with the Italian Conference and the Marseilles Conference which permits cargo originating in Switzerland to move with equal facility and at equal through rates to the United States via a Mediterranean or Continental Atlantic gateway.

In addition to the North Atlantic Westbound Freight Association, covering cargo from the United Kingdom and Ireland, traffic to American Gulf ports from continental European ports between Bayonne, France, and Hamburg, Germany, is controlled by the Continental-U.S.A. Gulf Westbound Freight Conference. Cargo from Europe to the Pacific Coast of the United States is regulated by the United Kingdom-United States Pacific Freight Association and the Outward Continental North Pacific Freight Conference;[13] while the two lines which connect Europe directly with the Great Lakes have formed the Great Lakes-London, Bordeaux, Hamburg Range Westbound Conference.

FREIGHT CONFERENCES ACCORDING TO TRADE GROUPS

Table IX-A shows the principal freight conferences in the United States foreign trade by trade groups, and lists the names of the executives in charge, the number of regular and other members, and the inter-conference agreements in which the conferences or their members participate. Although this table does not show the appreciable amount of overlapping in the memberships of conferences, especially

[13] In December 1950 the Commission approved an agreement creating the Mediterranean-North Pacific Coast Freight Conference.

TABLE IX-A

Principal Steamship Freight Conferences in United States Foreign Trade by Trade Groups
(Approved agreements on file with the United States Maritime Commission as of January 18, 1950) *

Trade Group	Name of Conference	Chairman or Secretary	No. of Regular Members	Other Members	Inter-Conference Agreements
EUROPE (including U.K., North Africa, and Mediterranean Asia)					
1. From N. Atlantic:	North Atlantic, United Kingdom, Freight Conference	C. R. Andrews	13	1	T. A. Assoc.[1]
	" Baltic "	"	17	—	"
	" Continental "	"	11	—	"
	" French Atlantic "	"	7	—	"
	" Mediterranean "	"	29	—	"
	" Spanish Conference	F. Rothe	3	1	1
	" Portuguese Freight Conference	E. A. McDowell	15	—	—
2. From S. Atlantic:	South Atlantic Steamship Conference	E. J. Middleton	5	—	—
3. From Gulf:	Gulf United Kingdom Conference	H. A. Carlys	7	—	Gulf Assoc.[2]
	" Scandinavian & Baltic Conference	"	3	—	"
	" French Atlantic Hamburg Freight Conference		9	—	"
	" Mediterranean Ports Conference		12	8 A.L.	"
4. From Pacific:	Pacific Coast European Conference	J. F. McArt	23	—	—
5. From Great Lakes:	Great Lakes London Bordeaux Hamburg Eastbound Conf.				
6. To N. Atlantic:	Norway North Atlantic Conference	H. M. Holden	2	—	—
	Spain Portugal North Atlantic Conference	W. Wilhelmsen	3	—	—
	N. Atlantic (U.K.) Westbound Freight Association	R. Garcia-Vitros	5	—	—
	Morocco, Algeria and Tunisia N. Atlantic Westbound	McDiarmid & Co.	9	—	—
	Middle East Mediterranean Westbound Conference	C. R. Andrews	13	—	T. A. Assoc.
	French-North Atlantic Westbound Conference	M. Lambert	3	4	4,5
	Continental N. Atlantic Westbound Freight Conference	E. R. Humphries	8	4	4,5
	"Italian" North Atlantic ...	G. G. Phi...	20		

	Conference	Representative	No.	Votes	Note
7. To Gulf:	Marseilles North Atlantic Freight Conference	J. Manescau	5	—	[5,7]
	Swiss North Atlantic Freight Conference	M. Lambert	7	[6,7]	[6,7]
	N. Atlantic (U.K.) Westbound Freight Association	McDiarmid & Co.	9	—	—
8. To Pacific:	Continental U.S.A. Gulf Westbound Freight Conference	A. Loots	6	—	—
	U.K.-U.S. Pacific Freight Association[8]	O. F. Johnson	4	{ 2 A.M. 2 A.L.	—
	Outward Continental N. Pacific Freight Conference[8]	A. DeWaard	6	1 A.M.	—
9. To Great Lakes:	Gr. Lakes London Bordeaux Hamburg Westbound Conf.	C. A. VanWankum	2	—	—
FAR EAST (China, Japan, Korea, Siberia, Philippines, Hong Kong, Indo-China)					
1. From Atlantic & Gulf:	Far East Conference	H. E. Hornung	19	10 A.L.	[9]
2. From Pacific:	Pacific Westbound Conference	W. G. Tait	19	8 A.M.	[9]
3. To Atlantic & Gulf:	Japan Atlantic Coast Freight Conference	H. E. Case	12	—	—
	New York Freight Bureau (Shanghai)	F. Marshall	18	—	[10]
	New York " (Hong Kong)	Lowe[11]	18	—	[12]
	Associated Steamship Lines (Manila) Conference[12]	F. M. Gisbert	20[14]	—	—
4. To Pacific:	Trans-Pacific Freight Conference of Japan	H. E. Case	16	—	—
	" " " North China	F. Marshall	17	—	—
	" " " (Hong Kong)	J. S. Sandolt	18	—	—
	Associated S.S. Lines (Manila) Conference	F. M. Gisbert	25[16]	—	—
INDIA, PAKISTAN, BURMA, CEYLON, PERSIAN GULF AND RED SEA					
1. From Atlantic & Gulf:	India, Pakistan, Ceylon & Burma Outward Freight Conf.	J. M. Phillips	6	3 A.M.	—
	Persian Gulf Outward Freight Conference	"	5	—	—
	N. Atlantic Red Sea & Gulf of Aden Freight Conf.	G. R. Andrews	7	—	T.A. Assoc.
2. From Pacific:	Pacific Coast European Conference[17]	J. F. McArt	23	—	—
3. To Atlantic & Gulf:	Calcutta U.S.A. Conference	D. H. Sackett	7	—	—
4. To Pacific:	Trans-Pacific Freight Conference (Hong Kong)	J. S. Landolt	18	—	—

TABLE IX-A Cont'd.

Trade Group	Name of Conference	Chairman or Secretary	No. of Regular Members	Other Members	Inter-Conference Agreements
INDONESIA, SINGAPORE, SIAM, MALAYA					
1. From Atlantic & Gulf:	Atlantic and Gulf Straits Settlements, Malay States & Siam Conference	Funch, Edye & Co.	11	—	—
2. From Pacific:	Pacific Straits Conference	H. E. Hornung	10	—	—
	Pacific Netherlands East Indies Conference	Kerr S. S. Co.	6	3 A.M.	—
	Pacific Westbound Conference[18]	H. E. Hornung	19	8 A.M.	9
		W. G. Tait			
3. To Atlantic & Gulf:	Straits–New York Conference	H. B. Noon	16	—	—
	Java–New York Rate Agreement[19]	L. Bliek	14	—	—
	Deli–New York " [19]	N. V. Stoomvart Maats.	17	—	—
4. To Pacific:	Straits–Pacific Conference[15]	H. B. Noon	15	—	20
	Java–Pacific Rate Agreement[19]	N. V. Stoom-Maat.	8	—	20
	Deli–Pacific "	"	11	—	—
	Trans Pacific Freight Conference (Hong Kong)[15]	J. S. Landolt	18	—	—
AUSTRALASIA					
1. From Atlantic & Gulf:	U.S. Atlantic & Gulf–Australia, N.Z. Conference	H. Jager	4	1 A.M.	—
2. From Pacific:	Pacific Coast–Australasian Tariff Bureau	J. P. Williams	5	—	—
3. To Pacific:	Australia, New Z. & the South Sea Islands–Pacific Coast Conference	"	4	—	—
AFRICA (west, south, and east—for north Africa see EUROPE.)					
1. From Atlantic & Gulf:	American West African Freight Conference	P. A. Bindrim	5	4 A.L.	—
	U.S.A.–South Africa Conference[21]	J. M. Phillips	6	—	—
	Gulf South & East African Conference[22]	H. A. Carlys	3	—	Gulf Assoc.

2. From Pacific:	Pacific Coast European Conference[17]	J. F. McArt	23	—	—
3. To Atlantic & Gulf:	American West African Freight Conference	P. A. Bindrim	5	4 A.L.	—
	South Africa–U.S.A. Conference	J. M. Phillips	6	—	—
SOUTH AMERICA					
1. From Atlantic & Gulf:	River Plate & Brazil Conference[23]	G. F. Foley	19	—	—
	East Coast S. America Reefer Conference[24]	"	16	—	—
	U.S. Atlantic & Gulf Netherlands West Indies and Venezuela Conference	A. J. Pasch	5	3 A.M.	—
	Atlantic & Gulf–West Coast of S. America Conf.	"	9	8 A.M.	—
	Leeward & Windward Islands & Guianas Conference	"	4	—	—
	East Coast Colombia Conference	"	6	—	—
	Oil & Cargo to Netherlands W.I. and Venezuela	"	4	—	—
2. From Pacific:	Pacific Coast River Plate Brazil Conference	J. F. McArt	6	—	—
	" Caribbean Sea Ports	"	18	—	—
	" West Coast of South America	"	9	—	—
3. To Atlantic & Gulf:	Mid-Brazil–U.S.–Canada Freight Conference	G. F. Foley	18	—	—
	North Brazil "	"	9	—	—
	Brazil " [23 25]	"	19	—	—
	River Plate " [23]	"	18	—	—
	" & Brazil–U.S. Reefer [24]	"	14	—	—
	East Coast Colombia Conference	A. J. Pasch	6	—	—
	West Coast S. America Northbound [26]	"	4	—	—
	Association of West Coast S.S. Companies [27]	Ca. Colombiana de Nav. Mar.	13	11 A.S.	—
4. To Pacific:	U.S. Atlantic & Gulf Neth., W.I. & Venezuela Conf.	A. J. Pasch	5	—	—
	Leeward & Windward & Guianas Conference	"	4	—	—
	Pacific River Plate Brazil Conference	J. F. McArt	6	—	—
	Association of West Coast S.S. Companies[27]	Ca. Col. Nav. Mar.	13	11 A.S.	—
	West Coast S. America–North Pacific Coast Conf.[26]	J. F. McArt	4	—	—
	Colpac[28] Freight Conference	"	14	—	—

TABLE IX-A Cont'd.

Trade Group	Name of Conference	Chairman or Secretary	No. of Regular Members	Other Members	Inter-Conference Agreements
CENTRAL AMERICA AND MEXICO					
1. From Atlantic & Gulf:	Atlantic & Gulf West Coast of Cent. America and Mexico Conference	A. J. Pasch	4	{ 3 A.M. 2 A.L.	—
	Atlantic & Gulf–Panama C. Z. Colon & Panama City Conference	"	6	2 A.M.	—
2. From Pacific:	Pacific Coast Panama Canal Freight Conference	F. J. McArt	10	—	—
	Capca[29] Freight Conference	"	7	—	—
	Pacific Coast Mexico Freight Conference	"	2	—	—
	Pacific Coast Caribbean Sea Ports [30]	"	18	—	—
3. To Pacific:	Canal, Cent. America Northbound Conference[31]	"	16	—	—
	Pacific Coast Mexico Freight[31]	"	2	—	—
	Camexco Freight Conference[32]	"	13	—	—
WEST INDIES AND BERMUDA					
1. From Atlantic & Gulf:	Havana Steamship Conference[33]	A. J. Pasch	7	[34]	[34]
	Gulf & S. Atlantic Havana Steamship Conference	A. J. Cooper	7	[34]	[34]
	Santiago de Cuba Conference	A. J. Pasch	3	—	—
	U.S. Atl. & Gulf Neth. W.I. & Venezuela Conference	"	5	—	—
	Leeward Windward Islands & Guianas Conference	"	4	—	—
	U.S. Atlantic & Gulf Haiti Conference	"	6	—	—
	U.S. " " Jamaica "	"	3	—	—
	U.S. " " S. Domingo "	J. W. de Bruycker	2	—	—
	Oil Co. Cargo to Neth. W.I. & Venezuela	A. J. Pasch	4	—	—
	U.S. Atlantic Bermuda Freight Conference	"	2	—	—
2. From Pacific:	Pacific Coast Caribbean Sea Ports Conference	J. F. McArt	18	—	—
3. To Atlantic & Gulf:	Havana–U.S. Atl. & Gulf Rate Agreement	A. J. Pasch	10	—	—
	Santiago de Cuba Conference	"	3	—	—

U.S. Atl. & Gulf-Neth. W.I. & Venezuela Conf.	"	5 —
" " Haiti Conference	"	6 —
Leeward & Windward Islands & Guianas Conference	"	4 —
U.S. Atlantic–Bermuda Freight Conference	"	2 —
U.S. Atlantic & Gulf Santo Domingo Conference	J. W. deBruycker	2 —

* Includes all conferences whose agreements are on file, except those operating exclusively to or from U.S. non-contiguous territories and port associations.

A.L.—Associated Line   E/B—Eastbound   W/B—Westbound

A.M.—Associated Member

Gulf Assoc.—Gulf Associated Freight Conferences

T.A. Assoc.—Trans-Atlantic Associated Freight Conferences

For definitions of A.L. and A.M. see Chapter VIII, pp. 139-140.

[1] Agreement between North Atlantic United Kingdom and North Atlantic Spanish Conferences.

[2] Agreement between Gulf United Kingdom and Gulf French Hamburg Conferences.

[3] Includes South Atlantic Range.

[4] Agreement between Continental Westbound and French Westbound Conferences.

[5] Agreement between Continental Westbound and French Westbound, Marseilles and Italy Westbound Conferences.

[6] Agreement between Swiss and Italy Westbound Conferences.

[7] Agreement between Swiss and Marseilles Westbound Conferences.

[8] Includes Hawaiian Islands.

[9] An Agreement between Far East Conference and Pacific Westbound Conference was negotiated after January 18, 1950.

[10] Agreement between N.Y. Freight Bureau (Shanghai) and Trans-Pacific Freight Conference, North China.

[11] Lowe, Bingham & Matthews.

[12] Agreement between N.Y. Freight Bureau (Hong Kong) and Trans-Pacific Freight Conference (Hong Kong).

[13] Includes Puerto Rico.

[14] Members serving Atlantic and Gulf ports.

[15] Includes Hawaiian Islands.

[16] Members serving Pacific Coast ports.

[17] Covers transshipment cargo only.

[18] To Siam.

[19] These conferences cover traffic from most of Indonesia, and the Java and Deli New York Rate agreement apply to all U.S. Atlantic and Gulf ports.

[20] Provides for observance of rates fixed by Java and Deli New York Rate Agreements on traffic to U.S. Gulf ports transshipped at Pacific Coast ports.

[21] From U.S. Atlantic ports only.

[22] From U.S. Gulf ports only.

[23] Excludes refrigerator cargo.

[24] Includes refrigerator cargo.

[25] Covers Victoria, Brazil (20° S) and ports South thereof.

[26] From Chile and Peru.

[27] From Ecuador and Colombian Pacific ports.

[28] From Colombian Atlantic ports.

[29] To Pacific Coast ports of Central America.

[30] Includes East Coast of Central America.

[31] Does not include green coffee.

[32] Covers green coffee from Central America and Mexico.

[33] From North Atlantic ports.

[34] Agreement between Havana S.S. Conference and Gulf and S. Atlantic Havana S.S. Conference.

those serving adjacent ranges, it does reveal in a general way the pattern of shipping conferences which regulate most of the liner-borne foreign trade of the United States. Several of these conferences cover Canadian trade as well, although only a few of them include that country in their title; but since the data filed with the Federal Maritime Board are not complete for Canadian traffic no attempt is made here to show when Canadian ports are included. An inspection of the table reveals that, unlike conferences covering trade to Europe, conferences on other routes do not belong to associations like the Trans-Atlantic Associated Freight Conferences and the Gulf Associated Freight Conferences. Coordination is achieved in different ways. Some, like those controlling the inbound traffic from the Orient, have organized "port" committees.[14] Others, like the outbound Far Eastern Conference and the Pacific Westbound Conference, cover virtually the entire range of ports with which there might be competition.

The Pacific Westbound Conference, for example, covers freight traffic to Japan, Korea, Formosa, Siberia, Manchuria, China, Hong Kong, Indo-China, Siam, and the Philippine Islands. The business of this conference from Northwestern ports is so different from its business from California ports that it is divided into two semi-autonomous districts, each with its own secretary-manager—one in San Francisco and the other in Seattle. Problems common to both sections are considered at joint meetings which are held not less frequently than three times a year. On other routes, such as those serving the Caribbean, for example, conferences cover only a small range of ports; but then transshipment facilities among the islands is generally incapable of providing the direct services from or to the United States with sufficient competition to require formal cooperation among the various conferences. Of course much coordination automatically develops from overlapping memberships and from the fact that the same person is chairman of nine of the eleven freight conferences connecting this part of the world with American Atlantic and Gulf ports. A common chairmanship also characterizes the routes from American ports to South America. The same phenomenon is found on some of the routes from Indonesia and the Far East to the

[14] In March 1950 the Commission approved an agreement creating the Pacific Coast Committee of Inward Trans-Pacific Steamship Lines. The New York Committee of Inward Far East Lines dates from 1936.

United States where the same person or concern acts as chairman of the conference controlling traffic to the Atlantic and Gulf as well as of the agreement regulating transportation to Pacific ports.

Some conferences cover traffic on what is only a segment of a route for other conferences. The Colpac Freight Conference (from Colombian Atlantic ports to the Pacific Coast of North America), for instance, has fourteen members—seven of which operate from Europe to the Pacific Coast, three of which are in the Northbound run from the East Coast of South America to American Pacific ports, and the remaining four members serve other Caribbean and Central American ports in addition to Colombia. The lines from Europe and the East Coast of South America call at Colombian ports only when there is sufficient inducement, and if they have unused carrying capacity. By the same token, individual lines frequently belong to several conferences when segments of their itineraries are covered by different agreements.

A few conferences are highly specialized. Between United States Atlantic and Gulf ports and the East Coast of South America separate conferences have been formed to regulate the movement of refrigerated cargo; and green coffee from the West Coast of Central America and Mexico to American Pacific ports is covered by its own conference. Developments such as this arise from special competitive conditions. Not all lines operating between the United States and Brazil, Uruguay, and Argentina have facilities for carrying refrigerated cargo; therefore a separate conference was formed so that carriers without such accommodations could not vote on matters pertaining to cargo of this type. The most highly specialized agreement is undoubtedly the one between four dry-cargo lines carrying cargo for oil companies, intended for their own use and not for resale, moving from Atlantic and Gulf ports to the Netherlands West Indies and Venezuela. These oil companies enjoy great bargaining strength vis-à-vis the conference lines, because their shipments of pipe and other company supplies comprise the backbone of the liners' business. In fact the volume of oil company business on this route is sufficient to permit them to charter tramps, if satisfactory arrangements cannot be made with the lines. By way of contrast, it should be remembered that other conferences, such as the Associated Steamship Lines (Manila), are almost ubiquitous. And other conferences, such as the Pacific Coast European Conference, for example, add to the area covered by direct service additional territory when the latter is served by transshipment.[15]

PASSENGER CONFERENCES

Turning from freight to passenger conferences, one finds that although the latter are neither so numerous nor so universal they nevertheless do control the heavily traveled passenger routes and quite a few of lesser importance. Table IX-B lists by trade groups the passenger conferences controlling United States traffic on January 1, 1950. The highly important route to Europe is covered by the Atlantic Conference, which is composed of a North Atlantic group and a Mediterranean group; and by the Trans-Atlantic Passenger Conference. The Trans-Pacific Passenger Conference controls the various trades in that area ranging from Australasia to all Oriental ports; and, in addition, has agreements with lines operating around-the-world passenger service, and other agreements covering travel from Europe to Australia, New Zealand, and the Orient. The Western Hemisphere Passenger Conference covers all of Latin America and the West Indies as well as "special cruises." And the North Pacific Coast-Europe Passenger Conference covers not only passage from North America to all European destinations and the West Indies, but also regulates travel between the United States and British Columbia, as well as transportation between the Pacific Coast of North America and the West Coast of Central America. With the exception of the North Pacific Coast-Europe Passenger Conference, which does not control passage from Europe or the West Indies to the United States unless a round-trip ticket is purchased in America, these conferences regulate transportation in both directions.

Limited non-conference competition is sometimes offered by freighters, many of which have accommodations for twelve or fewer passengers. However, as members of freight conferences are very apt to cooperate with passenger rings as associate members, most competition from this source is controlled. Independent freight lines, on the other hand, customarily also operate on a non-conference basis in the transportation of such passengers as their generally very limited capacity will accommodate. Consequently such non-conference passenger competition as exists is apt to come from this source,

---

[15] The Pacific Coast European Conference controls cargo from the Pacific range to India, Iraq, and South Africa when it is transshipped at European or Mediterranean ports covered by the agreement.

Passenger Conferences in United States Trades
By Trade Groups
(as of January 18, 1950)

Trade Group	United States Ports	Conference
Europe, North Africa and Mediterranean Asia	From Atlantic & Gulf	Atlantic Conference, and Trans-Atlantic Passenger Conference
	From Pacific	North Pacific Coast-Europe Passenger Conference
	To Atlantic & Gulf	Atlantic Conference, and Trans-Atlantic Passenger Conference
	To Pacific	None
Far East	From & to Atlantic & Gulf	None
	From & to Pacific	Trans-Pacific Passenger Conference
India, Pakistan, Burma, Ceylon, Red Sea, Persian Gulf	From & to Atlantic & Gulf	None
	From & to Pacific	None
Indonesia, Singapore, Siam, Malaya	From & to Atlantic & Gulf	None
	From & to Pacific[1]	None
Australasia and South Sea Islands	From & to Atlantic & Gulf	None
	From & to Pacific	Trans-Pacific Passenger Conference
Africa, West, South & East	From & to Atlantic & Gulf	None
	From & to Pacific	None
South America	From & to Atlantic & Gulf	Western Hemisphere Passenger Conference
	From & to Pacific	None
Central America, Mexico, Canal Zone	From & to Atlantic & Gulf	Western Hemisphere Passenger Conference
	From & to Pacific	North Pacific Coast-Europe Passenger Conf.
West Indies and Bermuda	From Atlantic & Gulf	Western Hemisphere Passenger Conference
	From Pacific[2]	North Pacific Coast-Europe Passenger Conf.
	To Atlantic & Gulf	Western Hemisphere Passenger Conference
Canada	From & to Atlantic & Gulf	None
	From & to Pacific	North Pacific Coast-Europe Passenger Conf.

[1] Covers Malaysia only.
[2] Does not include Bermuda.

and from the very limited and highly irregular sailings of tramp vessels.

Serious competition has been introduced by air transportation; for despite the strong preference of many to travel by ship, and the fact that air carriers generate much new business of their own, a large and growing proportion of the total traffic is directly and strongly competitive. On the route between the Pacific Coast of North America and Australasia the plane, in combination with other factors, has virtually eliminated the passenger liner. On all routes the airplane has severely limited the monopoly position of passenger conferences. The regular international airlines, however, are confronted by competitive problems similar to those faced by the shipping lines; and as a result have coordinated rate-making in the International Air Transport Association.[16] So far there appears to be no cooperation between air lines, or I.A.T.A., and shipping lines or conferences beyond arrangements for the interchange of traffic on some routes; although it is not impossible that they may work together at some future time.

NON-CONFERENCE OPERATORS

In addition to the liner services operated by conference members, sailings are made by concerns which do not belong to a conference. There are, roughly speaking, four types of independent operation. One type consists of those who intend to maintain a regular service on a given route on a more or less permanent basis and who generally charge the same rates as the conference lines. Sometimes these independents will subsequently join the conference, while in other instances their continued reluctance to join is based on the desire for greater freedom of action in regard to sailing schedules and other non-rate matters. Personality conflicts may also in some instances help to account for independent operations of this sort. Examples of lines with regular, permanent services, generally at the same rates as the conferences in their respective trades, are the Israel American Line, and the Robin Line which operates between the American North Atlantic range and South and East Africa.

A second type resembles the first in that the operators intend to maintain a regular and permanent service, but are distinguished from the members of the first group in that they customarily charge dif-

---

[16] The I.A.T.A. will be considered in more detail in Chapter XIII along with some of the basic features distinguishing air transport from water transport.

ferent rates (usually lower) than the conference tariff. Examples of this type of operation are the non-conference liner services of the States Marine Lines and all of the lines run by the Isbrandtsen Company. Some lines operate on this basis in order to become established on a route, and may subsequently apply for admission to the conference; while others, of which Isbrandtsen is a prime if not unique example, make it a matter of policy to operate independently.

A third type of operation is represented by those companies which provide a regular service while the trade is booming, but who drop out when business slacks off or when better opportunities appear elsewhere. Lines of this type follow a flexible rate policy which generally involves charging rates below the conference level. Since motives are extremely difficult to identify and all carriers are free to change their minds and to abandon a trade they have served, it is impossible to distinguish this type of operation from those in the second category in advance of the service's termination.[17] An illustration of this type of independent operation may be furnished by some of the Stevenson Lines' services. Prior to its withdrawal, in June 1950, from the Gulf-Mediterranean Ports Conference and the North Atlantic Mediterranean Freight Conference this company, like several others, operated some services as an independent and others as a conference member.[18] Subsequent to its resignation from these conferences this company's sailings from the Gulf became quite irregular, thereby suggesting that vessels were being placed on berth for general cargo either to top-off a bulk shipment, or when vessel position and cargo inducements rendered it attractive. There is some doubt, therefore, that these were still truly liner services by the year's end.

The fourth type consists of irregular services provided by tramps, which top-off a shipment of bulk cargo with some general cargo, and by an occasional vessel which is placed on berth for general cargo when the volume of traffic is exceptionally large. Such carriers will always try to charge all the traffic will bear, but are generally content to complete the loading of their vessel by cutting rates. According to the tariffs filed with the Commission these carriers often file rates on only one, two, or three commodities that they have transported on a common carrier basis; and at times they even specify

---

[17] It must be remembered that conference lines are also completely free to abandon a service and not infrequently do so.

[18] The States Marine Corp. and the U. S. Navigation Co., for example, operate some conference services as well as some non-conference lines.

the actual quantity of the commodity on which the rate was applicable, which indicates that some of them are not really common carriers at all, but are actually contract carriers or tramps filling up available space with some general cargo. The ability of tramps to secure full and balanced loads in this manner is of course a highly efficient method of ship utilization, but if it were to occur on a large scale it would be distressing to lines offering regular scheduled sailings. Such irregular service, however, is not at all attractive to many varieties of general cargo, and exclusive patronage contracts undoubtedly deter shippers of some other items from patronizing vessels of this type. There are surprisingly few such tariffs filed, so competition from this source is either unrecorded or relatively unimportant at this time. The abolition of the exclusive patronage contract system might stimulate such competition.

Table IX-C lists the non-conference liner services which were advertised as operating in November and December 1950 on United States trade routes covered by conference agreements, and therefore includes most, if not all, of the non-conference services of the first three types. These independent services generally operate on a non-conference basis on the inbound portion of their voyage as well as on the outbound segment; but there are exceptions. One of them, the States Marine Line service from the North Atlantic Range to India, belongs to the Calcutta U.S.A. Conference on the homebound voyage, although it sails outbound as a non-conference service. Occasionally a line sails outbound as a conference carrier, but returns as an independent. This has not been uncommon in the trade from Havana, where the huge volume of sugar has enabled vessels which sailed from the United States as common carriers to return as bulk or contract carriers. It should be noted that while Isbrandtsen's round-the-world service carries cargo both outbound and inbound as an independent, it does not return directly from the first range of foreign ports at which it calls, but continues in an eastward direction until it has circumnavigated the northern hemisphere.

NON-CONFERENCE COMPETITION

With the exception of the Robin Line and the Israel America Line, which customarily quoted conference rates, all other lines listed in Table IX-C have generally charged lower rates than those named by the conferences in their respective trades. As the agent for one independent line has stated, "Since a non-conference service is in competition with the conference services, lower rates are customarily charged than conference rates, though the non-conference service will naturally endeavor to obtain the best rates possible."[19] Several of the independents have made a practice of charging conference rates reduced by a fixed percentage (usually 10 per cent); while others file tariffs very similar, if not actually identical, to the conference tariff except for lower rates on the more important commodities. The Isbrandtsen Line, the oldest consistently independent operator, for example, generally charged conference rates less 10 per cent prior to World War II. Since the war, Isbrandtsen has filed replicas of conference tariffs on several of the routes it serves, having apparently copied them word for word including typographical errors, but has reduced the conference rates by various amounts for selected commodities. In the trade from United States North Atlantic ports to Europe, Isbrandtsen's rates between August 1946 and October 1949 ranged from 3.3 per cent to 53.4 per cent lower than those filed by the conference.[20] Independent lines may also enter contracts with important shippers, but since they are common carriers the same rates would presumably be available to other shippers of the particular commodities so covered. Prior to the last war, Isbrandtsen occasionally made such contracts, and there have been no complaints filed that the practice was discriminatory. Since common carriers which do not belong to conferences are not under the same obligation to file their inbound rates with the Commission as they are in respect to outbound rates, the rate practices they followed on import traffic is not easy to document. Nevertheless the available evidence indicates that the general pattern is the same.

How can an independent line exist in a trade where the conference employs the patronage contract system? It is difficult to be sure, and not very common; but it has happened. The Isbrandtsen Company, prior to World War II, operated lines in several trades on this basis. On some trades certain commodities are not covered by patronage contracts, and therefore are available to non-conference carriers. Additional business may be obtained from shippers who, regardless of their agreement with the conference, will ship via the independent lines. These violations do not always become known to the conference, but when they have, some of the violators were

---

[19] In a letter to the author.
[20] Recommended Decision of C. W. Robinson, examiner for the U.S. Maritime Commission, in Docket 684, pp. 14-15.

TABLE IX-C

Advertised Non-Conference Liner Services Operating on United States Foreign Trade Routes Covered by Conference Agreements[1]
(November and December 1950)

Trade Group	Route	Name of Line	Approx. Frequency of Sailings
Europe, North Africa & Mediterranean Asia	North Atlantic and Northern Europe	Isbrandtsen	biweekly
		U.S. Navigation	10 days
		Meyer	biweekly
		States Marine	10-20 days
	Gulf and Northern Europe	Isbrandtsen	biweekly
		Stevenson	irregular[3]
	North Atlantic and Mediterranean	Isbrandtsen[4, 5]	biweekly
		Costa[6]	biweekly
		Israel-America[7]	18-20 days
		Stevenson	1-2 weeks
	Gulf and Mediterranean Ports	Stevenson	irregular[3]
Far East	North Atlantic and Far East	Isbrandtsen[4]	biweekly
	Gulf and Far East	Stevenson	monthly
India, Pakistan, Ceylon, Burma, Persian Gulf, Red Sea	North Atlantic and India, Pakistan & Ceylon	Isbrandtsen[4]	biweekly
	North Atlantic & Gulf and Persian Gulf & India	States Marine	monthly

Region	Routes	Line	Frequency
Indonesia, Singapore, Malaya, Siam	North Atlantic and Singapore	Isbrandtsen[4]	biweekly
Australasia		None Advertised	
Africa (West, South & East)	North Atlantic and South & East Africa	Robin[8]	biweekly
	Gulf and South & East Africa	States Marine[9,2]	monthly
		States Marine[9]	monthly
South America	North Atlantic and Venezuela	Isbrandtsen[10]	weekly
	Gulf and Venezuela	States Marine	monthly
		Isbrandtsen[10]	weekly
Central America and Mexico		None Advertised	
West Indies[11]	North Atlantic and Cuba	Cubamar	biweekly
	From Cuba to North Atlantic	12	
	South Atlantic & Gulf to Cuba	Cubamar	biweekly
	From Cuba to Gulf	12	

[1] Based on advertisements in *The Journal of Commerce*, *The New York Forwarder*, and *Pacific Shipper*.
[2] Also calls at South Atlantic ports.
[3] This may not qualify as a liner service.
[4] Part of round-the-world service.
[5] Alexandria, Egypt only regular port of call.
[6] Only Italian ports advertised.
[7] Only Israeli ports advertised.
[8] Seas Shipping Co.
[9] South African Marine Corp., Ltd.
[10] Returns via Cuba.

[11] Several operators of small vessels participate from time to time as common carriers between South Atlantic & Gulf ports and various Caribbean destinations. Some charge conference rates, while others do not. Information regarding them is meager, but because of their limited carrying capacity they do not constitute an important competitive threat to the superior services provided by the conference lines.

[12] Several lines operate on a non-conference basis northbound. The principal cargo is sugar.

so important to the member lines that the infraction was forgotten, and no damages were collected. To the extent large shippers were favored—and it may be presumed that their infractions were more apt to be ignored than the transgressions of less important concerns —the practice was discriminatory. Most cargo carried by independent carriers, however, was for shippers who had refused to sign a patronage contract, or who voluntarily withdrew from their agreement with the conference after giving the specified advance notice. The Isbrandtsen Lines obtained much of their traffic from shippers in this latter category, and before World War II had contracts with such large concerns as the Ford Motor Co. and E. I. du Pont de Nemours to carry their exports to the Far East on a non-conference basis. Independent carriers may also carry cargo in which they have a proprietary interest.[21] In this respect the independent is like any other industrial carrier. There are many industrial carriers in the shipping business who operate as common carriers and who belong to conferences.[22] Since the war an additional and large source of business for the independents has appeared in the form of shipments made by the United States government, which does not enter into patronage contracts.

The amount of competition provided conferences by the independents offering regular services is extremely difficult to determine with accuracy. A comparison of sailings or carrying capacity, though interesting, is apt to be misleading; for any major independent operator can, at most times, charter additional tonnage. Furthermore, differences in frequency of sailings, speed of delivery, type of vessel accommodation, and other qualitative differences make mere quanti-

[21] The Isbrandtsen Company are merchants as well as ship operators, and it has been suggested that they carry an appreciable amount of cargo for their own account as traders. Mr. M. S. Crinkley, vice president of the Isbrandtsen Co., expressed his regret to the author that this had not been so, and explained that their business as merchants unfortunately had not materially assisted their shipping operations, although he hoped that someday it would.

[22] The advantages and disadvantages of industrial carriers are well-known and need not be argued here. Suffice it to say that many liner services have achieved a high degree of efficient vessel utilization by their ability to control a basic cargo in which they have a proprietary interest. On the other hand, discrimination against non-shipowning shippers is always possible; but, possibly because of the more competitive nature of shipping, such abuses have not been so serious as in railroading, where some shipment points rely entirely on one carrier. Trading for ship's account is one of the oldest traditions of merchant shipping, still one cannot help but wonder how consistent this ancient custom is with the more recent practice of performing as a common carrier.

tative comparisons misleading. Differences in schedules alone make comparison hazardous.

For example, twenty-two conference sailings and nine non-conference sailings were scheduled from New York to Hamburg for the month November 6 through December 5, 1950; but even if we assume that all the vessels were of approximately the same type and size, which they were not, we find other significant differences. Ten of the twenty-two conference vessels scheduled for Hamburg also called at Antwerp, while all nine of the non-conference sailings included Antwerp in their itinerary. Some of the conference vessels, as well as some of the non-conference sailings, also carried cargo for Amsterdam, Rotterdam, Bremen, and British ports, and changes in announced schedules are apt to have been made as inducements varied.

Competition, therefore, must be considered as existing between ranges rather than between ports, and the ever-present opportunities of changed itineraries and of transshipment make the range limits quite large and disconcertingly flexible. Suffice it to say that, on the basis of past experience, an aggressive independent operator can exert sufficient pressure to disrupt most trades, if he is foolish enough to push the matter that far.

Nonetheless, a comparison of sailings does occasionally disclose some comparative information concerning regular competition from independents. In the November 6 to December 5 period, seventeen conference vessels were advertised to sail from New York to Hong Kong, and although they were listed to discharge at a number of other ports their carrying capacity greatly exceeded the two non-conference sailings of Isbrandtsen's round-the-world service whose capacity on this leg of their long voyage is considerably reduced by the requirements of the numerous other segments of it. By way of contrast, non-conference competition appeared much more serious on the New York to Venezuela route where twelve conference sailings for the month were supplemented by five independent voyages.

But the greatest variable of all is the state of the freight market. If cargo is plentiful and tonnage scarce, there is apt to be plenty of business for all and the temptation to cut rates is minimized. However, when business is slack not only are the independents tempted to reduce rates, but it is quite easy for them to charter additional vessels if they succeed in capturing a large volume of traffic. The reduction of rates may not by itself be a bad thing, nor need the addition of new tonnage necessarily be contrary to the public interest, although it is apt to augment unused capacity under the circumstances described above. A review of the types of non-conference operations should illuminate the nature of the competition provided by independent carriers.

Non-conference operators who observe conference rates have substantially the same effect on the trade that they would have if they were conference members, and therefore their influence can be analyzed more appropriately in Chapter XII where intra-conference competition is discussed. Their existence, however, is not completely without unique significance, because they do suggest the probability of somewhat more flexibility in sailings in cases where the conference or an associated pool controls schedules. Furthermore these independents also tend to render the exclusive patronage contract system less binding, unless they participate in it.

The three other types of non-conference competition, on the other hand, are very apt to exert a direct and at times powerful influence on the trades they enter. The irregular participation of tramp vessels, which fill up spare carrying capacity with general cargo, may represent the maximum efficiency in the utilization of such vessels; but may also disrupt the orderly marketing of the products carried, and shift to other cargo the burden of maintaining the regular lines. If shippers of these commodities would be content to rely exclusively on the service provided by such tramp vessels, then we could conclude that they performed with utmost efficiency and presumably at low cost to shippers. But if traders in these commodities also count on the regular service of liners and whatever rate stability they maintain, then the participation of the tramp vessel will, unless the regular lines are shutting out cargo, tend to disrupt the market for the product and shift a burden to other shippers.

Independents, who operate regular services at less than conference rates may remain in a trade in slack times as well as in prosperous periods, or they may, as previously indicated, abandon the route when the volume of traffic falls off, or prospects elsewhere are better. In the latter case, they provide additional capacity when it is needed, but it cannot be taken for granted that the necessary extra tonnage would not otherwise be forthcoming, since conference lines may very well under such circumstances place more vessels in the trade.

The independent, it is true, may help to keep conferences from charging exorbitant rates; but when tonnage is scarce the independent will also attempt to charge all that the traffic will bear, while at other times the independent may exist, as uncontrolled truck carriers did in taking business from the railroads, by "skimming the cream" off the traffic. Rate concessions on highly remunerative commodity groups may provide adequate revenue to permit some carriers to operate profitably, but may render unremunerative operations restricted to the carrying of the less well-paying varieties. Or the independent may earn a satisfactory return by merely engaging in the trade in good periods, leaving the responsibility of maintaining good service in poor times to the more stable conference lines, thereby placing an unfair burden on them, or forcing them to charge higher rates whenever they can. If the burden of these boosted charges fell on the same persons that benefited from the independent competition, a crude justice would emerge, but there is no reason to believe that this would necessarily be the case. The elasticities of demand and other market forces are so apt to have changed with the altered conditions which led to the withdrawal of the independent service that the probabilities of achieving a balancing of the advantages and disadvantages of non-conference competition are quite remote.

Nonetheless, independent carriers are not without merit. This is especially true of the non-conference liner service which is maintained on a basis as permanent as that of the majority of conference lines. The self-regulation provided by conferences may at times achieve sufficient cohesion among those subscribing to the agreement so that rates may become excessive and service may deteriorate. The stimulus of outside competition can be extremely salutary whenever internal competition among conference members declines to such a point. However, while it may be assumed that the permanent, independent line will not automatically desert the trade when business slackens, thereby passing the burden of continuing the route to others, such a non-conference service may operate, nevertheless, on the well-established transportation principle of "skimming the cream." Or to vary the metaphor, the independent may "travel under the umbrella" held by the conference to shield the route from the tempests of cutthroat competition. In the presence of such independent competition, the "umbrella" may succeed primarily in keeping the less remunerative commodities off the independent's vessels.

It may always be asked, Why don't all liner services join conferences, or at least adhere to conference tariffs? Conferences, of course, by limiting membership, have often been far from blameless; a genuinely open membership policy is crucial where tying arrangements are employed. But in contemporary American trades the difficulty of bona fide common carriers joining the conference on an equal basis with other members has been pretty well solved by the policy of the Maritime Commission.[23] An enforced open membership policy, however, does not guarantee that conference rates will not be excessive; for the temptation to the members to keep rates high is great, even though some vessels may be sailing light.

The fact remains that non-conference services continue to operate independently, despite their ability to join the conferences; and furthermore they do not generally charge conference rates. Why is this so? They must operate independently because it is to their advantage to do so. An independent line may have more flexibility in scheduling, but it will invariably have more flexibility in rate-making than the conference lines which make rates by committee. (Except for the possibility of greater schedule flexibility, there is no reason why an independent line can operate at lower costs than conference members.) Furthermore, the independent, by charging lower rates, can frequently fill his ships when conference vessels are not able to sail fully loaded. By riding under the conference "umbrella" the independent may, if it does not cut rates too vigorously, enjoy the benefits of stability and still carry more than its normal share of remunerative cargo.

Committee rate-making, while conducive to stability, is by the same token apt to be hostile to change. Voting rules may be important in this respect, but, whatever they are, one or two important lines can often strongly influence conference policies. If such lines are opposed to change, inflexibility inevitably results. In any event, it is always more difficult for several persons to agree on a policy than it is for one executive to make up his mind. Since stability and flexibility are both desirable, the problem is to achieve them in the right proportions and at the right time. Both conferences and independents may err or serve the public interest, but tend to do so in opposite ways.

Independent carriers do not always reduce rates on the more attractive cargoes exclusively, but sometimes quote the entire conference tariff less some specified percentage. Independents may exist

[23] *supra.* pp. 122-124.

on this basis, not only by carrying better loads, but either because the conference rates are too high or because the independent's rates are too low. If conference rates are too high, an independent line charging lower rates may easily earn a satisfactory return. On the other hand, the independent's lower rates may not cover the full costs of operation. In depressed periods vessels can frequently be chartered well below their cost of replacement from owners who need some revenue desperately, or who, for some other reason, prefer not to lay up their vessels. The independent operator, therefore, may not be losing money, because his service might be "subsidized" by the losses of the owners of the vessels he charters. Conference lines may also charter ships, but they are more apt to own sizable fleets than the independents, who tend to rely more on chartered tonnage. Whenever a non-conference line maintains a regular, permanent service at less than conference rates, it can be assumed that the conference rates are too high, or that the independent is not charging full costs, or that the independent is "skimming the cream" off the traffic mix. If this competition goes beyond some point, which is determined more by considerations of strategy than by the traditional economic concept of profit maximization, a rate war will develop. But, short of this point, independent liner services may compete with conference carriers under conditions of reasonable rate stability.

A definite conclusion regarding the non-conference line operator is difficult to reach. At times the independent line may be like the predatory fish that fishermen sometimes place in the tanks of their vessels, where the marketable fish are kept alive, in order to prevent the catch from getting flabby before being brought to market. Some of the marketable fish are eaten as a result, it is true, but the survivors arrive on shore as fresh and firm as when first caught. Market competition, too, often has this virtue. At other times, however, rate-cutting by a non-conference service may lead to rate reductions by the conference lines, and then to successive reductions by both parties until individual rates, and sometimes entire rate structures, are below cost. This is not like the predatory fish keeping the others alert, but rather as if he had started a struggle for existence which would lead either to the annihilation of all the fish, or to the survival of one large specimen who has devoured all the others.

In summation, the foregoing analysis indicates that independent carriers may be extremely useful in helping to keep conference rates from remaining long at excessive levels; but that independents may also charge rates below costs, or, by directing their competition, exert rate pressure on selected groups of commodities, thereby leaving a greater burden of overhead costs to be carried by other goods which are often less capable of supporting them.

Indeterminateness of costs makes quantitative analysis difficult, but even if such data were available two debatable theoretical propositions remain: the cost-of-service principle versus the value-of-service principle of rate-making; and the related question of marginal-cost pricing versus full-cost pricing. This is not the appropriate place to settle these arguments. Deduction, however, indicates that independents are most apt to exercise a restraining influence on conference rates when the freight market is firm yet not so strong as to make chartered tonnage very dear. When the freight market is weaker than this, the independents are prone to "skim the cream" off the traffic; whereas when chartered tonnage becomes relatively costly they tend either to drop out or to charge conference rates. Independents are probably most damaging in periods of depression, for despite their salutary influence on the relative inflexibility of conference tariffs, it is at such times that selective rate-cutting is apt to be most harmful both to conference carriers and to the shippers of the less attractive commodities.[24] Furthermore, it is during severe depressions that independents are most apt to operate below cost. Public policy regarding the operation of independent liner services and respecting the measures adopted by conferences to restrict this competition should bear in mind the different impact of non-conference services under various conditions of the freight market.

ROUTES WITHOUT CONFERENCES

Table IX-A quite correctly gives the impression that conferences regulate almost all the ocean routes connecting the United States with the rest of the world. A number of less important American routes, however, are not covered by conference agreements; and Table IX-D lists those for which no conference agreements were on file in 1950. Since lines can enter and leave a trade at will, it is difficult to be certain how many are actually operating on these routes at any given time, especially in the import trades where non-conference carriers are not required to file tariffs. Nevertheless, a pat-

---

[24] For illustrations of the disruptive influence of non-conference operations, see: Section 19 Investigation, 1935 1 U.S.S.B.B. 470 (1935); and Cargo to Adriatic, Black Sea and Levant Ports, 2 U.S.M.C. 342 (1940).

tern emerges, and it does not indicate rate competition to be more common on these unorganized routes than on routes controlled by conferences. In some of these unorganized trades, e.g. the route between United States Atlantic ports and Canada, there is only one regular line in operation. On other routes all the lines—and generally

TABLE IX-D

Freight Liner Service on United States Foreign Trade Routes for which no Conference Agreements were on File in 1950

EUROPE, NORTH AFRICA AND MEDITERRANEAN ASIA
1. Mediterranean ports to Gulf range
2. Mediterranean ports to Pacific range[1]

FAR EAST
None

INDIA, PAKISTAN, BURMA, CEYLON, RED SEA & PERSIAN GULF
1. Pacific Coast to Persian Gulf
2. Pacific Coast to India
3. Red Sea & Gulf of Aden to Atlantic range
4. Bombay, Karachi, Madras & Colombo to Atlantic range
5. Calcutta to South Atlantic & Gulf ports
6. India, Pakistan & Burma to Pacific Coast

INDONESIA, SINGAPORE, MALAYA & SIAM
None

AUSTRALASIA
1. Australia & New Zealand to Atlantic range

AFRICA (West, South & East)
1. Pacific Coast to South & East Africa
2. South to East Africa to Pacific Coast

SOUTH AMERICA
None

CENTRAL AMERICA & MEXICO
1. Atlantic Coast to East Coast of Mexico and the East Coast of Central America
2. Gulf ports to East Coast of Mexico and the East Coast of Central America
3. East Coast of Mexico, Central America & Canal Zone to Atlantic range
4. East Coast of Mexico, Central America & Canal Zone to Gulf ports

WEST INDIES & BAHAMAS
1. Atlantic Coast to Bahamas

CANADA
No conferences cover freight traffic on any ocean routes between the United States and Canada

---

[1] A conference agreement in this trade was approved by the Federal Maritime Board on December 20, 1950.

there are not more than two or three—customarily charge the same rates, despite the fact that they have each filed a separate tariff. In some instances this is probably due to price leadership by one of the lines whose tariff is scrupulously followed by the others, while in other cases it seems to be a policy of "live and let live" that prompts the lines to charge the same rates without incurring the expenses involved in a formal arrangement.

Whatever the reasons may be, the fact remains that the several lines in most unorganized trades charge identical rates. This is exemplified by the three lines connecting United States North Atlantic ports with Tampico and Vera Cruz, Mexico; as well as by the following routes, to mention a few: from Mediterranean ports to the Pacific Coast;[25] from India, Pakistan, and Burma to the Pacific range; from Bombay, Karachi, Madras, and Colombo to the Atlantic Coast; from Australia to Atlantic ports; and from the Pacific Coast to the Persian Gulf. On several of these routes the lines are already cooperating with each other in a conference controlling traffic in the opposite direction (e.g. the United States Atlantic and Gulf-Australia, New Zealand Conference); or they may be working together in a conference which controls other segments of the route (e.g. the Pacific Westbound Conference). An interesting case exists on the route from the Pacific Coast to India where three lines sailing westward across the Pacific (American Presidents Line, Pacific Far East Line, and Java Pacific Line) have filed identical tariffs; but are subject to limited rate competition from the eastward sailing round-the-world service of the independent Isbrandtsen Line.

[25] An agreement creating the Mediterranean-North Pacific Coast Conference was approved by the Federal Maritime Board on December 20, 1950.

CHAPTER X

TYING ARRANGEMENTS

THE VARIOUS METHODS which conferences have employed to bind shippers to the member lines and to render the entry of a new carrier difficult have been among the most hotly criticized conference practices. The dissatisfaction in many countries with the widely used deferred rebate system, and the action of the United States Department of Justice after World War II in challenging the legality of the exclusive patronage contract, which conferences in the American trade had substituted for the forbidden deferred rebate, indicate that this problem is far from settled. The four principal devices used to secure the loyal patronage of shippers are the preferential contract, the deferred rebate, the agreement between conferences and shippers' associations, and the exclusive patronage contract.

Preferential contracts are agreements between a line or a conference, usually the former, and a large shipper for the transportation on a given route of either all his freight, or of certain important articles, at lower rates than those charged similar goods shipped by others presumably in smaller quantities. The ship operator may agree to provide a certain amount of carrying capacity for the accommodation of the contract shipper's cargo, and the shipper generally guarantees a minimum quantity of freight. To the extent that these preferential contract rates are demonstrably lower than can be justified by cost considerations they become unduly discriminatory, and in the United States trades run afoul of Sections 16 and 17 of the Shipping Act of 1916. This practice tends to distort the obligations of a common carrier by combining the function of a common carrier with that of a contract carrier. In general, these contracts have not been very popular with ship operators who prefer to encourage the business of a considerable number of shippers, whenever possible, rather than to become too dependent on one or a few large customers.

The deferred rebate system provides shippers, who agree to employ exclusively the steamers of conference members in a given route, a rebate of a certain percentage of their freight payments (usually 5 or 10 per cent). This rebate is computed for a designated period (usually three, six, or twelve months), but is not paid until after a certain period of deferment (usually six months) following the interval of time for which it is computed, and then only on the condition that during the entire time, both of the period for which the rebate was computed and of the deferment, the shipper has given his exclusive support to the conference lines. "The system of rebates or discounts to those who deal exclusively with a particular company," Alfred Marshall points out, "is very old; but the plan of withholding the rebate for a long time, in order to keep the shipper in what he regards as bondage, was begun late in the last [19th] century. . . ."[1] This practice appears to have been inaugurated in 1877 by the United Kingdom-Calcutta Conference. Deferred rebates, which were probably already rendered illegal by American anti-trust legislation, were specifically made unlawful by Section 14 of the Shipping Act of 1916.[2]

The procedure of tying shippers to member lines by agreements between conferences and associations of shippers was developed in the trades from Europe to South Africa, and from Australia and New Zealand to the United Kingdom. Since these agreements have been described in Chapter VI they will not be discussed in detail again. Suffice it to say that they impose obligations on both parties: the shipper must give the member lines all his business on their route; and the ship operators are required to provide adequate tonnage and regular sailings, and to maintain the agreed tariff. Penalties are sometimes stipulated for violations by either party. Their most serious limitation has been the difficulty of forming shippers' associations; since the disparate interests of various exporters, importers, brokers, manufacturers, merchants, and others are frequently greater and more decisive than the matters which concern them commonly.

The exclusive patronage contract is an agreement between a line, or a conference, and a shipper which provides that in return for the shipper's exclusive patronage on a specified route the shipper will be billed at contract rates which are lower (usually 10-20 per cent) than those specified in the tariff for shippers who do not agree to give the conference members their exclusive patronage.[3] Such con-

---

[1] Alfred Marshall, *Industry and Trade* (London: Macmillan, 1919), p. 439.
[2] 39 Stat. 733 (1916), 46 U.S.C. §812 (1934).
[3] While the differential between contract and non-contract rates usually ranges from 10 to 20 per cent, larger differentials are not unknown; and at one time contract rates for numerous commodities in the American-European trade were half those

tract rates and deferred rebates are generally available to large and small shippers alike, provided they are "loyal" to the conference; although they do not always apply to all commodities. The contracting lines generally agree to furnish adequate tonnage at regular intervals, and the shipper is temporarily released from his exclusive patronage obligation whenever, after designated advance notice, the conference carriers cannot accommodate his cargo. Deferred rebate arrangements also often incorporate provisions similar to those described in the foregoing sentence; so that the principal and essential distinction between the deferred rebate system and the exclusive patronage contract is that the former requires "loyalty" over a period of deferment in addition to "loyalty" during a period of performance, while the latter requires "loyalty" only during the contract or performance period. The exclusive patronage contract system is widely employed in the carrying of United States water-borne foreign commerce as a substitute (some say a subterfuge) for the deferred rebate which is unlawful in this country. Both deferred rebates and exclusive patronage contract rates are discriminatory in the sense that the difference in the amounts charged "loyal" and "disloyal" shippers is not based on differences in cost.

It is claimed that such tying arrangements are necessary and of advantage to shipper and shipowner alike. Proponents argue that without them the market structure on some routes would make it impossible to maintain regular schedules and stable rates; for non-conference competition would disrupt the trade by "skimming the cream" in seasons when business was flourishing, only to cut rates unduly or to abandon the route when traffic was slack. If lines providing regular year-round service are not able to have good loads at regular rates in good seasons, it is contended, then they will be unable to provide satisfactory service when business is quiet. Opponents of tying arrangements, on the other hand, forcibly denounce them for fostering discrimination and other monopoly abuses. Court action concerned with complaints about tying arrangements provide us with some of the earliest public evidence available regarding the practices of steamship conferences. In 1886 a United States federal court held that charging "disloyal" shippers higher rates was illegal

---

charged non-contract shippers. See U.S. Navigation Co. *v.* Cunard S. S. Co., 284 U.S. 474 at 479 (1932).

at common law;[4] while in 1892, in a British case, the House of Lords upheld the legality of the deferred rebate in that nation's ocean carrying trade.[5] The Alexander Committee of the House of Representatives was emphatic in its criticism of deferred rebates and of discriminatory practices such as preferential contracts, but took a more tolerant view of the exclusive patronage type of contract. The Committee concluded "That deferred rebate systems are objectionable and should be prohibited for the following reasons:

"(1) By deferring the payment of the rebate until three or six months following the period to which the rebate applies, shipowners effectively tie the merchants to a group of lines for successive periods. In this connection it is argued that the ordinary contract system does not place the shipper in the position of continued dependence that results from the deferred rebate system.

"(2) That the system is unnecessary to secure excellence and regularity of service, a considerable number of conferences being operated today without this feature."[6]

The Royal Commission on Shipping Rings, however, took a more tolerant view of the deferment principle, and the *majority* report concluded that although this device gave shipping conferences a limited but still very effective monopoly over the carriage of general merchandise, the deferred rebate system was necessary for effective control. They felt that as an alternative the contract rate system was inadequate and tended to lead to preferential contracts favoring large shippers and secret rates favoring exporters from the Continent of Europe. The *minority* observed that the conference system with the deferred rebate had created a monopoly "the limitations upon which are in many cases illusory and which generally tend to decline."[7] Still both the majority and minority reports made substantially similar recommendations for indirect control of conferences and neither report advocated legal abolition of the rebate system.[8] Despite its acceptance of the deferred rebate, the Royal Commission was not unaware of this system's shortcomings, and noted that "loyal" merchants were not always adequately protected

---

[4] Menacho v. Ward, 27 Fed. 529 (1886). For a description of the use of the deferred rebate system in American trade, see: U.S. v. Prince Line, 220 Fed. 230 reversed as moot 242 U.S. 537; and Thomsen v. Cayser, 243 U.S. 660.

[5] Mogul Steamship Co. v. McGregor, App. Cas. 25 (1892).

[6] Alexander Committee Report, *op.cit.*, Vol. 4, p. 307.

[7] Report of the Royal Commission on Shipping Rings, *op.cit.*, p. 114.

[8] See Chapter IV.

during rate wars, and that there was evidence of discrimination against ports not served by conference members.[9]

The Royal Commission carefully noted that the deferred rebate system was inapplicable under the following market structures: (1) when there was no need for regular and fixed sailings; (2) when there is a chronic deficiency of liner tonnage such as on some trades where the outbound and homebound volume of business is badly unbalanced; (3) when commodities which can be shipped in boatload lots are present in large quantity; (4) in the North Atlantic-European trade where the remunerative passenger traffic made available more than enough space for freight cargoes.[10]

The Alexander Committee, however, while recognizing that different market conditions required different types of controls,[11] did not sanction the use of deferred rebates under any circumstances.

The entire British Empire, however, was not completely satisfied with the deferred rebate system nor with the Commission's recommendations concerning it. As a result, the investigation of the system by the Imperial Shipping Committee, first requested by the Australian government in 1921, was broadened as representations from other sources were received. These additional complaints were submitted by crown agents for the colonies, various trade associations in the United Kingdom, several Indian trade associations, the Associated Producers and the Associated Chambers of Commerce of East Africa, the Association of West African Merchants, and the government of New Zealand. Australian dissatisfaction with the rebate system had been aggravated, it will be recalled, by the inability of a government-owned line to join the conference because it was unlawful for it to pay rebates. The discontent of other parts of the Empire with deferred rebates has also been discussed in previous chapters.[12] A unanimous report of the Indian Fiscal Commission, which held the system of shipping rebates to be one of the strongest buttresses of monopoly, helps to explain why all evidence put before the Imperial Committee by shippers in both inward and outward Indian trades was against the deferred rebate system;[13] and this attitude was fairly representative of many in the Dominions and Colonies as well as of some exporters and merchants in the United Kingdom.

[9] op.cit., pp. 71-72.   [10] ibid., p. 18.   [11] op.cit., pp. 54-55.
[12] See Chapters V and VI.
[13] S. N. Haji, "The Deferred Rebate System," *Indian Shipping Series*, No. 3 (Delhi, 1923).

The Committee, which operated solely in an advisory capacity, realized that its work was not only quasi-judicial but also diplomatic, and that to be effective its recommendations had to be both practicable and unanimous. It is not astonishing, therefore, that on this issue a compromise solution was required to prevent a deadlock.[14] The Committee observed that while regular sailings were made in some trades where nothing in the nature of a tie existed, an examination revealed that the exceptional position in these cases was attributable to the peculiar circumstances of the trade. "We have carefully considered the question of the necessity for a 'tie,'" the Committee reported, "and it appears to us that there is a clear mutual obligation—the shipper wants the ship on berth without fail and the shipowner wants the goods on the berth without fail. Hence we find that it is necessary for the Conferences to have some assurance of continuous support from shippers such as will constitute an effective method of preventing intermittent and irresponsible competition for berth cargo by outside ships."[15]

However, the Committee could not ignore the actual and potential abuses associated with the rebate system; and therefore recommended that shippers be given a running option between the deferred rebate system and a system of agreements between shippers' associations and shipowners such as existed in the South African trade.[16] Although the agreement covering the South African-European trade did not provide penalties for infractions of its terms, the Committee felt that in most instances such agreements should define penalties which would attach to breaches by either party. It is interesting to note that a few years later, when the Australian Oversea Transport Association began to function, its contracts provided such penalties.[17]

[14] H. J. Mackinder, "The Imperial Shipping Committee," *Brasseys Naval and Shipping Annual*, 1929, p. 176.

[15] Final Report of the Imperial Shipping Committee on the Deferred Rebate System, Cd. 1802 (1923), p. 19.

[16] *ibid.*, pp. 20-22. The Committee was not unaware of the difficulties of forming such associations, and stated, "On the other hand, it appears that these shippers associations have been difficult to form on a comprehensive basis because of the jealousies and divergent interests of the shippers and the natural fear that they may have to divulge their business to their competitors" (p. 24). Another method of coping with the problem was illustrated by the conference in the Straits Settlements-United Kingdom trade. This conference allowed that once every three years the overlapping of rebates should cease, at which time shippers would be free to leave the conference without loss of rebates. This opportunity was given in 1911, 1914, 1917, and in 1920. *ibid.*, p. 12.

[17] See Chapter VI.

The exclusive patronage contract is employed by the majority of conferences in trades to and from the United States;[18] but it has been challenged by the Departments of Justice and Agriculture, and by the independent Isbrandtsen Line. These contracts will, therefore, be examined in more detail. Exclusive patronage contracts should not be confused with either the agreement between the member lines which constitutes the conference, or with the contract of freightment between a shipping line and a shipper, known as an ocean bill of lading, which provides the conditions of carriage for an individual shipment. The exclusive patronage contract, sometimes referred to as a "steamship contract" or "freight contract," is an agreement between a shipper and a conference granting the former more favorable rates in order to secure his loyalty. Although these contracts vary in certain details they display considerable similarity in their essentials, which are briefly described hereunder.

(1) They are available, as a rule, to large and small shippers alike.

(2) The shipper agrees to ship all of his goods moving over the route controlled by the conference during the contract period (usually one year) on vessels operated by members of the conference, in return for which the shipper is entitled to rates lower (usually by 10 to 20 per cent) than those applicable to non-contract shipments. This agreement requires the shipper, or his agent, to employ conference vessels exclusively and penalizes their use of tramps or non-conference lines.[19] In its implementation, however, this provision is limited somewhat by the contract of sale which may give the control of the routing to another party. (For example, if an exporter has a contract with a conference, he is obligated to use conference vessels exclusively when the terms of sale leave the provision of freight space in his hands, such as when the terms of sale are c. & f., or c.i.f.; but when the sale is made f.a.s., or f.o.b. vessel then the obligation to provide freight space and to pay the freight charges are with the buyer.)

There is some uncertainty regarding: (a) the rights of a shipment

---

[18] In 1950, seventy-eight conferences out of ninety-six, or 81 per cent, employed patronage contracts; although two conferences had been temporarily enjoined, as described subsequently in this chapter, from using them. In 1940 the Maritime Commission reported that prior to World War II, sixty-eight conferences employed this device.

[19] In a few instances contract shippers are permitted to ship via an independent line which maintains the conference tariff.

to contract rates if the exporter has a contract but the shipment is controlled by an importer who does not have a contract; and (b) the responsibility of a contracting shipper to the conference when he no longer controls the routing of cargo in which he has an interest. One important American importer maintains, "The fundamental point would seem to be that the party who is obligated under the terms of the sales contract to provide the freight space should have the conference contract in order to obtain the benefit of the conference contract rate. Conversely, if an importer or exporter who is obligated to provide the freight space chooses to ship on a non-conference line, the conference contract held by the other party should not thereby be vitiated."[20] In short, the patronage contract should bind the shipper only for goods on which he may or must designate the carrier; but since judicial decision is lacking a degree of uncertainty and confusion remains.[21]

(3) The contract, or a supplement attached thereto, usually specifies the commodities that are covered and the rates applicable to them. Most contracts provide that if commodities, in addition to those enumerated, are subsequently dispatched they too are subject to the terms of the agreement; although in some instances contracts are specifically limited to the itemized commodities. A few conferences apply the contract system to only one or a small number of commodities, while others may specifically except certain items from contract treatment. Occasionally conferences agree in their contracts to provide firm freight rates for the term of the agreement (usually one year), but most permit rates to be increased on anywhere from ten to ninety days' notice.[22] Rate decreases made during the life of the contract are applicable to all contractors. To be legal in United

[20] By permission from *Techniques of International Trade*, by Morris S. Rosenthal. Copyright 1950 (McGraw-Hill Book Co., Inc.), pp. 45-48. The views of Mr. Rosenthal, president of both Stein Hall & Co., Inc., a major American importing firm, and the National Council of American Importers, Inc., have influenced much of this section.

[21] Similar difficulties have plagued the implementation of the deferred rebate system. According to the Royal Commission on Shipping Rings (Cmd. 4668) some conferences require the loyalty of both the principal and the forwarding agent, if the latter is employed; while others require loyalty from both consignor and consignee (pp. 30-31). The Alexander Committee found in 1914 that the lines carrying coffee from Brazil required the "loyalty" of shippers on shipments to both the United States and Europe. This unusual situation was made possible by the fact that several shipping companies operated in both trades as did some of the more important coffee importers.

[22] Prior to the Maritime Commission's investigation of the Pacific Coast European Conference in 1947 (3 U.S.M.C. 11), some contracts did not require the conference to give any advance notice of increases in contract rates.

States trades, contract rates presumably must be open to all shippers under like conditions, and the spread between the contract and non-contract rates must be reasonable.[23]

(4) While the shipper who signs a patronage contract may select for the carriage of his goods any vessel operated by any member of the conference, some agreements state that it is their spirit for the shipper to allocate his patronage equitably among the members. Contracts generally provide that if, after the stipulated advance notice, the member lines cannot accommodate the shipper's cargo, the shipper may use non-conference transportation without breaching the agreement.

(5) Various forms of penalties are provided for a breach of contract by a shipper. Prior to 1948 many freight contracts provided that in the event of a breach by the shipper the agreement immediately became null and void as to future shipments; and the shipper became liable for the payment of additional freight on all shipments made since he entered the contract (that is, for the difference between the contract and the non-contract rates in force at the time the shipments were made); but in the case of contracts which have continued in effect for several years the back payments for which the shipper became liable were limited to a specified period, usually one year. In 1948 the Commission, after investigating the Pacific Coast European Conference, ruled that such retroactive penalty clauses were unlawful; and suggested that a multiple of the amount of freight on the shipment which breached the contract might be justifiable as liquidating damages.[24] Recent contracts have been rewritten in the light of this decision, and several contracts now restrict the penalty to the amount of freight that would otherwise have been paid to the conference member for the carriage of the particular shipment which violated the contract by employing non-confer-

---

[23] It is also unlawful for a single line to employ the contract rate system. Eden Mining Co. v. Bluefields Fruit & S. S. Co., 1 U.S.S.B. 41 (1922).

[24] op.cit. See also Isbrandtsen v. North Atlantic Continental Freight Conference, 3 Federal Maritime Board 235 at 246 (1950).

In July 1951 an Oregon Circuit Court concluded that a shipper had violated his contract with the Pacific Westbound Conference by evasion and subterfuge, but refused to award liquidating damages because: (1) the damages sought were a penalty, which is illegal in Oregon; (2) differential rates for contract and non-contract shipments of the same commodity are discriminatory, and therefore in violation of Section 16 of the Shipping Act; and (3) the commodity in question was not similarly treated as a contract commodity when shipped from Canada and the arrangement was unjustly prejudicial to exporters from the United States. Pacific Westbound Conference v. Leval & Co., Inc.

ence transportation. The contracts do not customarily provide penalties for a breach by the conference or its members.

(6) These contracts permit either party to cancel the agreement after specified advance notice (usually 30 to 120 days); but war or its imminence, or government regulations affecting the operations of the carriers, may immediately relieve the lines of their obligation to maintain regular sailings.

(7) Exclusive patronage contracts also generally contain an arbitration clause requiring the shipper and carrier to submit their differences to a board of arbitrators. Mr. Morris Rosenthal states, "Even though there has been little arbitration between shippers and carriers, the inclusion of the clause has done much to improve relations between the two. The tendency of carriers to disregard the requests and claims of shippers, and the tendency of shippers to make unwarranted petty claims, have both lessened greatly with the use of the arbitration clause."[25]

ADVANTAGES AND DISADVANTAGES OF EXCLUSIVE PATRONAGE CONTRACTS

While the Shipping Act of 1916 provides that all conference agreements must be filed with the government, no such requirement applies to patronage contracts between a conference and shippers. As a result, it is not definitely known when they became widely prevalent in American trades, but it is generally thought that they came into fairly general use during the 1920's, after the war-created shortage of shipping turned into a plethora of tonnage. The Shipping Board's regulatory office did not usually concern itself with matters that were not causing complaints, and the Maritime Commission followed much the same policy. The Board, in fact, did not wish to be advised of such "details" as these contracts, so long as the conference employing them was covered by an approved agreement, which for all practical purposes generally meant any agreement which had been filed.[26] Anything done under such an agreement was presumed to be all right as long as there were no complaints. The result of this passivity has been to restrict public knowledge of this form of tying arrangement almost exclusively to court actions and to complaints made to the regulatory body. The courts have main-

[25] Rosenthal, op.cit., p. 50.
[26] Some conferences filed the contract form with their tariffs, but this practice was not universally followed.

tained that the propriety of the patronage contract system is primarily a matter for the regulatory agency to determine in the exercise of its administrative discretion, having regard to the conditions under which the system may be employed and its purpose and effect in relation to the facts of each particular case.[27] The Maritime Commission and its predecessors have endeavored to administer their authority on this basis whenever a case involving the contract system came before them. Where the contract system was found to be unnecessary or to be employed for an improper purpose it was forbidden;[28] but where the system was found to be necessary and beneficial its use has been authorized.[29] Although the Commission held in 1939 that patronage contracts which interfered with the flow of commerce through natural gateways were detrimental to the nation's commerce and therefore unlawful,[30] it was not until 1948 that the Commission carefully examined the details of the system and prescribed modifications in the terms of such contracts.[31]

Dissatisfaction with the Commission's tolerance of the contract system came to a head when the practice was revived after World War II. The attack was spearheaded by the Isbrandtsen Line, a well-known non-conference operator,[32] and by the United States Department of Justice, which attacked the dual rate aspect of the contract system as being discriminatory. The Department of Agriculture intervened in favor of the complainants,[33] while the Maritime Commission intervened in behalf of the defendants. As a result, the North Atlantic Continental Freight Conference and the Continental North Atlantic Westbound Freight Conference were temporarily restrained in January 1949 from making use of the dual-rate-exclusive-patronage contract by the United States District Court for Southern New York.[34] The Court stipulated that the Isbrandtsen Line should bring

[27] U.S. Navigation Co. v. Cunard S. S. Co., 284 U.S. 474; and Swayne & Hoyt v. U.S. 300 U.S. 297.

[28] Eden Mining Co. v. Bluefields Fruit & S. S. Co., 1 U.S.S.B. 41 (1922); Intercoastal Investigation, 1935 1 U.S.S.B.B. 400 (1935); and Gulf Intercoastal Contract Rates, 1 U.S.S.B.B. 524 (1936).

[29] Rawleigh Co. v. Stoomvart, 1 U.S.S.B. 285 (1933); and more recently the Federal Maritime Board in Isbrandtsen v. North Atlantic Continental Freight Conference, Docket 684 (1950).

[30] Contract Routing Restrictions, 2 U.S.M.C. 220 (1939).

[31] Pacific Coast European Conference Agreement, 3 U.S.M.C. 11 (1948).

[32] See Chapter IX.

[33] The Department of Agriculture has argued for open competition for ocean freights at the same time that it has favored international agreements to maintain the prices of key agricultural commodities.

[34] Isbrandtsen v. U.S., 81 F. Supp. 544. Also 96 F. Supp. 883.

before the Maritime Commission a complaint challenging the validity of the dual rate system; and in December 1950 the Federal Maritime Board upheld the practice.[35] Late in January 1951 the District Court, in disagreement with the Board's decision, ruled that the spread of the dual rate provisions in this case were arbitrary and therefore unlawfully discriminatory. In March the Court issued a permanent injunction against the use by the two North Atlantic conferences of the dual rate system. In March 1952 the U.S. Supreme Court, by a 4 to 4 vote, affirmed the findings of the lower court as to the arbitrariness of the rate differentials in the instant case.

In another action the Department of Justice proceeded in 1948 against the Far Eastern Conference in the United States District Court for New Jersey on the grounds that the exclusive patronage contract violated both the anti-trust laws and the Shipping Act.[36] In 1951 the District Court in New Jersey finally ruled that it had the authority to hear the case. The Court held that conference agreements containing the dual rate system were not illegal in themselves, but that each case must be tried on its merits. The authority of the Federal Maritime Board to approve conference agreements, the Court continued, is limited, and therefore such approval does not necessarily exempt participants from the Sherman Anti-Trust Act. The U.S. Supreme Court early in 1952 reversed the district court by a 6 to 2 vote when it ruled that the Federal Maritime Board has primary jurisdiction. As a result of the Supreme Court's holdings in the Isbrandtsen and Far Eastern Conference cases the legal status of the exclusive patronage contract in the United States remains unclear.

As a result of the litigious character of the contract system, numerous arguments pro and con have been declaimed. Some of these are specious and some are concerned exclusively with legal precedent, but a number of sound arguments relevant to an evaluation of the system have also been expressed. The significant arguments both for and against the contract system are essentially the arguments for and against conferences. Proponents contend that without an effective tying arrangement most conferences could not function effectively; and therefore the contract system deserves credit for:

(1) Avoiding the chaos of cutthroat competition.

[35] Isbrandtsen v. North Atlantic Continental Freight Conference, 3 F.M.B. 235 (1950).
[36] U.S. v. Far Eastern Conference, 94 F. Supp. 900.

(2) Assuring the stability of rates necessary to permit and encourage forward trading.

(3) Giving small shippers the same rates as large shippers (cut-throat competition, it is correctly maintained, tends to favor the large shipper).

(4) Avoiding the necessity of frequent bargaining for rates.

(5) Removing the emphasis from rate competition and placing it on service, thereby providing better vessels, regular schedules, proper terminal facilities, and improved handling of cargo.

(6) Helping the smaller (presumably efficient) lines by enabling them to participate in the patronage of large shippers who could not find service adequate to their needs in that provided independently by such lines. (Presumably the large shippers referred to here would, in the absence of a contract supported conference, enter into preferential contracts with one or more of the larger lines whose frequency of sailings more nearly met their needs.)

Opponents, on the other hand, argue that the contract system is not necessary for regularity of service or stability of rates, and in fact does not assure either, for the conferences do not customarily obligate themselves in regard to rates or schedules in the patronage contract. (The implicit assumption here is either that the conference does not require a tying arrangement in order to function effectively, or that rate stability and sailing schedules would be unaffected by the absence of the conference itself. The conference system has been openly attacked in recent litigation only by the Department of Agriculture, which, as an intervenor, has claimed that open competition would result in lower rates, and that shippers of agricultural products should be free to bargain for the cheapest rates without being penalized.) Furthermore, critics of the contract system maintain—and this is their most damaging challenge—that this practice, by enhancing the monopoly power of the conferences, assists them to charge excessive rates and engage in practices which are unduly discriminatory. Numerous other abuses directly associated with the implementation of these contracts are also cited.

Since the advantages and disadvantages of the conference system can be more appropriately considered in Chapter XII, we shall assume at this point that some form of self-regulation is necessary in this industry; and proceed to discuss in the remainder of this chapter the role, in such a scheme, of the exclusive patronage contract. In order to become more intimately acquainted with the contract system it is necessary to examine the faults it has demonstrated in practice.

The contract system has been held discriminatory on several grounds. Some commodities are excepted from the contracts, and it is maintained that this discriminates against commodities that are not permitted this freedom. Insofar as the excepted items are commodities such as grain and lumber, which are suitable for carriage by tramps and which do not generally require regular service, the alleged discrimination may be considered an inevitable consequence of the nature of the goods and the competitive structure of ocean shipping.

A more serious charge is that the government and other large shippers are sometimes accorded special treatment.[37] When government shipments are competitive with goods moving through commercial channels not similarly favored, or when large private exporters or associations of exporters are given consideration not extended to smaller organizations, prompt correction is indicated. It has also been pointed out that through the use of contracts conference carriers may discriminate against certain ports, and that they may attempt to control the routing of traffic moving through gateways they are not even in a position to serve.[38]

A final charge of discrimination arises from the practice of obligating a contract shipper to use the member lines for *all* his cargo. Consequently, if the conference gives notice of an increase in rates on any of the contract commodities, the shipper must agree thereto or else lose the benefit of contract rates on all his other goods. This is not only patently unfair, but also places firms handling several items at a disadvantage with firms handling only one or a few goods.

Another series of complaints has arisen from the contention that the patronage contract is a one-sided affair which favors conference carriers and does not offer shippers an adequate *quid pro quo*. The same service, it is pointed out, is provided to contract shippers and non-contract shippers. The non-contract shipper is compelled to

---

[37] The Pacific Coast European Conference, for example, accorded special treatment prior to 1948 to two powerful groups, the Dried Fruit Association and the Canners' League; and recently the North Atlantic Continental Freight Conference acceded to a request from the Automobile Manufacturers' Association to give its members the benefit of contract rates for sixty days prior to the effective date of their contracts.

[38] The North Atlantic Continental Freight Conference recently proposed to penalize contract shippers who utilized non-conference shipping sailing from Canadian ports. See also Contract Routing Restrictions, 2 U.S.M.C. 220 (1939); and footnote 24.

pay higher rates, it is true, but the contract rates themselves may be quite high enough, if not actually excessive. The patronage contract offered by the North Atlantic Continental Freight Conference in November 1948, for example, did not offer contract shippers rate reductions, but proposed to raise the rates charged non-signers by 20 to 30 per cent over the existing tariff, which was essentially the same as the War Shipping Administration had approved during the war when allowance was made for war risk insurance, bonus payments to seamen, and other war factors. Furthermore, it has been held that the spread between contract and non-contract rates are arbitrary and therefore unjustly discriminatory. Critics of the system point out that the conference carriers make no commitment to contractors to make space available beyond that required of them as common carriers, and that many contracts permit rates to be changed without any advance notice or within a period too short to be adequate for forward trading. Defenders point out that the patronage contract is clearly not intended as a firm space contract, and that the shipper signing a patronage agreement does not obligate himself to ship if he has no shipments to make.

Although it may be agreed that advance notice of rate changes should be given, the proper period which conferences should observe in notifying contract shippers of such changes is difficult to specify. Some maintain that 30 or 60 days should suffice, while others argue in favor of 90 days, one year, or the duration of the contract. Before the war, conference practice varied greatly. And since the requirements of different routes vary, no single solution would be universally applicable, although some minimum period might be required by administrative ruling for all conferences, with a provision allowing for exceptions in event of certain emergencies. Furthermore, while it is true that a shipper can generally cancel the contract on about thirty days notice, the complete absence or the inadequate service of non-conference lines on most trade routes reduces the attractiveness of this option; although it does tend to keep conferences from becoming as arbitrary as they might be under the more rigid deferred rebate system.

It has also been pointed out that the penalty provisions of patronage contracts protect the carriers from violations by shippers, but shippers in turn are not similarly protected if the carriers violate the contract, since penalties applicable against the member lines are not generally stipulated. In addition, the penalties have been charged with being unduly severe. But it was not until 1948 that the Commission, in the Pacific Coast European Conference Agreement Case, ruled against the retroactive penalty which characterized many patronage contracts.[39] Subsequent to this decision, penalty clauses have been modified, but there has been considerable difficulty in reaching a formula which will satisfy the regulatory agency whose scrutiny has become considerably sharper since the system has been under attack in the courts, and at the same time will offer the conferences a tie that is sufficiently binding. Proposals to give the member lines the option of declaring a contract terminated in the event of a breach by a shipper have been frowned on as potentially discriminatory.[40] And provisions which permit the conference to collect damages equal to some multiple of the freight that would have been payable on a shipment made in violation of the agreement have been criticized as being more in the nature of a penalty than liquidating damages. Penalties, it is contended by C. W. Robinson, trial examiner for the Commission, constitute a retaliation against a shipper for patronizing another carrier, and therefore would be in violation of Section 14 of the Shipping Act. Nevertheless, the Federal Maritime Board did not disapprove a contract which provided, in case of a violation, for liquidated damages equal to twice the amount of freight that would have been payable on the shipment constituting the violation.[41]

The Maritime Commission, in short, has generally endeavored to eliminate abuses associated with exclusive patronage contracts only after they were brought to its attention. Prior to World War II the Commission seems to have relied on its slowly developed policy of requiring conferences to admit to membership all qualified applicants, counting on this to place a check on the more extreme monopoly practices of conferences. This policy may have been adequate in the inter-war period during which there was generally a plethora of tonnage, although it does not seem sufficient in the prosperous situation that has existed on most trade routes since the outbreak of war in 1939. One cannot help suspecting, however, that if the Commission's recent attitude on this subject has become stricter, it is more the consequence of the critical attitude of the Department of

[39] op.cit., 3 U.S.M.C. 11.
[40] Himala International v. American Export Lines, 3 F.M.B. 232 (1950); and Isbrandtsen v. North Atlantic Continental Freight Conference, 3 F.M.B. 235 (1950).
[41] Isbrandtsen v. North Atlantic Continental Freight Conference, 3 F.M.B. 235 (1950).

Justice than of the altered relation of the supply of shipping to the demand for it.

The patronage contract system does not of itself guarantee that illegal rebates are not also paid. Since the penalty for such an infraction of Section 14 of the Shipping Act may involve both the loss of the right to enter United States ports and a fine which may run as high as $25,000 for each offense, it is certain that if any such payments are made great care would be exercised to keep them a carefully guarded secret. Nonetheless Professor Mears, while observing that on the whole conferences in American trades probably do not pay secret deferred rebates, does question, as a practical matter, how far the legal machinery of the United States is able to prevent the granting of such payments to shippers exporting to this country.

Conferences governing the inbound trades are often located in foreign countries where such rebates are quite legal and the shippers to whom the payments might be given would in most cases be citizens of foreign countries.[42] In the fifteen years that have elapsed since these doubts were expressed no evidence to support them has become public. If such secret rebates do in fact exist, the probabilities are that they are not common. That secret arrangements have at times existed in some parts of the world, however, cannot be denied. Mr. Haji, writing of deferred rebates in 1923, claimed, "It is an open secret that in the coastal rice trade of Burma, preference is shown to large shippers in respect of (1) rate of rebate, (2) period of deferment, and (3) facility of shipment."[43] If secret understandings between shippers and ship operators do occur in American trades, they are apt to be based on favored treatment in regard to space and shipment facilities, lenience in the payment of claims, and similar discriminatory treatment, the existence of which it is extremely difficult to prove. In fact such favoritism might be accorded large shippers by some lines unbeknownst to other members of the conference, and possibly even unbeknownst to the large shipper who might interpret the actions as "good service." Furthermore, it is possible that a conference, or its members, might in a reverse manner secretly discriminate against a shipper because he has been "disloyal," or for other reasons, and proof of such unfavorable treatment would also be exceedingly difficult to establish.

[42] E. G. Mears, *Maritime Trade of Western United States* (1935), pp. 345-346.
[43] S. N. Haji, *op.cit.*, p. 16.

The validity of any system of tying shippers to members of a conference presupposes the soundness of the conference system itself. If the conference system is not valid, then any tie employed to bind customers to the conference lines is obviously contrary to the public interest. Most complaints concerning deferred rebates and exclusive patronage contracts have not, however, seriously challenged the conference system itself. In fact, since the passage of the Shipping Act in 1916 the necessity of conferences has been taken pretty much for granted in litigation critical of patronage contracts. Therefore, we shall continue the assumption, made earlier, that shipping conferences are necessary (although this particular question will be carefully explored in Chapter XII), and shall now only inquire if under the terms of this assumption a system of tying is required, and if it is, how the public interest can be protected.

It should be clear, from what has preceded, that the ability of a conference on one trade route to operate successfully over a period of years without a tying arrangement, is no reason why, under altered circumstances in the market structure, the same or another conference might not find some form of tie imperative to the maintenance of rate stability and regularity of service. Of course, the mere existence of a tie does not confirm its necessity; and at times tying procedures are doubtlessly employed for exploitative purposes, whether or not that was their original intent. In short, an examination must be made of the particular structure of competition prevailing at a given time on the route in question if one is to reach a sound conclusion regarding the effect of a tie on the public interest.

The Royal Commission on Shipping Rings, for example, recognized and specified certain general market conditions which rendered tying arrangements unnecessary; and both the Alexander Committee and the Imperial Shipping Committee concluded that different market conditions required different types of controls. The explicit conclusions of both British committees, however, were to the effect that some form of tie was frequently necessary.

The American committee was not so clear on this point, and condemned deferred rebates while taking a more tolerant view of the contract system. The American group placed its principal reliance on government regulation. The evidence accumulated by the Maritime Commission and its predecessors reinforces the conclusion that some form of regulation or tying arrangement is required to control the competition of non-conference lines.[44] C. W. Robinson, trial examiner for the Commission, reached the conclusion in 1950 that, "The conference system is sapped of its vitality if there be no method of binding the majority of shippers in the trade. Without the contract system, or some other effective means, the life of a conference would be short in the face of rate manipulations by independent lines or the influx of tramp vessels. Respondents cannot be expected to put off the use of the system until trouble actually brews in the trade, for rate wars completely demoralize commerce and all interests suffer needlessly."[45] One may question the universal applicability of Mr. Robinson's conclusions, but conference experience throughout the world supports his contentions on a great many trade routes.

The danger of cutthroat competition has undoubtedly been enhanced by the over-supply of tonnage which in the past has prevailed during most peacetime years. Cyclical disturbances have acutely aggravated this situation, but the chronic condition of excess tonnage arose from war-stimulated construction, and war-stimulated disturbances in payments and the volume of trade.[46] The validity of both the conference system and its handmaiden, the tying arrangement, are largely predicated on the prevalence of such excess tonnage. Subsequent to World War II, there has been a shortage rather than a surplus of tonnage, and under such conditions the necessity for conferences is considerably reduced and the use of tying arrangements becomes extremely dubious.

The growth of state trading monopolies may materially alter the relationship between shipper and carrier; and so may the renewed development of discriminatory measures designed to favor the shipping of a particular nation, whether for currency, strategic, or other reasons. These developments have not yet progressed far enough to permit a drawing of definite conclusions regarding their effects on the continued need for the conference system; but it is obvious that, since they directly and materially affect the market structure of trade routes, they must be taken into consideration along with other

[44] For example, see Section 19 Investigation, 1935, 1 U.S.S.B.B. 470; Rates, Charges, and Practices of Yamashita and O.S.K., 2 U.S.M.C. 14; and Cargo to Adriatic, Black Sea, and Levant Ports, 2 U.S.M.C. 342.

[45] Examiner's Report in Isbrandtsen v. North Atlantic Continental Freight Conference, Docket No. 684 (1950).

[46] See Chapter III.

factors in determining the validity of a tying arrangement on a particular route.

A review of the four acknowledged methods of binding shippers to conference lines reveals that they all have their shortcomings. The preferential contract is inimical to the public interest, because it is almost invariably discriminatory. The deferred rebate, through its overlapping periods, permits conferences to obtain a strangle hold on many shippers. In addition, this tie is subject to other faults and abuses and may become discriminatory. Agreements between shippers' associations and conferences may also become unfairly discriminatory unless subjected to government supervision. The principal disadvantage of this device, however, is the difficulty encountered in reconciling the conflicting interests of a large number of shippers. It appears best suited to a route, such as the trade from Australia to Europe, where a few major commodities constitute almost the entire movement. The exclusive patronage contract, while potentially free from some of the disadvantages of the preferential contract and the deferred rebate system, also has been subject to abuses.

The crucial question is: Can any tying arrangement be sufficiently binding to perform effectively its purposes of assuring rate stability and regularity of service without being at the same time so strong as to be capable of being abused? There is much evidence to indicate that the answer to this query is negative; and this in turn points to the need for some form of external control. In short, if tying arrangements are necessary they must be strong to be effective; and if they are sufficiently strong, then unfair discrimination, excess profits, wasteful intra-conference competition, and other abuses become possible if not inevitable; and, therefore, supervision by an outside regulatory agency becomes necessary.

Shippers are frequently rendered quite helpless when bound to a conference by a tying agreement; and the interests of exporters, importers, manufacturers, brokers—and last but not least the interests of consumers—all should be protected from the improper use of such arrangements. Shippers should be assured a definite *quid pro quo* in return for committing their patronage. Conference members using these devices should be firmly obligated to provide regular service, to maintain reasonable rates, and to give adequate advance notice of rate changes.

Furthermore, such tying arrangements tend to give conferences using them the power to charge excessive rates. Unless freedom of entry into the trade, and freedom of entry into conference membership can be relied upon to prevent such abuses of monopoly power or rectify them soon after they appear, the probabilities are high that excessive rates and discriminatory practices will occur. While such freedom of entry, if strictly enforced, will tend to eliminate the earning of excessive monopoly profits and to curb the occurrence of abusive and discriminatory monopoly practices, freedom of entry does not guarantee reasonable rates or the absence of all unreasonable discrimination. In periods when tonnage is scarce freedom of entry will have little or no influence, while at times when tonnage is in oversupply it may lead to the operation of much unused carrying capacity.[47]

Some contend that non-conference competition should be relied on to keep the conferences from abusing what might otherwise be their monopoly position.[48] There is much truth in this contention, and the stimulus of competition may often be extremely salutary; but one must not forget that in businesses like shipping, characterized by indeterminate cost structures, the distinction between healthy rate competition and the quoting of rates below cost is, within rather wide limits, extremely difficult, if not impossible to ascertain. The potentialities of non-conference competition for good and evil were discussed in the preceding chapter.

In conclusion, it can be said that if the conference system is necessary, then, under certain circumstances, tying arrangements binding shippers to the conferences are also frequently requisite.[49] Tying agreements, however, not only contain flaws of their own, but by enhancing the monopoly power of the conferences increase the ability of the members to practice abuses. Neither freedom for independents to enter a trade, nor freedom of conference membership to all qualified applicants, appears to offer a satisfactory means of control. In other segments of the economy where indeterminate elements of costs are large and are aggravated by unused capacity, and decreasing costs, and the industry has distinct public utility characteristics, it has been customary to control both cutthroat competition and the abuses of monopoly power by government regulation. The interna-

[47] This argument is developed more fully in Chapter XII.
[48] This is essentially the position of the U.S. Dept. of Justice.
[49] cf. W. Arthur Lewis, "Notes on the Economics of Loyalty," *Economica*, New Series, Vol. 9, Feb. 1942, pp. 333-348.

tional shipping industry has endeavored to prevent cutthroat competition by combining the conference system with tying agreements. To the extent that this combination fails to eliminate rate competition it fails to accomplish its objective, while to the extent that it succeeds in controlling or eliminating such competition it achieves monopoly power. Some form of external regulation, therefore, appears to be necessary if the conference and tying agreement system is to be kept from abusing its monopoly position. An examination of the agencies and means which can most satisfactorily perform these regulatory functions is considered in the concluding chapter.

~·~

CHAPTER XI

TRAMP-LINER COMPETITION AND
TRAMP RATIONALIZATION

BOTH THE Alexander Committee and the Royal Commission on Ship-ping Rings looked at tramp shipping as a potentially important check on the monopolistic authority of liner conferences. They did so de-spite their knowledge that tramps specialized in the transportation of bulk shipments and rarely competed directly with the liners in the carriage of general merchandise.[1] Although their expectations might have been too sanguine, tramps may nevertheless under cer-tain circumstances impose limitations on the power of shipping con-ferences. It is necessary, therefore, to examine this source of com-petition and any changes in it that may have been brought by the passage of time.

The distinction between tramps and liners, one must remember, is real but not definitive. Although some vessels are typically cargo-boats or tramps and others unmistakably cargo liners, a distinction based on function rather than vessel type is more meaningful, be-cause a great number of ships may be employed interchangeably. The principal feature which distinguishes liners from tramps is the regularity of service. "A liner is any vessel that operates over a fixed route on a regular schedule of sailings. On the other hand, a tramp, or general trader, as it is sometimes called, is any vessel which has no fixed route and no regular time of sailing and which is ever seek-ing those ports where profitable cargo is most likely to be found."[2]

---

[1] The Royal Commission, for example, after noting that tramp competition would be more effective in some trades than in others, because of the nature of the cargo, or because transport conditions provided the areas with a large amount of tramp ton-nage, came to the following ambivalent conclusion: "We are of the opinion that in most cases they [tramps] do not constitute for the general merchant a practical alterna-tive to shipping by Conference vessels. We are further of the opinion that, were it not for the system of deferred rebates or some similar tie, many outside shipments of this character would be made and the position of regular lines be thereby seriously af-fected." op.cit., p. 34.

[2] U.S. 75th Cong. 3rd sess., House Document No. 520, Report of the United States Maritime Commission on Tramp Shipping Service (1938), p. 1. The relationship be-tween tramps and liners has occasionally been so intimate that a bastard type known as the tramp liner has been spawned. This term may be used to define two quite dif-ferent operations: (1) vessels which operate in one direction as common carriers on a

223

Tramp cargoes consist for the most part of commodities with the following characteristics: (1) value sufficiently low so that the cheapness of transport outweighs the value of speed and regularity of delivery; (2) relatively great bulk or weight; (3) require no exceptional facilities of the carrier for handling or preserving; (4) availability for shipment in full cargo lots, or capable of being handled in bulk and combined with other shipments without mark or count. Furthermore, when commodities are subject to a seasonal or highly variable movement, or if it is difficult to secure regularly adequate return cargoes, tramps are apt to carry the traffic or to supplement a liner service. Commodities commonly carried by tramps are grains, coal, ores, sugar, cotton, lumber, fertilizers, etc. But despite these limitations, competition between tramps and liners arises under various circumstances.

THE NATURE OF TRAMP-LINER COMPETITION

When trade is active and demand for space is high, liner companies will often charter additional vessels, many of which may have been operating as tramps. Furthermore, during such periods tramps may be placed on berth for general cargo by their agents. Generally these tramps will merely top off a load of bulk cargo with a parcel or so of other commodities, but if the freight market is sufficiently tight a tramp vessel may load largely with general cargo. It must be remembered, however, that the shippers of some commodities find the regularity of liner schedules or the shoreside facilities of the liner companies so indispensable that they rarely if ever would consider shipment via a tramp vessel which has been placed on berth. On most routes, therefore, the competitive impact probably comes principally from the need of conference and independent lines for the additional ships which can be chartered from the available supply of tramps. Nevertheless, if tying arrangements were abolished, tramps would probably be more apt to fill up with general merchandise the space left over by their bulk loads.

On the other hand, the extension of liner service to more and more of the world's routes and the increase in the size of vessels

---

liner basis and return as private or contract carriers on a tramp basis; and (2) vessels operated either under long time charters or for the account of their owners in fairly regular trades on which they carry bulk cargoes on irregular schedules most of the time. In the majority of cases, however, the requirements to operate on a *fixed route and on a regular schedule* quite successfully distinguishes the liner from the tramp, and in fact keeps a goodly number of so-called tramp liners in the tramp category.

have tended to enhance direct competition between liners and tramps. But this competition has been for bulk cargoes, the traditional mainstay of the tramps, rather than for such typical liner traffic as manufactured goods and semi-manufactured items. The liner must maintain its regular schedule, and if its carrying capacity is not required by shippers of general cargo, it enters the market for whatever cargo is offered for the route it serves. The space on a liner left unused after general cargo has been loaded may, and often does, enable it to compete for as big a bulk cargo as is carried by many tramps.[3]

The quotation of "open rates" by numerous conferences generally indicates the existence of such direct competition for cargo which otherwise might be moved exclusively by tramp ships. Competition of this type is aggravated, of course, in depression periods; and the general tendency of liner services in the inter-war period to be chronically overtonnaged rendered this type of competition both bitter and persistent. The rigidity of liner schedules increases the element of fixed costs and thereby subjects carriers of this type to declining costs to a greater extent than is the case for tramps.[4] In short, a liner may find it profitable to carry bulk items under certain circumstances for any rate in excess of the out-of-pocket expense involved, while tramp vessels will ordinarily require more than this.[5] Therefore, regardless of whether it is theoretically tramp or liner cargo (which is a meaningless distinction at best) the competition varies in intensity at different times. But liner operators have come to feel that in return for providing regular sailings they are entitled to first call on all business the route offers, whether the particular cargo requires this regularity or not. We need not be concerned with the merits of this point of view, but the survival of lines in slack periods may depend on their ability to carry such competitive cargo. The development of the tramp liner appears to have come from an attempt to obtain some of the advantages of operating on a fairly

[3] Liverpool Steamship Owners Association *Annual Report, 1934*, p. 18. It should be noted that while a great many tramps are much smaller than most cargo liners, this is not true of all tramp vessels. The concentration during World War II on the construction of relatively large vessels (10,000 deadweight and larger) has undoubtedly increased the average size of tramp vessels.

[4] *supra*, Chapter II.

[5] At times tramps will also handle cargo at any rate that exceeds handling costs in order to get to a more promising cargo area. They will frequently carry for less than full costs rather than go into lay-up; but unlike the liner the tramp generally does not have access to higher-paying cargo to offset losses incurred in transporting low-paying items, and is not obligated to observe a prearranged schedule.

regular route without incurring the full burden of fixed costs which result from relatively inflexible schedules.[6]

It appears, in conclusion, that it is in periods of active demand for carrying capacity that tramps are most apt to participate in the transportation of general cargo, although they might participate in this business to a somewhat greater extent if it were not for tying arrangements. On the other hand, competition between tramps and liners is no less active in slack periods, for it is then that liner services become increasingly dependent on the carrying of bulk commodities which they would otherwise be content to leave to the tramps. It seems, therefore, that on most routes tramps are in a position to temper the monopoly position of liner conferences only when trade is booming and space is scarce. But even at such times the additional carrying capacity required for general merchandise is much more apt to be provided by the chartering of additional tonnage by lines regularly serving the trade than it is by tramps being placed on berth for general cargo, although here again it may well be the tying arrangements which restrain shippers from using tramp vessels. Nevertheless, even if competition from tramps is thus relatively restricted, it still exists as a potential threat, if not as an active competitor; and therefore it becomes necessary to determine whether anything has occurred since the major investigations were made in the early part of the century which has affected the potency of this latent competition.

Statistics showing the total tonnage of tramp shipping have always been disputable; and so long as classification is of necessity based on functional definitions and the functions are subject to change and to a certain extent are interchangeable, then quantitative data concerning tramp shipping will doubtlessly remain debatable. In 1909 the Royal Commission on Shipping Rings presented two estimates of the proportion of the British merchant marine which consisted of tramp shipping. One estimate claimed that two-thirds of British merchant tonnage was composed of tramps, while the other estimate claimed that tramps composed 50 to 80 per cent of the tonnage;[7] and although these estimates are not contradictory they do indicate the existence of a serious definitional problem. This problem has remained unsolved and as a result it is difficult to

---

[6] cf. Walter A. Radius, *United States Shipping in Transpacific Trade 1922-1938* (Stanford University Press, 1944), p. 20.

[7] Cd. 4668 *op.cit.*, pp. 34, 95.

trace in the years that have followed more than the most general shifts in the relative quantities of tramp and liner tonnage.

For some years the extension of liner services encroached on the traffic domain of tramps, and, according to an authoritative shipping historian, "The prolonged slump which began in the summer of 1920 tilted the balance still further in favor of the lines; for the regular services were able to take care of a large proportion of the diminished volume of cargoes on offer."[8] The decline in coal exports from Great Britain was also a hard blow to tramp-owners. A series of studies made between 1926 and 1938 all testified to the decline of tramp shipping; and it was not until the latter year that a statistical study aroused suspicion that the decline of tramp shipping had been exaggerated and that much of the apparent decline had possibly been more cyclical than secular in nature.[9] Since World War II tramp shipping appears, for the time being at least, to have grown in importance.[10] This is probably due in large measure to the increased

[8] C. Ernest Fayle, A Short History of the World's Shipping Industry (George Allen & Unwin Ltd., 1933), pp. 296-297.

[9] The following publications all testified to the decline, in one way or another, of tramp shipping: E. S. Gregg, "The Decline of Tramp Shipping," Quarterly Journal of Economics, February 1926; E. T. Chamberlain, "Liner Predominance in Transoceanic Shipping," U.S. Dept. of Commerce Bulletin, 448, December 1926; Franz Lohse, Die Entwicklung der Trampschiffahrt in der Nachkriegzeit, dissertation, Christian Albrecht University, Kiel, 1934; Chamber of Shipping of the United Kingdom, Annual Report, 1934; M. O. Phillips, Tramp Shipping: Its Changing Position in World Trade, dissertation, University of North Carolina, 1937; and Report of the United States Maritime Commission on Tramp Shipping Service, Washington, 1938. It should be noted that Phillips' conclusions are based on Lohse's analysis, and the Maritime Commission based its report on the findings of Lohse, Phillips, and the Chamber of Shipping of the U.K.

Dr. Radius questioned these conclusions in 1944 on the basis that the years chosen by Lohse were not suitable for calculating a trend (op.cit., p. 182). A few years earlier Dr. L. Isserlis published some data concerning the classification of British tonnage which is highly significant not only because Great Britain was the world's premier operator of both tramp and liner tonnage, but because much of the alleged decline of tramp shipping in previous analyses was predicated on the fall of the British tramp industry. Dr. Isserlis' statistics show that British tramp tonnage not only expanded slowly from 1914 to 1929, and from 1929 to 1936; but that in relation to cargo liner tonnage, tramp tonnage declined very slightly from 1914 to 1929, and gained somewhat from 1929 to 1936. L. Isserlis, "Tramp Shipping, Cargoes and Freights," Journal of the Royal Statistical Society, Vol. ci, 1938.

Subsequent to writing the foregoing the author has had the opportunity of reading an unpublished dissertation entitled The Co-ordination of Market Forces in Ocean Tramp Shipping with Special Reference to the Period 1920-1939 submitted to the University of London by Hector Gripaios. Mr. Gripaios is also of the opinion that Lohse's estimates overstate the decline of tramp shipping. He believes that tramp shipping held its own in the dry cargo field during the interwar period, but that it has lost ground since the close of the Second World War.

[10] M. G. Kendall, "United Kingdom Merchant Shipping Statistics," Journal of the Royal Statistical Society, Vol. cxi, 1948. cf. Gripaios' views in Footnote 9.

volume of boat-load shipments which have resulted from the dispatch of relief and recovery cargoes financed by the United States government, and by the bulk purchasing of state trading monopolies. Regardless of whatever the long-run trend, or lack of trend, for tramp shipping may be, the available evidence strongly indicates that for the forseeable future competition between tramps and liners will not flag because of an overall insufficiency in tramp tonnage.

The total tramp tonnage, however, is far less important than the presence of tramp vessels at a specific time and place to make a bid for cargo which liners also want to carry. Beyond noting that large volumes of bulk cargoes traditionally attract tramps in large numbers to certain parts of the world and that tramp owners are constantly seeking the most profitable opportunities, there is nothing definite that can be said in this connection.

Of even greater significance to the competitive situation than the position of tramps is the fact that tramp service is not at all suitable for many commodities. In addition to the speed and predictable regularity required by many shippers of general cargo, and the fact that transportation costs are of little importance to many manufactured items, numerous commodities require specialized handling or carrying facilities that usually precludes all but vessels specially designed for the purpose. Refrigerator vessels for meat and fruits, some ore carriers, and tankers are the more obvious examples of vessel specialization; but the numerous general cargo carriers specially designed for particular routes are also of importance. These specialized carriers have of course developed much new traffic that would not otherwise have moved, but they may have carrying capacity left over after loading fruit or meat, for example, and they generally have no specialized cargo to carry on the return leg of their voyage; so they too may at times become competitive with tramps. To the extent that petroleum has encroached on coal, tankers have deprived tramps of one of their most important sources of freight, for coal is not only a typical tramp cargo, but coal exports, especially from England, provided tramps with an outbound cargo from Europe. To the extent, however, that the oil industry has developed new traffic it operates outside the orbit occupied by dry cargo carriers, tramp and liner alike.[11]

[11] On balance, the development of the petroleum industry has created traffic for dry cargo liners. Shipments of case oil and small lots of bulk oil transported in deep tanks are important liner cargoes, as of course are supplies for wells, refineries, and pipelines.

The growth of business requiring the speed and regularity which only liners provide, the development and operation of an increased number of specialized ships, and the indifference of some commodities to lower tramp rates have all conspired to reduce the area of competition between liners and tramps. Nevertheless, the prevalence of tying arrangements indicates that most conferences fear outside competition, and such competition might come from tramps more frequently if shippers' patronage were not bound.

It appears reasonable to conclude that although potential competition as well as actual competition between tramps and liners tend to be restricted to certain commodities, this competition is of considerable importance on some routes. Some potential competition is kept from becoming actual competition by binding shippers to conference members. The growth of specialized carriers has perhaps been more instrumental in developing new traffic than it has been in limiting further the competitive area, although the regular service provided on the return segment of the voyage might deprive tramps of some business. Furthermore, it appears that there is ample tramp shipping available to provide liners with competition, although not all routes will experience the pressure equally. The principal limiting factor now is much the same as it was when the Royal Commission and the Alexander Committee made their reports; namely, that tramps do not constitute a practical alternative for most shippers of general cargo.

In the middle 1930's, however, a development took place which reduced tramp and liner competition significantly; and since this occurrence still casts a large cloud over the future prospects for competition between these two types of shipping it is necessary to consider it at some length. This development was the inauguration of a cooperative rationalization scheme for tramp shipping which bears a close resemblance to certain international commodity agreements.

RATIONALIZATION SCHEMES

Two attempts to achieve international control of charter rates were made early in the present century when tramps were suffering serious losses, but these efforts were not markedly successful. In 1905 the Sailing Ship Owners' International Union, with the assistance of a bounty from the French government, essayed to set minimum rates, on a basis which afforded no profit, for sailing vessels on certain long, Europe-bound voyages. In the same year an agreement known as the Baltic and White Sea Conference was negotiated by a number of vessel owners carrying lumber from Russian and Scandinavian sources to Western European destinations. While minimum rates were established, this organization's lasting contribution was the drafting of a uniform charter party, and the formulation of rules for measuring lumber, loading, discharging, and insurance.[12] It was not until almost thirty years later that attempts to control tramp rates were repeated; and in view of the tramp industry's highly individualistic traditions all such attempts appear exceedingly strange at first glance. Obviously only the pressure of outrageous circumstance can explain such a basic alteration in behavior, and it was the length and severity of the Great Depression on top of a protracted period of poor financial results that produced the change.

In 1934 the acute depression in world tanker freights and the large volume of laid-up tonnage induced European tankship owners to form the International Tanker Owners' Association to operate an international pool. However, since tank vessels are not directly competitive with either dry cargo tramps or liners the formation of this pool would not be of concern to this study if this development had not influenced the creation in early 1935 of a rationalization scheme for dry cargo tramps.[13] There was sufficient community of interest in the tanker industry so that, once the active support of the big oil companies was gained, the industry was able to organize the tanker pool without government aid; but the tramp rationalization scheme, like the earlier Sailing Ship Owners' International Union, required governmental financial assistance to get started.

The British Shipping (Assistance) Act originally made available for one year a subsidy of £2,000,000 to owners of British tramp vessels, and provided a loan fund of £10,000,000 for advances to shipowners for scrapping obsolete vessels and building new ships or modernizing existing tonnage.[14] The scrap-and-build subsidy, which was intended at one and the same time to reduce the amount of old ton-

[12] J. F. Myhre, *Twenty Years with the Baltic and White Sea Conference* (Liverpool, 1927).

[13] For a description of various earlier proposals for international action to alleviate the distressed condition of shipping in the 1930's, see League of Nations, Notes by Economic Relations Section and the Communications and Transit Section on the Merchant Shipping Crisis (mimeographed; March 16, 1933), pp. 23-26.

[14] For details of these subsidies, see Great Britain, *Assistance to British Shipping,* Cd. 4754 (1934). The scrap-and-build subsidy provided loans at low interest rates to owners who were required to scrap two tons of old for every ton of new shipping built or one ton of old for each ton modernized.

nage and to modernize the British merchant fleet, applied to both tramps and liners. It had its counterpart in the maritime legislation of several other nations, and possessed no unique significance for this study. The program and experience of the tramp subsidy, however, are of the utmost importance, for it inaugurated a period of successful control of international tramp rates.

The Assistance Act, which was extended so that it ran for three years, authorized the payment of a subsidy to British owners on the basis of gross ton-days of operation of ships as tramps.[15] The total amount, which was not to exceed £2,000,000 per annum, was to be reduced if the average level of freight rates during the subsidy year rose above 92 per cent of the average level for the year 1929.[16] This payment procedure was unlike that of the Tanker Pool which collected a certain percentage of all freight revenues of vessels in operation for distribution to owners of laid-up tankers.

The British government's decision to pay their tramp subsidy to operating tonnage rather than to idle tonnage seems to have been due to its desire to increase the employment of British shipping. It was realized that the employment of British ships could be increased if the subsidy enabled British shipowners to undercut their foreign competitors; but if this were done the subsidy would be dissipated and the deplorable financial condition of many British owners would remain unaltered.[17] Therefore, it was decided that the Tramp Shipping Administrative Committee, on which both tramp and liner interests were represented and which had been created to assist the

[15] Eligible vessels were those registered at a United Kingdom port as a British ship as of January 1, 1934, and new vessels built in the United Kingdom so registered after that date. Tankers, passenger ships, and vessels with a substantial amount of refrigerated space were excluded. No better testimony to the difficulty of distinguishing a tramp from a liner exists than the fact that draftsmen of this legislation gave up in despair the attempt to make a statutory distinction. Parliament then proceeded to define a tramp voyage as one "in the course of which all the cargo carried is carried under charter party but does not include any voyage during any part of which more than twelve passengers are carried." Coastwise trade and some near-by trades were excluded.

[16] The amount of the subsidy payable was reduced by £250,000 for each percentage point over 92 that was achieved by the annual average level of freight rates; so that if the index reached 93 per cent the subsidy payable was reduced to £1,750,-000, and at 94 per cent the amount payable was cut to £1,500,000, etc. The index number of tramp shipping freights prepared by the Chamber of Shipping of the United Kingdom was employed.

[17] Answers to questionnaires issued by the Chamber of Shipping of the U.K. showed that British tramp shipowners as a whole were unable to make adequate provision for depreciation between 1929 and 1938. British Shipping in the Orient, *op.cit.*, p. 11. Also see Chapter XII.

Board of Trade with the administration of the subsidy program, should seek to control charter rates and in order to accomplish this would invite the cooperation of shipowners of other countries.[18] This cooperation was obtained from shipowner's organizations in all the principal tramp-owning countries except Japan, whose tramp ships operated mainly in Oriental and Pacific waters. Minimum freight rates were established in the Europe-bound trades from the River Plate, from Australia, and from the St. Lawrence-American North Atlantic range. These rates were gradually raised as conditions improved, and supplementary controls such as the regulation of ballast sailings to Argentine waters and the regulation of time charters were added.

Although there were difficulties, some loopholes, and some chiseling, the scheme was generally considered to have been successful. By 1937, however, the improvement in general business conditions had raised the freight rate index above the average 1929 level; so the subsidy scheme was terminated at the end of that year. As minimum rates were established for tramp cargoes, minimum rates for liner parcels were also established by agreements with liner companies and conferences. This cooperation from the liners not only contributed to the successful operation of the tramp program, but was obviously of advantage to the liner companies as well. One liner operator stated, "We have conference rates out to South America, but we have nothing to hold on to homewards except the Tramp Administrative Committee's minimum rate, so it is of considerable benefit to us to cooperate."[19] In the grain trade from the Atlantic Coast of North America, where liners and tramps are in permanent rivalry, the scheme could succeed only if this competition was stabilized.

Encouraged by the operation of the tramp rate control scheme, shipowners in the Baltic and White Sea-Western Europe trade once again attempted to establish minimum rates on timber. The Baltic and International Maritime Conference was organized for this purpose, and in January 1936 inaugurated minimum rates on timber for

[18] The control of rates was also unlike the methods of the Tanker Pool where each member retained complete freedom to charter at any rate he liked. The Tanker Pool worked for better rates by making the alternative of laying-up more attractive and thereby reinforcing the position of owners of active tonnage.

[19] A speech before shareholders of Lamport and Holt Line, Ltd., in March 1938 by Philip Haldin, printed in the *Times of Argentina*, April 18, 1938, according to Wickizer, *op.cit.*, p. 104.

both liners and tramps.[20] Although the Russian government did not approve the "Baltwhite Minimum Freight Scheme," this plan was renewed in 1937 and again in 1938.

The Soviet Union also firmly opposed, and exerted its utmost influence to get foreign shipowners to ignore, an attempt of the Tramp Shipping Administrative Committee, which was unsuccessful, to fix minimum rates from the Black Sea and Baltic to the St. Lawrence. The Soviet government claimed all its imports and one-half of its exports in the Baltic and White Sea-Western Europe route were carried in its own vessels by 1937.[21] The Russian attitude led the Chamber of Shipping of the United Kingdom to observe, "It is obvious that where, as in Russia, a foreign government controls the import, export and transport, only firm support by the British government can suffice to safeguard the interests of British shipping."[22] The Baltwhite scheme was suspended at the end of 1938.

EVALUATION OF TRAMP SHIPPING ADMINISTRATIVE COMMITTEE

An examination of the minimum rates established by the Tramp Shipping Administrative Committee reveals that between early 1935 and early 1937 the basic rates on bulk grain imports from the River Plate were gradually raised from the prevailing open market rate of around 12 shillings per long ton to 25 shillings. At the time it was estimated that 16 s. 6 d. barely covered the running expenses of the average British steamer, without allowing anything for repairs, surveys, depreciation, or interest on capital.[23] Shippers claimed, however, that 20s. permitted a modern tramp to come out in ballast and more than pay its way on the round trip.[24] As a result, River Plate shippers in 1938 held off chartering, going on strike as it were, and succeeded in driving the rate back to 20s.[25] The minimum rates on bulk grain from the St. Lawrence were gradually boosted from an open market rate of less than 1s. 6d. per quarter in 1935 to 2s. 9d. in January 1937; and the open market rate from Western Australia

---

[20] This conference, which reported a membership of 575 owners and brokers of 22 nationalities controlling 9,750,000 gross tons of shipping, should not be confused with the liner conferences which represent the principal subject of this volume. Liner conferences do not include brokers and owners of tramps.

[21] Chamber of Shipping of the United Kingdom, *Annual Report, 1936-1937*, pp. 77-78.

[22] *ibid.*

[23] Sanderson, "Control of Ocean Freight Rates in Foreign Trade," *op.cit.*, p. 70.

[24] Wickizer, *op.cit.*, p. 104.

[25] W. Arthur Lewis, "The Inter-Relations of Shipping Freights," *Economica*, New Series, Vol. VIII, No. 29, Feb. 1941, p. 71.

was stepped up from 19s. 3d. prevailing prior to the scheme to 31s. in January 1937.[26] Attempts made to control rates in other trades did not meet with the same degree of success as on the three aforementioned routes. On these three routes liner rates on grain moved correspondingly. Of course the scrapping of old vessels and the increased demand for tonnage which arose from the drought in the United States and from armament programs in Europe and Japan greatly assisted the rate control scheme, but the controls themselves were regarded unquestionably by the trade as an important factor in raising rates.

No more eloquent testimony to shipowners' satisfaction with the control program can be found than their determination to continue it after the expiration of the British subsidy. Prior to the termination of the subsidy the Tramp Shipping Administrative Committee had obtained agreement from the owners of over 90 per cent of all British tramp and liner tonnage to continue their cooperation. The liner companies promised to cooperate in the spirit of the scheme, and to be bound by its provisions when their ships operated as tramps; and furthermore, liner companies were given the right to veto the extension of the control agreement to areas in addition to the River Plate, Australian, and St. Lawrence trades.[27] An international conference of shipowners was held in London in December 1937 and assurances were obtained from the respective national shipowners' associations that they would support the continued cooperation of their members in the rate control program. An international Consultative Committee on which each of the countries would be represented was created. Denmark, Estonia, Finland, France, Germany, Greece, Yugoslavia, the Netherlands, Norway, Spain, and Sweden were represented at the meeting; and expressions indicating general willingness to continue cooperation were also received from Belgium, Canada, Italy, and Poland.[28] In September 1938 the Greek government enacted a law making the cooperation of Greek shipping compulsory.[29] During 1938 plans to form a compensation pool, similar to the Tanker Pool, to encourage the laying-up of ships, were drafted by British tramp shipowners; but as the freight market continued to

---

[26] Data on rates in this paragraph based on Sanderson, *op.cit.*, p. 71; and Wickizer, *op.cit.*, p. 104.

[27] Liverpool Steamship Owners' Association, *Annual Report, 1937*, pp. 17-18.

[28] Sanderson, *op.cit.*, p. 79. Also Sixth Report to the President of the Board of Trade on the Work of the Tramp Shipping Administrative Committee (1938) Cmd. 5750.

[29] Chamber of Shipping of the United Kingdom, *Annual Report, 1938-1939*, p. 85.

slump agitation was resumed for a government subsidy. Accordingly, in March 1939 a new British Shipping Assistance Bill was introduced in Parliament. Its financial provisions were more liberal than the 1935 Act, and it included proposals for considering methods of adjusting the supply of tonnage to its demand through the formation of an international tonnage pool.[30] However, during this period of unsubsidized voluntary cooperation minimum rate control was extended to the grain trade from United States South Atlantic and Gulf ports in order to fill the gap which existed between North Atlantic ports and River Plate ports; and the Chamber of Shipping of the United Kingdom reported the control program to be working well.[31] The outbreak of war in 1939 caused the suspension of the Tanker Pool and the tramp control program, and the shelving of the new Shipping Assistance Bill.

The respect paid the Tramp Shipping Administrative Committee by foreign as well as by British shipowners during the critical period in which it had no power to enforce its recommendations is conclusive demonstration of the ability, which had previously been frequently questioned, of tramp shipowners to cooperate voluntarily in a rate-fixing program. W. Arthur Lewis, in a penetrating study of the effects of control by the T.S.A.C., helps to explain this willingness to work together. He observes that shipowners are in almost unanimous agreement that the price elasticity of total demand for their services is zero. "It may make some difference," Lewis continues, "as between grain moving from the Plate, Australia, or North America, what relation exists between the freights from those ports. But provided that the proper relationship is maintained, there is little reason to believe that a general fall in grain freights from all ports would have any significant effect on the volume of trade in grain."[32] Although the application of this conclusion to commodities for which demand and supply are more elastic than they are for grain may be unwarranted, the small addition to costs that freight charges often represent argues in favor of its extension to many other commodities.

In addition, it should be remembered that tramps have important fixed costs, and since a tramp shipping company has no control over

---

[30] ibid., 1939-1940, p. 66.   [31] ibid., 1938-1939, pp. 84-85.
[32] Lewis, op.cit., p. 71. It should be pointed out that although the price elasticity of the total demand for shipping may be very low at any particular period of time the elasticity over longer periods may be large. No one, for instance, can gainsay that the declining price of ocean freights has been one of the most important factors in the great expansion of world trade that has taken place in the past ninety years.

the market there is little stimulus to lay up a ship so long as it can earn something more than its variable expenses. Ohlin explains that tramp shipping is in this respect like agriculture and certain manufacturing industries which produce standardized goods for large markets. "Supply reactions are not sensitive to rate reductions, until rates have reached the level of variable costs."[33] This analogy is even more poignant when one recalls that the world's principal charter market, the Baltic Shipping Exchange, operates very much like a security or commodity exchange.[34] It is not astonishing, therefore, that rationalization schemes for tramps and for tankers have borne more than a small resemblance to commodity agreements.

The effect of these shipping control schemes on the allocation of resources, however, arises from conditions more or less peculiar to the ocean transportation industry. Since it is impossible for ship pools to operate buffer stocks, because transportation service is a flow and cannot be stored, they have concentrated on restricting output and on raising prices by agreement. The freight market is apt to be far more complex than the markets for most basic agricultural and mineral products, for despite its standardization tramp shipping is still a rather varied industry affected not only by its own operating problems but also by the market for many of the world's bulk commodities and their peculiar fluctuations.

It is on the divergence of some rates from others that the world depends for a proper distribution of ships as conditions change. If all rates are fixed, this mechanism for controlling the flow of shipping ceases to function. A similar problem exists in railroading, but since the railroad company is under legal obligation to carry all the traffic that is offered additional trains are provided, within limits, without any change in rates. The shipping industry is under no such compulsion. The T.S.A.C. avoided this difficulty by fixing rates on a limited number of routes while leaving the others to adjust themselves in the market.[35] The great demand for shipping created by the war makes an analysis of the effect of the rate control schemes on

[33] Ohlin, *op.cit.*, p. 530.

[34] The Baltic Shipping Exchange was opened in 1883; but its functions had long been performed, in a less highly organized manner, at the Baltic Coffee House. On its spacious floor vessels all over the world are chartered in a highly competitive market. Since 1949 one small portion of the floor has been devoted to the chartering of aircraft. Prior to World War II it was also one of the chief commodity exchanges in Europe. Its membership includes shipowners, ship brokers, and buyers and sellers of bulk cargoes such as grain, timber, oil, oilseeds, and coal.

[35] Lewis, *op.cit.*, p. 76.

construction and scrapping unnecessary; but assuming that the volume of ocean-borne trade during the period covered by the control programs was abnormally low we can conclude that the cooperation of tramp shipowners was not inimical to the public interest.[36] A projection of this conclusion to cover the effects of possible future control schemes, however, is definitely not justified. Nevertheless, a persistent agitation for a renewal of the tramp freight control program is well under way.

Before the end of the war the British shipping industry in a statement of its postwar program expressed itself in favor of the restoration along prewar lines of liner conferences, a tanker pool, and a tramp control scheme.[37] In the immediate postwar prosperity only conferences were restored; but the drop in tramp freights that took place in the latter part of 1948 and continued through 1949 led to a revival of interest in a cooperative tramp pool, and the large postwar increase in tanker tonnage also regained interest for a new international tanker pool.

Direct controls over British shipping were not removed until the end of 1948, but indirect controls and interference continued; so proposals to create these pooling arrangements were not acted upon prior to the outbreak of war in Korea, after which the rate levels rapidly improved. However, it may be taken as a foregone conclusion that whenever rates again fall sharply the agitation to form new pools will once more become active, and if rates remain seriously depressed for a considerable period of time the prospects for the creation of such pools will become extremely good.

The relation of the Tramp Shipping Administrative Committee

[36] An excellent analysis of the Tanker Pool and of its effects is contained in Tjalling Koopmans, *Tanker Freight Rates and Tankship Building* (London: P. S. King & Son, 1939). After allowing for the basic differences in the methods of the tanker and dry cargo tramp rationalization programs there is still sufficient similarity to warrant quoting one of Koopmans' conclusions. "The problem of new building is the weak point of the Tanker Pool. As long as the Tanker Pool continues to ensure profitable investment to anyone who orders the construction of a tanker, capital will stream into the trade. Loss being eliminated, there remains a chance of considerable profit through a sudden rise in demand—a situation which cannot persist ad infinitum when free entrance to the trade is maintained" (p. 170). While the tramp scheme may not have ensured a profit, it did do much to enhance the prospects of profitable operation. In any case the outbreak of war created a demand both for tankers and dry cargo vessels of such vast proportions that the Allies can count as fortunate any factors which stimulated construction prior to 1939, regardless of what the economic consequences of these factors might have been if war had not occurred.

[37] General Council of British Shipping, *British Shipping Policy* (London: 1944), pp. 5-6.

to liner companies was intimate and clear. British liner companies were represented on the T.S.A.C. Competition between tramps and liners for general cargo was discouraged by the provision in the British subsidy program which limited payments to voyages "in the course of which all the cargo carried is carried under charter party"; and after the expiration of the subsidy the liner interests were given the right to veto an extension of control to new areas. Finally, liners customarily cooperated in the establishment and observation of rates in the controlled trades, although liner rates were as a rule differentially higher by small amounts. (Liners generally offered faster service, and at times were willing to book smaller parcels than most tramps; and therefore were entitled to somewhat higher rates.) To the extent that tramp control programs succeed in avoiding cutthroat competition in periods of severe depression they may be of temporary benefit to the world economy; but once started there is a strong tendency for them to remain active long after the "emergency" has ended. The long-run tendency, therefore, is for these control schemes to reduce still further the limited competition that exists between tramps and liners. Their effect on ship construction and scrapping will tend to increase and prolong a surplus of tonnage; but since political and strategic factors appear to dominate the construction cycle for dry cargo vessels this aspect of tramp control programs may not be of great significance.

It may be noted in conclusion that a device has been developed to cope with the condition of depressed ocean rates which has been chronic in such a large number of peacetime years since the turn of the century. This device has succeeded in gaining the approval of most tramp shipowners and of the governments of several of the more important tramp-owning countries.[38] Given a depression in ocean rates, the prospects for a restoration of a tramp control scheme are very good. Competition between tramps and liners for the carriage of general cargo was shown in the first part of this chapter to be rather severely restricted; and therefore it cannot be too much relied on to curb the monopoly power of liner conferences. A revival of tramp freight controls will reduce still further such limited competition as might otherwise prevail between these two types of shipping.

[38] The large amount of tramp tonnage registered under the Panamanian flag since World War II, in order to enjoy more freedom than is permitted by the restrictions of most other governments, may make it more difficult to obtain full cooperation in a new control scheme.

CHAPTER XII
THE ECONOMICS OF SHIPPING CONFERENCES

THE PRECEDING CHAPTERS have described the procedures for self-regulation developed by the operators of ocean liner services. Some form of regulation has been necessary; because both demand and supply functions in this industry tend to be rather inflexible, and therefore uncontrolled competition works badly. Costs are rendered indeterminate because of the importance of unused capacity, decreasing costs, joint costs, and opportunity costs; while demand often appears to be quite inelastic. Furthermore, the supply of tonnage is substantially influenced by political factors, wars especially, which tend to contribute to its redundancy, and since vessels are durable capital instruments with a life of many years the total supply of ocean transportation does not respond at all promptly to a reduction in rates. Only when scrapping and laying-up exceed new construction is the supply reduced, and laid-up tonnage still hangs over the market. Industries with these characteristics have customarily experienced cutthroat competition, combination of the competing units into a monopoly, or cartelization. The shipping industry has engaged all three of these alternatives; but since cutthroat competition cannot last for long, and because national-flag considerations have so far generally kept the combination movement from proceeding to its logical monopolistic conclusion, the formation of shipping conferences or rings has been the almost universal solution.[1] What have been the economic effects of this form of cartelization?

[1] It should not be inferred that the combination movement did not concentrate the ownership of much liner tonnage in the hands of a few companies. The tendency to combination in British shipping was accentuated by World War I. C. E. Fayle wrote in 1933 that "it would probably be safe to say that about a quarter of the tonnage on the Register of the United Kingdom has been controlled more or less directly, since the war, by one or the other of the 'Big Five'—the P. & O., Royal Mail, Cunard, Ellerman, and Furness Withy Groups." (*A Short History of the World's Shipping Industry*, George Allen & Unwin, Ltd., p. 298). Estimates of the ownership of British liner tonnage exclusively show even greater concentration. In 1926 it was estimated that 72 per cent of British liner tonnage was owned by seven large shipping combines; 14 per cent by eight other large corporations; 4 per cent by the Australian and Canadian governments; and less than 10 per cent by smaller concerns. (E. T. Chamberlain, "Liner predominance in Transoceanic Shipping," *op.cit.*, p. 37) The Great Depression gave further impetus to the combination movement, especially in Germany and in Italy. Nationalistic considerations, however, prevented the merging in

Although there have been several attempts to delineate the necessary conditions for workable competition and other efforts to measure the extent of concentration and monopoly power, there is no agreement among economists concerning the universality of criteria for determining the former, nor are there entirely satisfactory quantitative standards for evaluating the latter.[2] However, we know that liner services are characterized by fewness of sellers and that the threat of cutthroat competition has often compelled them to form a conference whose monopoly powers are restricted principally by: (1) intra-conference competition; (2) actual or potential competition from other lines,[3] which may or may not intend to join the conference; (3) alternate sources of supply or markets; (4) actual or potential competition from tramps; (5) the bargaining strength of shippers; and (6) government regulation or intervention. The influence of these limiting factors varies considerably from one route to another and from one commodity to another. Other characteristics of the industry are that: (1) it produces, with minor exceptions, an undifferentiated service for which the demand is derived; (2) there are usually many buyers of its service, and they are generally not organized to bargain collectively for shipping freights; and (3) entry of newcomers to the trade though difficult is not impossible.

PROFITS AND FREIGHT RATES

A careful study of profits and freight rates might shed much light on the effects of conferences; but unfortunately only fragmentary evidence regarding profits and rates are readily available. Several interesting indices of tramp freight rates are published, and despite the fact that they are necessarily subject to the inevitable weaknesses of sampling and the usual comparative shortcomings which are common to indices, they are nonetheless reasonably serviceable.[4] Unfortunately, however, no index of liner rates is available, and

---

the interwar period of major shipping companies operating under different flags. So on all the more important routes, and on most minor ones as well, several separate lines have been operating.

[2] For a review of the literature on this subject, see Joe S. Bain, "Price and Promotion Policies" in Howard S. Ellis ed., *A Survey of Contemporary Economics* (Philadelphia: The Blakiston Co., 1948).

[3] Including airlines where passenger conferences are concerned.

[4] The most carefully prepared index of tramp rates appears to be the "Index Number of Shipping Freights" prepared by the Chamber of Shipping of the United Kingdom. For a brief description of prewar freight indices, see Wickizer, *op.cit.*, pp. 112-114.

because of the magnitude of such an undertaking the preparation of one is more properly the function of a research organization than of an independent scholar.[5] Information concerning shipping company profits is even less accessible. The ownership of many liner companies is closely held and no information regarding their profitability is available to the public. Furthermore, the lack of a uniform system of accounting, plus the fact that many steamship companies engage in a variety of non-transportation activities, renders the use of those income statements which are published extremely unreliable.[6] Fragmentary rate data and some business annals concerned with the profits of liner companies, however, are available and do shed some illumination on these matters; and, although this type of informa-

[5] Liner rates are a carefully guarded secret in many parts of the world, but since the tariffs of almost all common carriers operating in United States ocean trade routes must be filed with the Federal Maritime Board a great abundance of rate data is accessible. The riches of this store of information, however, are so great as to be embarrassing to the independent scholar. Not only is the number of freight rate filings formidable—approximately 18,000 per year—but great differences in commodity descriptions and classifications and in port charges make such a study extremely laborious.

[6] A uniform system of accounting is observed by the few lines receiving subsidies from the United States government, but neither their operations nor the period of years for which these data are available can be considered representative.

Despite the numerous difficulties, *Fairplay*, the weekly British shipping periodical, publishes annually the available financial results of British liner and tramp operators. The number of companies and the amount of tonnage covered by these reports varies from year to year, but usually includes approximately two-thirds of the total liner tonnage of the United Kingdom and a very substantial amount of tramp tonnage. The accounting practices of the different concerns vary so much, however, that significant long-term comparisons are difficult to make. These figures, for what they may be worth, are presented in Appendix B.

Since both capitalization practices and depreciation and reserve policies differ, these statistics must be used with the utmost caution. It appears, however, that during the interwar period tramp concerns had a difficult time providing adequately for depreciation. The failure of tramp operators to accumulate sufficient reserves for replacements is supported by the observation made by *Fairplay* to the effect that for the fifteen years ending in 1937 the tramp concerns reporting showed a return of 6.71 per cent on the book value of their vessels. Since vessels are customarily written off in twenty years, or at the rate of 5 per cent per annum, it is clear that the rewards to British tramp operators were not handsome. (Book value tends to run higher than paid-up capital.) The Tramp Shipping Administrative Committee in the first complete report ever published of the earnings of all British tramp (cargo-boat) companies showed that in the six trading years ending in 1935 the owners of 913 tramps of 3,518,000 gross tons, which cost over £62,216,000, should have set aside £18,655,000 for depreciation, calculated at the rate of 5 per cent per annum; but that the profits of the voyages permitted only £2,966,000 to be set aside for this purpose. (*Fairplay*, January 12, 1939, pp. 149-150)

M. G. Kendall, after studying these data, came to the conclusion that general net earnings for the important British shipping industry are not known. "United Kingdom Merchant Shipping Statistics," *Journal of the Royal Statistical Society*, Vol. cxi Part ii, 1948, pp. 141-142.

tion will be referred to cautiously in the ensuing discussion, the reader should bear in mind the incompleteness and possible unrepresentativeness of such bits and pieces.

The available evidence on freight rates seems to indicate rather clearly that in general liner rates and tramp rates fluctuate in the same direction, but that liner rates are considerably more stable and less subject to such frequent alterations and to such large swings as tramp rates. Liner rates in general remain above tramp rates when times are bad, and somewhat below them when traffic is booming. Professor Robertson's observation, that "The liner companies are at once less sensitive to movements in market demand and more sensitive to movements in costs than the owners of tramps,"[7] lends support to this empirical conclusion. Accordingly, an index of tramp freights will provide only a rough picture of the general trend of liner rates over a period of years. It should also be remembered that limitations of rate data, improvements in vessel design and propulsion, and changes in the composition and direction of trade all limit the validity of such a comparison over long periods.

Taking the index, therefore, for what it might be worth, we find that tramp charter rates fell, with only relatively short and minor deviations caused by wars, from 1873 to an all-time low in 1908.[8] The fall in freights was greater than the partially concurrent decline in wholesale prices and continued for more than a decade longer. After rising to fanciful heights during World War I, ocean rates began another decline which was not significantly reversed until 1937. Dr. Wickizer concludes for this period that "If ocean freight rates are considered in relation to the general price level, they are found to have continued their long-term declining trend."[9] Improvements in ship architecture and engineering, badly depressed wage scales, and huge wartime profits helped the industry to remain solvent; but the trend of rates is evidence of the fact that in most peacetime years the tramp shipping industry was under strong competitive pressure.

We have seen that although tramps provide liners with only limited competition, the latter are nevertheless influenced to a considerable extent by major developments in the tramp market. The long and consistent fall in tramp rates inevitably affected the liners,

[7] D. H. Robertson, *Economic Fragments* (London: P. S. King & Sons, Ltd., 1931), p. 122.
[8] Wickizer, *op.cit.*, p. 69.　　　　[9] *ibid.*, p. 71.

for several reasons, not the least important of which was the temptation that the more stable liner trades offered shipowners to shift their investment from tramp to liner operation. The result has been to make shipping conferences in general defensive rather than aggressive cartels during the greater part of their history.

The most striking contrast between the stability of tramp and liner rates is provided by such cataclysmic changes as are brought about by the outbreak of war. Both liner and tramp rates increased by large and sometimes fantastic amounts during World War I. Both tramp and liner rates rose in some instances by several thousand per cent of prewar quotations. The rate on grain from United States North Atlantic ports to Le Havre, France, went from $2.28 per ton in 1914 to $74.95 in 1918, an increase of more than 3,000 per cent. The rate on general cargo on this route went from $5 per 40 cubic feet in 1914 to $66 in 1918, an increase in excess of 1,000 per cent. Largely as a result of increased costs, rates in 1939 were considerably higher than they had been in 1914, so wartime rate advances started from a higher base. Nonetheless, the actual as well as the percentage advances in World War II were relatively modest when compared to those of World War I.

This disparity between the increases in the two war periods can be partially explained by the fact that in 1939 the United States had a substantial number of vessels in its reserve fleet and in operation in its domestic trades which helped to fill the growing need for overseas transportation; but the principal difference rests in the earlier and more effective application of governmental rate control in World War II. As a result we find the rate on grain from United States North Atlantic ports to Le Havre to have increased from about $3.75 per ton in 1938 to $14.17 in 1945, an increase of about 280 per cent. The rate on general cargo rose from $20.00 in 1938 to $34.50 in 1945, or by 72 per cent.[10] Time charter rates are generally regarded as a reliable indicator of the tramp market. Lloyds List and Shipping Gazette show the average time charter rate paid for cargo tonnage of all sizes to have increased from 4 shillings in the first quarter of 1914 to 58 shillings in the fourth quarter of 1918. During most of World War I the average time charter rate was approximately 1,000

---

[10] The foregoing rates are taken from Merchant Marine Study and Investigation, *op.cit.*, p. 253. They are liner rates, but tramp rates for grain were substantially the same.

per cent higher than prewar;[11] while a small sample of time charters showed the average of such rates to be only 219 per cent higher in 1946 than in 1939.[12]

The reaction of rates to a substantial change in market conditions under more normal circumstances is demonstrated by their behavior since Great Britain abolished the direct control of rates late in 1948. Tramp rates fell during 1949 as the supply of tonnage increased more rapidly than the demand for it, until an increase in the volume of foreign commerce brought stability in 1950. With the outbreak of war in Korea and the acceleration of the American and Western European rearmament programs, rates began to climb slowly at first and then very rapidly with the result that ships were withdrawn from the American reserve fleet.[13] Liner rates remained fairly steady at their high postwar levels throughout the early part of this period. Late in 1949, however, a considerable downward movement of rates began on those commodities most susceptible to competition; and during the first half of 1950 the decline became more general.[14] In late 1950 liner rates began to rise, and in 1951, as tramp freights began to skyrocket, most of the liner conferences which had not already done so gave notices of general rate increases.[15]

[11] As reported in A. E. Sanderson, *Wartime Control of Ocean Freight Rates in Foreign Trade*, U. S. Dept. of Commerce, Trade Promotion Series No. 212 (Washington: 1940), pp. 8-9.

[12] U.S. Department of Commerce, Bureau of Foreign and Domestic Commerce, *Industry Report-Domestic Transportation* April-May 1946 (Processed), pp. 37-39. This issue and the February-March 1947 issue of the same report contain interesting comparative prewar and postwar rate information for both liners and tramps in selected American foreign trades. The regular tramp freight indices were not compiled during the war.

[13] Between the outbreak of war in Korea in June 1950 and the end of 1951 approximately 470 vessels were taken out of the American reserve fleet. The creation of the reserve fleet, whose function is similar to that of a stockpile of strategic goods, by removing more than two thousand vessels from active status, helped the shipping industry to remain profitable for a longer period after World War II than it would have without this program. However, as rates rose after the outbreak of the Korean War and after the rearmament program got under way, withdrawals from the reserve fleet tempered the rising market.

[14] U.S. Maritime Commission, *Annual Report for 1949*, p. 49. A spot check made in April 1950 disclosed approximately 2,200 rate reductions and only about 70 increases. *ibid.*, 1950, p. 45.

[15] Conferences on many American routes gave notice that their rates would increase by 10 per cent in thirty to ninety days. *New York Times*, December 16, 1950. Some conferences cited spiraling operation costs and noted that tariffs had not been increased since 1948. Additional conferences followed this pattern during the first quarter of 1951; but it should be noted that the total effect of these increases was considerably more than ten per cent for numerous commodities, because many of these conferences cancelled, as of January 1st, a substantial number of rate cuts on specific items that had been made to meet competition. *Pacific Shipper*, February 5, 1951, p. 57.

A sample comparison of the relative stability of tramp freights and liner rates during the past few years is presented in Table XII-A; but, like other statistical data in this chapter, these must be interpreted with care. The tramp freight index covers only fixtures in sterling; so it is largely influenced by the British import program, and it may have been affected by inconvertibility and by devaluation. The liner rates are presented as unweighted price relatives of the dollar rates for general cargo from New York to selected destinations covered by conference agreements.[16] June 1948 has been chosen as the base period in order to facilitate comparison with the tramp index which equalled 99.8 for that month. Since rates on general cargo apply to commodities not elsewhere specified in the tariff, such rates for different conferences are not comparable, nor does this rate necessarily cover the same items for any one conference at different periods. Specific commodity rates may vary independently of that quoted in the conference tariff for general cargo, but the latter usually provides a fairly representative picture of the "unweighted" trend of liner rates.[17] Despite these limitations, the relative stability of conference rates seems indicated. General cargo rates on some routes remained unaltered for more than three years, and then the changes were relatively modest. Another interesting feature is the tendency for conferences concerned with different parts of the world to respond to the cumulative effects of change at the same time. For example, five of the eight conferences covered in Table XII-A increased rates in April 1951, and four conferences raised their charges in October 1951.

The Economist of February 3, 1951, reported (p. 288) that shippers had been notified of rate increases by several shipping conferences. Freight rates from the United Kingdom to India, Pakistan, Ceylon which had remained unchanged since 1944 were to be increased by 25 per cent, as were homeward rates from India which had been unchanged since 1940 [sic]. Far Eastern conferences had notified shippers of increases up to 15 per cent.

Later in the year there was another round of rate increases.

[16] The Chamber of Shipping's sterling tramp index has been used because it is the best available. (No adequate dollar tramp index is currently published.) Dollar general cargo rates were employed because they were the only ones accessible to the author.

[17] The more volatile nature of some liner commodity rates is illustrated by a complaint of the American Institute for Imported Steel to the Federal Maritime Board. The Institute claimed that the rate on certain important steel items from Antwerp and Rotterdam to United States North Atlantic ports had increased every few months from $10.50 per ton in January 1950 to $17.00 in January 1952, and that a proposed increase would raise it to $18.75. (The Institute reported that the prewar rate had been $4.75 per ton.)

TABLE XII-A

A Comparison of Fluctuations in Tramp Freight Index[1] with Indices of Conference Rates for General Cargo (N.E.S.) from New York to Selected Destinations.[2] 1948-1951

	Index of Tramp Freights[1]	Index of Conference General Cargo Rates[2] from New York to:							
		Alexandria	Buenos Aires	Cape-town	Liverpool, London	Manila	Melbourne, Sydney	Singapore	Valparaiso
1948: Jan.	111.3	100.0	100.0	100.0	100.0	100.0	100.0	100.0	100.0
Feb.	104.5	"	"	"	"	"	"	"	"
March	105.5	"	"	"	"	"	"	"	"
April	102.7	"	"	"	"	"	"	"	"
May	104.6	"	"	"	"	"	"	"	"
June	99.8	"	"	"	"	"	"	"	"
July	99.4	"	95.2	"	"	115.2	"	"	91.2
Aug.	100.7	"	"	"	"	"	"	"	"
Sept.	97.2	"	"	"	"	"	"	"	"
Oct.	98.8	"	"	"	"	"	"	"	"
Nov.	88.8	"	"	"	"	"	"	"	"
Dec.	86.8	"	"	"	"	"	"	"	"
1949: Jan.	87.1	"	"	"	"	"	"	"	"
Feb.	100.5	"	"	"	"	"	"	108.5	"
March	95.0	"	"	"	"	"	"	"	"
April	94.6	"	"	"	"	"	"	"	"
May	99.7	"	"	"	"	"	"	"	"
June	86.7	"	"	"	"	"	"	"	"
July	73.3	"	"	"	"	"	110.0	"	"
Aug.	70.6	"	"	"	"	"	"	"	"
Sept.	71.6	"	"	"	"	"	"	"	"
Oct.	69.8	"	"	"	"	"	"	"	"
Nov.	66.5	"	"	"	"	..	111.0	"	112.8

Year	Month							
1950:	Dec.	72.8	"	"	"	"	"	"
	Jan.	"	"	"	"	"	"	"
	Feb.	75.5	"	"	"	"	"	"
	March	"	"	"	"	"	"	"
	April	74.4	"	"	"	"	"	"
	May	71.4	"	"	"	"	"	"
	June	74.3	"	"	"	"	"	"
	July	78.8	"	"	"	"	"	"
	Aug.	86.6	"	"	"	"	"	"
	Sept.	89.0	"	"	"	"	"	"
	Oct.	95.8	"	"	"	"	"	"
	Nov.	97.6	"	"	"	"	"	"
	Dec.	115.7	"	"	"	"	"	110.0
1951:	Jan.	151.9	"	"	"	"	"	"
	Feb.	164.7	"	"	"	"	"	"
	March	180.6	"	"	"	"	"	"
	April	176.8	110.0	104.8	115.4	118.8³	124.7	"
	May	203.8	"	"	"	"	"	115.0
	June	179.0	"	"	"	"	"	"
	July	179.6	"	"	"	"	"	126.5
	Aug.	149.3	"	"	"	"	"	"
	Sept.	166.5	"	"	"	"	"	"
	Oct.	190.4	"	"	"	"	"	"
	Nov.	172.9	121.1	"	132.4	"	137.1	134.8
	Dec.	168.5	"	"	"	"	"	"

[1] Weighted index of Tramp Shipping Freights (sterling) prepared by the Chamber of Shipping of the United Kingdom as reported by *The Economist*.

[2] Computed by the author on basis of rates reported in *Export Trade and Shipper*. To facilitate comparison with the tramp freight index, June 1948 has been used as the base period. These indices are simple price relatives. The rates used include surcharges where applicable and conference contract rates when available.

[3] An arithmetic mean of an increase of 17.6 per cent on measurement cargo and 20 per cent on weight cargo.

Deduction would lead one to expect rates in the highly competitive tramp market to be extremely volatile, and liner rates to demonstrate the stability of a controlled market. The available evidence supports these expectations. We find tramp rates to be very changeable, whereas liner rates, which can when necessary respond fairly quickly to competition, are nevertheless ordinarily quite stable and react rather slowly to general alterations in the patterns of demand or cost. Since rate stability is one of the principal justifications offered for shipping conferences, let us consider somewhat further the economic implications of such stability. Declining rates, like falling prices, may induce some shippers (buyers) to hold off in anticipation of further cuts; and rapidly fluctuating transportation rates, like rapidly changing exchange rates, add to the risk of doing business and thereby have the tendency of raising prices and curtailing volume.[18] With rigid prices there must be flexibility in the volume of output, if production is to be carried on economically. Since transportation service cannot be stored (manufactured for inventory), the result of price rigidity is apt to be unused capacity.[19] Efficient utilization of resources appears, therefore, to require price flexibility, while the minimization of business risk argues for stability. Both of these opposite qualities are necessary—the proper mixture depending on the elasticity of demand and the elasticity of supply to rate changes. The importance to many commodities of ocean rates is so small that a change in rates will have little or no effect on the volume shipped; but for other commodities ocean freights are an important determinant of the volume of business, and of the levels of employment and prosperity in some regions. We have seen, however, that ocean liner freights are far from absolutely rigid; they have both flexibility and stability—the degree of each depending on the commodity's susceptibility to transport competition. And, since these concepts are relative, the degree depends also on the time period one has in mind. Fortunately, many of the commodities to which rates are important (e.g. grains and cotton) move in quantities sufficiently large to enable them to utilize tramp shipping. But this does not ab-

[18] Frequent short-run fluctuations tend either to demoralize the trade, or to cancel out if rate reductions merely prompt cargo to move at one time instead of at another. Industries which rely on forward price quotations must either be able to hedge or they require rate stability. Prices of many manufactured products are quoted as orders are taken well in advance of delivery; and since there are no hedging facilities for these commodities, rate stability is extremely important to most manufactured items.

[19] *infra*, pp. 255-260.

solve the liner section of the industry from the responsibility of seeking to establish rates that will permit both efficient and reasonably
profitable operation on the one hand, and effective utilization of the
world's resources on the other hand. The extent to which these objectives are achieved is not entirely clear; but the analysis which follows indicates that the principal flaw has probably been in the efficiency with which ships have been utilized.

Satisfactory statistical information regarding profits is not available, for reasons previously described. However, it is well known that
the industry is of the feast-and-famine variety, and that until World
War II the periods of famine have been of considerably longer duration than the banqueting. Alfred Marshall, a most acute observer
and analyst of economic phenomena, wrote in 1919 that "There is,
even in peace time, about one year in ten, in which the net earnings
of a ship about equal its total cost; but, for every such year, there
are several in which a great many ships earn far less than their costs
of working."[20]

Net earnings of liner companies appear to be less volatile than
those of tramp operators (although some concerns operate both);
but the actual extent of the difference and the average net earnings
of each over a period of years remain an enigma. Nonetheless, there
is much reason to suspect that in the interwar period neither of the
two segments of the industry as a group earned excessively high
profits. A chronic oversupply of tonnage, originally stimulated by the
war and perpetuated by nationalistic ambitions, placed the industry
on a diet which it was able to survive only because of reserves of
"fat" accumulated during the war, government subsidies, and the
eternal hope that conditions would improve. By June 1920 the supply of shipping exceeded the demand with the result that "the *post-
bellum* boom in freights was followed, in the summer of 1920, by the
beginning of the worst and longest continued slump in the history
of shipping. Year after year, private shipping companies passed their
dividends or paid them out of accumulated reserves."[21] Though
tramps suffered worse financial indignities than liners, the latter were
not entirely exempt from the depression which hit ocean shipping
during a period in which most other industries were doing well; so
that when the Great Depression arrived it had little trouble in shov-

[20] Alfred Marshall, *Industry and Trade* (London: Macmillan, 1919), p. 334.
[21] Fayle, *op.cit.*, p. 294.

ing the shipping industry into the red.[22] Reporting to Congress in 1937, the Maritime Commission stated, "The unattractiveness of shipping to the investor is not peculiar to this period; nor is it confined to American companies. Shipping has been, in the financial sense, a sick industry for many years."[23]

World War II and its aftermath brought prosperity to the industry, but the rapidly increasing costs of operation and of replacements kept shipowners from being entirely satisfied.[24] And while we shall never know what the future would have brought the industry if war had not broken out in Korea, there is much reason to believe that without a war somewhere and without the expanded and accelerated rearmament program of the Western World the highly profitable postwar interlude would have come to an end. The *Pacific Shipper* observed that "Before Korea, shipping was steadily declining into a state in which only the ablest and best situated operators would be able to return a profit, and tonnage was progressively though erratically becoming less valuable, whether the value was measured by sale or charter or operating profits."[25] In its report for 1950 the Federal Maritime Board spoke of "the surplus of world tonnage," and of a decrease in cargo and a downward trend in rates.

THE NATURE OF CONFERENCE MONOPOLIES

One of the salient characteristics of shipping conferences, and one which has been influential in keeping profits from remaining excessive, has been the fact that conferences are not absolute monopolies. It is important to remember that shipping conferences are not combines linked by shareholdings or any other form of common ownership. It will be recalled that the Imperial Shipping Committee described them as follows: "A shipping conference is a meeting in which competitors face one another with the object of achieving

[22] In its *Annual Report for 1928-1929* the Chamber of Shipping of the U.K. claimed that "The British shipping industry has continued for the greater part of 1928 in a state of acute depression." (p. 54) And in its report for 1930-1931 it reported that "Whereas in 1929 few tramp companies were able to show a return on capital and make provision for depreciation, in 1930 many have made a direct loss. . . . Many liner companies have also failed to balance income and expenditure on their shipping business." (p. 62)

[23] U.S. Maritime Commission, *Economic Survey of the American Merchant Marine* (Washington: 1937), p. 35.

[24] Bunkers, wages, and port charges all increased materially in the postwar period. *The Economist* for December 23, 1950 reported that now it costs three times as much to construct a ship as the original cost of the vessel which it is to replace. p. 1158.

[25] *Pacific Shipper*, January 29, 1951, p. 16.

that minimum of co-operation which will suffice to prevent such chaotic competition as might render impracticable the liner system of working ships. Each member of a conference is seeking the minimum surrender of his competitive freedom which is compatible with this object; his attitude in debate is determined by the sources of strength which lie behind his diplomacy."[26]

Intra-conference competition and the potential threat of newcomers has generally been present in peacetime, and although such competition may have kept the industry from earning monopoly profits, it has not prevented all other abuses. The competitive strategy of the members of a cartel appears to resemble that of a military or diplomatic campaign more than it does the behavior ascribed by traditional economic textbooks to the efforts of competitive business units to maximize their profits. While the precise result of such pricing remains indeterminate, there is nevertheless a strong presumption that rates (prices) fixed by collective action will tend to be fixed so as to maximize the profits of the carriers as a group, or of the dominant members of the group; whereas if a rate is fixed in response to competitive influences, the presumption is that it reflects much more directly the costs of the most efficient competitors.[27] The cohesiveness of the conference group and its ability to exclude newcomers from its ranks are important factors in determining the extent of its monopoly power.

The economic character of the shipping industry is such that liner rates will rarely be identical to those that would be quoted if the industry could be highly competitive; but national-flag rivalry ordinarily prevents combinations from achieving the results of an absolute monopoly. Consequently the rate level of a shipping conference will deviate from that of a monopoly and towards the competitive level to the extent that the conference is vulnerable to internal or external competition. The members of a conference often compete bitterly for a larger share of the total volume of traffic, and unless a pooling arrangement stifles such competition it can do much

[26] British Shipping in the Orient, op.cit., p. 51.

[27] Professor Fellner's observations on spontaneous coordination, the maximization of joint profits, and the limitations thereto contain penetrating insights which appear to the author to provide the beginning of a systematic explanation of the formation of shipping conferences and the activities of their rate committees. William Fellner, *Competition among the Few* (New York: Alfred A. Knopf, 1949). A complete theory of shipping conferences may also be derived some day from John Von Neumann's and Oskar Morgenstern's *Theory of Games and Economic Behavior* (Princeton: Princeton University Press, 1947).

to keep the rate level from being excessively high. Conference members will be tempted to add more and more tonnage to the route if the rate level remains highly profitable to them for long. And as the importance of maintaining one's competitive position is usually regarded as extremely important, especially by corporations whose shares are not closely held by a few owners,[28] the introduction of new, faster, or additional tonnage by one member of a conference is usually met by a duplication of such a move by other members.

Of possibly greater importance, however, is the ease with which a new line may enter the trade. The effects of various types of independent, non-conference liner service and the procedures adopted by the conferences to throttle them have been described in Chapters IX and X. The great importance of freedom of entry to a trade route and freedom of entry to conference membership were discussed in those chapters; and the significance of the relative ease with which new lines can enter a route on equal terms with the lines already operating cannot be exaggerated as a means of alleviating such monopoly powers as a conference may acquire. Once a newcomer has applied for membership in a conference and has been admitted, his status becomes like that of the other members, and internal competition succeeds to actual or threatened external competition; but in the event of a showdown the bargaining power of the internal or external competitor depends in part on the efficiency of his operations, and ultimately on his financial resources. The financial resources of a shipping line may include the backing of a government which through subsidies or ownership can keep its chosen instrument in business come what may.

It has sometimes been maintained that large subsidized carriers are at the core of many conference agreements.[29] This point of view is supported by a Senate investigation which described "the conference system of foreign trade rate making" as that "which has done so much to make it possible for American flag lines to survive in berth services."[30] It is true that several governments have supported their

[28] It may, for example, be easier for the management of a corporation, the ownership of whose shares is widely distributed, to explain to the non-management members of its Board of Directors that although their company has lost money it has retained its competitive position as the second largest participant on a route than to explain a drop to fifth place, even though a profit was earned by doing so.

[29] John G. B. Hutchins, *The American Maritime Industries and Public Policy, 1789-1914* (Harvard University Press, 1941), pp. 523-527.

[30] U.S. Congress, Senate, Committee on Interstate and Foreign Commerce, *Final Report on Merchant Marine Study and Investigation*. 81st Congress, 2nd sess., S. Rept. 2494 (1950), p. 4.

national merchant marines for strategic, political, and commercial reasons which, whether sound or not, have displaced ordinary business criteria of success. Since low-cost operators do not generally need government assistance, unless they are required to provide a type of service which the market would not support, government-owned or subsidized carriers are frequently not the most efficient producers; and, therefore, they will not usually be rate cutters, but are apt to be conference-minded. (Many non-subsidized carriers are of course also conference-minded.) But even though subsidized carriers will rarely be aggressive rate slashers, the receipt of government financial assistance would by itself prevent the shifting of all ship operations to the low-cost producers.

A somewhat unusual subsidy program was presented by the policy of the Japanese government prior to World War II in giving subsidies to Japanese shipping companies, which already had a considerable wage advantage, in order to encourage the development of this highly strategic industry and to build up Japan's commerce in the Pacific area. For many years the Japanese companies virtually controlled the conference rate situation in these trades, for the subsidies which they received obligated them to charge very low promotional rates. According to Professor Mears, "Even the Japanese companies did not find the rates profitable, and occasionally faced a deficit in spite of the subsidies."[31]

The impact of United States subsidies has been quite different. As high-cost operators, neither the American lines, nor for that matter the Shipping Board and its successors, have as a general rule advocated cutting the level of rates on the routes on which American vessels operate. Since there is always a temptation for a cartel to establish prices that are satisfactory to its high-cost producers, one cannot help but suspect that the low-cost operators stand to make handsome monopoly profits if demand is inelastic. Unless demand is sufficiently elastic, only the threat of inviting competition—which as we have seen can come from within or without the conference—will restrain the cupidity of low-cost producers. While the principle of the operating-differential subsidy provided by the Merchant Marine Act of 1936 is to place high-cost American lines on a parity with an average of their composite foreign competition, it is doubtful that it has altered in any way the interest of subsidized American lines in a "remunerative" rate level which is quite satisfactory to their

---

[31] Mears, *op.cit.*, p. 353.

lower cost competitors.[32] But as we shall see, this is more apt to contribute to excess carrying capacity than to inordinately high profits.

In conclusion, it can be pointed out that the subsidization of high-cost liner operators has, along with demand and other cost factors, contributed to the industry's interest in self-regulation. Firstly, subsidies have encouraged the operation of excess tonnage. Secondly, the high-cost company does not wish to see its subsidy dissipated in a rate war. And thirdly, the unsubsidized lines do not seek to pit their financial resources against those of some nation's exchequer. The same considerations which tend to deter a subsidized company from cutting rates will ordinarily apply to government-owned lines; but, just as we have seen an exception to this rule in the case of subsidized Japanese lines, there can also be exceptions in the case of government-owned shipping companies. The Gran Colombiana Line, for example, was presumably founded by its owners, the governments of Colombia, Venezuela, and Ecuador, to protect the economies of their countries from conference rates which they believed were exorbitant.

If competitive and other limitations on the monopoly power of shipping conferences have generally prevented them from securing monopoly profits for their members, has the liner industry derived any benefits from the conference system besides the obvious advantage of avoiding cutthroat competition? Although the unsatisfactory nature of profit information precludes a definite statement, there is no reason to believe that the liner industry as a whole has not been able to earn a satisfactory return on its investment.[33] Rationalization of sailing schedules and of calls at outports, as well as the avoidance of cutthroat competition, have without doubt contributed to more remunerative operation; but the ability of a conference to control within fairly wide margins the rates of many commodities should not be discounted or despised just because such monopoly powers may not be sufficient to obtain full monopoly profits. Let us analyze the economic impact of the monopoly that the conferences have been able to exercise.

[32] For a description of the operating differential subsidy, see: Marx, "Current American Ship Operating Subsidies," *The Journal of Business of the University of Chicago*, Vol. xxi, No. 4, October, 1948, pp. 239-259.

[33] Some companies have of course fared better than others; and while some have needed subsidies, many have not.

UNUSED CARRYING CAPACITY

It is frequently claimed that, in their efforts to maximize profits, cartels, combines, and other monopolistic arrangements restrict output. This is probably generally true, and was unquestionably the dominant motive of the considerable number of cartels and combinations which were formed during the inter-war period to cope with the war-stimulated overexpansion of certain industries. This in essence was the program of the Tanker Pool and its system of compensated lay-ups. Liner conferences, however, because of the looseness of their control over the number of sailings, have not as a rule been able to restrict output. In the absence of pooling and an absolutely closed conference membership, internal and external competition will have a strong tendency, when rates are set so as to provide better than a "fair" return on the investment, to increase rather than decrease carrying capacity on the route.

Even with the existence of a pooling arrangement and a closed membership policy, internal competition alone may create redundant capacity if the rate structure is sufficiently remunerative to induce the more efficient operators to expand. Such an increase in capacity, however, is not nearly so apt to bring rates down as it is to raise costs through under-utilization of facilities until the profit level no longer invites either further expansion on the part of the conference members or the entrance of new companies.

Professor J. M. Clark had a situation much like this in mind when he wrote, "Where producers have power enough to prevent cutthroat competition, they probably have power enough to set prices above a fair return on the investment, unless some force intervenes which is more subtle and harder to bridle than the direct and obvious competition which they hold in check. Such forces exist, and may be grouped under the general term: 'potential competition.' . . ."[34] After pointing out that potential competition tends to lose force unless it occasionally takes the form of actual competition, Professor Clark continues, "Another unfortunate feature of this natural check [potential competition] on exploitation is that the consumer does not always get the benefit of the reduction of profits. When there is a definite agreement or understanding as to prices and the trade is open to anyone who chooses to come in, the natural

[34] John M. Clark, *The Economics of Overhead Costs* (Chicago: University of Chicago Press, 1933), p. 444.

result is that the newcomers should be taken into the understanding and maintain the same prices, unless they are so extortionate that it seems more profitable to take the chances of a price-cutting contest. This possibility would tend to keep the price sufficiently moderate so that a war would not promise large profits, and the trade would not be disrupted on every new arrival. Then the natural tendency would be for new competitors to come in, maintain prices, and share the existing business until ultimately profits came down, and prices and costs of production were brought together, not by bringing prices down to costs, but by bringing costs up to prices, by dividing the existing business up among so many competitors that they all had unused capacity and correspondingly high costs."[35] Professor Clark concludes his analysis by anticipating the constructive function of the independent, non-conference liner service by pointing out that "Fortunately this process could not go on absolutely indefinitely, for if it resulted in a very serious inefficiency, a new concern could cut prices, work to capacity, and operate at so much less expense per unit that it could make a profit."[36]

The application of this reasoning to shipping conferences presupposes the concept of the representative firm which would presumably average a "fair" profit. Less efficient firms, unless subsidized, would earn less, while more efficient operators would earn more. This, however, leaves unanswered a question confronting a more efficient operator: is it more prudent to earn such a better profit, or to enlarge its participation in the trade until a lower rate of profit is earned on a larger volume of business? While no definite answer can be given, the cost nature of the industry and the nationalistic interests involved seem to argue that within limits the more efficient operator will decide it wiser to be content with the share of the trade that can be carried with his existing facilities. But, outside of these limits, which are importantly influenced by the anticipated reaction of his competitors, the more efficient operation will be expanded. In short, a conference may include in its membership at the same time representative firms earning a "fair" return; firms earning less than this, some of which may be contemplating dropping out of the trade, or of agitating for an increased rate, a larger subsidy, or some discriminatory governmental assistance; and concerns earning larger than "fair" profits, some of which are content with their share of the business

---

[35] *ibid.*, pp. 445-446.
[36] *loc.cit.* and cf. Chapter IX.

and others of which may be induced by the favorable return to add more carrying capacity.

The foregoing analysis, therefore, strongly suggests the possibility of stable rates, of "fair" profits for the representative firm, and of under-utilization of carrying capacity. Rate stability is also supported by the relatively inelastic demand of many commodities for transportation service and by its importance to forward trading. The paucity of information regarding profits has already been discussed, and we discover in this analysis an additional reason for liner companies to obscure their financial results, lest new lines be attracted to their routes. Is there any evidence that under-utilization of carrying capacity has been a common phenomenon?

As usual, the evidence is not conclusive, especially when one considers that it is in the nature of a scheduled transport service to be only partially utilized at times; but, nonetheless, there is considerable data which supports the foregoing deductive analysis. The minority report of the Royal Commission on Shipping Rings observed in 1909 that "The [conference] system tends to inflate the amount of tonnage and consequently the amount of capital invested upon which interest has to be paid."[37] South African shippers had represented to the Commission that the number of ships kept on the run by the South African Line was considerably in excess of the needs of the traffic; and that the removal of the superfluous vessels would be less burdensome to the shippers than paying the rates which the Line found necessary to cover their swollen operation with profits. To this charge, an executive of the Line replied, "We do not know when busy times may come; and, if our tonnage were reduced considerably, we would not have the steamers there, and somebody else would put on the steamers."[38] Professor Marshall succinctly summarized the case, "The advantage is not South Africa's, yet they are made to pay for it."[39]

The Liverpool Steamship Owners' Association reported that in 1925 ships entering British ports came with 8,350,000 tons of vacant space, and that ships clearing from British ports sailed with 5,350,000 tons of unused space.[40] These statistics include tramps as well as liners; but the Liverpool Steamship Owners' Association, which is pri-

---

[37] op.cit., p. 114.
[38] Q 15, 214-6 as reported by Marshall, op.cit., pp. 441-442n.
[39] loc.cit.
[40] According to J. J. Kral, "International Trade in 1925," Trade Information Bulletin No. 446. Bureau of Foreign and Domestic Commerce (1925), p. 4.

marily interested in liners, regarded the situation as appalling. During World War I the average weight of imports per 100 net tons of cargo vessels carrying foreign commerce to the United Kingdom increased by 27 per cent.[41] In 1933 a section of the League of Nations which studied the impact of the Great Depression on merchant shipping reported a surplus of tonnage considerably in excess of 50 per cent, and concluded that "Partially employed tonnage is a very much heavier charge upon the shipping companies than the tonnage actually laid-up."[42] But even for such relatively good years as 1928 and 1929 the Liverpool Association reported that the average weight of imports per 100 net tons of foreign trade cargo shipping entering the United Kingdom had been 12½ per cent below the tonnage so carried in 1936 and 1937.[43]

Frequent references to under-utilization of vessels also appear in the reports of the Maritime Commission. The members of the U.S.A.-South Africa Conference reported the amount of unused space on their vessels to have averaged:[44]

32.3	per	cent in	1931
55.6	"	" "	1932
42.5	"	" "	1933
19.7	"	" "	1934
35.2	"	" "	1935

In 1939 the chairman of the North Atlantic Continental Freight Conference, the North Atlantic French Atlantic Freight Conference, and the North Atlantic United Kingdom Freight Conference testified that, on the average, conference vessels had had considerable unoccupied space for several years.[45] This was corroborated by more detailed evidence provided in the following year by two members of

[41] *Liverpool Steamship Owners' Association Annual Report, 1916*, pp. 8-9.

[42] Notes by Economic Relations Section and the Communications and Transit Section on the Merchant Shipping Crisis, *op.cit.*, p. 8.

[43] Based on Annual Reports of the Liverpool Steamship Owners' Association. Statistics covering vessels employed in bringing in the foreign trade of the United Kingdom show the estimated tons of cargo imported per 100 net tons of shipping entrances from 1928-1938 as follows:

1928 - 94		1934 - 100	
1929 - 96		1935 - 99	
1930 - 92		1936 - 107	
1931 - 91		1937 - 107	
1932 - 88		1938 - 98	
1933 - 92			

[44] Seas Shipping Co. *v.* American S. African Line, 1 U.S.S.B.B. 568 at 575 (1936).

[45] Waterman S. S. Corp. *v.* Arnold Bernstein Line, 2 U.S.M.C. 238 (1939).

the North Atlantic Continental Freight Conference. The Black Diamond Lines reported that the total tonnage transported eastbound by that company during 1938 represented 66 per cent of the deadweight and 63 per cent of the cubic capacity available; and that during the period June 15 to September 15, 1939, less than 47 per cent of the available deadweight capacity was occupied by cargo. The Belgian Line's eastbound carryings for 1938 were reported as 65 and 41 per cent respectively of deadweight and cubic capacity, and for the period July through September 1939, these percentages were 44 and 31 per cent.[46] (The westbound movement in these trades has customarily been lighter than the eastbound movement, so presumably there was much unused capacity on sailings in both directions.)

Several of the foregoing references to unused carrying capacity are for depression years, during which there was a very substantial amount of under-utilization of capital and of unemployment throughout the world in most branches of industry. It is impossible to say that under-utilization of facilities in shipping was greater than elsewhere in the economy during this troubled period. But there is reason to suspect that shipping has been one of the worst chronic sufferers from overcapacity, and that substantial amounts of unused carrying capacity was typical during the greater part of the interwar period. In addition to the plethora of tonnage contributed by wartime expansion and further aggravated by nationalistic considerations, the rather steady growth in the average size of ships has probably rendered the feat of regularly filling up a vessel increasingly difficult. Since average vessel size is still growing, this difficulty may be expected to continue.[47] Some unused capacity is also apt to result from strict adherence to advertised schedules and from seasonal fluctuations, although extra vessels are frequently added to a route during the active season. To the extent that the conference system has contributed to the operation of excess tonnage it has provided a modest increase in employment and has maintained in active status more strategically important vessels than would otherwise be in operation. If we assume that the principal burden fell on commodities whose demand for transportation was relatively inelastic, it

[46] Cosmopolitan Line v. Black Diamond Lines 2 U.S.M.C. 321, at 329-330 (1940).
[47] Prior to World War I ships employed in overseas trades were usually 3,000 gross tons or larger, while by 1923 very few ships of less than 4,000 gross tons were so employed. E. T. Chamberlain, op.cit., p. 6. Most of the merchant vessels built during and subsequent to the Second World War have exceeded 7,000 gross tons.

would seem that little harm was done to the volume of world trade. These higher rates either were absorbed in whole or in part by manufacturers, exporters, importers, or merchants; or they were passed on to the ultimate consumer. The principal impact on the world economy probably took place through the diversion of purchasing power.

CONFERENCE ABUSES

There are other disadvantages, shortcomings, and abuses in the conference system in addition to under-utilization. The practices of some conferences have long been the subject of controversy and investigation; and the results of such examinations and the steps taken by various governments to control the more flagrant conference abuses have been described in previous chapters. But even under such controls as now apply to ocean transportation in United States foreign commerce, which are as severe and thorough as any now in vogue, the conference system still displays shortcomings and abuses that are not consistent with the liner industry's "public utility" status as a common carrier.

Despite the usual stability of conference rates, the elements of internal and external competition, previously described as tending to protect the shipping public from monopoly exploitation, also contribute some instability. While these disruptive influences are more prevalent when the industry, or a particular trade, is depressed, they may occur at any time. Rate wars are not common, yet they do break out from time to time, and are apt to be pursued with great fury and intensity to the confusion of the trade.[48] A more common, though far less obvious, source of instability is the indisputably discriminatory practice that occasionally emerges from intra-conference rivalry.

[48] Rate wars are apt to be threatened by conference members dissatisfied with the existing agreement, by newcomers seeking admission, by an independent line, and by conferences serving competitive territory. Peaceful settlements are frequently negotiated, but when an acceptable compromise cannot be reached rate cutting often ensues. Some rate wars are quickly settled, others have dragged on for months, and some, with intermittent periods of peace, have lasted for several years. During a rate war reliable rate information becomes even more difficult to obtain than ordinarily, because of rapid changes and the quoting of special rates for individual shipments.

For an account of some rate wars before World War I, see: Paul Gottheil, "Historical Developments of Steamship Agreements and Conferences in the American Foreign Trade," *The Annals of the American Academy of Political and Social Science*, Vol. LV, September 1914, pp. 48-74; and the reports of the Royal Commission on Shipping Rings and the Alexander Committee. In the early twentieth century aggressive Ger-

The chiselling which takes place has been well described by an executive of an American shipping company who asked, "But what happens when all conference members do not get full cargoes?", and then replied, "Insinuations are made that someone in the conference is not sticking to the agreement." He continues, "Then there are more definite charges, such as rebates are being given, additional brokerage is being paid, someone is making valuable presents to brokers or traffic managers, someone is spending large sums for entertaining those who control bookings. Then there are more subtle ways of evading conference agreements, such as making a large shipper believe that by giving preference to one's line the representative of that line in the conference can get lower rates on the commodity in which the shipper is interested. Another way a conference member operating a service to ports not included in the conference agreement can get preference to which he is not entitled is by giving a shipper a low rate to some port in such non-conference service in exchange for preference of business at conference regulated rates. This is not an exhaustive list of the 'tricks of the trade.' I wish that phrase had never been coined. Its repeated use has in some degree taken away the stigma which otherwise would attach, if we referred to those acts as being dishonest."[49]

Additional evidence of this type of behavior is provided by the

---

man competition led to bitter struggles on several important routes. Freight rates were often cut by 50 per cent and sometimes by more. At one time steerage rates from Europe to North America fell to £1 10s. from several times that amount. Japanese lines had started rate wars in Oriental trades before World War I, but in the interwar period they took over the role formerly played by the Germans. (See: The Java-Japan Conference, *supra*, p. 82; and Rates, Charges, Practices of Yamashita and O.S.K., 2 U.S.M.C. 14).

German and Japanese lines, however, were not the only disturbers of the peace. Probably no more relentless warfare existed than in the United States intercoastal trade from 1923 to 1938. The Intercoastal Shipping Act of 1933 failed to bring stability, and therefore in 1938 the Maritime Commission was given minimum and maximum rate powers over common carriers on all domestic ocean routes. (See: Howard C. Kidd, "Regulation of Intercoastal Commerce," *University of Pittsburgh Bulletin*, Vol. 28, No. 21, June 15, 1932; and Intercoastal Investigation, 1935, 1 U.S.S.B.B. 400.) For examples of rate-wars in United States' foreign trades, see: Section 19 Investigation, 1935, 1 U.S.S.B.B. 470; and Seas Shipping Co. *v.* American South African Line, et al, 1 U.S.S.B.B. 568 (1936).

A recent spectacular struggle broke out in 1949 between Dutch and British lines in the Europe-India trade, with the sharing of the German prewar quota alleged as the bone of contention. Although the war only lasted about six weeks, rates were reported to have been cut by as much as 92 per cent.

[49] N. O. Pedrick, General Manager of the Mississippi Shipping Co., "Freight Conferences and the Merchant Marine," *Proceedings of the Sixth National Conference on the Merchant Marine* (Washington: Govt. Printing Office, 1933), pp. 61-63.

false billing cases. Members of conferences which controlled freight moving from Japan to the United States were found in 1940 to have been allowing transportation at less than regular tariff rates by means of falsely describing commodities and weights;[50] and in 1941 members of the Far East Conference were found to be similarly allowing false billing of freight moving from the United States to the Philippine Islands.[51]

Whenever such practices are prevalent, one can be certain that the members of the conference are not acting in the concert necessary for successful monopoly exploitation. If the chiselling becomes sufficiently serious, a rate war will be precipitated; and this likewise is inimical to the interests of both shippers and carriers. Eventually a conference agreement with adequate support to achieve workable stability will be negotiated. However, as soon as a shipping line assumes that all favors and cuts granted to shippers will automatically be met by their competitors they will begin to think in terms of total demand and act more like monopolists.

These observations should not be construed as a condemnation of the liner industry; they are intended to show the difficulty of retaining sufficient competition in the conference system to provide satisfactory protection against exploitation without introducing under-utilization, instability, and unreasonable discrimination. It is a very delicate balance that must be sought—too delicate one may suspect to bloom in the jungle of cutthroat practices or in the pampered garden of monopoly, without the aid of more control than persons or their corporate extensions are apt to impose voluntarily upon themselves.

The challenge to conferences offered by outside competition has been described in this and earlier chapters, and so have some of the efforts of conferences through tying arrangements to throttle independents and tramps, and by exclusive membership policies to prevent new lines from gaining admission to the conference. American experience since 1916 confirms the findings of earlier investigations and proves that constant vigilance is necessary if conferences are to be kept from employing unfair competitive tactics in their efforts to exclude new liner services from the trade and from conference membership. Many of the regulatory decisions of the Maritime Commission and its predecessors, described in Chapter VII, bear witness to

[50] Rates from Japan to United States, 2 U.S.M.C. 426 (1940).
[51] Rates from United States to Philippine Islands, 2 U.S.M.C. 535 (1941).

this. And in 1932 the Supreme Court reported that testimony had been presented regarding the efforts of conference members to keep a newcomer out of the trade which included, "giving rebates; spreading false rumors and falsely stating that the petitioner is about to discontinue its service; making use of their combined economic bargaining power to coerce various shippers, who are also producers of commodities used in large quantities by respondents, to enter into joint exclusive contracts with them; and threatening to blacklist forwarders and refuse to pay them joint brokerage fees unless they discontinue making, or advising shippers to make, shipments in petitioner's ships."[52]

Such resistance to newcomers is not confined to the American trades. The Australian government presented evidence to the Imperial Shipping Committee in 1921 showing that shippers who patronized the Commonwealth Government Line "besides incurring the loss of rebates, ran the risk of having cargo shut out by some of the Conference Lines from ships which were not full, on any occasion on which they might wish to make use of their services; and, further, that this refusal of space for cargo was likely to be extended to other trades in which they were engaged."[53]

Another striking attribute of conferences is that they have achieved sufficient monopoly power to form tariffs and to charge differential or discriminatory rates. The tendency is for a conference to charge the highest rate for each commodity that will not greatly check the flow of trade on its route; but charges may be oppressive to those who ultimately pay them, without exceeding this limit. The importance of liner freights to consumers, who in the final analysis probably pay most of them, is as difficult to ascertain as the incidence of taxes. Whether rates are a large or small proportion of a commodity's value they are frequently, when passed to the consumer, augmented by the pyramiding effect that results from including freight in the base for calculating mark-ups. Consumer interests are not represented in the conferences or in negotiations with them, except possibly when a government participates. Where well organized shipper groups exist, they are generally more concerned with their profits than with the consumers' welfare. Custom and the threat of

---

[52] U.S. Navigation Co. v. Cunard S. S. Co., 284 U.S. 474 (1932).
[53] Interim Report of the Imperial Shipping Committee on the Deferred Rebate System, Cmd. 1486 (1921), p. 5.

competition alone restrain the members from charging unreasonably discriminatory rates. Alfred Marshall was of the opinion that this situation generally did not get too far out of hand. After noting the substantial monopoly power which permits conferences to charge differential rates, he stated, "There is, however, less that is arbitrary and accidental in the apportionment of charges for ordinary consignments of different sorts of goods than appears at first sight. Long established usage, based in some degree on sound reason, has set up the general principle that goods are to be classified for high or low charges per ton (by weight or measurement) roughly as their values are high or low; provided the difficulty and risk of handling are about equal. . . . It is maintained in great measure even in an eager rate-war . . . rates may be lowered generally; but a proposal to carry first-class goods at fourth-class rates would be regarded as short-sighted even during the heat of combat."[54] It is highly unlikely that usage and the threat of competition succeed in preventing all undue discrimination, especially in the case of commodities which move in insufficient volume to attract competition for their transportation; but a rough justice seems to prevail in the majority of cases.[55]

Nonetheless, conference members can in numerous other ways act inimically to the interests of the shipping public. For example, in 1925 it was held that an agreement among a group of conferences in the trans-Atlantic trades had been negotiated with little, if any, consideration for the interests of the shipping public.[56] In 1937 it was found that members of the North Atlantic Spanish Conference had refused to accept cargo, despite the fact that they had space available, because of pressure brought to bear by competing shippers.[57] In 1939 the failure of the Pacific Coast River Plate Brazil Conference to agree on a reasonable rate for lumber was found detrimental to the commerce of the United States;[58] as was the division of revenue from joint through rates practiced by the Association of West Coast Steamship Companies in 1943.[59] And some conferences have stubbornly refused to give advance notice of contem-

[54] Alfred Marshall, op.cit., p. 436.
[55] See numerous cases involving reasonableness decided by the Maritime Commission, and its forebears, several of which are mentioned in Chapter VII. Also cf. Appendix A.
[56] Port Differential Investigation, 1 U.S.S.B. 61, at 72 (1925).
[57] R. Hernandez v. Bernstein Schiffahrtsgesellschaft, 1 U.S.M.C. 686 (1937).
[58] Pacific Coast-River Plate Brazil Rates, 2 U.S.M.C. 28 (1939).
[59] Restrictions on Transshipments at Canal Zone, 2 U.S.M.C. 675 (1943).

plated rate changes.[60] But the most sinister development has probably been the formation of pools which enable conference members, by operating more like a single unit, to organize their monopoly powers with increased effectiveness.[61]

Retarding the introduction of innovations is a very serious matter, and Professor G. C. Allen is of the opinion that "The real danger of monopoly arises when it is used to impede change."[62] Progressiveness depends upon incentive, and it may also be contingent on the scale of operations. Whereas the volume of business in some trades may be insufficient to permit operations on the most efficient scale, no such limitation exists on the world's major routes. Incentive may be adversely affected by the achievement of a monopoly on certain routes, but actual and potential competition is usually adequate to keep conference members alert. Although innovations in ship propulsion and design in recent years may not have been as breathtaking as developments in some other fields, they have been far more substantial than is generally appreciated by landlubbers. An atmosphere of conservatism is not uncommon to ancient industries with a romantic tradition; and while the shipping industry has not entirely escaped this heritage, it has, nevertheless, demonstrated sufficient progress to confirm the existence of competition's invigorating breath. As Professor J. M. Clark has indicated, competitive stimulus to efficiency does not require as large a number of competitors as workable price competition. "The best combination may be a moderate number of large and strong concerns, preferably still trying to expand, and the most efficient of which have a chance to grow to match their bigger rivals."[63] This situation is frequently approximated in shipping, though it may be seriously distorted by nationalistic considerations.

CONCLUSION

It should not be inferred from the foregoing, however, that monopoly profits are never earned in the liner trades. On routes where pooling agreements flourish, highly remunerative monopoly situations

[60] Pacific Coast-European Rates and Practices, 2 U.S.M.C. 58 at 60 (1939); and Pacific Coast European Conference, 3 U.S.M.C. 11 at 15 (1948).
[61] See Chapter VIII.
[62] G. C. Allen, "Economic Progress, Retrospect and Prospect," *Economic Journal*, Vol. LX, No. 239, September 1950, p. 474.
[63] J. M. Clark, "The Orientation of Anti-trust Policy," *American Economic Review*, Proceedings Vol. XL, No. 2, May 1950, p. 95.

can develop, especially if external and other competition is also restricted. But even without pooling, highly effective tying arrangements or other means of excluding newcomers may permit monopoly profits to be earned for a considerable period of time.[64] Lines belonging to a conference which has successfully restricted the entry of newcomers may earn monopoly profits until intra-conference competition has introduced excess carrying capacity. When conference membership is kept open, one may presume that although carriers will not on an average earn more than a normal, fair, or socially necessary profit for longer than a few years at a time, they will, nonetheless, make an attempt to average *at least* a normal rate of return over a period of years.[65] However, if the world supply of tonnage for any reason remains scarce for an appreciable length of time, all owners of vessels are in a position to make large profits.[66] Although freedom of entry, if strictly enforced, will tend to eliminate the earning of excess profits, it does not by itself guarantee either fair rates or the absence of all unreasonable discrimination. In a period when tonnage is scarce, freedom of entry may have little effect; while in a period when tonnage is in oversupply it may lead to the operation of much unused capacity and to unfair competitive practices.

The elements of competition, however, are not as a rule deeply buried. Airline competition is becoming increasingly formidable in the passenger, mail, and express freight business; and the relative ease with which cargo lines can be started through such plans as the

[64] The perseverance with which members of a conference will try to prolong a highly remunerative situation is illustrated by the following quotation describing one of the difficulties that confronted the efforts of the United States government to accumulate a strategic stockpile of rubber before the Japanese attack on Pearl Harbor. "There was not at this time enough cargo space to carry the available rubber. Stubbornly maintained steamship conference rules hindered the entry of additional lines into the rubber trade. Then part of the space was filled with non-essential but more profitable products. As a consequence, the movement of rubber from producing areas to the United States was interrupted." Herbert Feis, *Seen from E. A.* (New York: Alfred A. Knopf, 1947), p. 69.

[65] A precise economic evaluation of a particular conference would require in addition to the consideration of the profits of the member lines over a period of years sufficiently long to eliminate cyclical fluctuations a good deal of other information. It would be necessary to study the nature of the internal competition among the members of the conference as well as of the actual and more probable potential competition of tramps and of non-conference lines. The movement of the principal commodities would have to be considered as well as their alternate sources of supply and alternate markets at which they could be sold. The level of rates as well as individual rates and the behavior of both should also be examined. Such studies are confronted by the paucity of much of the necessary information; but for anyone with access to the data such studies should produce some interesting monographs.

[66] This situation prevailed after the close of the Second World War.

joint service agreement[67] makes the permanent tying up of a remunerative trade route exceedingly difficult. In fact, it could be argued that, since conferences occasionally break down and rate wars occur which disrupt trade, the conference system fails to provide the stability it claims as its justification. This is a failure it is true, but it does indicate the existence of substantial competitive elements which in turn tend to keep the member lines from abusing their monopoly position as badly as they might if such competition did not exist.

As we have seen, the liner trades are governed by two conflicting tendencies; they tend either to develop and exploit a monopolistic position, or to suffer from the wastefulness of competition. Monopolistic excesses range all the way from petty abuses to unreasonable discrimination and fairly secure monopoly profits; whereas the competitive aberrations include the failure to rationalize sailing schedules, under-utilization, unfair methods of securing traffic, and occasionally cutthroat rate wars. The market structure of the trade route and the phase of the trade cycle strongly influence the actual result. The open-membership policy which the Maritime Commission has promoted should help to achieve rate stability without producing monopoly profits, but at the cost of under-utilization. Unfair competitive methods and chiselling, which appear to be endemic in mankind, may break out in the liner industry at any time, but are most likely to assume epidemic proportions in depressed periods. Self-preservation, however, helps prevent rate wars from spreading and from becoming suicidal for all participants.

Nevertheless, the pathological aspects of the industry should not obscure the abundance of healthy tissue which enables many conferences to provide a reasonable degree of stability without indulging in excessive monopoly abuses or inordinate competitive wastes. Perhaps some monopoly profits or excess capacity are the social costs of industrial self-regulation. Are there alternatives to self-regulation which might provide a better solution to the problems which beset the liner shipping industry, or are there improvements in the methods now employed by the industry to regulate itself which ship operators could be compelled to adopt? After a description, in the following chapter, of various existing and proposed international organizations designed to facilitate the regulation of the shipping industry, alternatives to the existing situation will be considered in the final chapter.

[67] See Chapter VIII.

CHAPTER XIII
INTERNATIONAL SHIPPING ORGANIZATIONS

WHERE CONTACT between nations is as continuous as in aviation and shipping, the possibilities of friction are great. On the other hand, the successful conciliation of hotly disputed international differences not only requires great patience but also nurtures the elusive hope of a better world. As a result of "international" connections established by ships, treaties concerning navigation and trade are probably as old as civilization; but for the purposes of this study developments prior to the formation of shipping conferences can be taken for granted. Workable solutions had evolved to numerous matters of public and private international law. Freedom of the seas, for example, had become an accepted policy, although universal agreement as to its meaning under all circumstances did not exist; and the principle that there should be no openly discriminatory treatment of foreign-flag vessels in foreign commerce was predominant even though sometimes observed in the breach. Problems continued to arise, however, which called for international solution; and it is not surprising that numerous international meetings and several international organizations, some of which were intergovernmental and some of which were attended by representatives of private business interests, devoted themselves in whole or in part to various practices of ocean transport.

A number of meetings were concerned with maritime law and with technical and safety matters. The International Maritime Committee, for example, was founded in 1897 to deal with the legal aspects of international shipping. It is a non-governmental group representing shipowners, bankers, underwriters, and other commercial interests; and it has corresponding national associations in most important maritime and trading nations.[1] The Committee has drafted conventions dealing with matters such as collisions at sea, salvage, maritime mortgages, and bills of lading. These conventions have been submitted to diplomatic conferences which have in turn generally been convened by the Belgian government. Conferences con-

---

[1] Between 1897 and 1937 nineteen conferences were held by the Committee.

cerned with technical and safety matters have led to the formation of the International Hydrographic Bureau, International Ice Patrol and Ice Observation Service, and the International Commission of the Cape Spartel Light. Other *ad hoc* meetings have considered such subjects as tonnage measurements, oil pollution, construction of passenger ships, life-saving appliances, load-lines, radiotelegraphy, the buoyage and lighting of coasts, etc.[2]

Besides the International Maritime Committee there are two other non-governmental international organizations exclusively concerned with ocean transport, viz. the International Shipping Conference and the Baltic and International Maritime Conference.[3] The International Shipping Conference is not a "shipping conference" in the sense in which that phrase is employed in this volume. It is an international trade association. Founded in 1921, it has permanent headquarters in London and its membership is composed of some thirty shipowners' organizations representing the most important maritime countries. Plenary meetings are held periodically as circumstances require. This organization has dealt with a variety of subjects such as trade barriers, flag discrimination, safety of life at sea, maritime law, shipping documents, sanitary regulations, load-lines, tonnage measurement, passenger insurance, etc.[4] The International Shipping Conference, according to the Chamber of Shipping of the United Kingdom, "has never sought, and was not designed, to interfere with Liner Conferences or Tanker matters in settling (whether nationally or internationally) questions of freights, or tonnage, or sailings."[5] It will be recalled, however, that in the tramp sphere, where no conference machinery exists, the International Shipping Conference has offered a convenient agency to assist international self-regulation, and that the Tramp Shipping Administrative Committee obtained its assistance in the operation of minimum freight schemes in the late 1930's.

The Baltic and International Conference has already been briefly described in Chapter XI. This organization, whose membership in-

[2] For a summary of the activities of governmental and private international agencies concerned with maritime matters, see: Brig. Gen. Sir Osborne Mance, *International Sea Transport* (London: Oxford University Press, 1945).

[3] In the fall of 1951 a third group, the International Cargo Handling Coördination Committee, was formed. Its membership is to include shipbuilders, shipowners, manufacturers of cargo-handling equipment, exporters, packers, importers, stevedores and longshoremen, port authorities and harbor officials, and others concerned with moving vessels in and out of port.

[4] Mance, *op.cit.*, pp. 4-5.   [5] *Annual Report* 1945-1946, p. 54.

cludes both shipowners and brokers, has on several occasions fixed freight rates for both liners and tramps. Although its activities are mainly restricted to certain short trades, and its rate controls have concentrated on a few important commodities, it is of interest because it is a rare example of an international agency that has simultaneously and directly controlled both liner and tramp rates in peacetime.[6]

In addition to the foregoing, inter-governmental organizations such as the League of Nations, International Labor Organization, and Pan American Union, have also interested themselves in shipping. The League's Organization for Communications and Transit concerned itself, with some small success, in matters involving public international law such as the principle of equality of treatment in maritime ports of vessels of different flags, and with such other problems as the unification of tonnage measurements and buoyage systems. Broader economic issues, particularly ship subsidies, were discussed from time to time at economic conferences held under the League's auspices; but no progress was made toward the resolution of differences in these matters. In 1946 the League's functions were turned over to the United Nations.

The Pan American Union has been concerned on a regional basis with much the same types of questions as the League. But at the Inter-American Maritime Conference held in Washington in 1940 rate matters received an amount of attention that has rarely been permitted at intergovernmental conclaves.[7] Several Latin American countries registered dissatisfaction with ocean rate practices; as a result of which the final act of the Conference included Resolution VI concerning "Ocean Freight Rate Problems." The United States and other Latin American members, however, were satisfied with the prevailing practices; so the resolution was drafted with dextrous ambiguity. Nevertheless, the Colombian delegation in signing claimed that they understood that statements in Resolution VI admitted, "the necessity of giving special attention to the system of contracts and double freight rates which, in the form in which it has today de-

[6] It should be recalled that the Tramp Shipping Administrative Committee, with the cooperation of British liner companies, also controlled some tramp and liner rates. *supra.* pp. 237-238.

[7] It may be that the opposition of the United States government to the discriminatory practices of some Latin American countries could be argued only if the United States was in turn willing to permit the conference system, as regulated by the Maritime Commission, to be discussed and criticized.

veloped in certain regions of the Western Hemisphere, has created a special situation of monopoly, [and] which cannot be accepted by the countries affected."[8]

The matter was raised again at Bogotá in 1948 where the Venezuelan delegation recorded in the Minutes that, in approving Chapter VIII of the Economic Agreement of Bogotá and the annexed declaration, "it did so with [the] assurances that the phrase 'questions having to do with maritime transport' includes the problem relating to discriminatory practices and similar problems that appear in the maritime transport contracts that the conferences or associations of shipowners have in use, as was expressly approved in the work group to which the study of this chapter was assigned. It also understands that the foregoing sentence includes the study of the freight rates at present in effect and the means for ensuring that such rates be fair and equitable."[9]

Shipping and transportation questions were then referred to the Inter-American Economic and Social Council, and in 1951 this body passed a resolution over United States objections calling for expert study of ocean freight and insurance rates. The United Nation's Economic and Social Council, in response to an earlier proposal for international regulation of freight rates on South American routes, requested its Transport and Communications Commission to study them. In March 1952 the Inter-American Economic and Social Council reported, and "in view of the very specialized and complex nature of the problem" recommended further study and statistical analyses.

The International Labor Organization and its affiliated Joint Maritime Commission have been primarily concerned with labor matters. Since its inception in 1920, the I.L.O. has adopted a number of conventions and recommendations affecting maritime labor, the most ambitious of which was the minimum-wage resolution adopted at Seattle in 1946. Ratification of I.L.O. resolutions, however, has been slow and incomplete, with the result that actual accomplishment has not been too impressive.

These details are mentioned because they illustrate the reluctance

---

[8] Inter-American Maritime Conference, *op.cit.*, p. 458. Resolution VI also included the statement "that when freight rates are established, particular attention be given to the desirability of avoiding arbitrary differentials not based on normal and equitable trade considerations." pp. 476-477.

[9] According to a letter to the author from José Gil-Borges, commercial counselor, Venezuelan Embassy, Washington.

and inability of the aforementioned agencies to come to grips with rate problems.[10] This is not astonishing when one recalls that they were not created to handle such matters. Nevertheless, there has been agitation from time to time for giving authority over rates to an international agency. The principal early exponent of this concept was an American merchant and statesman, David Lubin, one of the founders of the International Institute of Agriculture at Rome. Mr. Lubin believed that shipping conferences enjoyed a monopoly power which they exercised to the detriment of world commerce. Although lacking proof, he alleged in 1914 that the great shipping trusts controlled not only the liner trades but the tramps as well, and that shipowners had sufficient advance knowledge of ocean freight rate changes to profit by operating on the grain exchanges. As a result, he pressed before the Congress of the United States a bill to create an International Commerce Commission to regulate ocean rates and to rationalize the movement of cargoes and ships.[11] This proposal was not greeted by any appreciable enthusiasm either in the United States or elsewhere; but the exigencies of war soon developed an acute need for complete centralized control of ocean transportation.

THE INTERGOVERNMENTAL MARITIME CONSULTATIVE ORGANIZATION

Since ordinary commercial considerations are subordinated to the strategic requirements of gaining victory, wartime control experience is not of great relevance. Nevertheless, the Allied Maritime Transport Council in World War I, and the British Ministry of War Transport, the United States War Shipping Administration, and the Combined Shipping Adjustment Board in the second global conflict accumulated significant experience in the problems of international control.[12] Even more important, perhaps, were the experiences of the United Maritime Authority and the Shipping Coordinating and Review Committee in the postwar period during which transportation problems and conditions began to resemble more closely those pre-

[10] Unofficial international organizations were also reluctant to tangle with rate problems. In 1948 the Sea Transport Committee of the International Chamber of Commerce agreed that "the International Chamber should not lend itself to purposes of controversy between shipowners and their customers."

[11] D. Lubin, *The Cost of Ocean Carriage*, S. Doc. 423, 62nd Cong. 2nd sess. (1914); and *Proposal for an International Conference on the Regulation and Control of Ocean Carriage by Means of an International Commerce Commission for the Purpose of Steadying the World's Price of Staples* (Rome: International Institute of Agriculture, 1914).

[12] For a complete description of the control of ocean transport in World War I, see: J. A. Salter, *Allied Shipping Control* (Oxford: The Clarendon Press, 1921).

vailing in ordinary peacetime. The United Maritime Authority was established by the Allies in 1944 to discuss the best methods for ensuring the continued availability of tonnage during the concluding phases of the war, and was terminated in 1946, six months after the end of hostilities, at which time the Shipping Coordinating and Review Committee was established to consider and review relief shipping requirements. The control of rates was left in the hands of such agencies of the individual governments as the Ministry of War Transport and the War Shipping Administration.

A second body, known as the United Maritime Consultative Council (U.M.C.C.), was also created upon the expiration of the United Maritime Authority, and its purpose was to provide a forum for the exchange of information and the discussion of mutual problems which might assist the Allied governments in forming their postwar shipping policies.[13]

Both the United Maritime Consultative Council and the Economic and Social Council of the United Nations favored the creation of an intergovernmental shipping organization as a specialized agency of the United Nations, and at its final session in October 1946 the U.M.C.C. agreed to recommend the establishment of an Intergovernmental Maritime Consultative Organization to its eighteen-member governments. Pending the formation of such an intergovernmental body, the U.M.C.C. provided for a Provisional Maritime Consultative Council. It was hoped that a permanent shipping organization would provide greater continuity and more satisfactory coordination than had been possible before the war under either the decentralized and sporadic maritime conferences with their diverse memberships or under previous permanent international bodies which were not exclusively concerned with shipping matters.

With this aspiration in mind, the United Maritime Consultative Council drafted a plan for an international shipping body, which, with the express approval of the Economic and Social Council, served as the basic working document at the United Nations maritime conference held in Geneva early in 1948. Three fundamental issues confronted this convention: (1) Was a separate maritime body necessary, or could some other commission of the United Nations deal adequately with problems involving ocean transport? (2) Should

13 For a brief account of these postwar agencies, see: Eula McDonald, "Toward a World Maritime Organization," *The Department of State Bulletin*, Vol. xviii No. 447 and 448 (Jan. 25, 1948; Feb. 1, 1948).

the scope of a new maritime organization be limited to technical matters, or should it be empowered to consider private shipping economics and the efforts of nations to promote their merchant fleets? (3) How should the interests of shipowning and ship-using nations be balanced in a new agency?

Since only Australia and New Zealand, out of the thirty-two governments represented, opposed the establishment of a separate maritime body, this question was easily disposed of, and it was soon agreed to establish the Intergovernmental Maritime Consultative Organization (IMCO).

Definition of the scope of the agency's authority, however, was a far more difficult matter. The Scandinavian countries and Finland favored restricting IMCO to technical matters and strenuously objected to giving the proposed organization any control of commercial shipping practices. Whether the granting of subsidies should be viewed as an unfair practice was also debated at considerable length. Both these issues were "solved" by compromises, whose nature is revealed in the first four articles of the proposed organization's charter. Because of their relevance to the problem of regulating shipping conferences, these articles are fully reproduced below *with italics supplied* to the most pertinent passages:

PART I

Purposes of the Organization

ARTICLE 1

The purposes of the Organization are:

(a) to provide machinery for co-operation among Governments in the field of governmental regulation and practices relating to technical matters of all kinds affecting shipping engaged in international trade, and to encourage the general adoption of the highest practicable standards in matters concerning maritime safety and efficiency of navigation;

(b) to encourage the removal of discriminatory action and unnecessary restrictions by Governments affecting shipping engaged in international trade so as to promote the availability of shipping services to the commerce of the world without discrimination; assistance and encouragement given by a Government for the development of its national shipping and for purposes of security does not in itself constitute discrimination, provided that such assistance and encouragement is not based on measures designed to restrict the freedom of shipping of all flags to take part in international trade;

(c) *to provide for the consideration by the Organization of matters*

274

concerning unfair restrictive practices by shipping concerns in accordance with Part II;

(d) to provide for the consideration by the Organization of any matters concerning shipping that may be referred to it by any organ or Specialized Agency of the United Nations;

(e) to provide for the exchange of information among Governments on matters under consideration by the Organization.

PART II

Functions

ARTICLE 2

The functions of the Organization shall be consultative and advisory.

ARTICLE 3

In order to achieve the purposes set out in Part I, the functions of the Organization shall be:

(a) subject to the provisions of Article 4, to consider and make recommendations upon matters arising under Article 1 (a), (b) and (c) that may be remitted to it by Members, by any organ or Specialized Agency of the United Nations or by any other intergovernmental organization or upon matters referred to it under Article 1 (d);

(b) to provide for the drafting of conventions, agreements, or other suitable instruments, and to recommend these to Governments and to intergovernmental organizations, and to convene such conferences as may be necessary;

(c) to provide machinery for consultation among Members and the exchange of information among Governments.

ARTICLE 4

"In those matters which appear to the Organization capable of settlement through the normal processes of international shipping business the Organization shall so recommend. When, in the opinion of the Organization, any matter concerning unfair restrictive practices by shipping concerns is incapable of settlement through the normal processes of international shipping business, or has in fact so proved, and provided it shall first have been the subject of direct negotiations between the Members concerned, the Organization shall, at the request of one of those Members, consider the matter."[14]

The objectives of IMCO are clearly twofold: (1) to set up machinery for international cooperation in technical and safety matters; and (2) to abolish discriminatory practices of governments and *unfair* restrictive practices of shipping concerns. The Organization,

[14] United Nations Maritime Conference, *Final Act and Related Documents* (Lake Success: 1948), pp. 29-30.

however, can act solely in a consultative and advisory capacity. Its recommendations become compulsory only when they are adopted by member governments as national laws. Of particular interest to shipping conferences is the provision on unfair restrictive practices of shipping concerns. Dr. J. J. Oyevaar, Director-General of Shipping for the Netherlands, and president of the United Nations Maritime Conference which drafted the IMCO Convention, stated that, "In adopting a provision on unfair restrictive practices by shipping concerns, the Conference acted on a directive of the Economic and Social Council which decided at its fourth session that the Conference should consider this matter."

Dr. Oyevaar goes on to point out that, "The provision has particular significance in relation to shipping conferences. There is hardly any subject of a shipping nature on which so many different and, I may add, unjustified views are now being held. A study of this phenomenon and of the argumentation for and against the justification of 'shipping conferences' would fill many volumes. The Organization's constitution wisely does not condemn restrictive practices as such; it concedes that they may be justified, but condemns unfair restrictive practices by shipping concerns. The Organization's machinery provides for its consideration of unfair restrictive practices by shipping concerns: when such matters are, in each particular case, incapable of being settled through the normal processes of the international shipping business, or have in fact so proved"; and, "provided they shall first have been the subject of direct negotiations between the governments concerned.

"As between the views of some that the restrictive practices of shipping concerns could never be unfair and of others that they are necessarily unfair in principle, the formulation adopted again appears as the result of wisdom and restraint."[15]

It was agreed that IMCO should have headquarters in London and that it should consist of an Assembly, Council, Maritime Safety Committee, and Secretariat. In both the Assembly and the Council each member shall have one vote, but the large shipowning countries are well protected by their power in the Council. For while all members are to be represented in the Assembly, the Council consists of sixteen members selected as follows: (a) six shall be governments of the nations with the largest interest in providing interna-

[15] J. J. Oyevaar, "The New Maritime Organization," *United Nations Bulletin*, Vol. IV, No. 6, March 15, 1948, p. 239.

tional shipping services; (b) six shall be governments of other nations with the largest interest in international seaborne trade; (c) two shall be elected by the Assembly from among the nations having a substantial interest in providing international shipping services; and (4) two shall be elected by the Assembly from among the governments of nations having a substantial interest in international seaborne trade. An annex stipulated that the first Council was to be composed of Greece, the Netherlands, Norway, Sweden, the United Kingdom, and the United States as shipowners; and of Argentina, Australia, Belgium, Canada, France, and India as ship-users. (It should be noted that some of the latter group also own and operate considerable merchant tonnage, whereas the former includes highly important ship-users.)

These twelve members of the Council are empowered to decide which countries are shipowners and which are ship-users for the purpose of election to the remaining four seats on the Council; and the eight shipowning members of the Council then have the power to determine the principal shipowners for membership in subsequent Councils. Control of the Council is, therefore, practically assured to shipowning nations (albeit they are frequently also important ship-users as well). This control may become important because the Assembly is required (by Article 16h) to refer all matters relating to Article 3 (a) and (b) to the Council for its formulation of recommendations or instruments; and, furthermore, any recommendations or instruments submitted to the Assembly by the Council and not accepted by the Assembly shall be referred back to the Council for further consideration with such observations as the Assembly may make. The decisions of the Council cannot be revised by the Assembly unless the latter's vote is unanimous. Decisions or recommendations by the Council can be either approved or rejected as whole, and if rejected they are to be referred back to the Council for reconsideration. The reason for this extraordinary provision, which prevents the Assembly from overriding the Council, stems from the fact that the shipowning nations feared they would be hopelessly outnumbered in the Assembly where each member country has one vote.[16] Several countries took a dim view of these voting provisions.

[16] This single-vote provision also applies in the Council. It would have been extremely difficult to have devised a weighted voting formula. Votes based on tonnage owned is easily calculated; but it is more difficult to reach agreement on how to weight votes based on the volume of foreign ocean-borne trade, because of differences in the composition of and the distance traveled by the commerce of various nations.

Panama withdrew formally from the conference promptly upon learning that it had been "overlooked" as an important shipowning nation; whereas China's objection to the constitution of the Council led her to oppose the Convention to establish IMCO in the final vote, and Egypt abstained for the same reason.[17]

The Intergovernmental Maritime Consultative Organization is to come into existence when twenty-one States, of which at least seven shall each have a total tonnage of not less than 1,000,000 gross tons of shipping, have approved the Convention. In the meanwhile, a Preparatory Committee composed of the twelve nations chosen for membership on the Council are to complete the preparations for the plenary body. The Convention to establish IMCO was expedited, on the one hand, by the desire of shipowning nations to establish a separate maritime organization, so that matters within its scope would not be handled by the proposed International Trade Organization (ITO); while, on the other hand, several ship-using nations were equally eager to establish a specialized agency in order to speed up international consideration of shipping questions. As a result of this alacrity, the final charter of the proposed ITO provided that shipping matters were automatically to be referred to IMCO.[18]

The decision of the United States Department of State not to urge the Senate to ratify the loopholed Havana Charter for the ITO has probably sealed the doom of that body, and this has not improved the prospects for activation of the Intergovernmental Maritime Consultative Organization. Nevertheless, IMCO may still come into existence, and as of July 1951 the following seven countries had ratified the Convention: Canada, October 1948; United Kingdom, February 1949; Netherlands, March 1949; United States, August 1950; Greece, September 1950; Ireland, February 1951; and Burma, July 1951. However, opposition to the constitution of the Council has

---

Furthermore, it would be difficult to reach agreement on the number of votes that nations, which are both important shipowners and ship-users, such as the United Kingdom and the United States, are entitled to.

[17] Besides Egypt, the following countries also abstained from voting: Denmark, Lebanon, Norway, New Zealand, Pakistan, and Sweden. The Scandinavian countries abstained because their instructions were to approve only an organization to consider technical matters. The following countries voted in favor of the Convention: Argentina, Australia, Belgium, Brazil, Canada, Chile, Colombia, Dominican Republic, Finland, France, Greece, India, Ireland, Italy, Netherlands, Poland, Portugal, Switzerland, Turkey, United Kingdom, and United States. In addition to Panama, Czechoslovakia and Peru were absent when the final vote was taken.

[18] Article 50 of the ITO charter.

grown, and was brought into the open by Hernan Plaza, the Chilean delegate to a meeting of the United Nations Transport and Communications Commission held in March, 1951. Mr. Plaza proposed revising the Convention so that smaller countries with small merchant fleets, but with a relatively large interest in seaborne commerce "would have the possibility of equitable representation."[19]

INTERNATIONAL AVIATION ORGANIZATIONS

Brief consideration of international organizations controlling air transportation may shed some additional illumination on the peculiarities of problems involved in international regulation of ocean transport. The International Civil Aviation Organization (ICAO) came into existence in 1947, and like IMCO has an Assembly, a Council, and a Secretariat.[20] Although each member government has one vote in both the Assembly and in the Council of twenty-one member states, the latter is *elected* by the Assembly which is required to give adequate representation to: (1) the states of chief importance in air transport; (2) the states not otherwise included which make the largest contribution to the provision of facilities for international civil air navigation; and (3) the states not otherwise included whose designation will ensure that all the major geographic areas of the world are represented. ICAO is endowed with broad jurisdiction in the field of international air navigation, but has only consultative and advisory functions in matters pertaining to the economics of international air transport and to private international air law. The aims and objectives of ICAO are defined as follows:

To develop the principles and techniques of international air navigation and to foster the planning and development of international air transport so as to:

(a) Insure the safe and orderly growth of international civil aviation throughout the world;

(b) Encourage the arts of aircraft design and operation for peaceful purposes;

(c) Encourage the development of airways, airports, and air navigation facilities for international civil aviation;

(d) Meet the needs of the peoples of the world for safe, regular, efficient and economical air transport;

(e) Prevent economic waste caused by unreasonable competition;

[19] *New York Times*, March 29, 1951.

[20] Prior to World War II the International Commission for Air Navigation (ICAN) administered the Paris Convention of 1919, and the International Technical Committee of Aerial Legal Experts (CITEJA) dealt with air law.

(f) Insure that the right of contracting States are fully respected and that every contracting State has a fair opportunity to operate international airlines;

(g) Avoid discrimination between contracting States;

(h) Promote safety of flight in international air navigation;

(i) Promote generally the development of all aspects of international civil aeronautics.[21]

In discharge of its responsibilities in economic matters ICAO has collected and studied statistics on the origin and volume of international air traffic and its relation to the facilities provided, as well as data on government subsidies, tariffs, and operation costs. It has also concerned itself among other things with the possibility of international ownership and operation of the world's trunk air routes; the problem of differentiating between scheduled and non-scheduled air services; the rules of procedure to govern the filing of aviation agreements and contracts between the member states or their airlines; the possibility of reducing international airmail rates; the standardization of charges at international airports; and the double taxation of international airline operators.

When the formation of ICAO was first officially discussed at an international conference in Chicago in 1944 there was a head-on collision between American and British concepts of economic regulation. The American government stood for free competition for world traffic, while the British favored some international control to protect the interests of the various countries providing air transport. Two years later a workable bilateral compromise was reached at Bermuda. The determination of equitable rates was delegated to the Traffic Conferences of the International Air Transport Association (IATA), with the stipulation that the rates could not become effective until both governments had approved them. It was hoped that this procedure would avoid unfair and cutthroat competition which might so easily arise from conflicting national aspirations as well as from purely economic considerations, and at the same time provide the traveling public with reasonably low rates. This bilateral arrangement between the United States and the United Kingdom was quickly followed by a series of more than sixty similar agreements contracted by these and other governments.

The International Air *Transport* Association was founded in 1945, and although it had no legal connection with any previous organiza-

[21] Article 44, Convention on International Civil Aviation, Chicago, Ill., 1944.

tion it was the direct inheritor of the principles, problems, and much of the personnel of the International Air *Traffic* Association, an international trade association established in 1919. The original organization did not ostensibly deal with rate matters, but concerned itself with technical and legal problems, the reconciliation of differing national codes, and such other matters as the coordination of timetables and interline connections, the settlement of interline accounts, arrangements for carrying airmail, etc. In addition to performing the services of its predecessor, IATA was, as a result of the Bermuda formula, officially designated to consider rates and fares, and in order to do so created three regional Traffic Conferences. Membership in IATA and its Traffic Conferences is open to all air transport enterprises operating a scheduled international air service authorized by a state eligible for membership in ICAO.

The Traffic Conferences, by means of resolutions, agree upon minimum rates and fares for scheduled operations. Rate action may be taken only upon the unanimous vote of all members represented at the meeting. Independent action by individual members of a conference is not prohibited, since the other carriers cannot bind a *dissenting* member. However, every member of a conference can stop a particular action by its right to veto it, and it is expected that all members will comply with agreements they have not chosen to veto. It should, of course, be remembered that all rates are subject to the approval of the contracting governments.

Dr. J. G. Gazdik, secretary of IATA's Legal Committee, reports that: "The effort to bring rates into relationship with costs has been a process of continuous development. When the old North Atlantic Traffic Conference held its first meeting in February, 1946, it was found that no appropriate cost figures were available for rate-making purposes. It was then necessary to develop a standard form for collecting cost data, but the successful drafting of such a form was not in itself enough to assure their availability. In some cases, some of this data was considered as confidential from either a national or commercial point of view, and special procedures for its confidential disclosure and transmittal had to be developed. In others, the accounting procedures of the airlines themselves had to be expanded or changed to gather the information required."[22]

The Traffic Conferences are too young to permit a meaningful ap-

---

[22] J. G. Gazdik, "Rate-Making and the IATA Traffic Conferences," *The Journal of Air Law and Commerce,* Vol. 16, No. 3, Summer, 1949, p. 312.

praisal of their ability to discharge their rate-making function; but, like most other transport rate authorities, they have taken into consideration "ability to pay" as well as the cost of providing the particular service.[23]

AVIATION AND SHIPPING ORGANIZATIONS CONTRASTED

It is interesting to speculate why operators of the young airline industry developed organizations for intergovernmental control earlier than descendants of the "ancient mariner." There are several plausible reasons for the more rapid growth of international control of air transport.

Firstly, there are far fewer scheduled international airline operators than shipping lines, so arrangements agreeable to the operators were both easier to reach and more urgently required. Secondly, there was a pressing need for achieving workable solutions to the technical and legal problems that confronted the new air transport industry. The airline industry did not have all antiquity to call upon for precedents, and the essence of air transport is to be in a hurry. Thirdly, the importance of aviation as a political and military instrument was frequently considered even greater than the strategic importance of surface transportation, which together with the universal need of air transport for government financial assistance widened the extent of government participation in all countries operating airlines.

Finally, as a result of the strategic nature of air transport "freedom of the air" has never meant the same thing as "freedom of the seas." While any nation may refuse to allow the aircraft of another nation to fly over the territory of the first nation or to land therein, current treaties of commerce and navigation would make the exclusion of the merchant vessels of another nation an unfriendly act. Accordingly, as John C. Cooper has pointed out, "These treaties . . . created a situation which made it most difficult for any nation, without good reason, to regulate the terms of entry, including freights to be charged, or to bar entirely foreign merchant vessels of another nation from entering one of its ports open to the foreign commerce of others."[24] On the other hand, the retention by individual nations of the author-

---

[23] *ibid.*, p. 316.

[24] John C. Cooper, *The Right to Fly* (New York: Henry Holt and Co., 1947), pp. 127-128. An interesting comparison of international law as it affects air transport and sea transport is contained in Chapter 7 of this work.

ity to exclude foreign aircraft from landing in their territory reserved to the nations of the world the right to regulate rates charged by all incoming air-carriers. Therefore, unless aircraft were to be accorded freedom of entry similar to that enjoyed by merchant vessels, intergovernmental accord was clearly necessary for the development of international air services, and these intergovernmental agreements could easily and logically include provisions for the control of rates.[25]

The IATA Traffic Conferences have not been without their critics, but no acceptable substitute has yet been proposed. Prior to the Bermuda Conference, according to Dr. Gazdik, the following three plans to solve the problem of rate regulation were discussed: (1) To subject rates to the approval of an intergovernmental aeronautical agency; (2) To fix international rates by means of bilateral agreements; and (3) To permit the carriers operating in a given trade to fix rates by agreement among themselves.[26] Few nations were willing to yield sufficient national sovereignty to an intergovernmental rate-regulating agency to permit the first suggestion to operate satisfactorily. It was felt that bilateral agreements would not be sufficiently flexible. The possibility that conflicting interests of third nations would create embarrassment and confusion that could be resolved only by the negotiation of additional bilaterals, which would in turn render the entire structure even more inflexible, created grave doubts as to the practicability of the second proposal. Leaving the determination of tariffs to agreement among the carriers had practical advantages; and it was felt that if rates so determined were made contingent on approval of the contracting governments then both cutthroat competition and exploitation of the public could be averted.

It appears that whereas the airlines have borrowed much of the conference concept from their elder maritime brothers, the principle of bilateral governmental supervision of rates determined by agreement among carriers may in turn be of precedential value for the regulation of liner rates. Important differences between the ocean liner industry and the airline industry should be noted, since they affect the transferability of such practices. Despite the strength of the combination movement, there are still a great many more operators of international shipping lines than there are of international

---

[25] It remains to be seen if the freedom of "innocent passage" by merchant vessels of foreign marginal seas will survive the atomic age.

[26] Gazdik, *op.cit.*, p. 307.

airlines where the tendency is for carriers to be restricted to one chosen instrument for each major trading nation. Partially as a result of this and partially because of the greater historical flexibility of shipping, it remains much easier to start a new shipping line than it does to inaugurate a scheduled air service.

The greater flexibility of ship operation stems from the tradition of freedom of the seas, and the resultant fact that nations neither limit the number of vessel entries nor exercise any control over the rates they charge. The pattern of self-regulation developed by ocean liner services has naturally been predicated on these characteristics which involve vessel mobility and imply the frequent threat of actual or potential competition. The heedless application to ocean liner shipping of the procedures developed by the airlines could not be expected to work satisfactorily unless both the flexibility and competitiveness of ocean transport were materially reduced, if not completely abandoned. Furthermore, ocean liners on a great many trade routes are dependent on a large variety of commodities, while the scheduled airlines have been primarily concerned with the transportation of passengers. Air transport is becoming increasingly interested in the carriage of an expanding number of goods, but the preponderant importance to them of passenger business greatly simplifies the rate-making process and its bilateral supervision.

OCEAN RATE REGULATION AND INTERNATIONAL COMMODITY AGREEMENTS

It is this multiplicity of items to be priced that renders the experience of intergovernmental commodity agreements even less apposite than airline procedure to the solution of the regulatory problem of ocean liner services. An examination of intergovernmental action concerning a few basic primary products reveals that they have all involved highly standardized commodities. This uniformity is singularly lacking in most liner trades, as an inspection of most conference tariffs will clearly reveal. In addition to this important difference, there are some similarities as well as some other differences between the problems of international commodity agreements and those of shipping conferences. Both have been significantly influenced by war-stimulated surplus capacity, and both seem frequently to be characterized by the failure of demand and supply to respond with sufficient promptness to changes in price. Since World War II trade in many of these basic primary commodities has been channeled by bilateral trade agreements; and although this procedure has not assumed great importance in ocean transport, the growth of discriminatory measures exerts a similar artificial influence. On the other hand, shipping is not affected by climate as are agricultural commodities, which constitute such a large number of the products subject to intergovernmental control; and shipping service, unlike both mineral commodities and controlled agricultural products, cannot be stored.[27] But the greatest difference for the administrative purpose of price regulation is the great multiplicity of shipping rates. Nevertheless, strong currents affecting the international control of prices in one segment of the world economy cannot fail to influence thought in others; and therefore it is advisable to mark certain criteria that have been recommended for intergovernmental commodity control.

The Havana Charter for an International Trade Organization, for example, recognized in its Chapter VI the need for: (a) Opportunity to any government to request and to participate in intergovernmental consultations regarding the problems of a commodity in which it considers itself substantially interested; (b) Adequate and specialized study of commodity problems before any formal intergovernmental agreement is made; (c) Adequate representation of importing and consuming countries in any arrangement; (d) Full publicity to any intergovernmental commodity agreement proposed or concluded; (e) Assuring the availability of adequate supplies and, when practicable, the expansion of world consumption; (f) Limiting the use of agreements regulating prices or restricting the production or trade in a commodity; and (g) Coordinating the activities of international organizations concerned with commodity problems.[28]

The Havana Charter recognized that restrictive arrangements in the international service industries required somewhat different treatment from the essentially negative admonitions addressed to international industrial cartels. The proposed charter for IMCO, despite its abstention from direct authority over rates, has, however, been influenced by the positive criteria outlined above for international commodity agreements.

[27] Ships can be laid up; but the service of providing transportation cannot be stored. This distinction is not without significance.
[28] I am indebted to a United Nations publication, the *Review of International Commodity Problems 1949* for this excellent summary of the principles incorporated in Chapter VI of the Havana Charter.

CONCLUSION

Some thoughtful students of international affairs believe functional organizations might constitute the most practicable beginnings of effective world government. Dr. Mitrany, for example, avers that "In this approach it is not a matter of surrendering sovereignty, but merely pooling so much of it as may be needed for the joint performance of the particular task."[29] The grave international tensions which threaten the peace of the world at the time this is written render all conjectures regarding the future organization of the world's commercial activities extremely hazardous; but this unhappy fact certainly does not reduce the need to provide for the amicable and equitable settlement of those differences of opinion and conflicts of interest in economic matters that may arise between the free countries. Therefore, regardless of the implications of IMCO for the peaceful evolution of a world government, if a sufficient number of nations desire the formation of an intergovernmental shipping organization, it is important that it should function well. To be eminently effective an international agency must have real tasks of government entrusted to it; and to perform the tasks of government satisfactorily the representatives of an intergovernmental organization must be both intimately acquainted with the problems of the industry and vested with sufficient responsibility to execute the decisions they have agreed upon. Success has been meager where action has depended upon persuading states to follow the lines of policy recommended by international experts. The Intergovernmental Maritime Consultative Organization, however, has been designed for the rather modest purposes of providing international cooperation and consultation, and of making recommendations.

If IMCO should come into existence, it will still remain to be seen how effective it may be in the handling of "matters concerning unfair restrictive practices by shipping concerns." Carefully conducted investigations may serve a highly useful purpose, although there is always the danger that an investigative and advisory body may become merely an apologist for the regulated industry and overlook the interests of consumers.

Professor Alfred Marshall has succinctly described the strength

[29] David Mitrany, "The Functional Approach to World Organization," *International Affairs*, Vol. xxiv, No. 3, July 1948, p. 358. See also his *A Working Peace System* (London: National Peace Council, 1946) Pamphlet No. 40; and J. B. Condliffe, *The Reconstruction of World Trade* (New York: Norton & Co., 1940), pp. 388-389.

and weakness of official inquiries, and since his observations apply to international investigations quite as well as to national examinations they are reproduced below. "Much helpful knowledge comes to a Commission of Inquiry spontaneously. For there are nearly always two, often more, sets of persons who have intimate technical knowledge of, and strong interest in the subjects investigated by it. Each set puts its own case vigorously, and spares no effort to bring to light any flaw in statements or arguments that make against it: and thus, so far as the trade interests of any important group of people in the country are concerned, the Commission may sometimes rest content with keeping a fair field for all combatants, and sifting out the vital from the secondary and even irrelevant issues that may be raised. But the interests of those who can offer careful, well-informed, and well-organized evidence are often less important in the aggregate than those of the public at large; who seldom have the special knowledge required for ascertaining exactly where lie their interests in the matter under discussion; or the organization required for setting out their case. The Commission is required to take some initiative in regard to the interests of the non-vocal multitude, in order that it may present a well-balanced picture of the whole position."[30]

The danger that the interests of consumers will be overlooked is certainly not reduced by the fact that the charter for IMCO leaves virtual control of ship-operating practices to the ship-operating nations. Even though most of the important ship-operating countries are also important ship-using countries, the relatively unorganized and non-vocal interests of consumers are very apt to be submerged by an inundation of evidence submitted by highly articulate and well-organized lobbies representing an industry of great military importance.

Some persons might suggest that it would be advantageous to give IMCO the authority to license conferences. However, even if the nations of the world would approve this proposal, which is extremely doubtful, their proponents should realize that so long as an international body must rely on national governments with different political and economic philosophies and different business standards for the enforcement of its rulings, the efficacy of international regulation is apt to be small. The importance of public opinion, however, should not be ignored. Therefore, the compulsory registration with IMCO of all conference agreements and exclusive patronage or de-

[30] *Industry and Trade* (London: Macmillan, 1919), p. 443.

ferred rebate contracts might be useful. Another improvement in its procedure would be to require conferences or independent lines, which, after a careful investigation, have been found engaged in an abusive practice, to report to IMCO after a specified number of months on their progress in correcting the condemned action.

Whether or not the shipping-conference system of industrial self-regulation requires intergovernmental supervision—and if the answer is in the affirmative, whether or not the proposed Charter for an Intergovernmental Maritime Consultative Organization provides a promising solution—is considered, together with alternatives, in the following chapter.

CHAPTER XIV
SUMMARY AND CONCLUSIONS

ARE SHIPPING CONFERENCES necessary, and do they possess the inherent vice of unregulated monopoly? Should they be abolished, let alone or regulated? These questions, which were raised in Chapter I, have been implicitly answered in the intervening chapters. Before attempting more explicit replies, let us review briefly the major observations and conclusions that have already been made.

We considered the indeterminate nature of both demand and cost in the liner shipping industry in Chapter II. The prominent roles of fixed costs, joint costs, opportunity costs, and unused capacity were emphasized. The consequences of these characteristics were found to be declining costs, discriminatory pricing, and other monopolistic arrangements.

Next, in Chapter III we briefly depicted the relation of ocean transport to international trade, to the location of industry, and to the international balance of payments. Fluctuations in the volume of world trade were compared with fluctuations in the tonnage of the world's shipping, and it was found that construction stimulated by war and defense considerations was responsible for a chronic oversupply of carrying capacity in the interwar period. The prevalence of subsidies and other nationalistic measures common to the shipping industry were found to produce still further distortion.

The findings of investigations into the operations of shipping conferences conducted by the United States, the United Kingdom, and several other countries were given in Chapters IV, V, and VI. Although the recommended solutions differ, there appears to be agreement that the industry requires some form of regulation. The consensus also held that the self-regulation of liner shipping by conferences may neglect the interests of shippers, and furthermore, that serious abuses may occasionally arise. There was considerable difference of opinion, however, regarding the frequency with which serious improprieties occur. Accordingly, the British, who have taken a rather more lenient view of shipping rings, have advocated the formation when necessary of shippers' associations to bargain collectively with the conferences. Australia and New Zealand have augmented the efficacy of their shippers' associations by legislation and indirect governmental participation. The United States, the Union of South Africa, and Brazil have favored governmental supervision and regulation of conferences; but at present only the United States has accumulated appreciable regulatory experience with shipping rings.

Consequently, Chapter VII described the Shipping Act of 1916, and the ensuing regulation of overseas shipping by the United States Shipping Board, Shipping Board Bureau, and Maritime Commission.[1] This chapter illustrated both the success and limitations of American regulatory activity, and provided additional evidence of the need for external supervision. The Maritime Commission and its predecessors enjoyed some success in correcting unreasonable discrimination and similar abuses, and in restricting the growth of monopoly power—especially by requiring conferences to maintain an open membership policy. The sanctioning of exclusive patronage contracts and pooling agreements, however, tended to augment the monopolistic authority of conferences. The principal limitation of the unilateral regulation of international shipping was its inability to control the general level of rates.

The organization, procedures, and geographical distribution of conferences in the United States' foreign trade were considered in Chapters VIII and IX. Conferences were found to exist on all of this country's principal trade routes and on most routes of lesser importance as well. It was shown that joint service agreements helped small shipping companies to compete with larger concerns. Pooling agreements were found to assist at times in the elimination of wasteful competitive practices, but they increased the danger of abusive monopoly practices. Careful regulation of pools by an external agency appears advisable. It was shown that independent or non-conference lines could be helpful in keeping conference rates from remaining long at excessively high levels; but non-conference carriers may also, by directing their competition, exert rate pressure on selected groups of commodities, and thereby leave a greater burden of overhead costs to be carried by goods which are less capable of supporting them. At other times the inde-

[1] The regulation of commercial practices of overseas shipping was successively administered by the independent United States Shipping Board, the U.S. Shipping Board Bureau of the Department of Commerce, the independent U.S. Maritime Commission, and is now again under the Commerce Department in its Federal Maritime Board.

pendent lines may charge rates that are less than the costs of operation. The general condition of the freight market significantly influences the character of non-conference competition.

Various tying arrangements employed by shipping lines and conferences to secure the loyal patronage of shippers were examined in Chapter X. It was found that some form of tying arrangement was frequently necessary for the effective operation of conferences. Tying agreements, however, not only have flaws of their own but enhance the monopoly power of the conferences. In short, tying arrangements must be strong to be effective, and when they are sufficiently strong they may lead to monopolistic excesses. Some form of external regulation appears necessary to prevent conferences using tying agreements from abusing the degree of monopoly so achieved.

Chapter XI analyzed the character of tramp-liner competition and described the operation of some pooling and rationalization schemes to stabilize tramp freights. Competition between tramps and liners for the carriage of general cargo was found to be restricted, and therefore cannot be relied on to curb the monopoly power of liner conferences. If tramp freight control schemes are revived, they will further reduce this competition.

The analysis of the economics of shipping conferences in Chapter XII suffers from the lack of precise data on profits and freight rates. Nevertheless, deduction, buttressed by business annals and such data as are available, reveals that liner trades are governed by two conflicting tendencies; they tend either to develop a monopolistic position or to suffer from the wastes of competition. Monopolistic excesses range all the way from petty abuses to unreasonable discrimination and monopoly profits; whereas the competitive ills include the failure to rationalize sailing schedules, under-utilization, unfair methods of securing traffic, and occasional cutthroat rate wars. The stronger the conference organization, the more prone it is to engage in monopolistic practices; and the weaker the conference, the more susceptible it is to competitive wastefulness. Under-utilization of carrying capacity has perhaps been the most common flaw of conferences which lack the power to achieve a monopoly position. The market structure of the trade route and the phases of the trade cycle exert an important influence on the actual result. By and large, however, conferences appear to provide a reasonable degree of stability without indulging in excessive monopoly abuses or inordinate competitive waste.

Chapter XIII reviews the nature of prewar international shipping agencies and then describes the organization and functions of the proposed Intergovernmental Maritime Consultative Organization. In a comparison with international commodity agreements and the international regulation of commercial aviation, some parallel and some unique characteristics of shipping were illuminated. The principal shortcoming of the proposed Intergovernmental Maritime Consultative Organization is the slim protection that it is apt to provide the consuming public. Whether or not an international organization of this type, or of some other form, is necessary, will now be considered along with other alternatives.

ALTERNATIVES

It can be argued, of course, that the *status quo* is quite satisfactory and that no more regulation is needed. The reader of the foregoing chapters will appreciate that many conferences operate for long periods of time without seriously abusing their power. Good behavior may be the result of business statesmanship or of the threat of actual or potential competition; but in either case these restraints disappear from time to time and monopolistic excesses emerge. The reader will also have found that the shortcomings of the conference system are fairly universal, occurring now and again in many different parts of the world, and that abusive practices have been all too common. An increasing number of nations have expressed their dissatisfaction with conferences. Furthermore, while non-conference competition was found salutary under certain circumstances, it was predatory and destructive under others.

To judge whether a rate or pricing system is satisfactory or unsatisfactory, it is necessary to consider it in relation to other practical and practicable alternatives. The foregoing analysis has indicated that unrestricted competition is generally unworkable in liner shipping with its largely indeterminate and frequently declining per unit costs. Some form of regulation is clearly necessary, and the foregoing chapters have reviewed the merits and shortcomings of the conference system of control.

Since it is apt to be precisely when a conference has adequate power to function smoothly that it also has sufficient strength to engage in monopolistic excesses, it appears advisable to eliminate these shortcomings insofar as possible, even though the monopoly power is not always abused. Improvements in the operations of conferences may be self-imposed, or may be brought about by increasing the bargaining power of shippers, by the international joint operation of lines on a route, or by regulation.

It is doubtful whether all conferences will exercise sufficient restraint to eliminate all serious abuses, but there is much that conferences can do to improve their relations with shippers. Some of the proposals made by the National Council of American Importers at the National Foreign Trade Convention in 1940 present examples. It was recommended that freight tariffs be published and made available to exporters and importers at cost, and furthermore, that these tariffs contain exact copies of the conference contract and bills of lading. It was also suggested that conferences should make public all contemplated changes in freight rates sufficiently early to permit shippers to present their views to the conferences. It was contended that conferences should follow the procedure of railroad rate-making agencies and publish their dockets, including the basis for the contention of a rate change, well in advance of the contemplated meeting of the rate committee. It was also recommended that shippers should be informed of all changes proposed in existing contracts at least four months prior to the effective date of the new contract; and "the terms of all conference contracts should be reasonable, fair and equitable both to conferences and American exporters and importers."

It will be recalled that the solution frequently recommended by various British committees was the creation of shippers' associations to bargain collectively with the conferences of shipping lines. The difficulties of organizing such associations of shippers have been described in previous chapters. Frequently there is not sufficient community of interests to permit the formation of an effective bargaining unit, but even when such a community of interests exists there is no reason to believe that a bilateral monopoly will assure the attainment of a socially desirable result. An association of shippers in a trade with adequate strength to counter a sound conference will usually also be in a position to exercise a monopoly influence on its own account which may well be abusive in character and inimical to the interests of the general public. Ultimate consumers cannot organize in this way, so representation tends to be by merchants, who are not primarily concerned with the consumers' interests.[2] In the

[2] A. C. Pigou, *The Economics of Welfare* (London: Macmillan, 1920), pp. 320-321.

293

few situations where shippers' associations have been effective, as in Australia and New Zealand, one finds that shipments consist almost entirely of a relatively small number of commodities. Furthermore, government supervision of, or participation in, the bargaining has apparently been necessary.

A variant of this proposal is that state trading monopolies would be better able to stand up to strong shipping conferences. But state trading monopolies create new problems which are outside the scope of this study. Suffice it to say that the logical concomitant to the development of state trading monopolies is the nationalization of merchant shipping. However, further developments along these lines, which may occur for other reasons, will not solve any of the problems with which we have been concerned. On the contrary, nationalization may, in addition to posing new difficulties, also aggravate the old ones. Professor Viner succinctly summarized the situation as follows: "When governments are also conductors of economic enterprise in the international field, what results is a pattern of intergovernmental relationships in which economic, political and military bilateral-monopoly-plus duopoly are all wrapped up in one package of international dynamite."[3]

It has sometimes been suggested that the industry's problems might be alleviated by international joint operation and agreement to limit the construction of new tonnage.[4] Although proposals of this type have been made in periods of depression with the intent of relieving the industry from financial difficulties, they do, nevertheless, introduce a possible method for the international control of seaborne commerce. An international line may serve a useful purpose on a few of the smaller trade routes where the lack of such cooperation might produce an unprofitable redundancy of tonnage if each nation participating in the trade attempted to run its own line. Unofficial joint service agreements, however, appear better suited to achieve satisfactory arrangements in such situations. Proposals for internationalization of shipping have met with very little enthusiasm, and internationalization on major trade routes is not likely to come before there is internationalization of political and military power.

After reviewing the foregoing alternatives one comes to the same

---

[3] Jacob Viner, "International Relations between State-controlled National Economies," *American Economic Review*, Supp. Vol. xxxix, No. 1, Pt. 2 (March, 1944), p. 319.

[4] The French government made such a proposal in 1933; but it did not receive any support from other countries.

general conclusion that was reached by the Alexander Committee in 1914 when it reported, "The Committee believes that the disadvantages and abuses connected with steamship agreements and conferences as now conducted are inherent, and can only be eliminated by effective government control. . . ."[5] Experience since World War I permits us to appraise the efficacy of unilateral government regulation, and to compare it with the relative advantages of bilateral and multilateral international control.

We have seen that unilateral regulation of the type practiced by the United States has checked the charging of flagrantly discriminatory rates and has curbed many of the other abuses of the conference system. Nevertheless, some undesirable practices remain.[6] It is debatable whether more forceful administration of the regulatory laws would have reduced the remaining disadvantages of conferences, or whether more aggressive enforcement would have introduced new and possibly more serious bureaucratic abuses. Any evaluation of the efficacy of the regulatory activities of the Shipping Board and its successors must bear in mind the severe limitations that are inherent in the unilateral regulation by one nation of an international industry. The regulatory agencies have had no general authority over rates and no power to control either the entrance of new lines to a trade route or the abandonment of a service by a line which has been operating. Nor is it feasible for an individual nation to exercise such authority. To take such action unilaterally would abrogate existing treaties of commerce and navigation, and would most probably provoke a spate of retaliatory actions. Retaliation is especially dangerous in an industry already characterized by subsidies and nationalistic discrimination. Cordell Hull, when Secretary of State, explained this in a letter to the Chairman of a Committee of the House of Representatives, which was considering a bill to provide for regulating ocean rates in United States foreign commerce:

"I think it important to keep clearly in mind the essential distinction between . . . [domestic] commerce which both begins and ends within our territory, and the foreign commerce which at one end or the other enters the jurisdiction of another government.

"I do not feel that an attempt by this Government to prescribe

---

[5] *op.cit.*, Vol. 4, p. 418.

[6] It is interesting to note that in the case of industries, which were not subject to the Shipping Act, 1916, the American antitrust laws provided the public with protection in some cases, but were also inadequate in others. J. B. Oseas, "Antitrust Prosecutions of International Business," *Cornell Law Quarterly*, Vol. xxx, Sept. 1944.

minimum rates which may be charged by foreign vessels on the cargoes which they carry between American and foreign ports would be in harmony with that basic principle in our treaty structure under which we have granted to foreign shipping the right of free access to our ports and in return have obtained for our ships the right of free access to foreign ports. Certainly such regulation would be in conflict with the generally accepted practices of international law. . . .

"In my opinion, a most serious objection to any unilateral attempt by this Government to fix rates in foreign commerce lies in the fact that this procedure would add one more form of restriction to the entangled and conflicting mass of nationalistic restrictions from which our foreign trade is suffering today. The impracticability of such unilateral regulation can readily be appreciated if one considers the impasse that would result if another government should adopt the same practice, but should prescribe rates covering its trade with us differing from those our authorities prescribed for the very same trade."[7]

Unless current concepts regarding freedom of the seas are discarded, bilateral control is also not a feasible method of regulating ocean transport. Unlike aircraft which require specific treaty permission to land and to participate in the carrying of passengers and cargo, ships can freely enter most of the world's harbors, and (subject only to certain safety requirements) can carry passengers and cargo moving in foreign commerce. It might be possible for the United States and Chile, for example, to agree on the rates to be charged on cargo moving between the two countries, but they would have no control over the number of lines or the number of vessels that would be allowed to operate. The difficulty of satisfying all the parties interested in domestic rate cases is well known. It does not appear that agreement between different sovereign nations would be more easily achieved, especially if competition from third nations is involved, or if one of the terminal nations is an important ship operator and the other is not.

In an industry where large elements of cost are indeterminate it is particularly difficult to find objective grounds for accord. But even if such agreements could be reached, it is extremely doubtful that the rate regulations would be effective so long as there was no control over the entrance of newcomers and over abandonments. If the rate level were low it would be difficult to keep ships on the run,

[7] Inter-American Maritime Conference, *op.cit.*, p. 467.

whereas if it were high the trade would tend to be overtonnaged. In either case there would be a great temptation for ship-operating countries to favor their own vessels. Subsidies would be apt to be paid if losses were common, and then there would be a demand for discriminatory legislation to cut the losses and eliminate the surplus capacity. (On the other hand, ship-using nations may try to keep rates unduly depressed.) Such actions would be as contrary to current treaties of commerce and navigation as the unilateral regulation of ocean freights.

Even a system of multilateral rate negotiation subject to bilateral approval, such as is in vogue in the aviation industry, would require fundamental changes in international law regarding freedom of the seas. Changes in this custom might loose a flood of discriminatory measures. In the event, however, that satisfactory preceptual alterations were made, there would still remain the great difficulty of reaching multilateral agreement on and then of securing governmental approval of a long and complex tariff containing rates on a great many commodities. Such a solution is not unthinkable, but it presents great difficulties.

Similar results might be achieved without appreciably altering the traditional interpretation of freedom of the seas through multinational regulation by an international organization; but the difficulties of obtaining agreement among competing carrier nations, not to mention the obstacles to achieving accord between the ship-operating powers and the ship-using countries, render the practicability of this solution extremely doubtful under current notions of sovereignty. It must be remembered that for an international organization to control rates effectively it would need authority to control entry to a route and abandonment, and presumably to control ship construction as well. This does not seem politically feasible at present. However, if the actual and potential competitive elements now inherent in the industry can be maintained and encouraged, it may not be necessary to control rate levels. But as long as shipping is considered important for national defense, for earning foreign exchange, and for prestige, the industry will be subsidized by some nations. So long as it is subsidized neither conference action nor external rate regulation can be expected to eliminate all high-cost operators.

A proposed international body, the Intergovernmental Maritime Consultative Organization, is now before the nations of the world for ratification. It will not have authority to regulate rates, only the power to conduct investigations and to report its findings. There is some doubt concerning the acceptability of even this modest attempt at international collaboration, since both some shipowning and some ship-using nations oppose it. In view of the hostile reactions of some ship-using nations to the charter proposed for IMCO, it is quite unlikely that they would find more acceptable the proposal of Brig. Gen. Sir Osborne Mance to have the shipping industry itself form an international association of liner conferences. Such an association, he suggests, could facilitate the continuity of policy between *ad hoc* diplomatic meetings; and, in conjunction with a similar international association for tramps and another for tankers, it would make it possible to entrust to one or another of these unofficial bodies the working out of measures for international agreement on their own initiative or in accordance with previously agreed upon official intergovernmental policy.[8]

How useful might an organization like IMCO be, if it is ratified in its present form? Lacking the power to regulate rates, will it be effective in curbing monopolistic excesses and in rectifying competitive wastes? It appears doubtful that it will be able to influence the level of rates, the rate of profits, the entrance of new lines to a route, or the abandonment of a service. But it may be able to bring about the correction of individual rates which are unduly discriminatory, and it may be able to curb some other monopoly abuses such as patently unfair provisions in exclusive patronage or deferred rebate contracts. It could scrutinize pooling agreements; and in time might establish sufficient confidence in its judgment, fairness, and integrity to help arrange for the more economical use of shipping in periods when there is a considerable oversupply of tonnage.

Is there any satisfactory and feasible program that might replace the conference system? Or is there any program for improving the system's operation which would not introduce new disadvantages as bad, or worse, than the shortcomings it is designed to correct? The retention of some form of self-regulation, and the conference system seems as good as any, appears to be necessary. The structure of the industry will not permit a competitive solution; and complete reliance on either unilateral or multilateral governmental regulation has been shown in foregoing paragraphs to be either unworkable or un-

[8] Brig. Gen. Sir Osborne Mance, *International Sea Transport* (London, Oxford University Press, 1945), pp. 165-168.

acceptable. Therefore, if shipping conferences cannot advantageously be replaced, let us see if it is possible to improve them.

CONCLUSIONS

It should be recalled that the structure of the liner shipping industry contains elements of competition and elements of monopoly, with the advantages and disadvantages of such a mixture. We have seen that the industry cannot be made sufficiently competitive to provide a workable solution; and that pure monopoly is unlikely in view of national interests in merchant shipping. Furthermore, such a monopoly would likewise leave much to be desired, even if it could be achieved. Some form of regulation, therefore, is needed to curb both competitive wastes and monopolistic abuses. The disadvantages of competition can be lessened by increasing the monopoly power of the lines. This is the principal justification for the shipping conference. But the existence of conferences sufficiently strong to reduce the shortcomings of competition inevitably creates monopoly power, which may in turn be abused. The disadvantages of a conference monopoly, even when somewhat offset by internal and external competition, frequently remain sufficiently great to require some form of governmental supervision.

Liner shipping, like many other segments of the economy, is a mixture; and the problem is to find the most desirable proportions for combining competition, monopoly, and government regulation. Let us remember that we do not seek absolute perfection, but merely a solution that will actually work, in the present imperfect world, more satisfactorily than any other acceptable alternative. With this humility of approach we shall examine the contribution that can best be made by the three components: competition, monopoly, and government regulation.

First, however, it is advisable to review the criteria by which a rate-making system may be judged. A satisfactory pricing system for ocean transportation should contribute to a reasonably economical allocation of resources both in the shipping industry and in world trade as a whole. In order to accomplish this the level of rates must not depart for long from costs, and individual rates must not be unduly discriminatory. The pricing system should be conducive to the introduction of innovations, and it should assist the industry to be sufficiently flexible to adapt itself promptly to changed conditions. Rewards for efficiency and penalties for inefficiency should keep

299

high-cost producers from setting either the price structure or the pace at which change takes place. Occasionally, certain social-welfare considerations may suggest deviations from a strict cost pattern, but usually such matters are better treated by open subsidies.

Competition can be most useful in providing a salutary stimulus to efficient operation, and it also assists the introduction of improvements. Competition, furthermore, can help to prevent rates from remaining excessive for overly long. Partnership monopolies, such as shipping conferences, are not generally noted for the elimination of high-cost operations; but they may, by producing sufficient stability, be helpful in encouraging investment in new vessels specifically designed for the requirements of a particular route. Governmental regulation is apt to be least effective in improving efficiency and quality, for it tends to be definitely restrictive rather than stimulating.[9]

Competition, however, cannot assure a satisfactory level of rates in an industry of this type, since it is likely to degenerate into cutthroat pricing. Unilateral government control, as we have seen, cannot regulate the level of rates; and, since the nations of the world are not prepared to delegate such authority to an international organization, multinational control is likewise not feasible. This unwillingness to entrust rate authority to an international agency should not be too much deplored. It is doubtful if at present either the wisdom or the administrative techniques exist for the satisfactory discharge of such a responsibility. The conflict of national interests and the bureaucratic disadvantages that might arise in an international organization with the power to regulate rates may well be greater evils than the ills they are intended to correct.

It appears advisable, therefore, to permit the industry to regulate itself; and the conference system, despite some shortcomings, has been a reasonably satisfactory form of self-regulation. This system tends to minimize the clash of national interests, and the intimate knowledge of member lines with business conditions on the route does much to produce a workable rate structure.[10] This does not deny

---

[9] Government regulation should not be confused with government subsidies or other forms of government assistance. Subsidies may encourage investment, but not necessarily in the most efficient operations.

[10] Though Professor Mears may have exaggerated the ability of conferences to ignore nationalistic considerations, there is considerable validity in his observation that: "Economic factors rather than national protectionism provide the real basis for efficient operation of commercial vessels; and yet chauvinism, patriotism and pride are more closely associated with a country's shipping and aviation than with any other

that such a concentration of power in the hands of shipping companies may be abused. In fact, we have seen the tendency toward such abuse. Therefore, some form of external regulation is needed to prevent the conferences from misapplying their authority. And so long as the nations of the world have such different economic philosophies and such different business standards, it will be advisable to have unilateral controls as well as an international body for investigations and consultations. Since an international organization will represent the lowest common denominator of agreement, some nations, like the United States, will wish to exercise more careful scrutiny and control of the shipping carrying their commerce.

Briefly summarized, we have reached the following conclusions: (1) self-regulation is necessary to prevent cutthroat competition, and to establish a workable tariff with differential prices or rates, which takes into account the traffic mix and the competition of alternate sources and markets while minimizing nationalistic considerations; (2) unilateral regulation, aided by an international investigative and consultative body, is needed to prevent undue discrimination and other monopolistic abuses; and (3) competition is required to provide incentives for efficient operation, and to prevent excessive profits from being earned for overly long. The combination of competition with monopolistically determined prices, however, is apt to encourage the operation of redundant tonnage.

A frequent maladjustment in the interwar period was the excessive unused carrying capacity maintained in operation by conference lines. Although partly a result of shipbuilding stimulated by war and defense needs, and further exacerbated by the Great Depression, the operation of excess tonnage is also partially attributable to conference rate levels sufficiently high to render it remunerative to operate vessels with more empty space than is normally unavoidable in the running of scheduled liners. The improper allocation of resources resulting from the support of such unused capacity may not be too high a price to pay, however, for the advantages that the retention of elements of competition offer. The disadvantages of operating redundant tonnage may, in view of the importance of shipping

---

form of national business." Still Professor Mears claimed that "The most arresting feature of the foregoing conferences is the demonstrated practice of private companies, operating under flags of leading maritime powers, in merging their spheres of enterprise and business secrets into semi-voluntary, international groups." E. G. Mears, *Maritime Trade of Western United States*, *op.cit.*, pp. 369-370.

to nations whose military strength is largely predicated on sea power, be unavoidable in any case. Furthermore, since the demand of many commodities for transport is relatively inelastic and since by differential pricing the added burden can be kept from falling too heavily on goods with an elastic demand for transport, the effect of this excess tonnage on the commerce of nations is probably quite small.[11]

It has been shown in previous chapters, however, that competition can be internal, among the conference members; or that it might be external, coming from tramps, independent non-conference lines, or from lines who are members of conferences serving alternate markets. The proper treatment of non-conference operations is particularly difficult to specify in detail. Despite the possibility that they might seriously disrupt the stability of rates, the advantages of their competition seem sufficiently great to warrant their existence. The problem of coordinating the regulation of tramp and liner shipping is similar in some respects to the problem of coordinating rail and road transport. (Tramps, like trucks, tend to base charges primarily on costs, whereas liners and railroads use a differential tariff in which value of service plays an important role.) It is certainly equally perplexing, and the prospect for a definitive solution that is not highly arbitrary is equally remote.

An even more difficult situation is presented by the competition of non-conference lines. Carefully supervised tying arrangements and an open conference membership policy appear to be the best way of coping with this problem. If conference membership is available to all properly qualified lines, few concerns will choose to operate independently unless some important conference rates are inordinately high. On the other hand, conferences must be allowed to protect themselves from competition which might selectively "skim the cream" off the traffic mix. Therefore, tying arrangements appear to be necessary for some trades. These ties should be carefully regulated, however, so that they will offer the shipper a genuine and adequate *quid pro quo*, and so that the tie will not be unfairly restrictive or unduly discriminatory. There is a great opportunity here for an international organization, such as IMCO, to formulate a code to govern the tying arrangements and other practices of international shipping rings.

---

[11] It should not be inferred from this statement that there may not be better ways of financing an instrument of defense than by "taxing" some of the peacetime users of the facility.

Before concluding, let us examine briefly some current trends. In a world characterized by nationalism and insecurity from attack, shipping, because of its strategic importance, will continue to be subsidized and in many instances governmentally owned and even governmentally operated. If peace prevails, this is almost certain in time to produce a redundancy of tonnage. Furthermore, the nationalization of shipping increases the danger of international misunderstandings in this field. An international organization could perform a highly useful function in helping to adjudicate such misunderstandings by conducting careful investigations either upon receiving complaints or on its own initiative. In the event of a serious plethora of tonnage such an international organization may assist in arranging rationalization programs that will protect ship-users as well as shipowners. The fact that Russian shipping and that of its satellites is relatively unimportant facilitates the achievement of such a program. At the same time, countries desiring more protection against conference abuses can employ regulatory methods like those of the United States, the Union of South Africa, or Australia. In the event of the outbreak of full-scale war the problem becomes quite different, since there is then more general agreement as to ends and a somewhat greater merging of national interests. In wartime the allocation of shipping becomes the dominant problem and this, too, is a highly controversial matter. But since in such a situation conferences would lapse into disuse it is not relevant to this study. Suffice it to say that an organization, the Defense Shipping Authority, has been agreed upon to coordinate this industry for the Western powers in the event of war. No one is wise enough to foretell what might follow the outbreak of general war. The postwar world might have achieved more integration, or possibly world government; or it might be fragmented into isolated, feudal segments; or it might not be appreciably different from the present so far as the problems of international shipping are concerned.

It should be clear by now that the conclusions reached are to take advantage of the constructive elements of conferences, competition, and regulation; and to eliminate the weaknesses and abuses of each insofar as possible. The retention of some competition, the improvement of conference procedures, the ratification of the proposed Intergovernmental Maritime Consultative Organization, and more effective unilateral regulation all appear desirable and practicable. It should be recalled that the critical problems are different when tonnage is scarce and when tonnage is plentiful; and therefore, such an eclectic solution has distinct advantages. Perhaps, in the future, it may become feasible to coordinate the planning of world ship construction, but this presupposes the prospect for a long, durable peace and a great reduction in national jealousies, rivalries, and sovereignty. But even with such cooperation the regulation of shipping would remain a highly complex problem, and complex problems often require complex solutions.

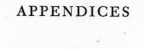

APPENDICES

A P P E N D I X A

A NOTE ON DIFFERENTIAL OR DISCRIMINATORY
PRICING

APPENDIX A
A NOTE ON DIFFERENTIAL OR DISCRIMINATORY PRICING

RAILROADS, public utilities, and similar service industries, which are often subject to under-utilization for considerable periods, have generally employed a classification system of pricing; i.e. different uses are classified and charged different rates. Such pricing is often discriminatory in the sense that rates or prices for different uses do not vary solely according to the cost of the service, but it is not necessarily or even customarily discriminatory in the sense that buyers of service in the same classification pay different rates for the same service. Classifications and rate differences both tend to be rather arbitrary but may or may not be unreasonable. (Reasonableness, like justice, requires judicial definition which takes into account all pertinent facts and circumstances.) Abuses have occurred, and either government regulation or the fear of competition has been necessary to keep them from being too flagrant. Nevertheless, while the results of this system have not been perfect, it has frequently given better than tolerable satisfaction to all concerned.

Another solution—marginal cost pricing and subsidies for industries which operate in a stage of declining unit costs—has long been popular in economic theory and has received the support of many economists. These economists have, it seems to me, left the domain of pure economic theory and have ventured into the realm of political economy without paying heed to that important signpost which reads, "administrative feasibility." Furthermore, some embarrassing questions have been raised concerning the premises carried in their baggage. In order to be more specific, let us review briefly some of the more influential literature on the subject.

The pricing problems of an industry with declining costs[1] have long been recognized.[2] Pigou treats the matter of discriminatory pricing in such industries at considerable length; but comes to a conclusion favoring the cost-of-service principle supplemented by bounties when necessary in order to expand production and achieve lower unit costs.[3] Marshall

---

[1] "Declining cost" is used here to cover what has previously been referred to as increasing returns and decreasing costs. Some of the authors cited below had the former in mind, others the latter. Although the impact on the allocation of new capital would differ, for the present purpose the distinction is not crucial.

[2] A. J. Dupuit, *Annales des ponts et chaussées* (1844).

[3] A. C. Pigou, *The Economics of Welfare* (London: Macmillan & Co., 1920), Chapters XIV and XV.

also favors bounties for production characterized by increasing returns, but explicitly abstracts from the "indirect evils of such artificial arrangements" (such as the costs of collecting the tax and administering the bounty), "and the danger that in the trade which had got a bounty and in other trades which hoped to get one, people would divert their energies from managing their own business to managing those persons who control the bounties."[4] Pigou was also aware that government authorities are liable to ignorance, political pressures, and personal corruption.[5] Furthermore, Pigou realized that the cost-of-service principle leads not to a single price for everybody, but to prices that vary with the incidental costs attaching to each service, and that these adjustments are often a very difficult accounting matter.[6] We may conclude, therefore, that Marshall and Pigou favored bounties for declining cost industries in principle, but had certain misgivings regarding the administrative difficulties.

The pricing problem under conditions of decreasing costs has received renewed attention recently as a result of the contributions of Hotelling[7] and Lerner;[8] and there has been considerable support and criticism by numerous other authors.[9] The well-known Hotelling-Lerner thesis may be stated briefly as follows: the price of a product should equal its marginal cost,[10] but since marginal costs are less than average costs when the latter are declining the difference should be covered by the government.

Proponents of marginal cost *cum* government aid pricing have neglected to consider the problems that would actually be involved in granting a government subsidy to a privately owned industry to compensate for the difference between marginal and average cost. Although Meade is not oblivious of fiscal difficulties involved in a program of government ownership of industries characterized by increasing returns,[11] he appears to underestimate the administrative obstacles. However, none of the recent proponents of this policy gives serious consideration to the alternative which is employed in actual practice and which in general does not work too badly, viz., discriminatory pricing or "charging what the traffic

---

[4] A. Marshall, *Principles of Economics* (London: Macmillan & Co., 1936), Eighth Ed., pp. 472-473.

[5] Pigou, *op.cit.*, p. 296.

[6] Pigou, *op.cit.*, p. 280.

[7] H. Hotelling, "The General Welfare in Relation to Problems of Taxation and of Railway and Utility Rates," *Econometrica*, July 1938.

[8] A. P. Lerner, *The Economics of Control* (New York: Macmillan Co., 1944); and earlier articles in the *Economic Journal* and *Review of Economic Studies*.

[9] The recent literature is well summarized in Nancy Ruggles' "Recent Developments in the Theory of Marginal Cost Pricing," *The Review of Economic Studies*, Vol. xvii (2), No. 43, 1949-50, pp. 107-126. Ruggles comes to an eclectic conclusion, not unlike my own.

[10] More correctly this proposition holds that the value of the marginal product of a factor should be equal to the price of that factor; or, still more accurately stated, the proposition is that the value of the marginal product should bear a constant ratio to that factor's price in all occupations.

[11] J. E. Meade, "Price and Output Policy of State Enterprise," *Economic Journal*, December 1944, pp. 338-339.

will bear." Lerner briefly discusses the possibilities of monopolistic discrimination and agrees that it will almost always tend to narrow the range by which the actual result will differ from the optimum result; but for public utility type industries in which this practice is generally employed he holds that "unintelligent compromise leads to unending regulation."[12] Marcus Fleming states the position more directly when he writes, *"In theory there is a third alternative, namely, two-part pricing combined with profit maximization, which might provide the best solution of all if it were possible to discriminate perfectly* in applying the standing charge to different customers, *but this is usually impossible."*[13]

These quotations are interesting in that they allow the theoretical advantages of discriminatory pricing, but reject it because it is not possible to discriminate or to regulate perfectly. Certainly no one familiar with public regulation or public subsidies can honestly argue that they work perfectly, but is not perfection in social institutions a relative matter? As Pigou has said in regard both to government intervention through regulation and to intervention through direct public operation: "It is not sufficient to contrast the imperfect adjustments of unfettered private enterprise with the best adjustment that economists in their studies can imagine. For we cannot expect that any state authority will attain, or will even wholeheartedly seek, that ideal. Such authorities are liable alike to ignorance, to sectional pressure and to personal corruption by private interest."[14] Who can doubt that the same shortcomings attend the administration of state subsidies and state-operated enterprises? Finally, the welfare postulates on which the theory of marginal cost pricing has been based have been gravely challenged and possibly annihilated by I. M. D. Little in his brilliant *Critique of Welfare Economics*.[15]

The crux of the matter lies in the existence of unused capacity and the slowness with which the number and size of large capital units such as ships are adjusted to the prevailing demand dimension. So long as there is unused capacity on a vessel which is being operated, any item carried which can be made to pay more than the identifiable expenses involved in its transportation (which is about as close to marginal cost as one can get) makes a contribution to the enterprise without which the profits of the ship would have been less or the burden on other cargo greater. Discriminatory pricing provides a rough justice. A "bounty," so to speak, is paid by the shippers (or consumers) of items which pay more than their fully allocated costs (if such imputation could be made), instead of by the government. Unless the monopoly power of the carriers is too great,

[12] Lerner, *op.cit.*, pp. 181-182, 190-197.

[13] Marcus Fleming, "Production and Price Policy in Public Enterprise," *Economica*, February 1950, p. 15. Italics added. Some time after writing this a conversation with Mr. Fleming revealed that he entertains a far more tolerant attitude towards discriminatory pricing by industries of the type considered here than is conveyed by the article referred to. His views will become known upon completion of an article currently (1951) in preparation.

[14] Pigou, *op.cit.*, p. 296.

[15] Oxford University Press, 1950. See especially Chapter XI.

there is a strong tendency, however, for these same shippers (or consumers) to be the beneficiaries, through somewhat lower rates charged them, of the contribution to the venture made by commodities which pay more than their out-of-pocket costs to the venture, but which presumably are unable to pay their full share of the expenses. It is a "marginal cost and bounty system" after all with "taxation" levied on a "benefit" basis which is crude, though probably far less crude and no more inequitable than a payment from general tax funds. Furthermore, since such discriminatory pricing eliminates the intercession of government, unless government regulation is required, there is no additional cost for the administrative services involved in tax collection and subsidy disbursement. The problems of administering governmental subsidy payments to declining cost industries for the purpose envisioned by advocates of the marginal cost pricing principle are staggering when applied to a multi-product industry like shipping with important joint costs and opportunity costs in addition to unused capacity.

Consequently if perfection cannot be achieved, a tolerably good solution will suffice. But according to Little's devastating analysis there is no reason to believe that marginal cost pricing coupled with government subsidies will produce tolerably good results in a declining cost industry. Price discrimination, however, has been providing socially satisfactory and eminently workable solutions in several industries with such cost characteristics. The greatest flaw in discriminatory pricing is that the discrimination may become unreasonable. In ocean shipping this abuse has occurred, but despite the fact that some monopoly power is necessary in order to discriminate, the presence of actual competition or the threat of potential competition has generally prevented flagrant abuse.

A P P E N D I X   B

BRITISH LINER, CARGO-LINER, AND CARGO-BOAT [TRAMP]EARNINGS

(Reports from companies representing approximately two-thirds of the total liner tonnage of the United Kingdom and a substantial amount of tramp tonnage. Source: *Fairplay*, January 10, 1952)

Forty-three Years of Liner and Cargo-Liner Earnings

Period	Paid-up capital £	Debentures and loans £	Reserves £	Sundry creditors £	Book value of fleet† £	Sundry debtors, investments, cash £	Dividend Amount £	Per cent. on capital	Per cent. on capital plus reserves	Fleet No.	Tons gross
Five year averages—											
1909—1913	22,828,765	15,196,092	11,150,210	12,611,176	47,238,768	14,545,472	1,560,476	6·83	4·59	889	4,275,919
1914—1918	34,487,900	18,183,374	23,649,174	33,178,877	71,915,370	37,583,956	3,884,694	11·26	6·68	935	5,042,398
1919—1923	45,534,090	18,221,306	30,301,520	72,239,193	118,300,904	47,995,204	4,291,425	9·42	5·66	789	4,639,567
1924—1928	73,413,004	33,477,645	36,900,691	58,623,317	159,718,145	45,899,192	4,169,114	5·68	3·78	1,159	6,400,791
Years—											
1929	80,906,031	40,837,903	29,314,948	43,618,956	147,945,940	51,523,745	5,043,589	6·23	4·58	1,321	6,315,412
1930	86,087,878	48,869,983	37,331,900	39,051,526	111,604,762	107,857,571	4,551,227	5·28	3·69	1,391	7,073,186
1931	103,862,949	82,033,950	35,369,426	31,684,702	116,723,578	140,856,759	2,421,356	2·33	1·74	1,110	6,792,165
1932	75,378,904	65,331,581	34,418,089	23,297,021	102,714,947	99,736,125	1,413,637	1·88	1·29	973	5,987,468
1933	87,094,566	60,273,758	29,609,245	19,691,112	102,684,645	96,319,811	1,357,609	1·56	1·16	1,017	6,628,395
1934	68,251,580	54,200,381	28,105,792	17,904,189	89,385,910	77,474,060	1,348,858	1·98	1·40	950	6,068,735
1935	73,276,083	47,836,892	34,723,050	18,911,704	90,235,493	88,217,627	1,634,280	2·23	1·51	918	5,916,848
1936	64,751,088	36,649,340	35,859,016	19,727,022	79,761,963	79,148,232	1,805,950	2·79	1·79	847	5,642,609
1937	64,053,588	38,776,304	34,322,284	19,068,170	77,524,043	81,290,911	2,124,801	3·32	2·16	838	5,616,262
1938	63,402,944	37,269,771	29,081,257	22,935,561	73,789,053	84,004,296	3,104,537	4·90	3·36	834	5,703,388
1939	63,225,569	37,417,788	30,186,828	22,081,943	77,429,284	80,993,636	2,735,322	4·33	2·93	826	5,591,491
1940	58,156,729	35,790,939	26,679,427	19,717,657	77,047,192	77,256,577	2,456,961	4·22	2·90	588	4,284,819
1941	62,445,164	29,432,513	49,545,100	31,904,688	59,867,720	121,145,216	3,171,698	5·08	2·83	715	4,832,322
1942	64,274,414	21,542,729	64,808,633	47,566,719	52,925,036	152,861,422	4,233,781	6·59	3·28	656	4,677,268
1943	61,831,680	14,200,510	82,526,366	48,211,589	45,910,433	168,438,322	5,206,488	8·42	3·61	591	4,290,448
1944	60,122,214	12,543,143	90,705,959	45,270,363	45,894,100	169,224,859	4,216,645	7·01	2·80	559	4,051,808
1945	61,608,244	11,730,942	100,082,989	50,941,187	41,832,243	190,470,171	4,341,472	7·04	2·68	517	3,811,441
1946	61,938,286	11,255,730	113,406,321	47,345,175	44,625,512	198,017,070	4,328,637	6·98	2·47	447	3,289,871
1947	61,938,286	10,628,870	121,609,457	49,324,022	57,132,267	194,070,793	4,704,034	7·60	2·57	488	3,507,380
1948	54,391,463	7,038,408	120,337,830	53,858,534	86,362,291	171,329,683	4,368,040	8·03	2·50	525	3,939,058
1949	64,978,606	6,683,739	161,845,122	79,253,475	111,758,909	202,536,823	5,871,970	9·04	1·93	619	4,585,447
1950	55,424,090	5,928,109	167,782,534	80,867,123	134,487,632	185,999,414	4,686,915	8·46	2·10	638	4,777,403
1951	54,778,915	5,752,379	176,209,885	83,676,500	149,714,632	182,396,650	5,298,637	9·67	2·29	642	4,802,115

† Including, in some instances, investments.

Reproduced through the courtesy of *Fairplay*.

Forty-eight Years of Cargo-Boat Earnings

Period Five year averages	Paid-up capital £	Debentures, loans, etc. £	Reserves £	Book value of fleet† £	Profit on voyages, etc. £	Dividend Amount £	Per cent. on capital	Per cent. on capital plus reserves	Fleet No.	Fleet Tons gross	Depreciation written off £	Depreciation at 5 per cent. £
1904—1908	8,608,632	3,892,040	=	12,661,860	921,486	321,764	3·74	=	463	1,419,093	322,079	760,896
1909—1913	10,076,439	5,668,818	=	15,480,886	2,267,483	573,160	5·69	=	545	1,852,934	1,158,752	945,972
1914—1918	13,227,492	8,775,012	=	19,608,484	5,581,064	1,929,667	14·59	=	502	1,912,136	2,143,198	967,377
1919—1923	22,562,176	12,471,974	=	36,863,451	3,815,048	1,779,972	7·89	=	361	1,300,883	1,298,995	1,593,858
1924—1928	26,802,107	10,959,605	14,289,079	42,100,509	2,914,700	1,286,980	4·80	3·13	477	2,106,137	1,485,809	2,004,644
Years—1929	18,134,035	8,564,998	8,399,164	29,226,189	1,466,690	928,391	5·12	3·49	489	2,070,359	605,487	1,525,013
1930	16,748,121	8,400,577	8,170,103	24,478,792	1,363,064	652,398	3·89	2·62	454	2,075,038	537,215	1,542,367
1931	15,722,698	7,712,101	6,668,071	22,418,769	607,023	241,438	1·53	1·08.	431	2,026,890	531,834	1,472,126
1932	14,585,461	5,887,248	6,399,196	19,611,259	626,325	229,905	1·58	1·09	387	1,850,556	551,887	1,226,534
1933	14,001,163	5,331,014	5,915,158	18,330,350	155,023	135,380	0·97	0·68	361	1,733,989	349,598	1,193,389
1934	14,636,389	5,811,210	4,826,803	19,223,343	88,653	208,246	1·42	1·07	347	1,701,940	134,304	1,190,607
1935	12,189,426	4,165,692	4,667,256	16,489,400	499,235	178,545	1·46	1·06	316	1,495,455	342,939	1,026,291
1936	12,451,926	3,914,198	4,681,434	16,177,984	1,082,889	260,435	2·09	1·52	309	1,464,487	673,578	1,005,275
1937	11,462,193	3,707,252	4,738,176	14,522,118	2,237,009	481,733	4·20	2·97	294	1,404,959	1,071,893	954,583
1938	12,178,135	2,860,526	6,156,943	14,717,444	4,546,688	1,123,207	9·22	6·13	329	1,664,945	2,510,317	1,005,488
1939	12,342,350	2,356,095	6,360,305	13,987,380	1,805,425	683,399	5·54	3·65	297	1,405,711	1,164,765	911,369
1940	12,451,034	3,365,569	7,543,344	13,107,426	1,736,263	787,343	6·32	3·94	289	1,373,310	718,744	846,020
1941	11,023,218	4,392,839	8,537,563	10,488,437	1,924,369	778,369	7·04	3·98	214	1,034,249	1,045,339	717,508
1942	11,784,770	5,196,986	13,195,335	10,602,441	1,575,303	837,506	7·11	3·35	206	986,705	833,244	686,481
1943	11,867,440	5,875,004	16,306,476	10,557,309	1,553,067	843,657	7·11	2·99	210	1,019,550	947,107	673,079
1944	11,756,420	6,265,460	17,887,130	11,367,087	1,355,389	826,913	7·03	2·79	235	1,127,744	937,246	706,072
1945	10,533,180	5,964,322	15,581,997	11,436,118	1,457,883	711,981	6·76	2·72	171	858,302	989,463	700,339
1946	10,129,270	4,207,348	18,303,998	9,057,898	2,169,300	805,304	7·95	2·83	131	739,479	1,633,046	542,677
1947	9,263,200	6,416,022	20,213,049	11,045,006	6,088,667	1,269,023	13·70	4·31	153	848,487	4,476,460	735,027
1948	9,873,420	7,692,427	21,596,569	11,096,106	6,863,104	1,548,055	15·68	4·92	155	883,706	4,559,589	826,858
1949	8,005,436	7,086,244	18,514,226	11,796,283	4,984,542	1,216,861	15·20	4·59	150	856,186	2,842,928	877,436
1950	11,731,075	6,614,470	24,381,426	16,910,209	4,100,991	1,304,418	11·12	3·61	165	986,082	2,426,330	1,194,783
1951	11,354,661	4,257,274	23,540,081	18,342,532	4,146,991	1,365,069	12·02	3·91	131	795,060	2,428,800	1,248,647

† Including, in some instances, investments.

Reproduced through the courtesy of *Fairplay*.

INDEX

A

Absorption of Insurance Premiums (3 U.S.M.C. 201), 116
Agreements 1438 & 5260-5264 (2 U.S.-M.C. 228), 160
Agreement 7620 (2 U.S.M.C. 749), 123
Agreements and Practices Re Brokerage (3 U.S.M.C. 170), 127
Agreement 7790 (2 U.S.M.C. 775), 126-127
air transport, 25, 73, 186, 266, 268, 292; international organizations of, 279ff
Alexander Committee, 4, 49ff, 127-128, 141n, 166-167, 204-206, 208n, 218, 223, 229, 260n, 295; report of, 56ff; recommendations of, 64ff
Allen, G. C., 265
Allied Maritime Transport Council, 272
amalgamations, *see* mergers
American Institute for Imported Steel, 245n
American President Lines, 125n, 200
Ames Harris Neville *v.* American-Hawaiian Steamship Co. (1 U.S.M.C. 765), 112n, 117
antitrust laws, 49, 52, 119-120
Application of G. B. Thorden for Conference Membership (2 U.S.M.C. 77), 122
Associated Chambers of Commerce of East Africa, 205
Associated Producers of East Africa, 205
Associated Steamship Lines of Manila, 103, 138, 141n, 183
Association of West African Merchants, 205
Association of West Coast Steamship Companies, 264
Association of West India Trans-Atlantic Steamship Lines, 138
Atlantic Conference, 146, 184
Atlantic-Eastbound Freight Association, Liverpool, 144, 169, 170
Atlantic & Gulf-West Coast of So. America Conference, 162
Atlantic Refining Co. *v.* Ellerman and Bucknall (1 U.S.S.B. 242), 117

Atlas Waste Manufacturing Co. *v.* The New York & Puerto Rico Steamship Co. (1 U.S.S.B. 195), 114
Australia, rates on wheat and flour, 78; experiences with shipping conferences, 93-96
Australian Industries Preservation Act, 76, 95
Australia-Japan Conference, 80
Australian Oversea Transport Association, 93-96, 206
Australian Royal Commission, 49
Australian Shipping Conference, 76
Austrian Lloyd, 80

B

Bahamas, 75
Bain, Joe S., 240n
balance of payments, 40ff; Norway, 42; United Kingdom, 42-43
Baltic Coffee House, 236n
Baltic and International Maritime Conference, 232, 269
Baltic Shipping Exchange, 10, 236
Baltic and White Sea Conference, 230
Barbour, David, 64
Belgian Line, 259
Berglund, Abraham, 100
Black Diamond Lines, 259
Black Diamond Steamship Corporation *v.* Cie Maritime Belge (2 U.S.M.C. 755), 124
Bland Forwarding Act, 127
Board of Trade (U.K.), 48, 62-64, 66, 91, 232
Bombay-Japan Conference, 80
bounties, *see* subsidies
Brazil, 98-99
British Iron Trade Association, 48
British Ministry of War Transport, 5, 272-273
British Shipping (Assistance) Act, 230-231, 235
British Shipping in the Orient, 79-82
Bruce, S. M., 93
Bureau of Steamboat Inspection and Navigation, 105

Date Due